SO YOU THINK YOU KNOW THE PRESIDENTS?

Also by Peter E. Meltzer

The Thinker's Thesaurus: Sophisticated Synonyms for Common Words
So You Think You Know Baseball? A Fan's Guide to the Rules

SO YOU THINK YOU KNOW THE PRESIDENTS?

FASCINATING FACTS ABOUT OUR CHIEF EXECUTIVES

BY PETER E. MELTZER

History Publishing Company
Palisades, New York

Copyright ©2014 by Peter E. Meltzer

Meltzer, Peter E., 1958-

So you think you know the presidents? : fascinating
facts about our chief executives / by Peter E. Meltzer.
-- 1st ed. -- Palisades, NY : History Pub. Co., c2013.

p. ; cm.

ISBN: 978-1-933909-73-8 (alk. paper) ;
978-1-933909-78-3 (ebk)
Includes bibliographical references and index.
Summary: Full of interesting insights and quirky
questions, this book goes beyond oft-discussed
presidential trivia and exposes the reader to the
stories that define our nation's chief executives as
individuals. A great reference guide for students and
avid history buffs alike.--Publisher.

1. Presidents--United
States--History--Miscellanea.
2. Presidents--United
States--Biography--Miscellanea.
3. Presidents--United States--Miscellanea.
4. Presidents--United States--Anecdotes. I. Title.

E176.1 .M45 2013   2013937209
973/.099--dc23   1306

LCCN # 2013937209

Published in the United States by
History Publishing Company LLC
Palisades, NY
www.historypublishingco.com

SAN: 850-5942

To my mom and dad and Fred and Judy Attea.

Four wonderful people.

TABLE OF CONTENTS

Introduction

This is a book about the American Presidents; not so much about their place in history or their domestic or foreign policies but rather about fascinating and little-known facts of their personal lives. It examines them more as people than as politicians. Take Herbert Hoover for example. I am interested in such facts as: (1) he was the only president who actually met with Adolf Hitler; (2) he was one of only two presidents who donated his entire salary to charity; (3) in 1964, the School of Engineering and Applied Science of Columbia University named him and Thomas Edison as the two greatest engineers in U. S. history; (4) he is mentioned in the theme song of the 1970's TV show *All in the Family*; (5) he wrote a book called *Fishing for Fun and to Wash Your Soul*; (6) he was the youngest member of Stanford University's first graduating class; (7) he made the *Star-Spangled Banner* our official national anthem; (8) he was one of four presidents who attended the same college as a Super Bowl winning quarterback, and (9) he is the only president who was never on the cover of *Time* magazine while president. Information about the presidents regarding causes, terms and effects of such things as the Smoot-Hawley Tariff Act of 1930, the 1929 Treaty of Lima, the Norris-La Guardia Act, or the Reconstruction Finance Corporation, all of which occurred during the Hoover administration, are not the type of information you will find in this book.[1] Those subjects are interesting in their

---

[1] I do confess however that I have a soft spot in my heart for the Smoot-Hawley Tariff Act of 1930 because it is famously discussed by Ben Stein, playing the economics teacher in *Ferris Bueller's Day Off*: "In 1930, the Republican-controlled House of Representatives, in an effort to alleviate the effects of the... Anyone? Anyone?... the Great Depression, passed the... Anyone? Anyone? The tariff bill? The Hawley-Smoot Tariff Act? Which, anyone? Raised or lowered?... raised tariffs, in an effort to collect more revenue for the federal government. Did it work? Anyone? Anyone know the effects? It did not work, and the United States sank deeper into the Great Depression." Whether Stein (who came up with this monologue himself) was aware that he was saying the names of Senator Reed Smoot and Representative Willis C. Hawley backwards is anyone's guess. Regardless, it's still a classic scene, though not relating to the presidents per se.

own right, of course, but they are not the subject of this book.

With regard to Richard Nixon, how much more can possibly be written about his political career, Watergate and his resignation? Yet I find it interesting (and largely unknown or unremembered) that: (1) he partially financed his first campaign for Congress through his poker winnings; (2) he argued a fascinating libel case before the Supreme Court stemming from a home invasion, a novel called *The Desperate Hours* and a *Life* magazine article; (3) he mediated a dispute between the Major League Baseball umpires and owners; (4) just before entering his first race, a committee of republicans placed an ad in several local papers seeking candidates to run against the incumbent (Nixon won); (5) he popularized the phrase "silent majority;" (6) he was the subject of an assassination attempt by a man who intended on flying a commercial plane into the White House; (7) although a lawyer, he refused to work on divorce cases because he was "severely embarrassed by women's confessions of sexual misconduct," and (8) he can be seen on YouTube playing his own piano composition.

There are two kinds of books which have been written which examine the lives of the presidents: those which are not in quiz format and those which are. On first impression, both of these may appear to cover similar terrain as that covered by my book. However, that is not the case. Books which fall into the former category are often excellent books but serve a very different purpose from mine. These include *Don't Know Much about the American Presidents* by Kenneth Davis, *The American Presidents* by David Whitney and *The Big New Book of U.S. Presidents* by Todd Davis. Books which fall into the latter category are often deeply flawed for reasons I will discuss.

1. Non-quiz books which are organized by president, focusing on one at a time

There are two major distinctions between this category of

books and mine. First is the obvious fact that they are not quiz books. I favor the quiz approach because it provides readers with an interactive experience which actually tests their knowledge of the presidents as opposed to a passive experience which does not involve reader participation, other than of course to read the book. Second, and more importantly, rather than focusing on topics such as those covered in the 31 chapters in this book, books in this category almost always discuss the presidents in order, focusing on one president per chapter. Often, they are like short biographies of each president. These can be valuable reference tools, but they have a different goal from my book.

The one-by-one format is limiting in certain important ways, at least in terms of what I set out to accomplish. For example, in books organized by president, there is no ability to compare and contrast the presidents, such as by comparing their relative rankings, their media appearances, their religions, etc. In addition, questions such as "How many presidents… ?," "Who was the only president who … ?" and, "who was the first president … ," cannot be included in a non-quiz book which examines each president in order. In fact, a main feature of this book is to consider the presidents vis-à-vis each other and not as islands unto themselves. For example, virtually every chart in this book considers all of the presidents inter se. In short, any book that is organized by president, while quite possibly an excellent source to learn about each president, is necessarily going to be a very different kind of book from this one.

2. Quiz books

While quiz books are more similar in format to my book, I concluded that, unlike many of the books which fall into the above category, these books leave a lot to be desired. In fact, if it wasn't for my disappointment at the quality of the question-and-answer books written on this topic, I would never have written this one.

Many of these books refer to themselves as "trivia" books, but I cringe at that word because it is derogatory and belittling and carries with it a suggestion that the topic matter is uninteresting. In fact, "trivial" means "of little importance or value; insignificant." That is not my view of the subject matter of this book, and as discussed below, I have tried to avoid questions which really are "trivial."

While I am reluctant to find fault with other books in the genre (even if only as a class), it is fair for readers to want to know how this book is different from, and an improvement over, books that seem to cover common ground. Therefore, it is appropriate that I answer that question.

There are four major flaws with other quiz books on this topic. I set out to write one which redresses all of them and which is hopefully informative and entertaining.

A. Lots of redundancy—little originality

Other books on this subject tend to cover the same material as each other. "If you've read one, you've read 'em all" is not an overstatement with these books because they all seem to repeat each other's information. I have tried to avoid that repetition and instead include as much original and interesting information in my book as possible.   A few examples:

Q: Calvin Coolidge's vice president accomplished two feats which it is safe to say will never again be accomplished by a vice president or likely any other person either. He won a Nobel Peace Prize and he was a co-writer of a song which reached no. 1 on the *Billboard* pop chart. Who was this man?

A: Charles Dawes. He won the Nobel Peace Prize in 1925 for the Dawes Plan, a program to enable Germany to restore and stabilize its economy after World War I. Unfortunately, the Plan proved unworkable and was replaced with a different plan in 1929.

His song was called *It's All in the Game*. Dawes, an amateur pianist, composed the tune in 1911. It was entitled *Melody in A Major*. In 1951, the year Dawes died, songwriter Carl Sigman added lyrics to it (although the tune was popular before then, so much so that Dawes grew to detest hearing it wherever he appeared). In 1958, it was recorded by Tommy Edwards. It reached number one on the *Billboard* pop chart on September 29 of that year, and stayed there for six weeks. Edwards' song ranked at #38 on *Billboard's All Time Top 100*, one ahead of *I Want to Hold your Hand*, by the Beatles. It has been recorded by Dinah Shore, Sammy Kaye, Louis Armstrong, Nat King Cole, Andy Williams, Robert Goulet, Cliff Richard, The Lettermen, Jackie DeShannon, The Four Tops, Cass Elliott, Van Morrison, Neil Sedaka, Merle Haggard and Johnny Mathis, among others. Imagine how tired Dawes would have become of the song if he had lived a few more years.

Q: Several future presidents appeared on the TV game show *"What's My Line?"* One of them appeared only two years before he was elected president and the panel did not know who he was, even though they were not blindfolded (i.e. he was not the mystery celebrity). Who was this president?

A: Jimmy Carter. He appeared while he was governor of Georgia on December 13, 1973. He signed his name with a large "X", indicating that the producers felt that he might be recognized by name though not by sight. One of the early exchanges that threw off the panel was when he was asked if his service "has to do with women" and his answer was, "Yes, it certainly does … but not enough." Although the panel eventually determined that he was a governor, none of them knew who he was and it was the host who had to identify him as "Jimmy Carter, governor of Georgia." A clip of the show can be seen on YouTube.

Two other future presidents also appeared on *What's My Line?* One was Gerald Ford. He appeared as a mystery guest in 1969 when he was a House Minority leader. The panel did not guess his identity. The other was Ronald Reagan who also appeared as a mystery guest in 1954. The panel had no trouble guessing his identity, though based on his fame as an actor at the time and obviously not as a politician.

Q: *Washington Crossing the Delaware* is an 1851 oil-on-canvas painting by German American artist Emanuel Gottlieb Leutze. It commemorates General George Washington's crossing of the Delaware River on December 25, 1776, during the American Revolutionary War. A future president (besides Washington) is depicted in the painting, immediately to the left of Washington. Who is it?

A: James Monroe. He was a lieutenant at the time and is seen holding the American flag, as designed by Betsy Ross. However, this is a historical anachronism. That flag had not yet been designed and did not fly until September 3, 1777, well after the scene depicted. The historically accurate flag would have been the Grand Union Flag, which was the first national flag. That flag resembles our national flag today except that, instead of the 50 stars, the upper left resembles a squared-off Union Jack, without the red diagonal lines.

Q: Based on the results of 13 major surveys of the "greatness" rankings of presidents prepared between 1948 and 2011, only one president appears in three different quartiles at least three times. Who is he?

A: Ronald Reagan appears in the first quartile five times, the second five times and the third three times.

In addition, the variety of the subject matters covered is much broader than in other books about the presidents. The chapter headings are as follows:

Activities and deeds when not president	Pets
	Political Parties
Appearance	Quotes by Presidents
Birth	Quotes about Presidents
Campaigning	Quotes by Presidents about Presidents
Currency and stamps	Rankings
Death	Religion
Education	Slavery
Elections	Subjective/whimsical
Events During	Supreme Court
Family	Vice Presidents as they relate to Presidents
General	
Inaugurations	War and Peace
Marriage	Wealth and Poverty
Media	Who was the first ...
Pardons	Who is the only ...

B. No backstory or supplemental information in the questions or answers.

This is another important flaw in most presidential fact books. The answers to the questions typically consist of simply identifying the president who is the correct answer (or some other one or two word answer which is the correct answer). Thus, the answers (in their entirety) are typically something like the following:

Rutherford B. Hayes	Benjamin Harrison
The Monroe Doctrine	Canada
The East Room	1847

In other words, there is no backstory or supplemental information provided at all. In my book, I try to provide not only the answer but as much additional information as I felt would interest the reader—in essence a narrative answer. Because of this distinction, even when there are questions in my book which also appear in others, I included them because I felt my answers would be more interesting to most readers than the usual one or two word answer.

For example, contrast following questions and answers:

Q: Which president was shot in the chest while campaigning?

A. Theodore Roosevelt.

Q: Which president was shot in the chest while campaigning?

A: Theodore Roosevelt. He was campaigning in Milwaukee, Wisconsin, on October 14, 1912, when a saloonkeeper named John Schrank shot him. The bullet lodged in his chest after penetrating his steel eyeglass case and passing through a thick (50 pages) single-folded copy of the speech he was carrying in his jacket. Roosevelt concluded that since he wasn't coughing blood, the bullet had not completely penetrated the chest wall to his lung, and so declined suggestions he go to the hospital immediately. Instead, he delivered his scheduled speech with blood seeping onto his shirt. He spoke for 90 minutes.

His opening comments to the gathered crowd were, "Ladies and gentlemen, I don't know whether you fully understand that I have just been shot; but it takes more than that to kill a Bull Moose." Afterwards, probes and an x-ray showed that the bullet had traversed three inches of tissue and lodged in Roosevelt's chest muscle but did not penetrate the pleura, and it would be more dangerous to attempt to remove the bullet than to leave it in place. Roosevelt carried it with him for the rest of his life. Schrank was declared insane on November 13, 1912 and committed to the Northern State Hospital for the Insane at Oshkosh, WI, and died at the Central State Hospital in Waupun, WI on September 15, 1943.

Since this occurred in 1912, and Roosevelt's term ended in 1909, it also makes Roosevelt the answer to the question: who is the only former president to have been the target of an assassination attempt?

C. Questions or facts presented in other books are either too obscure or trivial and uninteresting

Another common flaw with other presidential knowledge books is that the questions are obscure and/or the answers are uninteresting. Thus the readers' reaction to many of the questions will be: "I don't know and I wouldn't care if I did know." This is also often the case with books that are not set up in question and answer format and instead simply throw useless facts at the reader. Consider for example the following questions (or facts presented), culled from a variety of presidential knowledge books.

1. What was the favorite food of Theodore Roosevelt's family blue macaw? (Coffee grounds)
2. Which first lady once had menus for a White House dinner printed on satin? (Julia Grant)
3. Under whose name did Andrew Jackson register his racehorses to avoid bad press? (Andrew Donelson, who was Mrs. Jackson's nephew)
4. Whose Irish-born father immigrated to Pennsylvania in 1783? (James Buchanan)
5. George H.W. Bush was the first President born in June.

6. Which President was deemed by the American Conference Management Association to be the "father of the conference or retreat center"? (Dwight Eisenhower)
7. During the War of 1812, John Tyler was briefly a captain in what militia unit? (Charles City Rifles)
8. Who was president when Hudson Taylor went as a Christian Missionary to China? (Franklin Pierce)

Obviously most readers would not know the answers to these kinds of questions, nor would they really care if they did. This is not to say that I expect most readers will know the answers to many of my questions—I don't. But I do feel that the questions are interesting and the answers have depth and substance.

Another fault of other books on this topic is largely the opposite of the obscure questions fault, namely that, unless one has absolutely no interest in the presidents at all, the answers would be known to virtually everyone. The following are all actual questions from other books of this kind:

1. Who was the only President who resigned from office? (Richard Nixon)
2. Who were the only two Presidents to be impeached by the House? (Andrew Johnson and Bill Clinton)
3. Who was Jimmy Carter's vice president? (Walter Mondale)
4. Who, at the end of his first week in office, initiated his radio "fireside chats"? (Franklin Roosevelt)
5. Which election was finally decided by the Supreme Court? (Bush v. Gore in 2000)
6. What is the first George Bush's full name? (George Herbert Walker Bush)
7. The first ten Amendments to the Constitution, passed under George Washington, are known as what? (The Bill of Rights)

D. Answers are not sourced and are sometimes wrong

Rather surprisingly, there appears not to be a single book of this kind which has ever provided the specific sources for its answers. There are a few books which contain generalized bibliographies at the end, but they do not tie a particular source to any particular question. Perhaps not coincidentally, erroneous answers are not uncommon in these books. In my book, I provide the sources for many answers.

Q: Walt Whitman wrote a famous poem which begins:

> *O Captain! my Captain! our fearful trip is done;*
> *The ship has weathered every rack, the prize we sought is won;*
> *The port is near, the bells I hear, the people all exulting,*
> *While follow eyes the steady keel, the vessel grim and daring*

Who is this poem about?

A: Abraham Lincoln. It was written in 1865 just after the Civil War ended and Lincoln had been assassinated. Whitman was mourning his death. The last verse reads:

> *My Captain does not answer, his lips are pale and still;*
> *My father does not feel my arm, he has no pulse nor will;*
> *The ship is anchored safe and sound, its voyage closed and done;*
> *From fearful trip, the victor ship, comes in with object won;*
> *Exult, O shores, and ring, O bells!*
> *But I, with mournful tread,*
> *Walk the deck my Captain lies,*
> *Fallen cold and dead*

Reef, Catherine, *Walt Whitman*. Houghton Mifflin Harcourt. (2002)
Kaplan, Justin, *Walt Whitman: A Life*. Simon and Schuster (1979)

Q: Which former president later ran for office as a member of the Know Nothing Party?

A: Millard Fillmore. The Know Nothing Party was mainly active from 1854 to 1856, and was based on fears that the country was being overwhelmed by German and Irish Catholic immigrants, who were often regarded as hostile to Anglo-Saxon Protestant values and controlled by the Pope in Rome. It wanted only American-born Protestants elected to public office. In the 1856 election, Fillmore carried one state, Maryland.

Levine, Bruce. "Conservatism, Nativism, and Slavery: Thomas R. Whitney and the Origins of the Know Nothing Party" *Journal of American History* (2001).

Q: Who is the only president to have taught at an all-female college?

A: Woodrow Wilson, who taught at Bryn Mawr College on the Main Line outside Philadelphia. After receiving his doctorate in history from Johns Hopkins University in 1885, took a job teaching women at newly established college. He taught various courses, including Greece, Rome, English history and political science. At the time the college had only 42 students. In his diary he wrote: "Lecturing on the history and precepts of politics to young ladies is no more appropriate or profitable than lecturing to stone masons on the evolution of fashion in clothing. There seems to be a 'painful absenteeism of mind' among your listeners. Your speech generates no heat, because it passes through a vacuum." He disliked "women who meddled in the serious concerns of masculine life such as scholarship" which likely did not go over well at a school which scorned any implication of female inferiority. In 1888 he went to teach at Wesleyan University.

Dixon, Mark. *Scut Work—Like many job-hunting new graduates,*

Woodrow Wilson took what he could get. Main Line Times, May 20, 2010.http://www.sparknotes.com/biography/wilson/section3.rhtml

As between the novel questions and the full (and sourced) answers, I believe that the material in this book is fresh, original and entertaining. I hope you agree.

CHAPTER 1

Activities/Accomplishments When Not President

Q: Which president set an equestrian high jump record at West Point that lasted more than twenty-five years?

A: Ulysses Grant. As written in *Sports Illustrated*:

Grant was long remembered at West Point for the leap he made at the graduation exercises of the senior class. "The riding master placed a leaping bar higher than a man's head and called out 'Cadet Grant,'" wrote General James B. Fry. "A clean-faced, slender, blue-eyed young fellow, weighing about 120 pounds, dashed from the ranks on a powerfully-built chestnut sorrel horse and galloped down the opposite side of the hall. As he ... came into the stretch ... the horse increased his pace and, measuring his stride for the great leap before him, bounded into the air and cleared the bar, carrying his rider as if man and beast had been welded together. The spectators were breathless." Grant set the academy high-jump record which endured for some twenty-five years, but the exact height of the bar is questionable. One biography puts it at five feet, six inches, another at over six feet. [1]

Q: Which president came up with a proof of the Pythagorean Theorem? The Pythagorean Theorem states that in any right triangle, the area of the square whose side is the hypotenuse (the side opposite the right angle) is equal to the sum of the areas of the squares whose sides are the two legs (the two sides that meet at the right angle). It can be written as an equation relating the lengths of the sides a, b and c (often called the *Pythagorean equation*), as $a^2 + b^2 = c^2$.

A: James Garfield. He discovered the proof in 1876, five years before he become president. It was later published in *The New England Journal of Education*. [2]

Q: What president was named the president of a college at age twenty-six?

A: James Garfield. He was president of Hiram College (then named the Western Reserve Eclectic Institute) from 1857 to 1863. At the time they were called 'principals' rather than 'Presidents.' [3]

Q: Besides James Garfield, which other presidents were also college or university presidents?

A: Woodrow Wilson was president of Princeton from 1902-1910 and **Dwight Eisenhower** was president of Columbia from 1948-1953, although he took a leave of absence to become Supreme Commander of NATO from December, 1950 to May, 1952. In addition, **Millard Fillmore** was the first Chancellor of the University of Buffalo, although that University did not have presidents until later. People may assume that Thomas Jefferson was president of the University of Virginia, a reasonable assumption since he founded that University in 1819. However, that University did not have a president until 1904 and was instead governed by a Board of Visitors until that time. [4]

Q: Which President invented the swivel chair?

A: Thomas Jefferson. Jefferson actually invented or improved on existing forms of a number of products although he did not obtain patents for any, based on his belief that every invention should benefit all of society. These include: a dumbwaiter for wine bottles, which permitted them to be sent up from the cellar, the hideaway bed, a macaroni extruding device, the pedometer, the plow moldboard of least resistance, the polygraph (not a lie detector, but a copying machine), a revolving bookstand, the spherical sundial and a wheel cipher. [5]

Q: Only three presidents were also governors, senators and vice presidents. Who are they?

A: Martin Van Buren (New York), **John Tyler** (Virginia), and **Andrew Johnson** (Tennessee).

Q: Only one president was also governor of a state and a senator but not a vice president. Who is he?

A: James Monroe (Virginia). The 'of a State' qualifier was added because William Henry Harrison was a senator of Ohio and also a governor, but of the Indiana Territory (from 1800-1812), which was not a state. The Indiana Territory consisted of the future states of Indiana, Illinois, Michigan, Wisconsin and the eastern portion of Minnesota. [6]

Q: Which president, after office, mediated a dispute between Major League Baseball and the owners regarding the umpire's demand for more compensation?

A: Richard Nixon. In 1985, the umpires wanted extra compensation for working seven games instead of five in the American and the National League playoffs. *People Magazine* reported: "According to eyewitnesses at the arbitration, Nixon presided over the meeting between the umpires' lawyers and representatives from both leagues in his Manhattan office with aplomb and dignity, sipping soda from a glass with the presidential seal and listening to the arguments pro and con." [7]

Q: There has only been one book written by a president specifically about another president. Who was the author and who was the subject? As a hint, the author served under the president as head of the Food Adminstration but was from a different political party.

A: Herbert Hoover wrote *The Ordeal of Woodrow Wilson* in 1958. The book is generally favorable to Wilson. In a review of the book for *The Atlantic*, David Burner wrote, "Hoover's book was meant as a tribute to his former chief, but it is easy to suspect that anger and hurt might underlie a portrayal that presents the worst as well as the best in one of our greatest statesmen. What makes Hoover's memoir especially valuable to readers already familiar with the story are matters of tone and interpretation which Hoover himself ... probably did not notice that he was making available." [8]

Q: Which president declined an honorary degree from Oxford, explaining on some occasions that it was because he had done nothing to deserve the honor (or in his words, he had "neither literary nor scientific attainment") and on other occasions that it was because he said he couldn't read Latin (or in his words "no man should accept a degree he cannot read")?

A: Millard Fillmore. [9]

Q: Rank the following in terms of which of the three offices has produced the most presidents: governor of a state, senator, vice president.

A: Governors and senators are tied, with sixteen each.

1. The sixteen governors:
    Thomas Jefferson: Governor of Virginia from 1779-1781.
    James Monroe: served as Governor of Virginia from 1799-1802, and again served for a brief period from January through April in 1811.
    John Tyler: Governor of Virginia, serving from 1825-1827.
    Martin Van Buren: Governor of New York in 1829.
    James Polk: Governor of Tennessee, serving from 1839-1841.
    Andrew Johnson: Governor of Tennessee from 1853-1857. and then appointed by Lincoln to serve as military governor of Tennessee from 1862-1864.
    Rutherford Hayes: Governor of Ohio from 1868-1872 and again from 1876-1877.
    Grover Cleveland: Governor of New York from 1883-1885.
    William McKinley: Governor of Ohio from 1892-1896.
    Woodrow Wilson: Governor of New Jersey from 1911-1913.
    Calvin Coolidge: Governor of Massachusetts from 1919-1921.
    Franklin Delano Roosevelt: Governor of New York from 1929-1933.
    Ronald Reagan: Governor of California from 1967-1975.
    Jimmy Carter: Governor of Georgia from 1971-1975.
    Bill Clinton: Governor of Arkansas for two separate terms, from 1979-1981, and from 1983-1992.
    George W. Bush: Governor of Texas from 1995-2000.

2. The sixteen senators:
    James Monroe: Senator from Virginia from 1790-1794.
    John Quincy Adams: Senator from Massachusetts from 1803-1808.
    Andrew Jackson: Senator Tennessee from 1797-1798 and from 1823-1825.
    Martin Van Buren: Senator from New York from 1821-1828.
    William Henry Harrison: Senator from Ohio from 1825-1828.
    John Tyler: Senator from Virginia from 1827-1836.

Franklin Pierce: Senator from new Hampshire from 1837-1842.
James Buchanan: Senator from Pennsylvania from1834-1845.
Andrew Johnson: Senator from Tennessee from 1857-1862.
Benjamin Harrison: Senator from Indiana from1881-1887.
Warren G. Harding: Senator from Ohio from 1915-1921.
Harry S. Truman: Senator from Missouri from 1935-1945.
John F. Kennedy: Senator from Massachusetts from 1953-1960.
Lyndon B. Johnson: Senator from Texas from 1949-1961.
Richard M. Nixon: Senator from California from 1950-1953.
Barack Obama: Senator from Illinois from 2005-2008.

3. Vice presidents: fourteen. The names in bold are the men who became president by running for the office and winning as opposed to succeeding to the office through the death or resignation of their predecessor. Of these, Nixon was the only one who did not succeed the man under whom he served as vice president. **John Adams**, **Thomas Jefferson**, **Martin Van Buren**, John Tyler, Millard Fillmore, Andrew Johnson, Chester Arthur, Theodore Roosevelt, Calvin Coolidge, Harry Truman, Lyndon Johnson, **Richard Nixon**, Gerald Ford, **George H. W. Bush**.[10]

Q: One of the presidents was formerly the fourth youngest governor in history. Who was he?

A: Bill Clinton. He was thirty-two when first elected Arkansas governor in 1978. The other three were Stevens T. Mason of the Michigan Territory, who was elected in 1835 having just turned twenty-four. He was still governor when Michigan was admitted to the Union in January 1837, when he was twenty-five, and he was re-elected in November 1837, at age twenty-six. The second youngest governor ever elected was J. Neely Johnson of California (age thirty in 1855), and the third youngest was Harold Stassen of Minnesota (age thirty-one in 1938).

Q: Which president had previously been a public execution-er and personally hanged two murderers?

A: Grover Cleveland. Cleveland was elected sheriff of Erie County, New York at age thirty-three. In that role, he hanged two murderers, Patrick Morrisey, on September 6, 1872 and John Gaffney on February 14, 1873. Morrisey had murdered his mother. Although Cleveland had the option of paying a deputy $10 to perform the task, and had qualms about the hanging, he nevertheless opted to carry out the duty himself.[11]

Q: Which president was retained as an attorney to represent the Republic of Venezuela in their boundary dispute with the United Kingdom, during which he filed an eight-hundred page brief?

A: Benjamin Harrison. The two nations disputed the border between Venezuela and British Guiana. An international trial was agreed upon and the Venezuelan government hired Harrison to represent them in the case. Harrison traveled to Paris where he spent more than twenty-five hours arguing in court. Although he lost the case, his legal arguments won him international renown.[12]

Q: Which president played in the first two college baseball World Series?

A: George H.W. Bush. His Yale teams lost to California in 1947 and to USC in 1948. Bush was captain of the 1948 team. In the 1948 Series, he got to meet Babe Ruth and there is a photo of the two of them shaking hands. Ruth died later that year. Of the meeting, Bush said, "I was the captain of the ball club, so I got to receive him there. He was dying. He was hoarse and could hardly talk. He kind of croaked when they set up the mike by the pitcher's mound. It was tragic. He was hollow. His whole great shape was gaunt and hollowed out."[13]

Q: Which president lost sight in his left eye while boxing at the White House?

A: Theodore Roosevelt. [14]

Q: Which president formed a company called "Adventurers for Draining the Great Dismal Swamp?"

A: George Washington in 1763. The Great Dismal Swamp lies across the Virginia-South Carolina tidewater country. It is about 750-square miles in size. In May 1763, George Washington made his first visit to the Swamp and suggested draining it and digging a north-south canal through it to connect the waters of Chesapeake Bay in Virginia and Albemarle Sound in North Carolina. Joining with several other prominent Virginians and North Carolinians, he formed two syndicates known as the Dismal Swamp Land Company and the Adventurers for Draining the Great Dismal Swamp. This group hoped to drain the swamp, harvest the trees, and use the land for farming.

The company purchased 40,000 acres of Swamp land for $20,000 in 1763. Washington directed the surveying and digging of the five-mile long ditch from the western edge of the Swamp to Lake Drummond, known today as Washington Ditch. The ditch provided a way to transport logs out of the swamp and drain it as well. The adventurers soon realized, however, that the task of draining the Swamp was enormous and gave up that part of their plan to concentrate on lumbering. [15]

Q: Who is the only president who was a published poet?

A: John Quincy Adams. His poems, published in *Poems of Religion and Society* (1848), included *To the Sun-Dial* [1840] and *The Wants of Man* [1841]. Was he a talented poet? At least one reviewer, commenting on Adams's byline with respect to his long poem, *Dermot MacMorrogh or the Conquest of Ireland*, wrote:

"Indeed, it is that short sentence of four words—By John Quincy Adams—to which Dermot MacMorrogh will be solely indebted for all the attention it will receive. Were it not for this magic sentence, we doubt if many readers would get further than the middle of the first Canto; and we are quite certain that none would ever reach the end of the second."[16]

Q: Which presidents received posthumous law degrees from Columbia in 2008?

A: Theodore Roosevelt and **Franklin Roosevelt**. Both Presidents attended and but did not graduate from Columbia Law School. Theodore was meant to be a member of the Class of 1882 and Franklin the Class of 1907, but both departed early to embark on their political careers, never receiving their juris doctor degrees.[17]

Q: What president was given the title Chief Scout Citizen by the Boy Scouts of America, the only person to hold that designation?

A: Theodore Roosevelt. Of course, Roosevelt was not a scout himself since the organization was not established until 1910.[18]

Q: Which president became close friends with author Nathaniel Hawthorne while the two were students at Bowdoin College in Maine?

A: Franklin Pierce. Hawthorne would go on to write the official Franklin Pierce campaign biography, and in 1853, Pierce appointed him as United States consul in Liverpool, England.[19]

Q: Which president juggled Indian clubs to build his muscles?

A: James Garfield. [20]

Q: A PBS series called _The American Experience_ noted that this President desperately wanted to join the Navy but he was concerned about his flat feet and that he was too thin. To combat the flat feet, he rolled them over Coke bottles to strengthen the arches. To gain weight, he went on a banana diet. He was accepted into the Navy. Who was he?

A: Jimmy Carter. [21]

Q: Which president attained a third degree brown belt in judo?

A: Theodore Roosevelt. He was the first American ever to attain this rank. In 2007, The United States Judo Association posthumously presented him with an honorary black belt for embracing the sport of judo at a ceremony at Sagamore Hill in Oyster Bay, NY. [22]

Q: Which future president, at the age of thirty-two, became the youngest Solicitor General in U.S. history?

A: William Howard Taft in 1890. He was appointed by Benjamin Harrison.

Q: The personal library of which president effectively established the initial collection of the Library of Congress?

A: Thomas Jefferson. On April 24, 1800, president John Adams approved legislation that appropriated $5,000 to purchase "such books as may be necessary for the use of Congress." The first books, ordered from London, arrived in 1801 and were stored in the U.S. Capitol, the Library's first home. The collection consisted of 740 volumes and three maps. In 1814, the British army invaded the city of Washington and burned the Capitol, including the 3,000-volume Library of Congress. By then retired to

Monticello, Jefferson offered to sell his personal library, the largest and finest in the country, to the Congress to "recommence" its library. The purchase of Jefferson's 6,487 volumes for $23,940 was approved in 1815. The library that Jefferson sold to Congress not only included over twice the number of volumes that had been in the destroyed Library of Congress, it also expanded the scope of the library far beyond the bounds of a legislative library devoted primarily to legal, economic, and historical works. The Library's initial collection after the 1814 fire therefore, for a time, consisted of Jefferson's personal library. [23]

Q: Which president was a noted newspaper publisher?

A: Warren Harding. He was the owner and publisher of the *Marion Daily Star* from the 1880's until 1923, the last year of his presidency. It is still published today and is now owned by Gannett.[24]

Q: Which president wrote a book called *Fishing for Fun—and to Wash Your Soul?*

A: Herbert Hoover. It was 86 pages long and published by Random House in 1963.

Q: Which president wrote a book called *Fishing and Shooting Sketches?*

A: Grover Cleveland. It was published by Library Reprints in 1906.

Q: Which president tried to tackle Jim Thorpe in a football game?

A: Dwight Eisenhower. The play took place on November 9, 1912 when Thorpe's Carlisle team played Army, on which

Eisenhower played. Thorpe had recently won gold medals in the 1912 Olympics in Stockholm, Sweden. On the third play of the game, Thorpe ran off tackle. Eisenhower met him in the hole and Thorpe ran right through him, knocking him out of the game with a broken nose. Carlisle wound up winning 27-6. Eisenhower's football career ended the very next week when he suffered a severe knee injury against Tufts University. An entire book was written about the Carlisle game by Lars Anderson called *Carlisle vs. Army: Jim Thorpe, Dwight Eisenhower, Pop Warner, and the Forgotten Story of Football's Greatest Battle* (Random House, 2007).

There is also some evidence that Eisenhower may have briefly played semi-professional baseball in Kansas City in 1911. While there does not exist a great deal of evidence about this, Major League star Mel Ott said, "The General admitted that as a youth he had done so (played semi-pro ball), under the assumed name of Wilson." *The Baseball Reference Guide* does list a player by the name "Wilson" on the 1911 roster of the Junction City Soldiers minor league team of Junction City, Kansas. He played in nine games and batted .355.

In 1912, he attended the United States Military Academy at West Point. Student athletes entering the Academy have to pledge that they have never played professional sports because if they have done so, they would have to forfeit their amateur status. If Eisenhower did play semi-professional baseball, even if briefly, he would have had to sign such a pledge and if he pledged falsely, it would have been a violation of the Cadet Honor Code (although the Honor Code would not be formalized for several years). If this had been discovered, it could have derailed his military career and thus his political career thereafter. [25]

Q: Who is the only president to have parachuted out of a plane (twice voluntarily and once involuntarily)?

A: George H.W. Bush in 1944, 1997 and 2004. In World War II, he had to bail out of a crippled Navy Avenger bomber. [26]

Q: What 20th-century president was President of Columbia University?

A: Dwight Eisenhower. [27]

Q: What president got in trouble in high school for exploding a toilet seat with fire crackers?

A: John Kennedy. This occurred at Choate where he was a member of the class of 1935. In the ensuing chapel assembly, the strict headmaster, George St. John, brandished the toilet seat and spoke of certain "muckers" who would "spit in our sea." [28]

Q: Which Boy Scouts became president?

A: John Kennedy and **Gerald Ford**, the latter being the only Eagle Scout who became president. [29]

Q: Which president was a reasonably accomplished piano player who also composed pieces of his own?

A: Richard Nixon. A 1961 clip of Nixon playing one of his own pieces on *The Jack Paar Program* can be seen on YouTube. Harry Truman was also a piano player. A brief clip of Truman playing is at http://www.criticalpast.com/video/6567502423. During Nixon's appearance on Paar's show, he took a little jab at Truman: "Jack, you asked a moment ago whether I had any future political plans to run for anything. If last November didn't finish it, this will because, believe me, the Republicans don't want another piano player in the White House."

Q: Which president helped his college football team to two consecutive undefeated seasons and NCAA titles and was the only president who was offered contracts by teams in the National Football League?

A: Gerald Ford. His 1932 Michigan team was 8-0 and the 1933 team was 7-0-1. It has often been written that Ford "starred" on these teams but that is not the case. In fact, he was not a starter on either team, though he was the starting center on the 1934 team that unfortunately went 1-7. In 1932, he won the Meyer Morton award, given to the football player who shows the greatest development and most promise as a result of the annual spring practice. Following his graduation in 1935 with a Bachelor of Arts degree in economics, he turned down contract offers from the Detroit Lions and Green Bay Packers of the NFL to take a coaching position at Yale and apply to its law school.

Ford is also the answer to the question: Who is the only president to tackle a Heisman Trophy winner? In a game against the University of Chicago on October 13, 1934, he tackled Jay Berwanger, who went on the win the first Heisman Trophy award in 1935. [30]

Q: Which president personally approved the redesign of the Presidential seal so that the eagle's head faced to the left rather than the right?

A: Harry Truman. In 1877, President Hayes was the first president to use the Presidential seal on White House invitations, although the basic design existed before that time. Although it is not entirely clear when the basic design first came into being, virtually all versions of it depict an eagle, wingtips up, holding an olive branch in its dexter (left) talon and arrows in its sinister (right) talon, with an arc of cloud puffs between the wings, stars scattered below the arc and a scroll in its mouth reading *E Pluribus*

Unum. (Some designs predate Washington's presidency.) From Hayes' term onward, the eagle always faced towards the right.

In 1945, Arthur E. DuBois, the chief of the Heraldic Section of the Army's Office of the Quartermaster General (forerunner to the Army Institute of Heraldry), made several suggestions. including changing the direction the eagle faced. Truman liked the fact that the eagle would now face towards the olive branches (which he felt was symbolic of a nation on the march and dedicated to peace). On October 25, 1945, President Truman issued Executive Order 9646, which officially defined the presidential coat of arms and seal for the first time. That order read in part "By virtue of the authority vested in me as President of the United States, it is hereby ordered as follows:"

> The Coat of Arms of the President of the United States shall be of the following design:
>
> SHIELD: Paleways of thirteen pieces Argent and Gules, a chief Azure; upon the breast of an American eagle displayed holding in his dexter talon an olive branch and in his sinister a bundle of thirteen arrows all Proper, and in his beak a white scroll inscribed "E PLURIBUS UNUM" Sable.
>
> CREST: Behind and above the eagle a radiating glory or, on which appears an arc of thirteen cloud puffs proper, and a constellation of thirteen mullets Argent.
>
> The whole surrounded by white stars arranged in the form of an annulet with one point of each star outward on the imaginary radiating center lines, the number of stars conforming to the number of stars in the union of the Flag of the United States as established by the act of Congress approved April 4, 1818.

The only changes since have been to add stars to the outer circle in 1959 and 1960, with the addition of Alaska and Hawaii to statehood. [31]

Q: What president shot a hole-in-one during a Pro-am golf tournament?

A: Gerald Ford, at the 1977 Danny Thomas Memphis Classic at the Colonial Country Club in Memphis, Tennessee. [32]

Q: Which president co-founded the University of Buffalo?

A: Millard Fillmore, in 1846. Today there is a Millard Fillmore College at the University. [33]

Q: Which president announced Chicago Cubs games on radio?

A: Ronald Reagan. His descriptions of the action on the field were largely improvised, and were based solely on telegraph accounts of games in progress. On June 7th, 1934, something dramatic happened. The telegraph went out. This is how Reagan described what happened next:

"There were several other stations broadcasting that game and I knew I'd lose my audience if I told them we'd lost our telegraph connections so I took a chance. I had (Billy) Jurges hit another foul. Then I had him foul one that only missed being a home run by a foot. I had him foul one back in the stands and took up some time describing the two lads that got in a fight over the ball. I kept on having him foul balls until I was setting a record for a ballplayer hitting successive foul balls and I was getting more than a little scared. Just then my operator started typing. When he passed me the paper I started to giggle—it said: 'Jurges popped out on the first ball pitched." [34]

Q: During college, which president was a lifeguard and is credited with saving seventy-seven lives?

A: Ronald Reagan. [35]

Q: While modeling for a sculpting class in 1940, this president was deemed as having "the most nearly perfect male figure" by the Division of Fine Arts at the University of Southern California. Who was he?

A: Ronald Reagan. [36]

CHAPTER ONE NOTES:

1) Durant, John, *Horses for the General*, Sports Illustrated, 8/13/56.
   http://2009famousamericans.pbworks.com/w/page/798957/UlyssesSGrant
2) http://math.colgate.edu/faculty/dlantz/pythpfs/garfldpf.html James A Garfield (1876). *The New England Journal of Education* 3: 161.
3) http://www.hiram.edu/visitors/about/historyofhiram.html
   http://bioguide.congress.gov/scripts/biodisplay.pl?index=G000063
4) http://www.britannica.com/EBchecked/topic/630010/University-of-Virginia
5) http://cti.itc.virginia.edu/~meg3c/classes/tcc313/200Rprojs/jefferson_invent/invent. html Fahlman, Bradley D., *Materials Chemistry* (Springer, 2007)
   http://www.tititudorancea.org/z/james_a_garfield.htm
6) Owens, Robert M., *Mr. Jefferson's Hammer: William Henry Harrison and the Origins of American Indian Policy.* University of Oklahoma Press (2007).
7) *Richard Nixon Is Called Off the Bench to Make a Close Baseball Decision*, People Magazine, November 24, 1985
8) http://books.google.com/books/about/The_Ordeal_of_Woodrow_Wilson.html
9) http://www.juntosociety.com/uspresidents/mfillmore.html
   http://ourwhitehouse.org/prespgs/mfillmore.html
   http://www.librarything.com/topic/51523
   http://www.potus.com/mfillmore.html
   http://www.pbs.org/wgbh/americanexperience/features/biography/presidents-fillmore
10) http://www.senate.gov/artandhistory/history/common/briefing/senators_became_president.htm
11) Jeffers, H. Paul, *An Honest President: The Life and Presidencies of Grover Cleveland*, Harper Perennial (2002), p. 34.
    Nevins, Allan. *Grover Cleveland: A Study in Courage*, Dodd, Mead (1932), p. 61-62. Nevins' book won a Pulitzer Prize.
12) Moore, Chieko and Hale, Hester Anne, *Benjamin Harrison: Centennial President*, Nova Publishers (2006).
    Calhoun, Charles William, *Benjamin Harrison*. Macmillan (2005).
13) http://www.baseball-reference.com/bullpen/College_World_Series
    http://www.baseball-almanac.com/prz_qgb.shtml
14) *Theodore Roosevelt Dies Suddenly at Oyster Bay Home; Nation Shocked, Pays Tribute to Former President, The New York Times* Obituary, January, 1919

Blind in Left Eye, Roosevelt Admits; Colonel Reveals That He Lost Sight of Organ in Boxing Bout Years Ago, The New York Times, 10/22/1917, p. 10

15) http://www.albemarle-nc.com/gates/greatdismal
http://www.dismalswampwelcomecenter.com/History.php
http://www3.cesa10.k12.wi.us/ecosystems/wetlands/types/greatdismalswamp/index.htm

16) http://theotherpages.org/poems/poem-ab.html#jqadams
http://www.loc.gov/rr/program/bib/prespoetry/jqa.html

17) http://www.law.columbia.edu/media_inquiries/news_events/2008/october2008/roosevelts_jds

18) Scott, David; *We Are Americans, We Are Scouts: The Chief Scout Citizen on Building a Scouting Way of Life,* Red Honor Press (2008).
http://www.sossi.org/scouters/roosevelt.htm

19) McFarland, Philip, *Hawthorne in Concord.* Grove Press (2004).
Hawthorne, Nathaniel, *Life of Franklin Pierce,* Fredonia Books (2002)(originally published in 1852).

20) http://www.geni.com/people/James-A-Garfield-20th-President-of-the-USA/6000000003044154591

21) http://www.pbs.org/wgbh/americanexperience/features/transcript/carter-transcript/

22) http://www.fightingarts.com/content01/putin.html
http://mysite.verizon.net/resptwx6/roosevelt.htm
http://www.healthleader.uthouston.edu/archive/presidential_health/2008/teddyroosevelt.htm

23) http://www.loc.gov/loc/legacy/loc.html

24) http://www.mondotimes.com/1/world/us/35/5186/15488

25) http://archive.sportschatplace.com/sports-history/today-in-sports-history/42930-sports-historynovember-9-jim-thorpe-against-future-president-dwight-eisenhower-of-army.html
http://www.techrepublic.com/article/geek-trivia-out-at-first-but-ruled-safe/5224902
http://www.baseball-almanac.com/prz_qde.shtml
http://www.baseball-reference.com/minors/team.cgi?id=3c5a942c

26) http://www.usvetdsp.com/story46.htm

27) http://c250.columbia.edu/c250_celebrates/remarkable_columbians/dwight_d_eisenhower.html

28) http://privateschool.about.com/od/profiles/a/Jfk-At-Choate.htm
http://www.ldcfitzgerald.com/77-years-ago-jfk-graduates-from-high-school

29) Townley, Alvin *Legacy of Honor: The Values and Influence of America's Eagle Scouts.,* St. Martin's Press (2007).

30) Perry, Will. *The Wolverines: A Story of Michigan Football.* The Strode Publishers (1974).
http://nbcsports.msnbc.com/id/16367165/
http://www.npr.org/templates/story/story.php?storyId=4529638
http://mvictors.com/?p=655

31) Patterson, Richard. *The Eagle and the Shield: A History of the Great Seal of the United States*, University Press of the Pacific (2005).

32) http://www.wmctv.com/story/5863857/fords-hole-in-one

33) http://www.buffalo.edu/search/search?q=millard+fillmore

34) http://www.justonebadcentury.com/chicago_cubs_celebrity_fans_32.asp
http://radio.about.com/od/djsandhostsqt/a/aa060704a.htm

35) Ronald Reagan (1911-2004): "Small town to Tinseltown." CNN, 2004

36) http://ivn.us/history-unspun/2012/07/31/president-profile-of-the-day-ronald-reagan/

CHAPTER 2

Appearance

Q: Who was the tallest president?

A: Abraham Lincoln and Lyndon Johnson were both 6'4".[1]

Q: Who was the shortest president?

A: James Madison was 5'4".[1]

Rank	President	Height
1	Abraham Lincoln Lyndon B. Johnson	6' 4"
3	Thomas Jefferson	6' 2$^{1/2}$ "
4	Franklin D. Roosevelt George H. W. Bush Bill Clinton	6' 2"

7	George Washington	6' 1$^{1/2}$"
8	Andrew Jackson Ronald Reagan Barack Obama	6' 1"
11	James Monroe John Tyler James Buchanan James A. Garfield Chester A. Arthur Warren G. Harding John F. Kennedy Gerald Ford	6' 0"
19	William Howard Taft Herbert Hoover Richard Nixon George W. Bush	5' 11$^{1/2}$"
23	Grover Cleveland Woodrow Wilson	5' 11"
25	Dwight D. Eisenhower	5' 10$^{1/2}$"
26	Franklin Pierce Andrew Johnson Theodore Roosevelt Calvin Coolidge	5' 10"
30	Jimmy Carter	5' 9$^{1/2}$"
31	Millard Fillmore	5' 9"

	Harry S. Truman	
33	Rutherford B. Hayes	5' 8$^{1/2}$"
34	William Henry Harrison James K. Polk Zachary Taylor Ulysses S. Grant	5' 8"
38	John Quincy Adams	5' 7$^{1/2}$"
39	John Adams William McKinley	5' 7"
41	Benjamin Harrison Martin Van Buren	5' 6"
43	James Madison	5' 4"

Q: Which presidents generally had mustaches but no beard?

A: Chester Arthur, Grover Cleveland, Theodore Roosevelt and William Howard Taft.

Q: Of whom was Harry Truman speaking in the following quote? "[He] was one of the best-looking men ever in the White House. He was also one of the most vain, which I guess was on account of the fact that he was so good-looking. But, though he looked the way people who make movies think a president should look, he didn't pay any more attention to business as President of the United States than the man in the moon, and he really made a mess of things ... [He] was the best looking president the White House ever had—but as president he ranks with Buchanan and Calvin Coolidge."

A: Franklin Pierce.[2]

Q: Who was the last president to wear a beard?

A: Benjamin Harrison.

Q: Who was the first president to wear a beard?

A: Abraham Lincoln.

Q: Which president had porkchop (or muttonchop) sideburns?

A: Chester Arthur.

Q: Who was the only president between numbers seventeen (Andrew Johnson) and twenty-eight (Woodrow Wilson), who had no facial hair?

A: William McKinley.

Q: Who was the heaviest president?

A: William Howard Taft, who weighed between 335-340 pounds when he left the White House.[3]

Q: Who was the last president with facial hair?

A: William Howard Taft, who wore a mustache.

Q: Which president often recited the following limerick to describe his own appearance?

> *"For beauty I am not a star,*
> *There are others more perfect by far,*
> *But my face I don't mind it,*
> *For I am behind it,*
> *It is those in front that I jar."*

A: **Woodrow Wilson**. It was Wilson's favorite and he recited it so often that people assumed, mistakenly, that he had written it. In fact, many books still perpetuate this myth. However, this limerick is from Anthony Euwer's book, The *Limeratomy*, published in 1917.[4]

Q: Who was the first president with a mustache?

A: **Ulysses Grant**.

Q: Once, when he was accused of being "two-faced," this president replied, "If I had two faces, would I be wearing this one?" Who was he?

A: **Abraham Lincoln**.[5]

Q: All of our presidents wore powdered wigs up to and including which president?

A: **James Monroe**, our fifth president.[6]

Q: While most presidents did not have facial hair, there were six in a row who did. Who were they?

A: **Ulysses Grant, Rutherford Hayes, James Garfield, Chester Arthur, Grover Cleveland and Benjamin Harrison** (followed by Cleveland again).

Q: Which president wore mostly dresses until he was five-years-old?

A: **Franklin Roosevelt**. In analyzing one childhood photo of FDR, The *Smithsonian* stated: "Little Franklin Delano Roosevelt sits primly on a stool, his white skirt spread smoothly over his lap, his hands clasping a hat trimmed with a marabou feather. Shoulder-length hair and patent leather party shoes complete the ensemble. We find the look unsettling today, yet social convention of 1884, when FDR was photographed at age two and one half, dictated that boys wore dresses until age six or seven, also the time of their first haircut. Franklin's outfit was considered gender-neutral." [7]

Q: Why did Abraham Lincoln decide to grow a beard?

A: Because an eleven-year-old girl named Grace Bedell wrote him a letter suggesting that he do so. The letter was written on October 15, 1860, just before the 1860 election. The letter, exactly as written, stated:

"Hon A B Lincoln...Dear Sir
My father has just home from the fair and brought home your picture and Mr. Hamlin's. I am a little girl only 11 years old, but want you should be President of the United States very much so I hope you won't think me very bold to write to such a great man as you are. Have you any little girls about as large as I am if so give them my love and tell her to write to me if you cannot answer this letter. I have got 4 brothers and part of them will vote for you any way and if you let your whiskers grow I will try and get the rest of them to vote for you you [sic] would look a great deal better for your face is so thin. All the ladies like whiskers and they would tease their husbands to vote for you and then you would be President. My father is going to vote for you and if I was a man I would vote for you to but I will try to get every one to vote for you that I can. I think that rail fence around your picture makes it look very pretty I have got a little baby sister she is nine weeks old and is just as cunning as can be. When you direct your letter direct to Grace Bedell Westfield Chautauqua County New York.
I must not write any more answer this letter right off
Good bye
Grace Bedell"

The original of the letter is now housed in the Detroit Public Library. Lincoln's response was as follows:

"Springfield, Ill Oct 19, 1860
Miss Grace Bedell
My dear little Miss
Your very agreeable letter of the 15th is received—I regret the necessity of saying I have no daughters— have three sons—one seventeen, one nine, and one seven years of age—As to the whiskers have never worn any do you not think people would call it a silly affection if I were to begin it now?
Your very sincere well wisher
A. Lincoln"

The February 19, 1861 edition of the *New York World* recounted the meeting as follows:

"At Westfield an interesting incident occurred. Shortly after his nomination Mr. Lincoln had received from that place a letter from a little girl, who urged him, as a means of improving his personal appearance, to wear whiskers. Mr. Lincoln at the time replied, stating that although he was obliged by the suggestion, he feared his habits of life were too fixed to admit of even so slight a change as that which letting his beard grow involved. To-day, on reaching the place, he related the incident, and said that if that young lady was in the crowd he should be glad to see her. There was a momentary commotion, in the midst of which an old man, struggling through the crowd, approached, leading his daughter, a girl of apparently twelve or thirteen years of age, whom he introduced to Mr. Lincoln as his Westfield correspondent. Mr. Lincoln stooped down and kissed the child, and talked with her for some minutes. Her advice had not been thrown away upon the rugged chieftain. A beard of several months' growth covers (perhaps adorns) the lower part of his face. The young girl's peachy cheek must have been tickled with a stiff whisker, for the growth of which she was herself responsible." [8]

OFFICIAL WHITE HOUSE PORTRAITS:

What follows are some questions about presidential portraits. Excluding Barack Obama (whose term has not ended), every president has an official White House portrait. George W. Bush's portrait for the National Portrait Gallery (which is separate from the White House portrait) was released several weeks before his administration had ended. Painted by Robert A. Anderson, it was unveiled at the National Portrait Gallery of the Smithsonian Institution in Washington, D.C. on December 19, 2008. President Bush opened the unveiling with "Welcome to my hanging," resulting in the room erupting in laughter. [9]

The caption at the National Portrait Gallery beside President Bush's portrait originally read that his administration was "marked by a series of catastrophic events [including] the attacks on September 11, 2001, that led to wars in Afghanistan and Iraq." Vermont Senator Bernie Sanders wrote a letter to the director of the National Portrait Gallery, noting the link between the terrorist attacks and the Iraq war had been "debunked." Director Martin E. Sullivan assured him the label would be changed to delete "that led to." [10]

Q: Every president but one has been painted wearing a suit (or the equivalent of a suit given the era in which the president served). Who is that one president?

A: Zachary Taylor, who was painted in full military garb and holding a sword.

Q: Who is the first president whose portrait includes a United States flag?

A: Surprisingly, it's **Bill Clinton**.

Q: Whose portrait is the only one painted by an African-American artist?

A: **Bill Clinton**, whose portrait was painted by Simmie Knox.

Q: Who is the only president portrayed with his arms crossed and looking downward?

A: **John Kennedy**.

Q: Only one president is portrayed with his mouth open, who also happens to be the only president who is smiling. Who is it?

A: **Ronald Reagan**.

Q: Which president, who was known as a dapper dresser, is portrayed wearing a luxuriant knee-length coat with fur on the lapels and sleeves?

A: **Chester Arthur**.

Q: Which president is portrayed holding a pipe?

A: **Gerald Ford**.

Q: Which president is described in the following backstory of the painting?

"The two men surveyed the house and Sargent attempted to make sketches of his subject in various rooms trying to find the best lighting and pose, but nothing was working. This didn't sit well with the ever restless President. As they climbed the stairs to try and find a better arrangement on the second level, [the President] brusquely remarked that he didn't think Sargent had a clue as to what he wanted. Sargent, also losing patience, shot back that he didn't think the President knew what was needed to pose for a portrait. [The President], whom by then had reached the landing, planted his hand on the balustrade post, turned onto the ascending artist and said, "Don't I!"

Sargent had found his picture. Though Sargent would eventually hit a home run with the portrait, the rocky beginnings were telling signs of the entire commission. [The President] wouldn't stay still and would only consent to a half-hour a day after lunch. Aides and secretaries were constantly moving in and around him disrupting his concentration, and there was hardly enough time for Sargent to even reach his emotional groove for painting."

A: **Theodore Roosevelt**, painted by John Singer Sargent.[11]

Q: **Two presidents are painted wearing eyeglasses and one is holding a pair of eyeglasses. Who are they?**

A: **Theodore Roosevelt** and **Harry Truman** are wearing glasses. **Dwight Eisenhower** is holding glasses.

Q: **Which president sent a cable to his Secretary of War, Elihu Root which stated: "Went on a horse ride today; feeling good." Root replied, "How's the horse?"**

A: **William Howard Taft**, who weighed over 300 pounds.[12]

CHAPTER TWO NOTES:

1) http://en.wikipedia.org/wiki/Heights_of_Presidents_of_the_United_States_and_presidential_candidates
2) Margaret Truman (editor). *Where the Buck Stops: The Personal and Private Writings of Harry S. Truman*, Warner Books (1989).
3) Pringle, Henry F. *The Life and Times of William Howard Taft: A Biography.* Farrar & Rinehart, Inc. (1939)

4) *The Papers of Woodrow Wilson*, ed. Arthur S. Link and others, Vol. 56: March 17-April 4, 1919 (Princeton: Princeton University Press, 1987)
5) http://www.smithsonianeducation.org/educators/lesson_plans/lincoln/index.html
6) http://www.digitalhistory.uh.edu/database/article_display.cfm?HHID=567. Whitcomb, John. Real Life at the White House:Routledge (2002)
7) http://www.smithsonianmag.com/arts-culture/When-Did-Girls-Start-Wearing-Pink.html#ixzz1a3qSV5ZB
8) http://en.wikipedia.org/wiki/Grace_Bedell
   http://www.loc.gov/loc/lcib/0903/letter.html
   http://www.ext.nodak.edu/extnews/newsrelease/2004/020504/04plains.htm
9) Bush in Philadelphia: 'Welcome to my hanging.'" CNN. http://politicalticker.blogs.cnn.com/2008/12/06/bush-in-philadelphia-welcome-to-my-hanging/.
10) http://www.huffingtonpost.com/kriston-capps/text-for-president-bushs_b_157472.html.
11) http://www.jssgallery.org/Paintings/President_Theodore_Roosevelt.htm#Pic
12) http://familypedia.wikia.com/wiki/William_Howard_Taft_(1857-1930)/biography Pringle, Henry F. *The Life and Times of William Howard Taft: A Biography* (Farrar & Strauss) (1939).

CHAPTER 3

Birth

Q: Since George Washington was born in 1732 until and including the 1940's, at least one president has been born in every decade but two. Which ones?

A: The 1810's and the 1930's. There have also, as of 2014, been no presidents born in the 1950's although Barack Obama was born in 1961.[1]

Q: Only two presidents were born on the same day, November 2. Which ones? As a hint they were born in 1795 and 1865.

A: James K. Polk (1795) and **Warren Harding** (1865).

Q: Who was the only president born on July 4?

A: Calvin Coolidge, born on July 4, 1872.

Q: Who was the last president born who was not a naturally born U. S. citizen?

A: William Henry Harrison. He was born in 1773 as a British subject.

Q: Who was the last president born in a log cabin?

A: James Garfield.

Q: Who was the only president born in New York City?

A: Theodore Roosevelt. He was born on October 27, 1858 in a four-story brownstone at 28 East 20th Street in the modern-day Gramercy section of New York City.

Q: Of our 44 presidents (counting Cleveland twice), over half of them (23) have been born in only four States. Which ones?

A: Virginia (8), Ohio, (7), New York (4) and Massachusetts (4). Incredibly, seven of our first twelve Presidents were from Virginia and seven of the presidents between numbers 18 and 29 were from Ohio. In the former group are George Washington, Thomas Jefferson, James Madison, James Monroe, William Henry Harrison, John Tyler and Zachary Taylor. In the latter group are Ulysses Grant, Rutherford Hayes, James Garfield, Benjamin Harrison, William McKinley, William Taft, and Warren Harding.

Q: Who was the last president born in the 19th-century?

A: Dwight Eisenhower.

Q: Who was the last president born before 1800?

A: James Buchanan in 1791. Millard Fillmore was born in 1800.

Q: Three presidents were born after their fathers died. Who were they?

A: Andrew Jackson was born March 15, 1767, three weeks after the death of his father Andrew Jackson, Sr. in a lumber accident.

Rutherford B. Hayes was born in 1822, 10 weeks after his father died.

Bill Clinton was born August 19, 1946, three months after his father William Jefferson Blythe, Jr. drowned following a car accident.

Q: Who was the first president born after the death of a former president?

A: Millard Fillmore. Washington died less than a month before Fillmore's birth on January 7, 1800.

Q: Who is the only president who's State of birth is uncertain?

A: Andrew Jackson. His father died in 1767, just three weeks before Jackson was born. His mother made an arduous 12-mile trip after burying him, back to the farm where her family lived in what was then a backwoods wilderness on the North Carolina--South Carolina border called the Waxhaws. The land was so remote that it had not been officially surveyed yet and thus it is not known which State he was born in. Of course, Jackson went on to become a Tennessean, moving there in his 20's and claiming that State as his own for the rest of his life.[2]

Q: Who was the first president born after adoption of the Constitution?

A: John Tyler, who was born in 1790. The Constitution was adopted in 1787.

CHAPTER THREE NOTES:

1) http://en.wikipedia.org/wiki/List_of_Presidents_of_the_
   United_States_by_date_of_birth
2) Collings, Jeffrey. *Old fight lingers over Old Hickory's roots. The Washington Post* (March 7, 2011).

CHAPTER 4

Campaigns and Primaries

Q: What president may have had a child out of wedlock? This led to a campaign slogan against him, "Ma, Ma, where's my Pa?" When the situation became public, about ten years after it occurred, and while the president was campaigning, he was asked how to handle the situation and his advice was "tell the truth."

A: Grover Cleveland. He was a thirty-six year old bachelor in 1873 when he met Maria Halpin, who was thirty-five. She was a widow with two children. When a son was born to her on September 14, 1874, she named him Oscar Folsom Cleveland, clearly identifying Cleveland in her mind as the baby's father. Cleveland had no desire to marry Maria and was not certain that he was the child's father. Cleveland's friends later reported that Maria herself did not know who the father of her child was. Nevertheless, Cleveland took responsibility for supporting the child.

Gradually, Cleveland lost contact with both Maria and her son. Then, on July 21, 1884, an article appeared in a Buffalo newspaper called *The Evening Telegraph* under the title of *A Terrible Tale*. It revealed Cleveland's clandestine love affair with Halpin in 1873 and the resulting birth of their illegitimate child. When the news of the affair spread in the midst of the 1884 Presidential campaign, the Republicans rejoiced and the Democrats despaired. One of Cleveland's supporters in Buffalo sent him a frantic telegram, asking for advice. Cleveland wrote back: "Tell the truth." Taking his own advice, Cleveland prepared a statement describing his past affair with Maria.

The timing of the news was fortunate for Cleveland in the sense that it broke one month after the Democratic Convention in June, 1884, but well before the general election in November, enough time for the story to die down a bit. Although Republican candidate James Blaine had some scandals of his own to deal with, Republican parades featured men dressed as women pushing baby carriages, each carriage containing a large doll. As they marched, they cried in falsetto voices, "Ma! Ma! Where's my Pa?"

In the election which followed, Cleveland won by a slim majority. He carried New York with a plurality of slightly over a thousand votes out of a total of over a million votes cast. A shift of about five hundred votes in New York would have given the election to Blaine. After he won, the "Ma, Ma ..." attack phrase gained a classic rejoinder: "Gone to the White House. Ha! Ha! Ha!"[1]

Q: In which post-Civil War election did neither candidate for president personally campaign?

A: The 1892 election won by **Grover Cleveland** over **Benjamin Harrison**. It was, according to Cleveland biographer Allan Nevins, "the cleanest, quietest, and most creditable in the memory of the post-war generation," in part because Harrison's wife, Caroline, was dying of tuberculosis. Harrison did not personally campaign, and Cleveland followed suit out of sympathy to his political rival so as not to exploit Mrs. Harrison's illness. [2]

Q: Which president was shot in the chest while campaigning, and nevertheless proceeded to speak for ninety minutes with blood on his shirt?

A: Theodore Roosevelt. Since this occurred in 1912, it also makes Roosevelt the answer to the question: Who is the only former president to have been the target of an assassination attempt? Campaigning in Milwaukee, Wisconsin, on October 14, 1912, a saloonkeeper named John Schrank shot him, but the bullet lodged in his chest after penetrating his steel eyeglass case and passing through a thick (50 pages) single-folded copy of the speech he was carrying in his jacket. Roosevelt concluded that since he wasn't coughing blood, the bullet had not completely penetrated the chest wall to his lung, and so declined suggestions he go to the hospital immediately. Instead, he delivered his scheduled speech with blood seeping on to his shirt.

He spoke for ninety minutes. His opening comments to the gathered crowd were, "Ladies and gentlemen, I don't know whether you fully understand that I have just been shot; but it takes more than that to kill a Bull Moose." Afterwards, probes and x-rays showed that the bullet had traversed three inches of tissue and lodged in Roosevelt's chest muscle but did not penetrate the pleura, and it would be more dangerous to attempt to remove the bullet than to leave it in place. Roosevelt carried it with him for the rest of his life. Schrank was declared insane on November 13, 1912 and committed to the Northern State Hospital for the Insane at Oshkosh, WI. He died at the Central State Hospital in Waupun, WI on September 15, 1943.[3]

Q: What was the first presidential campaign to receive widespread newsreel coverage?

A: The 1920 campaign. The election that year was won by Warren Harding.

Q: Which was the first presidential campaign to use the power of Hollywood and Broadway stars?

A: Warren Harding's campaign in 1920. Al Jolson, Lillian

Russell, Douglas Fairbanks, and Mary Pickford were among the luminaries to make the pilgrimage to Harding's house in Marion, Ohio. Business icons Thomas Edison, Henry Ford, and Harvey Firestone also lent their cachet to the campaign. From the onset of the campaign until the November election, over 600,000 people travelled to Marion to participate.[4]

Q: Which president was able to partially finance his first campaign for Congress through his poker winnings?

A: Richard Nixon. In his autobiography, he wrote: "I learned that the people who have the cards are usually the ones who talk the least and the softest; those who are bluffing tend to talk loudly and give themselves away." [5]

Q: Which presidents used the following campaign songs:
A. *Happy Days Are Here Again*, by Milton Ager (music) and Jack Yellen (lyrics)
B. *High Hopes*, by Jimmy Van Heusen (music) and Sammy Cahn (lyrics)
C. *California Here I Come*, by Buddy DeSylva and Joseph Meyer
D. *This Land Is Your Land*, by Woody Guthrie
E. *Don't Stop*, by Fleetwood Mac
F. *I Won't Back Down*, by Tom Petty

Answers:
A. **Franklin Roosevelt** (1932)
B. **John F. Kennedy** (1960)
C. **Ronald Reagan** (1980)
D. **George H. W. Bush** (1988)
E. **Bill Clinton** (1992)
F. **George W. Bush** (2000)
Note: Tom Petty threatened to sue Bush if he did not cease use the song at campaign events, which he did. Petty's song suggests

a struggle against the odds, defying powers that be. To Bush, it was the perfect song for a political campaign. However, Petty had his publisher, Randall Wixen of Wixen Music Publishing Inc., send the Bush campaign a "cease and desist" letter to stop his campaign from using the song. Wixen said in his letter to Bush that the use of the song "creates, either intentionally or unintentionally, the impression that you and your campaign have been endorsed by Tom Petty, which is not true." Michael Toner, a lawyer for Bush's campaign, wrote back, saying, "We do not agree that the mere playing or use of a particular song at a campaign event connotes any impression, either intentionally or unintentionally, of endorsement." Nevertheless, Toner confirmed that the Bush campaign would not use the song at any future campaign events. "So we backed down," said Bush spokesman Dan Bartlett, jokingly, to reporter Jake Tapper, covering the issue for *Salon.com*.

Also, one cannot easily imagine Woody Guthrie endorsing George H.W. Bush. [6]

Q: Who was the first president to campaign actively for office and whose campaign featured slogans, songs, and a carefully manufactured image?

A: William Henry Harrison in the 1840 campaign.

Q: Which president had a campaign ditty that went as follows:

> *"Let Van from his coolers of silver drink wine*
> *And lounge on his cushioned settee,*
> *Our man on a buckeye bench can recline,*
> *Content with hard cider is he?"*

A: William Henry Harrison. This was Harrison's attempt to portray himself as a man of the common people from the rough-

and-tumble West, as contrasted to his opponent, Martin Van Buren, who he was attempting to portray as a rich snob. [7]

Q: There has only been one occasion since 1952 when a Republican-elected president did not win the New Hampshire primary. What year was it and which man lost?

A: In the 2000 primary, **George W. Bush** lost.

Q: Who beat George W. Bush in that primary?

A: John McCain.

Q: Which president campaigned frequently from the front porch of his house?

A: Warren Harding. His house was in Marion, Ohio.

Q: There have only been two occasions since 1956 when a Democrat-elected president did not win the New Hampshire primary. What years were these primaries and which men lost?

A: In the 2008 primary, **Barack Obama** lost and in the 1992 primary, **Bill Clinton** lost.

Q: Who beat Barack Obama and Bill Clinton in those primaries?

A: In 2008, Senator Hillary Clinton beat Obama and in 1992, Senator Paul Tsongas beat Clinton.

Q: There has been only one occasion since 1952 where a sitting president did not win the New Hampshire primary. What year was it and which man lost?

A: In the 1952 primary, President **Harry Truman** lost to Estes

Kefauver. Incidentally, the New Hampshire primary has been taking place since 1920, but before 1952, the delegates were unpledged.

Q: Whose famous campaign slogan was "Tippecanoe and Tyler, too?"

A: William Henry Harrison. Tippecanoe referred to Harrison's military victory over a group of Shawnee Indians at a river in Indiana called Tippecanoe in 1811. Tyler was of course Harrison's running mate.

Q: In what presidential campaign did supporters of one of the candidates urge voters not to vote for the other candidate by spelling his last name backwards?

A: Martin Van Buren against William Henry Harrison in 1840. No sirrah!

Q: True or false: There have been no occasions where a party's nominee did not come in first or second in the New Hampshire primary?

A: True.

Results of New Hampshire primaries (winners of their Party's nomination underlined):

Democrats

Primary Date	Winner	Runners-Up
January 10, 2012	President Barack Obama	(no viable opposition)

Primary Date	Winner	Runners-Up
January 8, 2008	Senator Hillary Clinton	<u>Senator Barack Obama</u>, Former Senator John Edwards, Governor Bill Richardson, Representative Dennis Kucinich and Former Senator Mike Gravel.
January 27, 2004	<u>Senator John Kerry</u>	Former Governor Howard B. Dean III, General Wesley K. Clark, Senator John Edwards, Senator Joseph I. Lieberman, Congressman Dennis J. Kucinich and Reverend Al Sharpton.
February 1, 2000	<u>Vice President Al Gore</u>	Former Senator Bill Bradley
February 20, 1996	<u>President Bill Clinton</u>	(no viable opposition)
February 18, 1992	Senator Paul Tsongas (33.20%)	<u>Governor Bill Clinton</u> (24.78%), Senator Bob Kerrey (11.08%), Senator Tom Harkin (10.18%), Former Governor Jerry Brown (8.15%)
February 16, 1988	<u>Governor Michael Dukakis (36%)</u>	Congressman Richard A. "Dick" Gephardt (20%), Senator Paul Simon (17%), Reverend Jesse L. Jackson (8%), Senator Al Gore (7%), Governor Bruce Babbitt (5%), and former Senator Gary Hart (4%)
February 28, 1984	Senator Gary Hart	<u>Former Vice President Walter Mondale</u>, Senator John Glenn, Reverend Jesse L. Jackson, and Former Senator George McGovern

Primary Date	Winner	Runners-Up
February 26, 1980	President Jimmy Carter	Senator Edward Kennedy, and Governor Jerry Brown
February 24, 1976	Governor Jimmy Carter	Congressman Mo Udall, Senator Birch Bayh, Former Senator Fred R. Harris, and Former Ambassador R. Sargent Shriver
March 7, 1972	Senator Edmund Muskie	Senator George McGovern and Mayor Samuel William Yorty
March 12, 1968	President Lyndon B. Johnson	Senator Eugene McCarthy
March 10, 1964	President Lyndon B. Johnson	(no viable opposition)
March 8, 1960	Senator John F. Kennedy	Businessman Paul C. Fisher
March 13, 1956	Senator Estes Kefauver	Former Governor Adlai Stevenson
March 11, 1952	Senator Estes Kefauver	President Harry S. Truman

Republicans

Primary Date	Winner	Runners-Up
January 10, 2012	Governor Mitt Romney (39.25%)	Congressman Ron Paul (22.88%), Governor Jon Huntsman (16.88%), Speaker Newt Gingrich (9.42%), Senator Rick Santorum (9.40%), Governor Rick Perry (0.71%)

Primary Date	Winner	Runners-Up
January 8, 2008	<u>Senator John McCain</u> (37.00%)	Governor Mitt Romney (31.56%), Governor Mike Huckabee (11.22%), Mayor Rudy Giuliani (8.48%), Congressman Ron Paul (7.65%), Senator Fred Thompson (1.23%), Congressman Duncan Hunter (0.50%)
January 27, 2004	<u>President George W. Bush</u>	(no viable opposition)
February 1, 2000	Senator John McCain (48.53%)	<u>Governor George W. Bush</u> (30.36%), Malcolm S. "Steve" Forbes, Jr. (12.66%), Ambassador Alan Keyes (6.37%), and Gary L. Bauer (0.69%)[19]
February 20, 1996	Pat Buchanan (27.25%)	<u>Senator Bob Dole</u> (26.22%), Governor A. Lamar Alexander (22.59%), Steve Forbes (12.22%), Senator Richard G. "Dick" Lugar (5.19%), and Ambassador Alan Keyes (2.67%
February 18, 1992	<u>President George H. W. Bush</u> (53.19%)	Patrick J. "Pat" Buchanan (37.53%)
February 16, 1988	<u>Vice President George H. W. Bush</u> (38%)	Senator Bob Dole (29%), Congressman Jack F. Kemp, Jr. (13%), Governor Pierre S. "Pete" du Pont IV (10%), and Reverend Marion G. "Pat" Robertson (9%)
February 28, 1984	<u>President Ronald Reagan</u>	(no viable opposition)

Primary Date	Winner	Runners-Up
February 26, 1980	Governor Ronald Reagan	Ambassador George H. W. Bush, Senator Howard H. Baker, Jr., Congressman John B. Anderson, Congressman Philip M. "Phil" Crane, and Senator Bob Dole
February 24, 1976	President Gerald R. Ford	Governor Ronald Reagan
March 7, 1972	President Richard Nixon	Congressman Paul N. "Pete" McCloskey, Jr. and Congressman John M. Ashbrook
March 12, 1968	Vice President Richard Nixon	Governor George Romney
March 10, 1964	Ambassador Henry Cabot Lodge, Jr.	Senator Barry M. Goldwater, Governor Nelson A. Rockefeller, and former Vice President Richard Nixon
March 8, 1960	Vice President Richard Nixon	(no viable opposition)
March 13, 1956	President Dwight D. Eisenhower	(no viable opposition)
March 11, 1952	General Dwight D. Eisenhower	Senator Robert Taft and Governor Harold E. Stassen
1948	Governor Harold Stassen	Governor Thomas E. Dewey

Q: Although it seems like the Iowa caucuses have existed forever, in fact, the first Iowa Democratic caucus was only in 1972 and the first Iowa Republican caucus was only in 1976. There have been two occasions when the man who came in third in the Iowa caucuses won the presidency. When did these occur?

A: In 1988, **George H.W. Bush** (19%) lost to Bob Dole (37%) and Pat Robertson (25%). In 1992, **Bill Clinton** lost to Tom Harkin (76%—not surprising since he was an Iowan), "uncommitted" (12%) and Paul Tsongas (4%). Clinton garnered only 3%.

Q: There has been one occasion when a sitting president failed to capture at least 98% of his party's vote in the Iowa caucuses. In that case, a challenger won 31%. When did that occur and who were the candidates?

A: In 1980, **Jimmy Carter** won 59% and Ted Kennedy won 31%. (The rest went to others.)

Past winners of Iowa caucuses
(winners of the Party's nomination underlined):

Democrats

January 3, 2012	Barack Obama (98%), "Uncommitted" (2%)
January 3, 2008	Barack Obama (38%), John Edwards (30%), Hillary Clinton (29%), Bill Richardson (2%), Joe Biden (1%)
January 19, 2004	John Kerry (38%), John Edwards (32%), Howard Dean (18%), Dick Gephardt (11%), and Dennis Kucinich (1%)

January 24, 2000	Al Gore (63%) and Bill Bradley (37%)
February 12, 1996	Bill Clinton (98%), "Uncommitted" (1%), Ralph Nader (1%)
February 10, 1992	Tom Harkin (76%), "Uncommitted" (12%), Paul Tsongas (4%), Bill Clinton (3%), Bob Kerrey (2%), and Jerry Brown (2%)
February 8, 1988	Dick Gephardt (31%), Paul Simon (27%), Michael Dukakis (22%), and Bruce Babbitt (6%)
February 20, 1984	Walter Mondale (49%), Gary Hart (17%), George McGovern (10%), Alan Cranston (7%), John Glenn (4%), Reubin Askew (3%), and Jesse Jackson (2%)
January 21, 1980	Jimmy Carter (59%) and Ted Kennedy (31%)
January 19, 1976	"Uncommitted" (37%), Jimmy Carter (28%) Birch Bayh (13%), Fred R. Harris (10%), Morris Udall (6%), Sargent Shriver (3%), and Henry M. Jackson (1%)
January 24, 1972	"Uncommitted" (36%), Edmund Muskie (36%), George McGovern (23%), Hubert Humphrey (2%), Eugene McCarthy (1%), Shirley Chisholm (1%), and Henry M. Jackson (1%)

Republicans

2012	Mitt Romney (25%), Rick Santorum (25%), Ron Paul (21%), Newt Gingrich (13%), Rick Perry (10%), Michele Bachmann (5%), and Jon Huntsman (0.6%)

2008	Mike Huckabee (34%), Mitt Romney (25%), Fred Thompson (13%), <u>John McCain</u> (13%), Ron Paul (10%), Rudy Giuliani (4%), and Duncan Hunter (1%)
2004	<u>George W. Bush</u> (unopposed)
2000	<u>George W. Bush</u> (41%), Steve Forbes (31%), Alan Keyes (14%), Gary Bauer (9%), John McCain (5%), and Orrin Hatch (1%)
1996	<u>Bob Dole</u> (26%), Pat Buchanan (23%), Lamar Alexander (18%), Steve Forbes (10%), Phil Gramm (9%), Alan Keyes (7%), Richard Lugar (4%), and Morry Taylor (1%)
1992	<u>George H. W. Bush</u> (unopposed)
1988	Bob Dole (37%), Pat Robertson (25%), <u>George H. W. Bush</u> (19%), Jack Kemp (11%), and Pete DuPont (7%)
1984	Ronald Reagan (unopposed)
1980	George H. W. Bush (32%), <u>Ronald Reagan</u> (30%), Howard Baker (15%), John Connally (9%), Phil Crane (7%), John B. Anderson (4%), and Bob Dole (2%)
1976	<u>Gerald Ford</u> and Ronald Reagan

Q: The phrase *54° 40' or Fight!* is wrongly said to have been a campaign slogan but in fact it was not used until after the election to which the issue related. What was the issue and which president's campaign is erroneously associated with it?

A: The president was **James Polk** and the line is misremembered as being part of the 1844 election. There are two reasons this would not and could not have been a Polk campaign slogan. First, it was not used until 1846, by William Allen, a senator and governor of Ohio. Second, it expresses a policy which Polk did not share.

54° 40' refers to a particular line of latitude which defined the northern-most extent of the Oregon Country, a territory which was disputed and claimed jointly by both the United States and Great Britain. The territory under dispute included all of the modern states of Oregon, Washington, Idaho, and parts of Montana, Wyoming, and the Canadian province of British Columbia. Various proposals to resolve the joint claims of sovereignty were proposed, but proponents of "Manifest Destiny" thought that the United States should resolve the conflict with Great Britain by insisting on taking the entire territory (all the way North to the 54° 40' line) and if necessary to fight (go to war) to do so. Polk feared that if he pressed the issue, it could provoke war with Great Britain. He ultimately resolved the dispute peacefully in the Oregon Treaty of 1846, by extending the border between the United States and British North America along the 49th parallel, which tracks the present-day northern border of the State of Washington.[8]

Q: Which post-World War II president had a one-word campaign slogan?

A: Barack Obama, 2012: Forward

Q: Which of the following were official campaign slogans:
    A. Read my lips: No new taxes. George H.W. Bush, 1988
    B. It's the economy stupid. Bill Clinton, 1992
    C. Hope and change. Barack Obama, 2008
    D. All of them
    E. None of them

A: The correct answer is E. "Read my lips: No new taxes" was spoken by Bush at the 1988 Republican National Convention as he accepted the nomination. However it was not a campaign slogan. It was written by speechwriter Peggy Noonan. Although Bush had secured the nomination by the time of the convention, there was a concern over lack of enthusiastic support for him in the conservative wing of the Republican Party. Taxes were an issue that, according to Bush adviser James Pinkerton, "unified the right and didn't antagonize anybody else." Bush stated:

> "And I'm the one who will not raise taxes. My opponent now says he'll raise them as a last resort, or a third resort. But when a politician talks like that, you know that's one resort he'll be checking into. My opponent won't rule out raising taxes. But I will. And the Congress will push me to raise taxes and I'll say no. And they'll push, and I'll say no, and they'll push again, and I'll say, to them, 'Read my lips: no new taxes.'"

Although the line is considered to have been helpful for Bush in winning the 1988 election, it was used against him effectively by Bill Clinton in the 1992 election because Bush did agree to a compromise with Congressional Democrats to raise several taxes as part of a 1990 budget agreement. Although technically there were no new taxes in this agreement, Bush in the 1988 speech also ruled out raising existing taxes.

"It's the economy, stupid" was also not a campaign slogan but rather a slight variation of the phrase "The economy, stupid" which Clinton campaign strategist James Carville had coined during Bill Clinton's 1992 campaign. It was one of three themes meant for Clinton's campaign workers as a way to keep them on message during the campaign. A sign in the campaign's headquarters read:

> "1. Change vs. more of the same.

2. The economy, stupid.
3. Don't forget health care.

Finally, "hope and change" was also never a campaign slogan. Rather, in the 2012 campaign it became a derisive way for Republicans to reference Barack Obama's 2008 campaign for president, arguing that the "hope" and "change" he promised was never realized in his first term as president. It is true that there was a famous Obama campaign poster that had he word "hope" at the bottom and that another version of the same poster had the word "change." He also had a poster that said, "Hope. Action. Change." He also of course talked frequently about the need to change the direction of the country in the 2008 campaign and in fact his slogan was "Change we can believe in." However, "hope and change" per se was never a campaign slogan.[9]

With respect to the following campaign slogans, state the president with whom they are associated and the year of the campaign.

Q: Vote as You Shot.

A: Ulysses Grant, 1868, reminding voters about his role in the Civil War. Grant's opponent, Horatio Seymour, had a campaign slogan that would be unthinkable today: "This is a White Man's Government!"

Q: Peace and Prosperity.

A: Dwight D. Eisenhower, 1956.

Q: He kept us out of war.

A: Woodrow Wilson, 1916. Of course, that slogan did not stay true for long in terms of American involvement in World War I.

Q: Don't swap horses in midstream.

A: Abraham Lincoln, 1864, an obvious reference to the ongoing Civil War.

Q: Grant us another term.

A: Ulysses S. Grant, 1872, almost as self-evident as "who is buried in Grant's tomb?

Q Four more years of the full dinner pail.

A: William McKinley, 1900.

Q: Return to normalcy.

A: Warren Harding, 1920. This was in the aftermath of World War I. The use of the word "normalcy" (instead of "normality") was unusual and there was some question as to whether "normalcy" was a neologism (i.e. an invented word) or a legitimate word. However, while less common than normality, its use dates date at least to the 1850's.[10]

Q: Sunflowers die in November.

A: Franklin Roosevelt, 1936. Roosevelt's opponent Alf Landon was from Kansas and its official state flower is the sunflower. November is of course when the presidential elections take place.

Q: Let's make America great again.

A: Ronald Reagan, 1980.

Q: Morning Again in America.

A: Ronald Reagan, 1984.

CHAPTER FOUR NOTES:

1) Nevins, Allan, *Grover Cleveland, A Study in Courage*, Dodd Mead (1932)
   Welch, Richard E., *Grover Cleveland*, University Press of Kansas (1988)
   Merrill, Horace S., *Bourbon Leader: Grover Cleveland and the Democratic Party*, Little Brown (1957)
   http://www.angelfire.com/il/ClevelandFamilyChron/Prez.html
2) Nevins, Allan. Grover *Cleveland: A Study in Courage*, Dodd, Mead (1932)
3) http://www.wisconsinhistory.org/museum/artifacts/archives/001692.asp
   http://www.doctorzebra.com/prez/z_x26a_g.htm
   http://www.theodoreroosevelt.org/life/timeline.htm
4) http://www.paralumun.com/presharding.htm
5) RN: *The Memoirs of Richard Nixon*, Simon & Schuster (1990)
6) http://blogs.ocweekly.com/heardmentality/2011/06/tom_petty_vs_republicans_top_t.php
   http://www.pophistorydig.com/?tag=tom-petty-and-politics
7) Remini, *Robert Henry Clay: Satesman for the Union*, Norton (1993)
   http://www.historynet.com/american-history-1840-us-presidential-campaign.htm/2
8) Rosenboom, Eugene H. *A History of Presidential Elections: From George Washington to Richard M. Nixon.* Macmillan (1970).
   Baily, Thomas A. and Kennedy, David M. *The American Pageant.* Heath and Company (1994).
9) Kelly, Michael, *The Democrats—Clinton and Bush Compete to Be Champion of Change; Democrat Fights Perceptions of Bush Gain, The New York Times*, October 31, 1992
10) http://www.cjr.org/resources/lc/normalcy.php

CHAPTER 5

Currency and Stamps

Q: Who is the most recent president portrayed on a U.S. coin?

A: John F. Kennedy is on the half dollar, first minted in 1964. Discussions regarding the issuance of the coin begin within days of Kennedy's assassination on November 22, 1963. However, there was a legal hurdle to overcome: Under existing law, U. S. coin designs could not be changed more often than every 25 years. The problem was that the half dollar with Benjamin Franklin's image on it was then only 15 years old, having first been minted in 1948. Its replacement would require an act of Congress. Partisan disputes were set aside in recognition of the nation's and the world's loss, and Congress managed to pass legislation permitting a change in the half dollar's design after only a few weeks' debate. The Act of December 30, 1963 made the Kennedy half dollar a reality.

Initially, the die was used with accented hair (i.e. the hair strands were more defined), but the president's widow, Jacqueline Kennedy, allegedly disliked the heavy hair lines above the ear. New dies were prepared to smooth out some of the details. It is estimated that about one to three percent (40,000-100,000) of the proof halves are of the earlier type.

Ironically, the Kennedy half dollar caused the slow disappearance of half dollar circulation. Meant to be a circulating coin, the Kennedy half dollar was hoarded by the public and few were actually spent. Before 1964, half dollars were a regular part of American commerce and every cash drawer had space for half dollars. After the release of the Kennedy half dollar coin, the general public hoarded most of the production which created a shortage. In 1965, the United States removed silver from circulating coinage except for the Kennedy, which was issued with a lower silver content. Because of this, all half dollars, as well as pre-1965 dimes and quarters were hoarded for their silver content, creating a further shortage. By 1971, when silver was removed from the half dollar, demand and use for the coins had dramatically diminished.[1]

Q: Who is the most recent president portrayed on U.S. paper currency in current circulation?

A: Ulysses S. Grant is on the front of the $50 bill.

Q: Who is the only president on a U.S. coin in current circulation who faces to the right?

A: Abraham Lincoln. The likeness of President Lincoln on the one-cent coin is an adaption of a plaque executed by Victor David Brenner, a Lithuanian who emigrated to this country in 1890, at age 19. Theodore Roosevelt, thought that American coins were pedestrian and uninspiring. That included the Indian Head penny, which had been around since 1859. Roosevelt knew Brenner, having seen his work. Brenner showed Roosevelt a bas-relief he had made of Lincoln, based on a photograph from Mathew Brady. Roosevelt was so impressed with Brenner's design that he recommended to the Secretary of the Treasury that this design be placed on a coin to be issued on Lincoln's 100th birthday in 1909. The direction that Lincoln faces on the cent was not mandated—this was simply Brenner's choice.

Up until then, the only figures on everyday American coins were allegorical figures, like Liberty. Putting real people on them, the thinking went, smacked of monarchy; even George Washington hadn't rated such treatment. Brenner, who received one thousand dollars for the commission, adapted his bas-relief Lincoln for the new coin, warming him up along the way. The revised Lincoln, he explained, would be "more intimate, deeper, more kindly. I read everything I could find describing the man's personal side," Brenner later recalled. "I studied his portraits and the death mask until I believed I knew him. My mind was full of Lincoln."

Production of the new penny began at the United States Mint in Philadelphia on July 10, 1909. It has been reproduced roughly half a trillion times. It is the longest-running design in United States Mint history. [2]

Q: Up until 1999, who was the only president featured on both sides of the same coin?

A: Abraham Lincoln on the Lincoln Memorial penny, although his image on the reverse side, showing him at the Lincoln Memorial, requires a magnifying glass to see. The reverse side was introduced on February 12, 1959, the 150th anniversary of Lincoln's birth. It was designed by Frank Gasparro, then assistant engraver at the Philadelphia Mint, who prepared the winning entry, selected from a group of twenty-three models that the engraving staff at the Mint had been asked to present for consideration. The initials "FG" appear on the right, near the shrubbery. The release of the New Jersey state quarter in 1999, depicts George Washington crossing the Delaware River on the reverse. He is of course on the front of that coin as well. [3]

Q: Which president's image appeared on the $20 bill before Andrew Jackson?

A: Grover Cleveland. His image was on the large size $20 bill, first issued in 1914. It was switched over to Jackson in 1929.

Q: In 1926, a commemorative half dollar was issued with two president's images on it, the only time this has occurred. Who were the two presidents? The answer to this question is also the answer to another question: **When is the only time a president appeared on a coin in his lifetime?**

A: America celebrated her 150th anniversary in 1926. As part of that event, the U.S. Mint issued a coin known as the Sesquicentennial Half Dollar. The coin features a portrait of **George Washington** and **Calvin Coolidge** on the obverse, with the Liberty Bell on the reverse. They are both right-facing, with Coolidge's image in the background and Washington's image in the foreground.[4]

Q: Who was the only bald president to appear on a U.S. coin?

A: Dwight Eisenhower on the dollar coin. It was minted from 1971-1978.[5]

Q: True or false: Prior to the 20th-century, no American president ever appeared on the face of a coin in general circulation?

A: True.

Q: Which president opposed to use of the phrase "IN GOD WE TRUST" on a coin?

A: Theodore Roosevelt. His opposition however was not based on Constitutional grounds (i.e. separation of church and state), as has sometimes been said, but rather because he thought it was "irreverent." On November 11, 1907, he wrote a letter to the Rev. Roland C. Dryer of Nunda, New York, defending the omission of the motto IN GOD WE TRUST from newly minted ten dollar and twenty dollar gold coins designed by Augustus Saint-Gaudens. Dryer protested the omission of the motto, which had appeared on numerous U.S. coins since 1864. Roosevelt defended the removal of the phrase citing legal precedent: "When the question of the new coinage came up we lookt [sic] into the law and found there was no warrant therein for putting 'IN GOD WE TRUST' on the coins..."

Roosevelt also cited his personal reasons for disliking the motto on coinage. "My own feeling in the matter is due to my very firm conviction that to put such a motto on coins, or to use it in any kindred manner, not only does no good but does positive harm, and is in effect irreverence which comes dangerously close to sacrilege. A beautiful and solemn sentence such as the one in question should be treated and uttered only with that fine reverence which necessarily implies a certain exaltation of spirit. Any use which tends to cheapen it, and, above all, any use which tends to secure its being treated in a spirit of levity, is free from every standpoint profoundly to be regretted. It is a motto which it is indeed well to have inscribed on our great national monuments, in our temples of justice, in our legislative halls, and in buildings such as those at West Point and Annapolis. In short, wherever it will tend to arouse and inspire a lofty emotion in those who look thereon. But it seems to be eminently unwise to cheapen such a motto by use on coins, just as it would be to cheapen it by use on postage stamps, or in advertisements."

Congress forced the issue on March 8, 1908 by passing "An Act Providing for the restoration of the motto, 'IN GOD WE TRUST' on certain denominations of the gold and silver coins of the United States. Be it enacted by the Senate and House of Representatives of the United States of America in Congress assembled, that the motto 'IN GOD WE TRUST,' heretofore inscribed on certain denominations of the gold and silver coins of the United States of America, shall hereafter be inscribed upon all such gold and silver coins of said denominations as heretofore..."

Roosevelt, in a letter to Senator Thomas Carter, called the legislation "not necessary, it is rot; I repeat, it is rot, pure rot; but I am telling the Congressman if Congress wants to pass a bill reestablishing the motto, I shall not veto it." True to his word, in his letter to Rev. Dryer, Roosevelt signed the act into law on May 18, 1908. The motto has continued in use to this day on most U.S. coinage and in 1957 began appearing on U.S. currency as well.

The original of Roosevelt's letter was sold at auction on November 3, 2005.[6]

Q: Rank the following coins in current circulation in order from the oldest one to first bear the image of a president to the newest: Penny, nickel, dime, quarter, half dollar and dollar?

Answer:

Penny: Abraham Lincoln-1909
Quarter: George Washington-1932
Nickel: Thomas Jefferson-1938
Dime: Franklin Roosevelt-1946
Half Dollar: John F. Kennedy-1964
Dollar: Dwight Eisenhower-1971

Q: Which president and what new product was the following poem that appeared in a New York newspaper referring to?

The millionaire may seldom
Those noble outlines grasp,
But childhood's chubby fingers
The image oft will clasp.
The poor man will esteem it,
And mothers hold it dear -
The plain and common people
He loved when he was here.

A: Abraham Lincoln and the Lincoln penny, just released in 1909. The article appeared in the *New York Sun*. Carl Sandberg told the *Milwaukee Daily News* that year: "If it were possible to talk with that great, good man, he would probably say that he is perfectly willing that his face is to be placed on the cheapest and most common coin in the country. Follow the travels of the penny and you find it stops at many cottages and few mansions. ... The common, homely face of 'Honest Abe' will look good on the penny, the coin of the common folk from whom he came and to whom he belongs."[7]

Q: Which president's image appears on the largest denomination currency ever issued by the Federal Reserve, whether or not ever in general circulation?

A: Woodrow Wilson's, on the $100,000 bill. These notes were only ever printed over twenty-two days, from December 18, 1934 through January 9, 1935. They were issued by the Treasurer of the United States to Federal Reserve Banks only against an equal amount of gold bullion held by the Treasury Department. The notes were used only for official transactions between Federal Reserve Banks and were not circulated among the general public.[8]

Q: Prior to 1866, who were the three presidents honored by having their image on a stamp?

A: George Washington (1847), **Thomas Jefferson** (1856) and **Andrew Jackson** (1863).

Q: Who is the only president who appeared on a Confederate States of America stamp before he appeared on a United States stamp?

A: Andrew Jackson, appeared on a two-cent C.S.A. stamp in 1862, one year before he appeared on a U.S. stamp.

Q: Besides Jackson, who are the only presidents who appeared on Confederate States of America stamps?

A: George Washington and Thomas Jefferson.

Q: Who was president when the first postage stamp was issued?

A: James Polk in 1847.

Q: Which president had the longest gap between the date of his death and the first time he appeared on a stamp?

A: John Adams died in 1826 but did not appear on a stamp until 1938. Note that living presidents do not appear on stamps.

Q: Four presidents who served before 1900 have appeared on new stamp issues since 1999 (as of 2014). Who are they?

A: George Washington, who appeared on a twenty-cent stamp in 2000 and a twenty-three-cent stamp in 2002, **James Madison**, who appeared on a thirty-four-cent commemorative stamp in 2001, celebrating the 250th anniversary of his birth, **Zachary Taylor** (2001) and **Benjamin Harrison**.

Q: There have been more stamp issues—eight—honoring this largely forgotten 19th-century president than any president since 1890, including both Roosevelts, Woodrow Wilson, Harry Truman, Dwight Eisenhower, John Kennedy, Lyndon Johnson, and Ronald Reagan. Who is he?

A: James Garfield, which is remarkable considering he was in office for less than seven months.

Q: Who is the only president to appear on a U.S. airmail stamp?

A: Abraham Lincoln. His airmail stamp was first issued on April 22, 1960.

Q: Which president was an avid stamp collector, having over one million stamps in his collection when he died?

A: Franklin Roosevelt.

Q: In 1938, a stamp was issued by the Post Office bearing the image of every president who had served until that point (other than Herbert Hoover). Similarly, in 1986, at the AMERIPEX International Stamp Show, a stamp was again issued by the Post Office bearing the image of every president who had served until that point. Aside from these two issues that honored all the presidents, which eight presidents have never had their image on a stamp individually.

A: Martin Van Buren, John Tyler, Millard Fillmore, Franklin Pierce, James Buchanan, Andrew Johnson, Chester Arthur, and Calvin Coolidge.

Q: True or false: Excluding the 1938 and 1986 issues referenced in the preceding question, there have been about as many stamp issues of George Washington as every other president combined.

A: True: Excluding the 1938 and 1986 issues mentioned above, which covered every president who had died up to those times, the list of stamp issues is as follows:

George Washington
- 1847: 10 Cents
- 1851/56: 3, 10, 12 Cents
- 1857/61: 3, 10, 12, 24, 90 Cents
- 1861/67: 3, 10, 12, 24, 90 Cents

- 1869: 6 Cents
- 1870: 3 Cents
- 1883: 2 Cents
- 1887: 3 Cents
- 1890: 2 Cents
- 1894/95: 2 Cents
- 1898/1900: 2 Cents
- 1903: 2 Cents
- 1903/08: 2 Cents
- 1908/10: 2, 4, 5, 6, 8, 10, 13, 15, 50 Cents, $1
- 1910/13: 2, 4, 5, 6, 8, 10, 15 Cents
- 1912/14: 1, 2, 7 Cents
- 1917: 2 Cents
- 1914/16: 1, 2, 3, 4, 5, 6, 7 Cents
- 1916/22: 1, 2, 3, 4, 5, 6, 7 Cents
- 1918/21: 1, 2, 3 Cents
- 1922/34: 2 Cents
- 1925: 1 Cent, Battle of Lexington-Concord
- 1928: 2 Cents, Valley Forge
- 1930: 2 Cents, Braddocks's Field
- 1931: 2 Cents, Yorktown
- 1932: 1/2, 1, 1 1/2, 2, 3, 4, 5, 6, 7, 8, 9, 10 Cents, 200th Birthday of George Washington
- 1932: 3 Cents
- 1936: 1 Cent, Washington with General Greene
- 1939: 4 Cents, George Washington First President
- 1947: 3 Cents, Stamp Centenary
- 1947: 10 Cents in block, 100th Anniversary United States Stamps
- 1949: 3 Cents, 200th Anniversary Washington and Lee University
- 1951: 3 Cents, Battle at Brooklyn
- 1952: 3 Cents, Betsy Ross
- 1952: 3 Cents, Mt. Rushmore

- 1954: 1 Cent
- 1962/63: 5 Cents
- 1966: 5 Cents
- 1967/81: 5 Cents
- 1976: four blocks with 13, 18, 24, 31 Cents
- 1977: 13 Cents, Princeton
- 1982: 20 Cents, 250th Birthday of Washington
- 1984: 20 Cents, National Archives
- 1985: 18 Cents
- 1989: 25 Cents, Bicentennial Executive Branch
- 1994: $5, Washington and Andrew Jackson
- 1997: 60 Cents, Stamp Exhibition PACIFIC'97
- 2001: 20, 23 Cents
- 2002: 23 Cents

John Adams
- 1983: 20 Cents, Bicentennial of Treaty of Paris

Thomas Jefferson:
- 1851/56: 5 Cents
- 1857/61: 5 Cents
- 1861/67: 5 Cents
- 1870: 10 Cents
- 1890: 30 Cents
- 1894/95: 50 Cents
- 1903: 50 Cents
- 1904: 2 Cents
- 1923/34: 9 Cents
- 1952: 3 Cents, Mt. Rushmore
- 1954: 2 Cents
- 1968: 1 Cent
- 1993: 29 Cents

James Madison
- 1894: $2
- 1903: $2
- 2001: 34 Cents, 250th birthday of James Madison

James Monroe
- 1904: 3 Cents
- 1923/27: 10 Cents
- 1953: 3 Cents, Louisiana Purchase
- 1954: 5 Cents
- 1958: 3 Cents, 200th Birthday of Monroe

John Quincy Adams
- 1983: 20 Cents, Bicentennial of Independence

Andrew Jackson
- 1863: 2 Cents
- 1870: 2 Cents
- 1883: 4 Cents
- 1894: 3 Cents
- 1903: 3 Cents
- 1946: 3 Cents, Tennessee, 150th Anniversary of Statehood
- 1963/66: 1 Cent
- 1965: 5 Cents, Battle of New Orleans
- 1967: 10 Cents
- 1994: $5, Washington and Jackson

Martin Van Buren
None

William Henry Harrison
- 1950: 3 Cents, Indiana Territory

John Tyler
None

James K. Polk
- 1995: 32 Cents, 250th Birthday of James K. Polk

Zachary Taylor
- 1975: 5 Cents

Millard Fillmore
None

Franklin Pierce
None

James Buchanan
None

Abraham Lincoln
- 1866: 15 Cents
- 1869: 90 Cents
- 1870: 6 Cents
- 1882: 6 Cents
- 1890: 4 Cents
- 1894/95: 4 Cents
- 1898: 4 Cents
- 1903/08: 5 Cents
- 1909: 2 Cents, 100th Birthday of Lincoln
- 1922/34: 3 Cents
- 1940: 3 Cents, 13th Amendment of Constitution
- 1942: 5 Cents, China 1937-1942
- 1948: 3 Cents, Gettysburg Address
- 1952: 3 Cents, Mt. Rushmore
- 1954: 4 Cents
- 1958: 4 Cents. Lincoln - Douglas debates
- 1959: 1, 3, 4 Cents, Lincoln's 150th birthday
- 1960/66: 25 Cents, Air Mail
- 1965/66: 4 Cents
- 1984: 20 Cents, National Archives

- 1984: 20 Cents, Nation of readers
- 1995: 32 Cents, Persons of American Civil War

Andrew Johnson
None

Ulysses Grant
- 1890: 5 Cents
- 1894/95: 5 Cents
- 1898: 5 Cents
- 1903: 4 Cents
- 1922/34: 8 Cents
- 1937: 3 Cents, Grant with Sherman and Sheridan
- 1995: 32 Cents, Persons of American Civil War

Rutherford B. Hayes
- 1922/34: 11 Cents

James Garfield
- 1882: 5 Cents
- 1888: 5 Cents
- 1890: 6 Cents
- 1895: 6 Cents
- 1898: 6 Cents
- 1903: 6 Cents
- 1922/34: 6 Cents

Chester Arthur
None

Grover Cleveland
- 1922/31: 12 Cents

Benjamin Harrison
- 1902: 13 Cents
- 1926: 13 Cents
- 1959: 12 Cents

- 2003: 37 Cents, Old Glory stamp

William McKinley
- 1904: 5 Cents, Louisiana exhibition in St. Louis
- 1923/34: 7 Cents

Theodore Roosevelt
- 1925: 5 Cents
- 1939: 3 Cents, 25th Anniversary Panama Canal
- 1952: 3 Cents, Mt. Rushmore
- 1955: 6 Cents
- 1998: 32 Cents in block, 1900s Celebrate the Century

William Howard Taft
- 1930: 4 Cents

Woodrow Wilson
- 1925: 17 Cents
- 1956: 7 Cents
- 1998: 32 Cents in block, 1910s Celebrate the Century

Warren Harding
- 1923: 2 Cents, Death of President Harding
- 1925: 1 1/2 Cents
- 1930: 1 1/2 Cents

Calvin Coolidge
None

Herbert Hoover
None

Franklin Roosevelt
- 1945/46: 1, 2, 3, 5 Cents, Death of President Roosevelt
- 1966: 6 Cents
- 1968: 6 Cents
- 1982: 20 cents, 100th Birthday of Roosevelt

Harry Truman
- 1973: 8 Cents, Harry S. Truman
- 1984: 20 Cents
- 1995: 32 Cents in block, 1945: Victory at Last
- 1999: 33 Cents in block, 1940s Celebrate the Century

Dwight Eisenhower
- 1969: 6 Cents, Death of Dwight D. Eisenhower
- 1970: 6 Cents
- 1971: 8 Cents
- 1990: 25 Cents 100th Birthday of Eisenhower

John F. Kennedy
- 1964: 5 Cents, 1917—John F. Kennedy—1963
- 1967: 13 Cents

Lyndon Johnson
- 1973: 8 Cents, Death of Lyndon B. Johnson

Richard Nixon
- 1995: 32 Cents, Death of Richard Nixon

Gerald Ford
- 2007: 41 Cents, Death of Gerald Ford

Ronald Reagan
- 2005: 37 Cents, Death of Ronald Reagan.
- 2011: Forever, 100th birthday of Reagan. [9]

CHAPTER FIVE NOTES:

1) http://coinsite.com/CoinSite-PF/pparticles/50ckenn.asp
   http://www.ipotad.com/pages/ah2.html (showing pictures of the accented hair variety and contrasting with the later variety)
   http://www.ngccoin.com/news/viewarticle.aspx?NewsletterNewsArticleID=69
2) David Margolick, *Penny Foolish*, *The New York Times*, 2/11/07.
   http://www.usmint.gov/faqs/circulating_coins/index.cfm#anchor14
3) http://www.nytimes.com/2001/10/03/us/frank-gasparro-92-of-mint-art-is-on-100-billion-pennies.html

4) http://www.coinsite.com/content/commemoratives/sesquihalf.asp
5) Yeoman, R.S. *A Guide Book of United States Coins*, Whitman Publishing, 2004
6) http://coins.ha.com/c/item.zx?saleNo=392&lotNo=6501
   http://query.nytimes.com/mem/archivefree/pdf?res=9406E2D8103EE033A25757
   C1A9679D946697D6CF (*The New York Times* article which appeared on
   November 13, 1907)
7) David Margolick, *Penny Foolish*, *The New York Times*, 2/11/07.
   http://www.nps.gov/carl/historyculture/abraham-lincoln.htm
8) http://www.treasury.gov/resource-center/faqs/Currency/Pages/denominations.aspx
9) http://sammler.com/stamps/president_stamps.htm
   Kloetzel, James E., ed. *Scott Specialized Catalogue of United States Stamps and
   Covers*. Scott Publishing Company (2010).
   http://en.wikipedia.org/wiki/U.S._Presidents_on_U.S._Postage_stamps

CHAPTER 6

Death/Assassinations

Q: What president's famous last words were "Thomas Jefferson still lives" (or "Thomas Jefferson still survives")?

A: John Adams, stated on his deathbed on July 4, 1826, the day he died.

Q: Was Adams correct?

A: Not if his statement was intended to be taken literally. Jefferson had actually died about five hours earlier, also on July 4, 1826, fifty years to the day after the signing of the Declaration of Independence. James Monroe also died on July 4, though five years later. [1]

Q: Which president's death was the only one in presidential history not to be officially mourned in Washington D.C., and in fact was not even officially recognized?

A: John Tyler, because of his allegiance to the Confederacy.

Q: Who is the only president who died in office who was not elected in a year ending in 0?

A: Zachary Taylor, who was elected in 1848. Of the others who died while President:

1840 - **William Henry Harrison**, who died in 1841 during his first term;

1860 - **Abraham Lincoln**, who died in 1865 during his second term;

1880 - **James A. Garfield**, who died in 1881 during his first term;

1900 - **William McKinley**, who died in 1901 during his second term;

1920 - **Warren G. Harding**, who died in 1923 during his first term;

1940 - **Franklin Delano Roosevelt**, who died in 1945 during his fourth term;

1960 - **John F. Kennedy**, who died in 1963 during his first term. [2]

Q: Who were the only presidents who actually died in the White House itself?

A: William Henry Harrison and **Zachary Taylor**. [3]

Q: Who is Charles J. Guiteau?

A: The assassin of James Garfield. Guiteau, a lawyer, had written a speech in support of Ulysses S. Grant called "Grant vs. Hancock," when it was thought that Grant may run for a third term. However, he revised it to "Garfield vs. Hancock" after Garfield won the Republican nomination in the 1880 presidential campaign. He changed little more than the title. The speech was delivered by Guiteau twice, at most, but he believed himself to be largely responsible for Garfield's victory. He insisted he should be awarded an ambassadorship for his vital assistance. His personal requests to Garfield and to cabinet members were continually rejected.

Guiteau then decided that God had commanded him to kill the ungrateful President. Borrowing fifteen dollars, he went out to purchase a revolver. He knew little about firearms, but did know that he would need a large caliber gun. He had to choose between a .44 caliber Webley British Bulldog revolver with wooden grips and one with ivory grips. He wanted the one with the ivory handle because he wanted it to look good as a museum exhibit after the assassination, but he could not afford the extra dollar it cost. (The revolver was recovered by the Smithsonian in the early 20th-century but has since been lost). He spent the next few weeks in target practice—the kick from the revolver almost knocked him over the first time—and stalking Garfield.

On one occasion, he trailed Garfield to the railway station as the President was seeing his wife off to a beach resort in Long Branch, New Jersey, but he decided to shoot him later, since Garfield's wife, Lucretia, was in poor health and Guiteau did not want to upset her.

On July 2, 1881, he lay in wait for Garfield at the (since demolished) Baltimore and Potomac Railroad Station, getting his shoes shined, pacing, and engaging a cab to take him to the jail after the deed was done. Garfield was on his way to Williams College for his 25th college reunion. As Garfield entered the station, looking forward to a vacation with his wife in Long Branch, New Jersey, Guiteau stepped forward and shot Garfield twice from behind. As he surrendered to authorities, Guiteau said: "Arthur is president now!"

After a long, painful battle with infections, possibly brought on by his doctors' poking and probing the wound with unwashed hands and non-sterilized instruments, Garfield died on September 19th, eleven weeks after being shot. Most modern physicians familiar with the case state that Garfield would have easily recovered from his wounds with sterile medical care, which was common in the United States ten years later. Guiteau was hanged on June 30, 1882, about a year after the assassination.[4]

Guiteau is also the answer to the question, which presidential assassin survived the longest after his act? He survived nearly a year. Leon Czolgosz was alive for 45 days; John Wilkes Booth was alive for 12 days and Lee Harvey Oswald was alive for 2 days.

Guiteau, at age 40, was also the oldest presidential assassin. Czolgosz was 28, Booth 26 and Oswald 24.

Q: Which presidents died in office but were not assassinated?

A: William Henry Harrison, Zachary Taylor, Warren Harding, and **Franklin Roosevelt.**

Q: Who is the only president to have predeceased both parents?

A: John Kennedy.

Q: Besides Kennedy, who are the only two presidents to have predeceased their mothers?

A: James Garfield and **James Polk.**

Q: Besides Kennedy, who is the only president to have predeceased his father?

A: Warren Harding.

Q: Which three presidents died on the 4th of July?

A: John Adams and **Thomas Jefferson** (died on the same day, in 1826) and **James Monroe** in 1831.

Q: Who are the only presidents buried in Arlington National Cemetery?

A: William Howard Taft and **John Kennedy.**

Q: Which president served the shortest term (31 days)?

A: William Henry Harrison. He died of pneumonia. His inaugural address, the longest ever at one hour and 45 minutes, was delivered outside on a cold and wet day without a hat or overcoat. Some historians maintain that this was the cause of his death while others maintain that there was no connection, noting that the onset of the illness did not come until three weeks after the inaugural. [5]

Q: Who is the only president to have predeceased a grandparent?

A: John F. Kennedy. His grandmother, Mary Josephine Hannon Fitzgerald, died in 1964 at the age of 98.

Q: Which president's will states in part his request to free all slaves that he owns at the time of his death?

A portion of this president's will is as follows:

"Upon the decease of my wife, it is my Will and desire, that all the slaves which I hold in my own right, shall receive their freedom. To emancipate them during her life, would, tho' earnestly wished by me, be attended with such insuperable difficulties on account of their intermixture by Marriages with the Dower Negroes, as to excite the most painful sensations, if not disagreeable consequences from the latter ... The negroes thus bound, are (by their Masters or Mistresses), to be taught to read and write; & to be brought up to some useful occupation ... And I do hereby expressly forbid the sale, or transportation out of the said Commonwealth of any Slave I may die possessed of, under any pretence whatsoever. And I do moreover most pointedly, and most solemnly enjoin it upon my Executors hereafter named, or the survivors of them, to see that this clause respecting Slaves, and every part thereof be religiously fulfilled at the Epoch at which it is directed to take place; without evasion, neglect or delay, after the Crops which may then be on the ground are harvested, particularly as it respects the aged & infirm."

A: George Washington. [6]

Q: Match the president with the weapon that killed him:

A. .32 caliber Iver-Johnson revolver
B. .44 caliber Webley British Bulldog revolver
C. .44 caliber Philadelphia Derringer
D. 6.5 mm Carcano-type Model 91/38 rifle

1. James McKinley
2. James Garfield
3. Abraham Lincoln
4. John Kennedy

Answers: A.1, B.2, C.3, D.4

Q: Who is the only president considered to have died outside the United States?

A: John Tyler, because his place of death, Richmond, Virginia, was part of the Confederate States at the time of his death in 1862.

Q: Which president served only sixteen months and died from heat stroke (or gastroenteritis)?

A: Zachary Taylor.

Q: The remains of which president were exhumed on June 17, 1991 to determine if he had died of poisoning?

A: Zachary Taylor. It was concluded that poisoning was not the cause of death. Rather, it was concluded that on a hot July day, Taylor had attempted to cool himself with large amounts of cherries and iced milk. In the unhealthy climate of Washington at the time, with its open sewers and flies, Taylor came down with cholera morbus, or acute gastroenteritis as it is now called. He might have recovered, according to Samuel Eliot Morison in his *Oxford History of the American People*, but his doctors "drugged him with ipecac, calomel, opium and quinine (at forty grains a whack), and bled and blistered him, too. On July 9, he gave up the ghost." [7]

Q: Who was the oldest president at his death?

A: Gerald Ford. 93 years, 165 days. He outlived Ronald Reagan by 45 days.

Q: Which president wrote his own epitaph, which made no mention of the fact that he was president?

A: Thomas Jefferson

HERE WAS BURIED THOMAS JEFFERSON
AUTHOR OF THE
DECLARATION OF AMERICAN INDEPENDENCE
OF THE STATUTE OF VIRGINIA FOR RELIGIOUS FREEDOM
AND FATHER OF THE UNIVERSITY OF VIRGINIA

Q: Which president is in the largest mausoleum in North America?

A: Ulysses Grant, whose mausoleum is in New York City.

Q: Which 20th-century president was shot at and almost killed while President-elect?

A: Franklin Roosevelt. In 1932, Giuseppe Zangara was a 32-year old Italian immigrant. He was an uneducated bricklayer. On February 15, 1933, two weeks before Roosevelt was to be inaugurated, he was giving an impromptu speech from the back of an open car in the Bayfront Park area of Miami, Florida. Zangara lived there, working the occasional odd job, and living off his savings. Zangara was armed with a .32-caliber pistol he had bought at a local pawn shop. However, being only five feet tall, he was unable to see over other people and had to stand on a wobbly folding metal chair to get a clear aim at his target.

After the first shot, bystander Lillian Cross grabbed his arm, and he fired four more shots wildly. Five people were hit, including Chicago mayor Anton Cermak, who was standing on the running board of the car next to Roosevelt. En route to the hospital, Cermak had allegedly told FDR, "I'm glad it was me and not you, Mr. President," words now inscribed on a plaque in Bayfront Park. Neverthless, Cermak died from his wounds just a few weeks later, on March 6, 1933.

On March 20, 1933, after spending only 10 days on death row, Zangara was executed in Old Sparky, the electric chair at Florida State Prison in Raiford, Florida. Zangara became enraged when he learned no newsreel cameras would be filming his final moments. Zangara's final statement was "Viva Italia! Goodbye to all poor peoples everywhere! Push the button!" There has always been controversy over whether Zangara's real target was Roosevelt or Cermak.[8]

Q: Who was the only president who had two assassination attempts against him by gunshot?

A: Gerald Ford. In 1975, Lynette "Squeaky" Fromme, was a twenty-six year old follower of incarcerated cult leader Charles Manson. She wanted to bring attention to the issue of the California redwoods, which she felt were endangered. She wanted to talk to the president about it but realized that would be impossible and needed some other way to get his attention. On September 5, 1975, in Sacramento, California, she pointed a semi-automatic .45-caliber pistol at the president. The pistol's magazine was loaded with four rounds, but none was in the firing chamber when the agent grabbed it. Ford later said: "I reached out to shake a hand and I looked down and instead of a hand to be shaken, there was a gun in a hand pointed directly at me."

At her trial, Fromme pleaded not guilty, arguing that she had not actually intended to shoot the president. She subsequently told *The Sacramento Bee* that she had deliberately ejected the cartridge in her weapon's chamber before leaving home that morning, and investigators did later find a .45 cartridge in her bathroom. She was convicted, sentenced to life in prison.

She remained a dedicated disciple of Manson. In December, 1987 she escaped from the Alderson Prison after she heard that Manson, also imprisoned, had cancer. After forty hours roaming the rugged West Virginia hills, she was caught on Christmas Day, about two miles from the prison. Five years were added to her life sentence for the escape. She was released from prison on August 14, 2009.

Just seventeen days later, Ford was the victim of a second assassination attempt. Sara Jane Moore was a forty-five-year old five-time divorcee. On September 21, 1975, she had been picked up by police on an illegal handgun charge, but was released from arrest. The police confiscated her .44 caliber pistol and 113 rounds of ammunition.

The next day, she was standing in the crowd across the street from the St. Francis Hotel in San Francisco holding a .38 caliber revolver she had bought in haste that same morning. She was standing about forty feet away from president Ford when she fired a single shot at him. Moore's attempt was thwarted by a bystander, Oliver Sipple, who grabbed Moore's arm when she raised the gun. Sipple's actions may have caused the bullet to miss. After realizing she had missed, she raised her arm again, but

Sipple dove towards her and prevented her from getting off a second shot. The bullet which Moore did fire from her revolver ricocheted off the entrance to the hotel and slightly injured a bystander. On December 31, 2007, at the age of 77, Moore was released from prison on parole after serving thirty-two years of her life sentence.

Gerald Ford is also the answer to the question, who is the only president who had not one but two assassination attempts against him by women? [9]

Q: Which president's father died as a result of having saved two friends from drowning in a boating accident, when the father was thirty-three and his son was only three?

A: Andrew Johnson. In the winter of 1811, his father Jacob was winter fishing, along with Colonel William Polk, *Raleigh Star* editor Thomas Henderson, Jr., and a Scottish merchant remembered only as Callum. A canoe carrying Henderson and Callum toppled into the icy water of Walnut Creek, NC. Jacob plunged in and saved both men from drowning, and soon afterward became very ill. Jacob's many friends called on him to wish him a speedy recovery. It was later, in early January 1812, when Jacob was attending to his duties as Raleigh's bell-ringer, tolling for a funeral on a bitterly cold day, that he collapsed from exhaustion and weakness. On January 4, 1812, Jacob succumbed to his illness, and was buried in the Citizen's Cemetery, now called Raleigh City Cemetery, with a marker inscribed simply "J.X.J." [10]

Q: Which president died in the United States Capitol?

A: John Quincy Adams, in 1848. [11]

Q: Aside from John F. Kennedy, who was the only president to die before reaching age 50?

A: James Garfield. He was 49 years and 304 days when he died.

Q: Which presidents lost both of their parents before reaching age fifteen?

A: Andrew Jackson, age 14, and **Herbert Hoover,** age 9.

Q: Who is the only president buried in Washington, D.C.?

A: Woodrow Wilson, who is buried at the Washington National Cathedral.

Q: Who is buried in Grant's tomb?

A: There are two possible correct answers. One is President Grant and his wife Julia. The other is nobody, since they are technically entombed there, not buried.

BURIAL SITES OF PRESIDENTS:

George Washington	Mt. Vernon	Alexandria, VA
John Adams	United First Parish Church	Quincy, MA
Thomas Jefferson	Monticello	Charlottesville, VA
James Madison	Montpelier	Orange County, VA
James Monroe	Hollywood Cemetery	Richmond, VA
John Quincy Adams	United First Parish Church	Quincy, MA
Andrew Jackson	The Hermitage	Nashville TN
Martin Van Buren	Kinderhook Cemetery	Kinderhook, NY
William Henry Harrison	William Henry Harrison Tomb State Memorial	North Bend, OH
John Tyler	Hollywood Cemetery	Richmond, VA
James K. Polk	Tennessee State Capitol	Nashville, TN
Zachary Taylor	Zachary Taylor National Cemetery	Louisville, KY
Millard Fillmore	Forest Lawn Cemetery	Buffalo, NY
Franklin Pierce	Old North Cemetery	Concord, NH
James Buchanan	Woodward Hill Cemetery	Lancaster, PA
Abraham Lincoln	Oak Ridge Cemetery	Springfield, IL
Andrew Johnson	Andrew Johnson National Cemetery	Greeneville, TN

Ulysses Grant	Grant's Tomb	New York, NY
Rutherford Hayes	Spiegel Grove	Fremont, OH
James Garfield	Lake View Cemetery	Cleveland, OH
Chester Arthur	Albany Rural Cemetery	Menands, NY
Grover Cleveland	Princeton Cemetery	Princeton, NJ
Benjamin Harrison	Crown Hill Cemetery	Indianapolis, IN
William McKinley	McKinley National Memorial	Canton, OH
Theodore Roosevelt	Youngs Memorial Cemetery	Oyster Bay, NY
William Howard Taft	Arlington National Cemetery	Arlington, VA
Woodrow Wilson	Washington National Cathedral	Washington, D.C.
Warren Harding	Harding Memorial	Marion, OH
Calvin Coolidge	Notch Cemetery	Plymouth Notch, VT
Herbert Hoover	Herbert Hoover Presidential Library and Museum	West Branch , IA
Franklin Roosevelt	Home of Franklin D. Roosevelt National Historic Site	Hyde Park, NY
Harry S Truman	Harry S Truman Library and Museum	Independence, MO
Dwight Eisenhower	Eisenhower Presidential Center	Abilene, KS
John F. Kennedy	Arlington National Cemetery	Arlington, VA
Lyndon Johnson	LBJ Ranch	Stonewall, TX
Richard Nixon	Richard Nixon Presidential Library and Museum	Yorba Linda, CA
Gerald Ford	Gerald R. Ford Presidential Museum	Grand Rapids, MI
Ronald Reagan	Ronald Reagan Presidential Library	Simi Valley, CA

Q: Which president was the youngest upon his death who was not assassinated?

A: James Polk was 53 years, 225 days when he died.

Q: Who is Leon Czolgosz?
A: The man who assassinated **William McKinley** in Buffalo on

September 6, 1901. Czolgosz was a 28 year-old laborer who became entranced with the anarchist movement, especially after hearing a speech by Emma Goldman earlier that year. "Under the galling yoke of government, ecclesiasticism, and a bond of custom and prejudice, it is impossible for the individual to work out his own career as he could wish." Czolgosz was mesmerized by Goldman's speech. "My head nearly split with the pain ... She set me on fire!" Czolgosz said later. He left the lecture hall that day convinced that it was up to him to bring social change to America. He decided he had to kill McKinley, who he saw as a symbol of America's woes. The day before the shooting, he bought a .32 caliber Iver-Johnson revolver in downtown Buffalo.

On September 6, McKinley was scheduled to give a speech at the Temple of Music at the Pan-American Exposition after greeting visitors. McKinley stood in the center of the room as the crowd, in single file, moved past him, shaking hands as they passed. At 4:07 p.m. Czolgosz was in front of the president. As the president extended his hand, Czolgosz pushed it aside and pulled out the revolver, wrapped in a handkerchief, from his pocket. He fired two quick shots into McKinley's torso. "I would have shot more but I was stunned by a blow in the face, a frightful blow that knocked me down and then everybody jumped on me!" Czolgosz said later. One bullet had never penetrated the flesh, but the other passed through McKinley's stomach, damaging the pancreas and a kidney. McKinley died of his wounds on September 14, 1901.

Czolgosz was convicted of first degree murder on September 24, 1901 after the jury deliberated for only one hour. On September 26, the jury unanimously recommended the death penalty. He was electrocuted in Auburn Prison on October 29, 1901, just 45 days after his victim's death. His last words were: "I killed the president because he was the enemy of the good people —the good working people. I am not sorry for my crime." As the prison guards strapped him into the chair, however, he did say through clenched teeth, "I am only sorry I could not get to see my father."[12]

Q: Who was the only president who had a child who died in the White House itself?

A: Abraham Lincoln. His son Willie died there on February 20, 1862.

Q: Besides Lincoln, which presidents had children who died while they were president?

A: John Adams—son Charles
Thomas Jefferson—daughter Mary "Polly" Jefferson
John Kennedy—son Patrick.

Q: Which president (one of our best remembered) who delivered the eulogy for another president (one of our least remembered) before the former became president?

A: Abraham Lincoln delivered the eulogy for **Zachary Taylor** in Chicago on July 25, 1850, a full ten years before Lincoln became President. The fact that Lincoln had done so was unknown until 1922. [13]

Q: Which president's Will consisted of one sentence?

A: Calvin Coolidge. His Last Will and Testament stated in its entirety: "Not unmindful of my son John, I give all my estate, both real and personal, to my wife, Grace Coolidge, in fee simple." [14]

CHAPTER SIX NOTES:

1) http://www.heritage.org/research/reports/2001/02/thomas-jefferson-still-live
2) http://en.wikipedia.org/wiki/List_of_presidents_of_the_United_States_by_date_of_death
3) http://politicalgraveyard.com/death/white-house.html

4) http://www.robinsonlibrary.com/america/unitedstates/1865/1881/garfield/
    death.htm
    http://en.wikipedia.org/wiki/Charles_J._Guiteau#CITEREFJune1999
    A President Felled by an Assassin and 1880's Medical Care, The New York Times,
    July 25, 2006.
5) Cleaves, Freeman. Old Tippecanoe: William Henry Harrison and His Time. C.
    Scribner's Sons (1939).
6) http://www.pbs.org/georgewashington/collection/other_last_will.html
7) http://www.nytimes.com/1991/07/04/opinion/l-scandal-and-the-heat-did-
    zachary-taylor-in-998691.html
    Morrison, Samuel, *Oxford History of the American People*, Oxford University
    Press (1965).
8) Boertlein, John, *"A Little Luck for the President-Elect." Presidential Confidential: Sex,*
    Scandal, Murder and Mayhem in the Oval Office. Clerisy
    Press (2010).
    http://www.spartacus.schoolnet.co.uk/USAcermak.htm
    Dwyer, Jim, ed. *"An Assassin's Bullets for FDR." Strange Stories, Amazing Facts*
    of America's Past. The Reader's Digest Association (1989).
9) Bravin, Jess *Squeaky: The Life and Times Of Lynette Alice Fromme.* St. Martin's
    Press (1997).
    http://www.history.com/this-day-in-history/ford-assassination-attempt-thwarted
    "The Evolution of the Personal Protective Function." House Security Review.
    Prop1.org. 1995-05. http://prop1.org/park/pave/rev8.htm.
    http://www.bittenandbound.com/2009/08/05/lynette-squeaky-fromme-parole-
    photos-video/
    Time magazine, *The Assailant: Making of a Misfit,* 10-6-1975
    http://www.history.com/search?search-field=president+ford+surviv&x=12&y=13
    Evans, Harold, "The Imperial Presidency: 1972-1980." *The American Century.*
    Random House. (1998).
10) http://www.raleighpublicrecord.org/opinion/2009/01/04/andrew-johnsons-
    father-a-hero-in-his-own-right/
11) Donaldson, Norman and Betty. *How Did They Die?* Greenwich House (1980).
12) Seibert, Jeffrey W. *I Done My Duty: The Complete Story of the Assassination*
    of President McKinley, Heritage Books (2002)
    http://www.trutv.com/library/crime/terrorists_spies/assassins/mckinley/2.html
    Assassin Czolgosz is Executed at Auburn; He Declared That He Felt No Regret
    for His Crime. Autopsy Disclosed No Mental Abnormalities, The New York Times,
    October 30, 1901
13) Collected works. *The Abraham Lincoln Association, Springfield, Illinois.* Roy P.
    Basler, editor; Marion Dolores Pratt and Lloyd A. Dunlap, assistant editors.
    Lincoln, Abraham, 1809-1865. New Brunswick, N.J: Rutgers University Press,
    1953.
    http://www.archive.org/stream/genzacharytaylor00lincrichgenzacharytaylor
    00lincrich_djvu.txt
14) http://www.juntosociety.com/uspresidents/ccoolidge.html

CHAPTER 7

Education

Q: Which three of the first ten presidents attended the same college, and which college was it?

A: Thomas Jefferson, James Monroe and **John Tyler**. They attended the College of William and Mary, and they were three of the first six presidents who actually graduated from college.

Q: Which presidents went to Yale Law School?

A: Gerald Ford and **Bill Clinton**.

Q: Who is the only president with an earned Ph.D.?

A: Woodrow Wilson. He received his Ph.D. in history and political science from Johns Hopkins. His doctoral dissertation was entitled *Congressional Government: A Study in American Politics* and may be read online.[1]

Q: Who was the only president in the 20th century not to earn a college degree?

A: **Harry Truman.** From 1923-1925, he did take night courses at the University of Kansas City Law School, but he did not graduate. [2]

Q: **Which president's college thesis was later published under the title *Why England Slept*?**

A: **John Kennedy's.**

Q: **Who was the first president to graduate from law school?**

A: **Rutherford Hayes**, who attended Harvard Law School.

Q: **Who was the only president who studied to become a doctor?**

A: **William Henry Harrison.** In 1791, he enrolled at the University of Pennsylvania Medical School to study under Dr. Benjamin Rush, a noted physician. Later that year, following his father's death and without funds to continue school, he withdrew.

Q: **Which president was the youngest member of Stanford University's first graduating class?**

A: **Herbert Hoover**, who graduated in 1895.[3]

Q: **Who is the only president to have been enrolled, at various times, at Princeton, Stanford and Harvard?**

A: **John Kennedy.**

Q: **Which president did not know how to read until he was about seventeen years old, and was the only president with no formal education?**

A: **Andrew Johnson.** [4]

Q: Besides Andrew Johnson, which three presidents had only minimal formal education?

A: George Washington, Zachary Taylor and **Abraham Lincoln.** George Washington received the equivalent of an elementary school education from a variety of tutors. Zachary Taylor had very little formal education. Abraham Lincoln had, by his own admission, only about one year of formal education.[5]

Q: Who is the only president with an M.B.A.?

A: George W. Bush.

Q: Between 1972 and 2004 inclusive, every election had a presidential or vice presidential candidate who attended this University. Which one and who were the candidates?

A: Yale.

1972—Sargent Shriver
1976—Gerald Ford (Law School)
1980—George H.W. Bush
1984—George H.W Bush
1988—George H.W. Bush
1992—Bill Clinton (Law School) and George H.W. Bush
1996—Bill Clinton (Law School)
2000—George W. Bush
2004—George W. Bush

Q: Who was the last president who never attended college at all?

A: Grover Cleveland.

Q: Besides Harvard and Yale, there are three colleges who can claim more than one future president as an undergraduate attendee. Which are they and who attended?

A: Three presidents attended William and Mary: **Thomas Jefferson**, **James Monroe** and **John Tyler**. However, Monroe dropped out to fight in the Revolutionary War. **James Madison** and **Woodrow Wilson** both graduated from Princeton although when Madison graduated in 1771, it was called the College of New Jersey. Finally, **Ulysses Grant** and **Dwight Eisenhower** both graduated from West Point. Ulysses Grant ranked 21st out of thirty-nine in his 1843 graduating class. Eisenhower ranked 61st out of 164 in his 1915 graduating class.[6]

PRESIDENT	EDUCATION
John Adams	Harvard University
Thomas Jefferson	College of William and Mary
James Madison	Princeton University
James Monroe	College of William and Mary
John Quincy Adams	Leiden University (transferred to Harvard University)
William Henry Harrison	Hampden-Sydney College (withdrew) University of Pennsylvania Medical School (withdrew)
John Tyler	College of William and Mary
James K. Polk	University of North Carolina at Chapel Hill
Franklin Pierce	Bowdoin College
James Buchanan	Dickinson College
Ulysses Grant	United States Military Academy
Rutherford Hayes	Kenyon College; Harvard Law School
James Garfield	Williams College
Chester Arthur	Union College
Benjamin Harrison	Miami University
William McKinley	Allegheny College; Albany Law School
Theodore Roosevelt	Harvard University Columbia Law School (withdrew)
William Howard Taft	Yale University University of Cincinnati College of Law

Woodrow Wilson	Davidson College
	Princeton University
	University of Virginia School of Law (withdrew)
	Johns Hopkins University (Ph.D.)
Warren G. Harding	Ohio Central College
Calvin Coolidge	Amherst College
Herbert Hoover	Stanford University
Franklin D. Roosevelt	Harvard University
	Columbia Law School (withdrew)
Harry S Truman	University of Missouri-Kansas City School of Law (withdrew)
Dwight D. Eisenhower	United States Military Academy
John F. Kennedy	London School of Economics
	Princeton University
	Harvard University
	Stanford Graduate School of Business (withdrew)
Lyndon B. Johnson	Texas State University-San Marcos
	Georgetown University Law Center (withdrew)
Richard Nixon	Whittier College Duke University School of Law
Gerald Ford	University of Michigan, Yale Law School
Jimmy Carter	Georgia Southwestern College
	Georgia Institute of Technology
	United States Naval Academy
Ronald Reagan	Eureka College
George H. W. Bush	Yale University
Bill Clinton	Georgetown University
	University of Oxford (Rhodes Scholar)
	Yale Law School
George W. Bush	Yale University
	Harvard Business School

Barack Obama   Occidental College
                        Columbia University
                        Harvard Law School[7]

Q: Five students at the College of William and Mary founded Phi Beta Kappa in 1776. well before George Washington became president. It is the country's oldest academic honor society. **Which of the following presidents graduated Phi Beta Kappa?**

John Adams   William McKinley
Thomas Jefferson   Herbert Hoover
James Madison   John F. Kennedy
James Monroe   Richard Nixon
James Polk   Barack Obama
Abraham Lincoln

A: None of them. Interestingly, it seems that, of our presidents who are considered great, almost none of the pre-20th-century presidents were Phi Beta Kappas, while most of the 20th-century presidents were. The seventeen who were are as follows:

John Quincy Adams   Chester A. Arthur
Martin Van Buren   Grover Cleveland
Franklin Pierce   Theodore Roosevelt
Rutherford B. Hayes   William Howard Taft
James A. Garfield   Woodrow Wilson
Calvin Coolidge   Jimmy Carter
Franklin D. Roosevelt   George H.W. Bush
Harry S. Truman   Bill Clinton [8]
Dwight D. Eisenhower

Q: Which president graduated from college in two-and-one-half years?

A: George H.W. Bush.[9]

Q: Four presidents attended colleges that also produced Super Bowl winning quarterbacks.

Name the presidents, the quarterbacks and the colleges.

Answers:

1. **Jimmy Carter** and Roger Staubach both graduated from the Naval Academy. Staubach won Super Bowls VI and XII with the Dallas Cowboys.

2. **Herbert Hoover** and John Elway both graduated from Stanford. Elway won Super Bowls XXXII and XXXIII with the Denver Broncos. Jim Plunkett also attended Stanford and won Super Bowl XV.

3. **Gerald Ford** and Tom Brady both graduated from Michigan. Brady won Super Bowls XXXVI, XXXVIII and XXXIX.

4. **Benjamin Harrison** and Ben Roethlisberger both graduated from Miami of Ohio. Roethlisberger won Super Bowls XL and XLIII.

CHAPTER SEVEN NOTES:

1) http://www.archive.org/details/congressionalgov00wilsa
2) Hamby, Alonzo L. *Man of the People*, Oxford University Press (1995)
3) http://www.ecommcode.com/hoover/hooveronline/hoover_bio/stan.htm
4) Trefousse, Hans L. *Andrew Johnson: A Biography*. Norton (1989)
5) http://www.u-s-history.com/pages/h1789.htm
   Chernow, Ron. *Washington: A Life*, Penguin Press (2010)
   Bauer, K. Jack. *Zachary Taylor: Soldier, Planter, Statesman of the Old Southwest*. Rrtff
   Donald, David Herbert. *Lincoln*. Simon and Schuster (1996)
   Ketcham, Henry. *The Life of Abraham Lincoln*, Empire Books (2011)
6) http://www.u-s-history.com/pages/h1789.html
7) http://en.wikipedia.org/wiki/List_of_Presidents_of_the_United_States_by_education
8) www.pbk.org/infoview/PBK_InfoView.aspx?t=&id=59
9) http://www.archives.gov/publications/prologue/2007/spring/schoolhouse.html

CHAPTER 8

Elections

Q: When was the last election before 2008 in which no incumbent president or vice president was on the ticket?

A: 1952, when **Dwight D. Eisenhower** and **Richard M. Nixon** defeated Adlai Stevenson and John Sparkman.

Q; What president won of 58% of the popular vote the first time he ran and under 40% the second time?

A: **Herbert Hoover.**

Q: Which president carried 49 States?

A: **Richard Nixon** in 1972. He failed to carry only Massachusetts and the District of Columbia.

Q: Which president's only defeat in a political race was when he ran for president?

A: **Gerald Ford** in 1976.

Q: Which president was not successful in his bid for the presidency until his fourth try for the office?

A: James Buchanan (1844, 1848, 1852 and 1856)

Q: In a particular race for Congress in California, a group calling itself *A Committee of One Hundred Men* wanted to unseat a sitting 5-term Congressman, named Jerry Voorhis. So they placed an ad placed in 26 newspapers which read:

> "WANTED—Congressman candidate with no previous political experience to defeat a man who has represented the district in the House for ten years. Any young man, resident of district, preferably a veteran, fair education, no political strings or obligations and possessor of a few ideas for betterment of country at large may apply for the job. Applicants will be reviewed by 100 interested citizens who will guarantee support but will not obligate the candidate in any way."

The man who won this Congressional race went on become President of the United States. Who was he?

A: Richard Nixon. Nixon was in the Navy at the time and apparently did not see the ad. However, on September 29, 1945, Herman Perry of the Whittier branch of the Bank of America, wrote Nixon and asked if he would be interested in entering the race. Nixon's October 6, 1945 response stated: "I feel very strongly that Jerry Voorhis can be beaten and I'd welcome the opportunity to take a crack at him. An aggressive, vigorous campaign on a platform of practical liberalism should be the antidote the people have been looking for to take the place of Voorhis' particular brand of New Deal idealism. You can be sure that I'll do everything possible to win if the party gives me the chance to run," he wrote. "I'm sure that I can hold my own with Voorhis on the speaking platform, and without meaning to toot my own horn, I believe I have the fight, spirit and background which can beat him."[1]

Q: On four occasions, presidents have defeated each other on successive elections. What were these occasions?

1796—John Adams beat Jefferson; 4 years later Jefferson won.

1824—John Quincy Adams beat Andrew Jackson; 4 years later Jackson won.

1836—Martin Van Buren beat William Henry Harrison; 4 years later Harrison won.

1888—Benjamin Harrison beat Grover Cleveland; 4 years later Cleveland won.

Q: Who was the only vice president who defeated his President?

A: Thomas Jefferson beat John Adams in the election of 1800.

Q: Who were the only presidents who won an election who did not run for re-election after their first term was over?

A: James Polk, James Buchanan and **Rutherford Hayes.**

Q: Which was the only election where the winner lost both the popular vote and the electoral vote?

A: The election of 1824 in which **Andrew Jackson** won both and yet **John Quincy Adams** was elected president. The reason is because no candidate secured a majority of the electoral vote. As a result, it was decided under the Twelfth Amendment, which provides that when no candidate secures a majority of the electoral vote the choice of the president is turned over to the House of Representatives The breakdown of the race was as follows:

Presidential Candidate	Party	Home State	Popular Vote		Electoral Vote
			Count	Percentage	
Andrew Jackson	Democratic-Republican	Tennessee	151,271	41.3	99
John Quincy Adams	Democratic-Republican	Massachusetts	113,142	30.9	84
WilliamHarris Crawford	Democratic-Republican	Georgia	40,856	11.2	41
Henry Clay	Democratic-Republican	Kentucky	47,531	13.0	37
(Massachusetts unpledged electors)	None	N/A	6,616	1.8	0
		Other	6,437	1.8	0
		Total	365,833	100.0%	261
				Needed to win	131 [2]

Q: In the eleven elections between 1952 and 1992, at least one of three men were on the Republican ticket in nine of those elections. Who were they?

A: Richard Nixon (1952 and 1956 as Dwight Eisenhower's vice presidential running mate, and 1960, 1968 and 1972 as presidential candidate), **Ronald Reagan** (1976, 1980 and 1984 as presidential candidate) and **George H.W. Bush** (1980 and 1984 as Ronald Reagan's vice presidential running mate, and 1988 and 1992 as presidential candidate).

Q: Which presidents tried to win a third non-consecutive term?

A: Ulysses Grant and **Theodore Roosevelt.** Grant ran for President in 1880 and Roosevelt ran for president in 1912.

Q: Which presidents lost the popular vote but were still elected?

A: Four presidents took office without winning the popular vote. They were elected, instead, by the electoral college or, in the case of John Quincy Adams, by the House of Representatives after a tie in the electoral votes. They were:

- John Quincy Adams who lost by 44,804 votes to Andrew Jackson in 1824.
- Rutherford B. Hayes who lost by 264,292 votes to Samuel J. Tilden in 1876.
- Benjamin Harrison who lost by 95,713 votes to Grover Cleveland in 1888.
- George W. Bush who lost by 543,816 votes to Al Gore in 2000.

Q: Who was the only person who became president despite having lost to an opponent who won an absolute majority (i.e. more than 50%) of the popular vote (as opposed to a mere plurality)?

A: Rutherford Hayes. He won 4,034,311 votes, Samuel Tilden won 4,288,546 votes and Peter Cooper of the Greenback Party won 75,793 votes. In the other three races above, the losing candidate still had less than 50% of the total popular vote.[3]

Q: Which presidents never held elective political office before being elected president?

A: George Washington, Zachary Taylor, Ulysses Grant, Herbert Hoover, William Howard Taft and **Dwight Eisenhower**. Grant, like Taylor and Eisenhower, had no elective positions between the Army and the White House. Hoover was

Secretary of Commerce which is not an elective office. Taft held numerous government positions before assuming the presidency, but they were all appointive, not elective.[4]

Q: Which president was only elected to one office prior to being elected president, which was vice president?

A: Chester Arthur.

Q: Who was the only non-elected president who did not seek to be elected president at the end of his term?

A: Andrew Johnson.

Q: Who was the first non-elected president who later won an election?

A: Theodore Roosevelt. The other non-elected presidents were John Tyler, Millard Fillmore, Andrew Johnson, Chester Arthur, Calvin Coolidge, Harry Truman, Lyndon Johnson, and Gerard Ford.

Q: Who was the only president to make three unsuccessful bids for president after serving?

A: Martin Van Buren. He was the Democratic nominee for president in 1840 but lost to William Henry Harrison, who became president. In 1844, he lost the Democratic nomination to James K. Polk, who also became president. Finally, in 1848, he ran as a member of the Free Soil Party. Although he won 10% of the vote, he had no electoral votes and did not win any individual States.[5]

Q: Who are the only presidents elected twice without winning 50% of the popular vote either time?

A: Grover Cleveland, Woodrow Wilson and **Bill Clinton.**

1884	Grover Cleveland	48.85%
1892	Grover Cleveland	46.02%
1912	Woodrow Wilson	41.84%
1916	Woodrow Wilson	49.24%
1992	Bill Clinton	43.01%
1996	Bill Clinton	49.23%[6]

Q: Who are the only presidents elected twice who won once with more than 50% of the popular vote and once with less?

A: Abraham Lincoln, Richard Nixon and **George W. Bush**

1860	Abraham Lincoln	39.65%
1864	Abraham Lincoln	55.03%
1968	Richard Nixon	43.42%
1972	Richard Nixon	60.67%
2000	George W. Bush	47.87%
2004	George W. Bush	50.73%[7]

Q: Who was the only president elected unanimously?

A: George Washington

Q: Besides Washington, who was the only president who ran for the office effectively unopposed?

A: James Monroe in the election of 1820. The two major parties at the time were the Democratic-Republican party, of which Monroe was a member, and the Federalist party. However the Federalist party effectively disappeared as a major political party, dating back to their opposition to the War of 1812. The Federalists did not even name a candidate. However, the election was not unanimous because one elector, William Plumer from New Hampshire, cast a vote for then-Secretary of State John Quincy Adams. Plumer thought Monroe was a mediocre president and that Adams would be a better one.[8]

Q: Who was the only president elected to the House after his presidency?

A: John Quincy Adams. Adams ran for and was elected to the Massachusetts House of Representatives in the 1830 elections as a National Republican. He was elected to eight terms, serving as a Representative from 1831 until his death in 1848.

Q: Who was the only elected president (as opposed to a vice president who succeeded to the position) to fail to be re-nominated by his party for a second term?

A: Franklin Pierce. James Buchanan defeated Pierce in his bid for re-nomination.

One-term elected presidents	Reason for failure to be reelected
John Adams	Defeated by Thomas Jefferson in general election
John Quincy Adams	Defeated by Andrew Jackson in general election
Martin Van Buren	Defeated by William Henry Harrison in general election
James Polk	Did not run for reelection, fulfilling campaign promise
Franklin Pierce	Democratic party nominated James Buchanan to run for President

James Buchanan	Did not run for reelection
Rutherford Hayes	Did not run for reelection, fulfilling campaign promise
Grover Cleveland	Defeated by Benjamin Harrison in general election
Benjamin Harrison	Defeated by Grover Cleveland in general election
William Taft	Defeated by Woodrow Wilson in general election
Herbert Hoover	Defeated by Franklin Roosevelt in general election
Jimmy Carter	Defeated by Ronald Reagan in general election
George Herbert Walker Bush	Defeated by Bill Clinton in general election

Q: Who were the only non-elected presidents who were not re-nominated by their party for a second term?

A: **Millard Fillmore, Andrew Johnson** and **Chester Arthur.** Fillmore, who became president when Zachary Taylor died in 1850, did not gain the Whig party nomination for a second term. Johnson's situation was murkier because of his ambiguous party affiliation. He had been elected as Lincoln's running mate as a "Union Democrat." However, after Lincoln was assassinated and he ascended to the presidency, he faced a Republican congress that despised him. After being impeached, he attempted to win the Democratic nomination in 1868. Since several Confederate states hadn't yet rejoined the Union to vote in that election, and he was not well-liked by north-ern Democrats either, he failed to win support from either major party. Chester Arthur, who took over upon Garfield's assassination, did not gain his party's nomination for a second term.

It's worth noting that all of these elections occurred before the modern era of party primaries being decided by voters. These

Presidents had to win the approval of their own party officials, not the public at large.

Q: Which was the first president elected after there was a popular vote for president?

A: John Quincy Adams in 1824.

Q: What was the only election in which voters could choose from among four men who all either had been or would be president? (Hint: At the time, voters selected a vice president as well).

A: The election of 1840. **Martin Van Buren, William Henry Harrison, John Tyler** and **James Polk.**

Q: Which president, besides Franklin Roosevelt, won the popular election three times?

A: Grover Cleveland. In 1888, Cleveland won the popular vote over Benjamin Harrison but lost the electoral vote.

Q: Since 1860, when was the only election in which a candidate other than a Democrat or Republican came in second place?

A: The election of 1912. Theodore Roosevelt, running for re-election as a Progressive (nicknamed the "Bull Moose Party"), won 27% of the popular vote and 17% of the electoral vote. Democratic Woodrow Wilson won the election and Republican William Howard Taft, running for re-election, came in third.

Q: Since 1860, who are the only third-party candidates besides Roosevelt to have won at least 10% of the popular vote? For extra credit, identify their respective parties.

A: In the 1924 election, won by Calvin Coolidge, Robert ("Fighting Bob") La Follette from Wisconsin, garnered 17% of the popular vote, running as a member of the Progressive Party. In the 1968 election, won by Richard Nixon, George Wallace of Alabama won 14% of the vote, running as a member of the American Independent Party.

Q: Who was the only Democrat elected president between 1860 and 1912?

A: Grover Cleveland.

Q: There have been nine presidents who ascended to the presidency through the death or resignation of their predecessors. Of those, only four were then elected president. Of those four, only one announced that he would not run for a second elected term before the campaign began, even though he was eligible to run. Who was it?

A: Calvin Coolidge. The four presidents who would have been possibly correct answers to this question are Theodore Roosevelt (who won the 1904 election), Coolidge (who won the 1924 election), Harry Truman (who won the 1948 election) and Lyndon Johnson (who won the 1964 election). Roosevelt ran for re-election as a member of the Bull Moose Party in 1912 and lost to Woodrow Wilson. Of the others, Coolidge was the only one who clearly announced his intention not to run for re-election in advance of the upcoming 1928 election. While on vacation in the summer of 1927, he issued this terse statement: "I do not choose to run for President in 1928." He stated, "If I take another term, I will be in the White House till 1933 ... Ten years in Washington is longer than any other man has had it-too long!"

In his memoirs, Coolidge explained his decision not to run: "The presidential office takes a heavy toll of those who occupy it and those who are dear to them. While we should not refuse to spend and be spent in the service of our country, it is hazardous to attempt what we feel is beyond our strength to accomplish."

Truman did not make his announcement not to run until after the 1952 campaign was underway. In 1951, the 22nd Amendment to the Constitution was ratified, making a president ineligible to be elected for a third time, or to be elected for a second time after having served more than two years of a previous president's term. The latter clause would have applied to Truman in 1952, except that a grandfather clause in the amendment explicitly excluded the current president from this provision. Therefore Truman could have run and in fact his name was on the ballot in New Hampshire (a race which was won by Estes Kefauver).

Truman did not formally announce his decision not to run for re-election until March 29, 1952. However, he wrote in his memoirs that his decision had been made well before his defeat by Kefauver. Thus, whether his decision had been made previously or was made because he saw the handwriting on the wall cannot be stated with certainty. However, he did not actively campaign for President in the 1952 election.

In 1968, Lyndon Johnson ran for a second full term, but dropped out of the race after he only narrowly won the New Hampshire primary against Eugene McCarthy, which was considered a sign of a major weakness for the incumbent president. After Robert Kennedy joined the race on March 16, 1968, Johnson announced that he would not run for another term a mere two weeks later (March 31). At the conclusion of an address to the nation, he stated:

> "I have concluded that I should not permit the presidency to become involved in the partisan divisions that are developing in this political year. With America's sons in the fields far away, with America's future under challenge right here at home, with our hopes and the world's hopes for peace in the balance every day, I do not believe that I should devote an hour or a day of my time to any personal partisan causes or

to any duties other than the awesome duties of this office—the presidency of your country. Accordingly, I shall not seek, and I will not accept, the nomination of my party for another term as your president."

Interestingly, even though Truman and Johnson withdrew from their respective races at about the same time in their campaign seasons, Johnson clearly ran and then withdrew from his race while Truman is considered not to have run at all. In any event, neither of them withdrew far in advance of the race as Coolidge.[9]

Q: Who were the only presidents who were never elected president?

A: John Tyler, Millard Fillmore, Andrew Johnson, Chester Arthur and **Gerald Ford.**

Q: Who were the only presidents who were not elected president who ran and lost after serving out their predecessor's term?

A: Millard Fillmore in 1852 and **Gerald Ford** in 1976.

Q: Who was the first president who became president through the death or resignation of his predecessor and who ran and won after serving out his predecessor's term?

A: Theodore Roosevelt in 1904. The fate of the other presidents besides Fillmore and Ford who became president through the death or resignation of their predecessors is as follows:

PRESIDENT	WHAT HAPPENED AT THE END OF THEIR TERM
John Tyler	Did not run for reelection in 1844
Andrew Johnson	Did not run for reelection in 1868
Chester Arthur	Did not run for reelection in 1884

Calvin Coolidge   Ran and won in 1924
Harry Truman   Ran and won in 1944
Lyndon Johnson   Ran and won in 1964

Q: When was the first presidential election covered by radio?

A: The 1920 election, won by **Warren Harding**.

Q: Only two presidents were elected with less than 40% of the popular vote. Who were they?

A: **John Quincy Adams** won the 1824 election with only 30.92% of the popular vote and **Abraham Lincoln** won the 1860 election with only 39.65% of the popular vote.

Q: Only four presidents were elected with more than 60% of the popular vote. Only one of them ever won another election. Who were they?

A: **Warren Harding** won the 1920 election with 60.32% of the popular vote, **Franklin Roosevelt** won the 1936 election with 60.80% of the popular vote, **Lyndon Johnson** won the 1964 election with 61.05% of the popular vote (the only President to break the 61% barrier) and **Richard Nixon** won the 1972 election with 60.62% of the popular vote.

Q: Of the presidents who won two consecutive terms, only two received a lower percentage of the popular vote the second time. Who were they?

A: **Andrew Jackson** in the 1836 election and **Barack Obama** in the 2012 election. Franklin Roosevelt did receive a fewer percentage of the popular vote in the 1940 and 1944 elections than he did in 1936. In addition, Grover Cleveland received a received a fewer percentage of the popular vote in the 1892 election than he did in 1884, but those were non-consecutive elections.

Q: In percentage terms, based on the electoral college vote, what was the most lopsided presidential election since 1824?

A: In 1936, during FDR's second run, he garnered 523 electoral votes to Alf Landon's eight. The 1824 election was anomalous because it is the only election which was decided by the House of Representatives. The 1800 election took place before adoption of the Twelfth Amendment to the Constitution. This Amendment required each elector to cast distinct votes for president and vice president, instead of two votes for president. Under the original procedure for the Electoral College, as provided in Article II, Section 1, Clause 3 of the Constitution, each elector could cast two votes. This created problems with the election of 1800.

   A history of the presidential elections follows, first by electoral college and then by popular vote. The first chart is ranked by percentage of electoral votes won, going from lowest to highest and the second is chronological.

Rank	Year	Winner	# of Electors	Votes cast for winner	Votes cast for runner-up	Percentage
1.	1824	draw: Andrew Jackson, John Quincy Adams, William Crawford	261	84	99	32.18%
2.	1800	draw: Thomas Jefferson, Aaron Burr	138	73	73	52.90%
3.	1876	Rutherford B. Hayes	369	185	184	50.14%
4.	2000	George W. Bush	538	271	266	50.37%
5.	1796	John Adams	138	71	68	51.45%
6.	1916	Woodrow Wilson	531	277	254	52.17%
7.	2004	George W. Bush	538	286	251	53.16%
8.	1884	Grover Cleveland	401	219	182	54.61%
9.	1976	Jimmy Carter	538	297	240	55.20%
10.	1968	Richard Nixon	538	301	191	55.95%
11.	1848	Zachary Taylor	290	163	127	56.21%

Rank	Year	Winner	# of Electors	Votes cast for winner	Votes cast for runner-up	Percentage
12.	1960	John F. Kennedy	537	303	219	56.42%
13.	1948	Harry S Truman	531	303	189	57.06%
14.	1836	Martin Van Buren	294	170	73	57.82%
15.	1880	James A. Garfield	369	214	155	57.99%
16.	1888	Benjamin Harrison	401	233	168	58.10%
17.	1856	James Buchanan	296	174	114	58.78%
18.	1812	James Madison	217	128	89	58.99%
19.	1860	Abraham Lincoln	303	180	72	59.41%
20.	1896	William McKinley	447	271	176	60.63%
21.	2012	Barack Obama	538	332	206	61.71%
22.	1844	James K. Polk	275	170	105	61.82%
23.	1892	Grover Cleveland	444	277	145	62.39%
24.	1900	William McKinley	447	292	155	65.32%
25.	1908	William Howard Taft	483	321	162	66.46%
26.	2008	Barack Obama	538	365	173	67.84%
27.	1828	Andrew Jackson	261	178	83	68.20%
28.	1992	Bill Clinton	538	370	168	68.77%
29.	1808	James Madison	175	122	47	69.71%
30.	1996	Bill Clinton	538	379	159	70.45%
31.	1904	Theodore Roosevelt	476	336	140	70.59%
32.	1924	Calvin Coolidge	531	382	136	71.94%
33.	1868	Ulysses S. Grant	294	214	80	72.79%
34.	1920	Warren G. Harding	531	404	127	76.08%
35.	1832	Andrew Jackson	286	219	49	76.57%
36.	1988	George H. W. Bush	538	426	111	79.18%
36.	1840	William Henry Harrison	294	234	60	79.59%
38.	1944	Franklin D. Roosevelt	531	432	99	81.36%
39.	1912	Woodrow Wilson	531	435	88	81.92%
40.	1872	Ulysses S. Grant	349	286	42	81.95%
41.	1952	Dwight D. Eisenhower	531	442	89	83.24%
42.	1928	Herbert Hoover	531	444	87	83.62%
43.	1816	James Monroe	217	183	34	84.33%
44.	1940	Franklin D. Roosevelt	531	449	82	84.56%
45.	1852	Franklin Pierce	296	254	42	85.81%
46.	1956	Dwight D. Eisenhower	531	457	73	86.06%

Rank	Year	Winner	# of Electors	Votes cast for winner	Votes cast for runner-up	Percentage
47.	1932	Franklin D. Roosevelt	531	472	59	88.89%
48.	1964	Lyndon B. Johnson	538	486	52	90.33%
49.	1980	Ronald Reagan	538	489	49	90.89%
50.	1864	Abraham Lincoln	233	212	21	90.99%
51.	1792	George Washington	132	132	77	100%
52.	1804	Thomas Jefferson	176	162	14	92.05%
53.	1972	Richard Nixon	538	520	17	96.65%
54.	1984	Ronald Reagan	538	525	13	97.58%
55.	1936	Franklin D. Roosevelt	531	523	8	98.49%
56.	1820	James Monroe	232	231	1	99.57%
57.	1789	George Washington	69	69	34 [10]	100%

Year		Pct. of pop. vote	Margin	Pop. vote	Margin	Electoral College runner-up	Voter Turnout
1824	John Adams	30.92%	10.44%	113,142	-38,221	Andrew Jackson	26.9%
1828	Andrew Jackson	55.93%	12.25%	642,806	140,839	John Quincy Adams	57.87%
1832	Andrew Jackson	54.74%	17.81%	702,735	228,628	Henry Clay	55.40%
1836	Martin Van Buren	50.79%	14.20%	763,291	213,384	William Henry Harrison	57.80%
1840	William Henry Harrison	52.87%	6.05%	1,275,583	145,938	Martin Van Buren	80.20%
1844	James K. Polk	49.54%	1.45%	1,339,570	339,413	Henry Clay	78.91%
1848	Zachary Taylor	47.28%	4.79%	1,360,235	137,882	Lewis Cass	72.71%
1852	Franklin Pierce	50.83%	6.95%	1,605,943	219,525	Winfield Scott	69.60%

Year		Pct. of pop.vote	Margin	Pop. vote	Margin	Electoral College runner-up	Voter Turnout
1856	James Buchanan	45.29%	12.20%	1,835,140	494,472	John C. Frémont	78.91%
1860	Abraham Lincoln	39.65%	10.13%	1,855,993	474,049	John C. Breckinridge	81.20%
1864	Abraham Lincoln	55.03%	10.08%	2,211,317	405,090	George B. McClellan	73.80%
1868	Ulysses S. Grant	52.66%	5.32%	3,013,790	304,810	Horatio Seymour	78.1%
1872	Ulysses S. Grant	55.58%	11.80%	3,597,439	763,729	Horace Greeley	71.3%
1876	Rutherford B. Hayes	47.92%	-3.00%	4,034,142	-252,666	Samuel J. Tilden	81.8%
1880	James A. Garfield	48.31%	0.09%	4,453,337	1,898	Winfield Scott Hancock	79.4%
1884	Grover Cleveland	48.85%	0.57%	4,914,482	57,579	James G. Blaine	77.5%
1888	Benjamin Harrison	47.80%	0.83%	5,443,633	-94,530	Grover Cleveland	79.3%
1892	Cleveland, Grover	46.02%	3.01%	5,553,898	363,099	Benjamin Harrison	74.7%
1896	William McKinley	51.02%	4.31%	7,112,138	601,331	William Jennings Bryan	79.3%
1900	William McKinley	51.64%	6.12%	7,228,864	2,546,677	William Jennings Bryan	73.2%
1904	Theodore Roosevelt	56.42%	18.83%	7,630,557	304,810	Alton Brooks Parker	65.2%
1908	William H. Taft	51.57%	8.53%	7,678,335	1,269,356	William Jennings Bryan	65.4%
1912	Woodrow Wilson	41.84%	14.44%	6,296,284	2,173,563	Theodore Roosevelt	58.8%
1916	Woodrow Wilson	49.24%	3.12%	9,126,868	578,140	Charles Evans Hughes	61.6%
1920	Warren G. Harding	60.32%	26.17%	16,144,093	7,004,432	James M. Cox	49.2%

Year		Pct. of pop.vote	Margin	Pop. vote	Margin	Electoral College runner-up	Voter Turn-out
1924	Calvin Coolidge	54.04%	25.22%	15,723,789	7,337,547	John W. Davis	48.9%
1928	Herbert Hoover	58.21%	17.41%	21,427,123	6,411,659	Al Smith	56.9%
1932	Franklin D. Roosevelt	57.41%	17.76%	22,821,277	7,060,023	Herbert Hoover	56.9%
1936	Franklin D. Roosevelt	60.80%	24.26%	27,752,648	11,070,786	Alf Landon	61.0%
1940	Franklin D. Roosevelt	54.74%	9.96%	27,313,945	14,966,201	Wendell Willkie	62.5%
1944	Franklin D. Roosevelt	53.39%	7.50%	25,612,916	3,594,987	Thomas E. Dewey	55.9%
1948	Harry S Truman	49.55%	4.48%	24,179,347	2,188,055	Thomas E. Dewey	53.0%
1952	Dwight D. Eisenhower	55.18%	10.85%	34,075,529	6,700,439	Adlai Stevenson	63.3%
1956	Dwight D. Eisenhower	57.37%	15.40%	35,579,180	9,551,152	Adlai Stevenson	60.6%
1960	John F. Kennedy	49.72%	0.17%	34,220,984	112,827	Richard Nixon	62.77%
1964	Lyndon B. Johnson	61.05%	22.58%	43,127,041	15,951,287	Barry Goldwater	61.92%
1968	Richard Nixon	43.42%	0.70%	31,783,783	511,944	Hubert Humphrey	60.84%
1972	Richard Nixon	60.67%	23.15%	47,168,710	17,995,488	George McGovern	55.21%
1976	Jimmy Carter	50.08%	2.06%	40,831,881	1,683,247	Gerald Ford	53.55%
1980	Ronald Reagan	50.75%	9.74%	43,903,230	8,423,115	Jimmy Carter	52.56%
1984	Ronald Reagan	58.77%	18.21%	54,455,472	16,878,120	Walter Mondale	53.11%
1988	George H.W. Bush	53.37%	7.72%	48,886,597	7,077,121	Michael Dukakis	50.15%

Year		Pct. of pop.vote	Margin	Pop. vote	Margin	Electoral College runner-up	Voter Turn-out
1992	Bill Clinton	43.01%	5.56%	44,909,806	5,805,256	George H.W. Bush	55.23%
1996	Bill Clinton	49.23%	8.51%	47,400,125	8,201,370	Bob Dole	49.08%
2000	George W. Bush	47.87%	-0.51%	50,460,110	-543,816	Al Gore	51.30%
2004	George W. Bush	50.73%	2.46%	62,040,610	3,012,171	John Kerry	55.27%
2008	Barack Obama	52.87%	7.27%	69,499,428	9,549,105	John McCain	57.48%
2012	Barack Obama	51.06%	3.85%	65,899,557	4,967,598	Mitt Romney	57.5%

CHAPTER EIGHT NOTES:

1) http://thenewnixon.org/2008/09/29/herman-perry%e2%80%99s-letter-to-richard-nixon/
Ralph Toledano, Nixon, Duell, Sloane and Pearce (1960).
2) http://en.wikipedia.org/wiki/United_States_presidential_election,_1824
3) http://www.u-s-history.com/pages/h221.html
4) http://www.u-s-history.com/pages/h221.html
5) Cole, Donald B. *Martin Van Buren and the American Political System.* Princeton University Press (1984)
Silbey, Joel H. *Party Over Section: The Rough and Ready Presidential Election of 1848.* University Press of Kansas (2009)
6) http://uselectionatlas.org/RESULTS
7) http://uselectionatlas.org/RESULTS
8) Turner, Lynn W. *"The Electoral Vote against Monroe in 1820-An American Legend." The Mississippi Valley Historical Review* (1955) — http://www.jstor.org/stable/1897643. Retrieved 22 March 2010.
"America President: James Monroe: Campaigns and Elections." Miller Center of Public Affairs.
http://millercenter.org/academic/americanpresident/monroe/essays/biography/3. Retrieved January 8, 2010.
9) Sobel, Robert. *Coolidge: An American Enigma.* Regnery (1998).
White, William Allen. *A Puritan in Babylon: The Story of Calvin Coolidge.* Macmillan (1938).
Coolidge, Calvin. *The Autobiography of Calvin Coolidge.* Cosmopolitan Book Corp. (1929).
McCullough, David. *Truman.* Simon and Schuster (1992).
http://millercenter.org/scripps/archive/speeches/detail/3388
10) In that election the votes for Adams were for vice president and not president.

CHAPTER 9

Events During Their Presidency

The following questions relate to events which occurred during a given person's presidency or were actions taken by the given president:

Q: While this person was president, six states were admitted to the Union, more than during the term of any other president, even though he only served one term. Who was he?

A: Benjamin Harrison with six.

North Dakota	November 2, 1889
South Dakota	November 2, 1889
Montana	November 8, 1889
Washington	November 11, 1889
Idaho	July 3, 1890
Wyoming	July 10, 1890

Q: True or false: No president who served less than one full term ever had a state admitted to the Union during his presidency.

A: False, but it happened only once. Nebraska was admitted during Andrew Johnson's presidency.

Q: True or false: Prior to Woodrow Wilson, there was no president who was elected twice who did not have at least one State admitted to the Union during his term?

A: False, although this is a little tricky since the answer is William McKinley, who was assassinated shortly into his second term, so he did not serve a full eight years.

Q: True or false: George Washington was president when the first thirteen States were admitted to the union?

A: False. Actually, Washington was president only for the last two of these, North Carolina and Rhode Island. There was no president for the first eleven.

State	Capital	Admitted to Union	President at Admission
Delaware	Dover	December 7, 1787	None
Pennsylvania	Harrisburg	December 12, 1787	None
New Jersey	Trenton	December 18, 1787	None
Georgia	Atlanta	January 2, 1788	None
Connecticut	Hartford	January 9, 1788	None
Massachusetts	Boston	February 6, 1788	None
Maryland	Annapolis	April 28, 1788	None
South Carolina	Columbia	May 23, 1788	None
New Hampshire	Concord	June 21, 1788	None
Virginia	Richmond	June 25, 1788	None
New York	Albany	July 26, 1788	None
North Carolina	Raleigh	November 21, 1789	George Washington
Rhode Island	Providence	May 29, 1790	George Washington

State	Capital	Admitted to Union	President at Admission
Vermont	Montpelier	March 4, 1791	George Washington
Kentucky	Frankfort	June 1, 1792	George Washington
Tennessee	Nashville	June 1, 1796	George Washington
Ohio	Columbus	March 1, 1803	Thomas Jefferson
Louisiana	Baton Rouge	April 30, 1812	James Madison
Indiana	Indianapolis	December 11, 1816	James Madison
Mississippi	Jackson	December 10, 1817	James Monroe
Illinois	Springfield	December 3, 1818	James Monroe
Alabama	Montgomery	December 14, 1819	James Monroe
Maine	Augusta	March 15, 1820	James Monroe
Missouri	Jefferson City	August 10, 1821	James Monroe
Arkansas	Little Rock	June 15, 1836	Andrew Jackson
Michigan	Lansing	January 26, 1837	Andrew Jackson
Florida	Tallahassee	March 3, 1845	John Tyler
Texas	Austin	December 29, 1845	James Polk
Iowa	Des Moines	December 28, 1846	James Polk
Wisconsin	Madison	May 29, 1848	James Polk
California	Sacramento	September 9, 1850	Millard Fillmore
Minnesota	St. Paul	May 11, 1858	James Buchanan
Oregon	Salem	February 14, 1859	James Buchanan
Kansas	Topeka	January 29, 1861	James Buchanan
West Virginia	Charleston	June 20, 1863	Abraham Lincoln
Nevada	Carson City	October 31, 1864	Abraham Lincoln
Nebraska	Lincoln	March 1, 1867	Andrew Johnson
Colorado	Denver	August 1, 1876	Ulyssess Grant
North Dakota	Bismarck	November 2, 1889	Benjamin Harrison
South Dakota	Pierre	November 2, 1889	Benjamin Harrison
Montana	Helena	November 8, 1889	Benjamin Harrison
Washington	Olympia	November 11, 1889	Benjamin Harrison
Idaho	Boise	July 3, 1890	Benjamin Harrison
Wyoming	Cheyenne	July 10, 1890	Benjamin Harrison
Utah	Salt Lake City	January 4, 1896	Grover Cleveland
Oklahoma	Oklahoma City	November 16, 1907	Theodore Roosevelt

State	Capital	Admitted to Union	President at Admission
New Mexico	Santa Fe	January 6, 1912	William Taft
Arizona	Phoenix	February 14, 1912	William Taft
Alaska	Juneau	January 3, 1959	Dwight Eisenhower
Hawaii	Honolulu	August 21, 1959	Dwight Eisenhower

Q: Excluding the Louisiana Purchase, under whose presidency did the land mass of the continental United States increase by 1/3 (based on addition of territory, not admission of states to the Union)?

A: James Polk. Under Polk, the United States grew by more than 500,000 square miles, adding territory that now includes the states of Arizona, Utah, Nevada, California, Oregon, Idaho, Washington, much of New Mexico, and portions of Wyoming, Montana, and Colorado. Most of this came as a result of The Treaty of Guadalupe Hidalgo, officially the Treaty of Peace, Friendship, Limits and Settlement Between the United States of America and the Mexican Republic. That treaty between the United States and Mexico, largely dictated by the United States, ended the Mexican-American War (1846-48) on February 2, 1848. The treaty added 1.2 million square miles of territory to the United States. Mexico's size was halved, while that of the United States increased by a third. The treaty also recognized the annexation of Texas. Mexico received a payment of $15 million. It was therefore under Polk's presidency that the U.S. became a coast-to-coast nation.[1]

Q: Which president purchased the area now comprising southern Arizona and part of southern New Mexico (an area comprising about 30,000 square miles) for $10,000,000?

A: Franklin Pierce. This was known as the Gadsden Purchase because the land was purchased by the United States in a treaty signed by James Gadsden, the American ambassador to Mexico at the time, on December 30, 1853. A bit on the Jimmy Fallon show discusses this transaction. A plant in the audience interrupts Fallon to ask "Why haven't you done any jokes about the Gadsden Purchase?" He brought a visual aid with him to show the land acquired by the transaction. When Fallon inquired what jokes could be made about a 150 year-old land treaty, the audience member said "Franklin Pierce, James Gadsden, and topographical issues about the construction of the transcontinental railroad. The jokes practically write themselves!" Another audience plant then chimed in that the Gadsden purchase would never have happened but for the Treaty of Guadalupe Hidalgo, which he claimed was the best Treaty.[2]

Q: Which member of George Washington's cabinet became president?

A: Thomas Jefferson, who was Secretary of State of 1790-1793.

Q: During whose presidency were gaslights installed in the White House?

A: James Polk. This occurred in 1848.[3]

Q: Which president, together with his wife, obtained Congressional funds to establish the White House library?

A: Millard Fillmore. His wife was Abigail Fillmore.

Q: Who was president when America purchased Alaska from Russia for $7.2 million?

A: Andrew Johnson. The purchase was negotiated by his Secretary of State William Seward. On March 30, 1867, he completed negotiations for the territory, which involved the purchase of 586,412 square miles of territory (more than twice the area of Texas), or approximately two cents per acre. Despite the price, at the time, some in the press criticized the purchase, calling it

"Seward's Folly" or "Seward's Icebox," on the theory that it was useless land. The *New York Tribune* commented that the country was now "burdened with territory we had no population to fill" and the land "contained nothing of value but fur-bearing animals, and these had been hunted until they were nearly extinct." However, when asked what he considered to be his greatest achievement as Secretary of State, Seward replied, "The purchase of Alaska—but it will take the people a generation to find it out." He turned out to be prescient. Public opinion of the purchase had changed markedly by 1890 once it was discovered that the land was rich in resources, including gold, copper, and oil.

Two years earlier, Seward was one of the intended targets of the men who assassinated Abraham Lincoln on April 14, 1865. He was stabbed repeatedly with a knife but survived. [5]

Q: Which president established the nation's first national park and what was it?

A: Ulysses Grant established Yellowstone National Park in 1872.

Q: Which president dedicated the Statue of Liberty?

A: Grover Cleveland in 1886. The statute (whose formal title is Liberty Enlightening the World) was designed by a young Frenchman, Auguste Bartholdi. He was inspired by a comment made by French law professor and politician Édouard René de Laboulaye in 1865. Laboulaye was an ardent supporter of the Union in the Civil War which had just ended. He stated: "If a monument should rise in the United States, as a memorial to their independence, I should think it only natural if it were built by united effort—a common work of both our nations." In 1872, Bartholdi found the right location for the proposed statue, Bedloe's Island located in New York Harbor. Construction of the statute began in France in 1876. The statue was built near the Parc Monceau in Paris.

The hand holding the torch was sent to the United States and displayed at the Centennial Exposition in Philadelphia on May 18, 1876. In 1883, Emma Lazarus composed the sonnet *The New Colossus*, the words of which are engraved on a plaque on the pedestal of the statue. The most famous portion of the sonnet are the last words: "Give me your tired, your poor, your huddled masses yearning to breathe free, the wretched refuse of your teeming shore. Send these, the homeless, tempest-lost to me. I lift my lamp beside the golden door!" In 1885, the statue was disassembled in Paris and shipped to the United States. It was placed in storage for a year while the pedestal was completed. On October 23rd, 1886, the statue was completed and it was dedicated five days later. Cleveland saluted Bartholdi as "the greatest man in America today." [6]

Q: Who was president when California was admitted to the Union?

A: Millard Fillmore. California was admitted in 1850.

Q: Although Thomas Jefferson was president when the Louisiana Purchase was signed, which president actually negotiated the purchase?

A: James Monroe. In 1803, the United States acquired 828,000 square miles of France's claim to the territory of Louisiana. The U.S. paid sixty million francs ($11,250,000) plus cancellation of debts worth eighteen million francs ($3,750,000), for a total sum of fifteen million dollars (less than three cents per acre) for the territory ($233 million in 2011 dollars, less than 42 cents per acre). The Louisiana territory encompassed all or part of fifteen current U.S. states and two Canadian provinces. It more than doubled the size of the United States at the time. [7]

Q: Under whose administration was the United States Naval Academy founded?

A: James Polk's. It was established in 1845.

Q: Which president had electricity installed in the White House for the first time by Edison General Electric Company, but he and his wife would not touch the light switches for fear of electrocution and would often go to sleep with the lights on?

A: Benjamin Harrison. This occurred in 1891.[8]

Q: Which president sent Commodore Matthew C. Perry to Japan to open trade with that country?

A: Millard Fillmore. [9]

Q: Which president appointed Brigham Young as the first governor of the Utah Territory?

A: Millard Fillmore.

Q: Which president approved the Star-Spangled Banner as our national anthem?

A: Herbert Hoover in 1931. At least one president, Harry Truman, didn't like it. When asked about his home state song, *The Missouri Waltz*, he stated: "It's a ragtime song and if you let me say what I think, I don't give a damn about it, but I can't say it out loud because it's the song of Missouri. It's as bad as *The Star-Spangled Banner* as far as music is concerned."[10]

Q: What president championed the interstate highway system?

A: Dwight Eisenhower. The Interstate Highway System is officially known as the "Dwight D. Eisenhower National System of Interstate and Defense Highways" in his honor. Construction began in 1956.

Q: Which president created the Department of Education and Department of Energy?

A: Jimmy Carter.

Q: How many posts were there in George Washington's original cabinet, and which posts were they?

A: Four: Secretary of State, Secretary of the Treasury, Secretary of War, Attorney General. All of these still exist today, with the exception of Secretary of War. Since 1947, that position has been filled by the Secretary of Defense.

Q: Match the cabinet position (and first person holding it) with the person who was president when the position was first filled:

CABINET POSITION	PRESIDENT
1. Secretary of Veteran's Affairs (Ed Derwinski)	a. John Adams
2. Secretary of Energy (James R. Schlesinger)	b. Zachary Taylor
3. Secretary of Agriculture (Norman Jay Coleman)	c. Grover Cleveland
4. Secretary of Commerce and Labor (George Cortelyou)	d. Theodore Roosevelt
5. Secretary of the Navy (Benjamin Stoddert)	e. Dwight Eisenhower
6. Secretary of Homeland Security (Tom Ridge)	f. Lyndon Johnson
7. Secretary of Health, Education and Welfare (Oveta Culp Hobby)	g. Lyndon Johnson

8. Secretary of Housing and   h. Jimmy Carter
   Urban Development
   (Robert Clifton Weaver)
9. Secretary of Transportation   i. George H.W. Bush
   (Alan Stephenson Boyd)
10. Secretary of the Interior   j. George W. Bush
    (Thomas Ewing)

A: 1.i; 2.h; 3.c.; 4.d (later divided into two separate cabinet positions); 5.a; 6.j; 7.e; 8.f; 9.g; 10.b

CHAPTER NINE NOTES:

1) http://millercenter.org/president/polk/essays/biography/print
   http://avalon.law.yale.edu/19th_century/guadhida.asp
   http://www.archives.gov/education/lessons/guadalupe-hidalgo/
   Seigenthaler, John, *James K. Polk: 1845-1849: The American Presidents Series*,
   Times Books (2004).
2) http://www.whitehousemuseum.org/special/renovation-1825.htm
3) http://www.whitehousehistory.org/whha_shows/whitehouse_timemachine/b.swf
4) http://avalon.law.yale.edu/19th_century/mx1853.asp
   Kluger, Richard. *Seizing Destiny: How America Grew From Sea to Shining Sea.*
   Knopf (2007)
   Whitehouse.gov/history/presidents
5) *Up the St. Elias Alps, The New York Times,* 09-20-1886.
   http://www.americainfra.com/news/alaska/
   Goodwin, Doris Kearns. *Team of Rivals: The political genius of Abraham
   Lincoln.* Simon and Schuster (2005).
6) Harris, Jonathan. *A Statue for America: The First 100 Years of the Statue of
   Liberty.* Four winds Press (1985). http://www.nps.gov/stli/index.html
7) Kukla, Jon. *A Wilderness So Immense: The Louisiana Purchase and the Destiny
   of America.* (Anchor, 2004)
   http://www.gatewayno.com/history/LaPurchase.html
8) http://www.whitehousehistory.org/whha_timelines/timelines_technology-02.html
9) http://millercenter.org/academic/americanpresident/fillmore/essays/biography/5
10) http://www.trumanlibrary.org/trivia/waltz.htm

CHAPTER 10

Family

Q: Which 20th-century president had three sisters named Rebekah, Josefa, and Lucia?

A: Lyndon Johnson.

Q: How many presidents were only children?

A: Including half-siblings, the answer is none. Excluding half-siblings, the answer is four: **Franklin Roosevelt, Gerald Ford** and **Bill Clinton** and **Barack Obama.**

Q: Excluding half-brothers and half-sisters, which president had the most brothers and sisters?

A: James Buchanan with ten.

President	Total	Brothers	Sisters	Half Brothers	Half Sisters
George Washington	9	3	2	2	2
John Adams	2	2			

President	Total	Brothers	Sisters	Half Brothers	Half Sisters
Thomas Jefferson	8	2	6		
James Madison	7	4	3		
James Monroe	4	3	1		
John Quincy Adams	3	2	1		
Andrew Jackson	2	2			
Martin Van Buren	7	2	2	2	1
William H. Harrison	6	2	4		
John Tyler	7	2	5		
James K. Polk	9	5	4		
Zachary Taylor	8	5	3		
Millard Fillmore	8	5	3		
Franklin Pierce	7	4	2		1
James Buchanan	10	4	6		
Abraham Lincoln	2	1	1		
Andrew Johnson	1	1			
Ulysses S. Grant	5	2	3		
Rutherford B. Hayes	1		1		
James Garfield	4	2	2		
Chester A. Arthur	7	1	6		
Grover Cleveland	8	3	5		
Benjamin Harrison	11	6	3		2
William McKinley	8	3	5		
Theodore Roosevelt	4	2	2		
William H. Taft	5	2	1	2	
Woodrow Wilson	3	1	2		
Warren G. Harding	7	2	5		
Calvin Coolidge	1		1		
Herbert Hoover	2	1	1		
Franklin D. Roosevelt	1			1	
Harry S Truman	2	1	1		
Dwight D. Eisenhower	6	6			

President	Total	Brothers	Sisters	Half Brothers	Half Sisters
John F. Kennedy	8	3	5		
Lyndon B. Johnson	4	1	3		
Richard M. Nixon	4	4			
Gerald R. Ford	6			4	2
James E. Carter	3	1	2		
Ronald Reagan	1	1			
George H. W. Bush	4	3	1		
William F. Clinton	1			1	
George W. Bush	5	3	2		
Barack Obama	8	0	0	6	2

[1]

Q: Which presidents adopted children?

A: George Washington, Andrew Jackson, James Buchanan, Grover Cleveland, and Ronald Reagan

PRESIDENT	ADOPTED CHILD	NOTES
George Washington	Eleanor Parke Custis	She was the daughter of Washington's stepson, John Parke Curtis
Andrew Jackson	Andrew Jackson, Jr.	Adopted at birth
	Lincoya Jackson	Adopted Creek Indian orphan
James Buchanan	Mary Elizabeth Spear Lane	Adoptive daughter; niece (daughter of sister Jane Buchanan and Elliot Tole Lane)
	Harriet Rebecca Lane	Adoptive daughter; niece (daughter of sister Jane Buchanan and Elliot Tole Lane)
Grover Cleveland	Oscar Folsom Cleveland	Alleged illegitimate child; adopted as "James E. King" into the family of James King in 1879
Ronald Reagan	Michael Reagan	

Q: Which president had the most children?

A: John Tyler: fifteen

With Letitia Tyler:

Child	Lifetime
Mary Tyler	1815 - 1848
Robert Tyler	1816 - 1877
John Tyler, Jr.	1819 - 1896
Letitia Tyler aka Letty	1821-1907
Elizabeth Tyler aka Lizzie	1823-1850
Anne Contesse Tyler	1825-1825
Alice Tyler	1827-1854
Tazewell Tyler	1830-1874

With Julia Tyler:

Child	Lifetime
David Gardiner Tyler	1846-1927
John Alexander Tyler	1848-1927
Julia Gardiner Tyler	1849-1871
Lachlan Tyler	1851-1902
Lyon Gardiner Tyler	1853-1935
Robert Fitzwalter Tyler	1856-1927
Pearl Tyler	1860-1947

Q: There were only two married presidents who had no children, including by legal adoptions. Who were they?

A: James Madison and **James Polk.** James and Dolley Madison had no children together but did raise John Payne Todd, Dolley's son from her first marriage. Polk and his wife Sarah also had no children of their own, but did raise a nephew, Marshall Tate Polk (1831-1884).

Q: Excluding adoptions, how many married presidents had no children and who were they?

A: George Washington, James Madison, Andrew Jackson and **James Polk.**

Q: Who is the only president to be the father of twins?

A: George W. Bush. The twins' names are Jenna and Barbara.

Q: Who was the last president to send a child to public school?

A: Jimmy Carter sent Amy to public schools, although she did attend Woodward Academy in Georgia for her senior year.

Q: Which president's daughter had her high school prom at the White House?

A: Gerald Ford's daughter Susan in 1975. As reported in *People Magazine*:

> "Her mom and dad were thousands of miles away on a historic European diplomatic mission, but Susan Ford was making some modest history on her own back home. She played host to the first high school senior prom ever held in the White House. Susan, 17, who is headed for Mount Vernon Junior College in the fall, invited 73 graduating classmates of the exclusive Holton Arms School in Bethesda, Md.—and their dates—to 1600 Pennsylvania Ave. In the East Room, they did "The Bump" to the music

of two rock 'n' roll bands, the Outer Space and the Sandcastle. In the State Dining Room they drank spikeless punch and munched on Swedish meatballs, quiche and chicken in sweet and sour sauce. 'I'm having a great time,' the jersey-gowned Susan coolly observed, 'but it's really like any other prom we've had.'

Many of her friends were less blasé. It isn't every teenage prom goer whose date had to be cleared before the dance by the Secret Service and whose chaperones included White House aides and microphone-jabbing newswomen. The Class of '75, which paid $1,300 for the prom out of class funds, petitioned headmaster James Lewis to ask Susan if she could arrange for them to use the White House. One classmate put it in simple teenage English: 'No one in the class didn't want it here.'" [2]

Q: Only two presidents had exactly one natural-born child. Who are they?

A: Harry Truman (Margaret) and **Bill Clinton** (Chelsea).

Q: This president was born during the second year that George Washington was president (1790) and had a child who died when Harry Truman was president, a span of 32 presidents and 157 years. Who was he?

A: John Tyler. Tyler was born in 1790, during Washington's first term. The last of his 15 children, Pearl, was born in 1860 when Tyler was 70 and she died in 1947.

Q: Which president had three children who all tragically died before age 12?

A: Franklin Pierce.

Franklin Pierce, Jr. (February 2, 1836-February 5, 1836) died three days after birth.

Frank Robert Pierce (August 27, 1839-November 14, 1843) died at the age of four from epidemic typhus.

Benjamin "Bennie" Pierce (April 13, 1841-January 16, 1853) died at the age of eleven in a tragic railway accident in Andover, Massachusetts which his parents witnessed, one month before the inauguration of his father. He was thrown from the car and crushed to death before their eyes. Pierce's wife Jane was emotionally devastated by Bennie's death and would spend time writing letters to her dead son while she lived in the White House. A sample of one of her heartbreaking letters, written on January 23, 1853, can be found of the website of the New Hampshire Historical Society. [3]

Q: Which president had two daughters who both tragically died before reaching age five?

Q: William McKinley. Katherine died at age three after developing typhoid fever and Ida died in infancy in 1873.

Presidents as a whole have had unusual misfortune when it comes to the premature deaths of their children, especially before the age of five. While mortality rates in the 1800's were much higher than they are now, the early deaths of presidential children has been unusual and tragic by any measure. Only 17 of the 44 presidents (through Obama) had all their children live to see them take office.

President	Child	Lifetime	Cause of Death (if known)
John Adams	Elizabeth	1777	Stillborn
Thomas Jefferson	Jane	1774-1775	
	Unnamed son	1777	
	Lucy I	1780-1781	
	Lucy II	1782-1784	Worms and whooping cough
James Monroe	James	1799-1801	

President	Child	Lifetime	Cause of Death (if known)
John Quincy Adams	Unnamed son	1806	
	Louisa	1811-1812	Winter illness
Martin Van Buren	Unnamed son	1814	
	Unnamed daughter		
	Unknown	Stillborn	
William Henry	Lucy	1800-1826	
Harrison	Carter	1811-1839	
	James	1814-1819	
John Tyler	Anne	1825	Died in infancy
	Elizabeth	1823-1850	
	Alice	1827-1854	
James Garfield	Eliza	1860-1863	Diptheria
	Edward	1874-1876	Whooping cough
Zachary Taylor	Sarah	1814-1835	Malaria
	Octavia	1816-1820	Malaria
	Margaret	1819-1820	Malaria
Millard Fillmore	Mary	1832-1854	
Franklin Pierce	Franklin, Jr.	1836	
	Franklin	1839-1843	Typhus fever
	Robert		
	Benjamin	1841-1853	Train accident
Abraham Lincoln	Edward	1846-1850	Consumption
	Willie	1850-1862	Typhoid fever
	Tad	1853-1871	
Andrew Johnson	Robert	1834-1869	Suicide
Rutherford Hayes	Joseph	1861-1863	Dysentery
	George	1864-1866	Scarlet fever
	Manning	1873-1874	
James Garfield	Edward	1874-1876	Whooping cough
Chester Arthur	William	1860-1863	Convulsions
Benjamin Harrison	unnamed daughter	1861	Died in infancy
Grover Cleveland	Ruth	1891-1904	Diptheria
William McKinley	Katherine	1871-1875	Typhoid fever
	Ida	1873	Died in infancy
Theodore Roosevelt	Quentin	1897-1918	Died in combat in WWI

President	Child	Lifetime	Cause of Death (if known)
Calvin Coolidge	Calvin, Jr.	1908-1924	Blood poisoning
Franklin Roosevelt	Franklin, Jr.	1909	Died in infancy
Dwight Eisenhower	Doud	1917-1921	Scarlet fever
John Kennedy	Arabella	1956	Stillborn
	Patrick	1963	Premature birth
Ronald Reagan	Christine	1947	Died shortly after birth
George W. Bush	Pauline	1949-1953	Leukemia [4]

Q: Which president had a daughter who was younger than his four grandchildren?

A: Benjamin Harrison. His daughter Elizabeth was born in 1897, when her father was 64 years old. His son Russell had a daughter, Marthena, who was born in 1888 and a son, William, who was born in 1896. His other daughter Mary, had a son and daughter, Benjamin and Mary, born in 1887 and 1888 respectively.

Q: Which president's children did not attend their father's second marriage because they disapproved?

A: Benjamin Harrison. In 1896 Harrison, age 62, was remarried to Mary Scott Lord Dimmick, the niece and former secretary of his deceased wife. A widow herself, she was 37 at the time, a full 25 years his junior. Harrison's two children were adults, Russell, 41 years old at the time, and Mary (Mamie) McKee, 38, disapproved of the marriage and did not attend the wedding. Benjamin and Mary had one child together, Elizabeth (1897-1955).[5]

Q: What president's children had nineteen marriages and fifteen divorces between them?

A: Franklin Roosevelt's.

Q: Which president had a son whose first and middle name were the name of a president and another son whose first and last name were also the name of a president?

A: John Quincy Adams. He had one son named George Washington Adams (April 12, 1801-April 30, 1829) and another named John Adams (II) (July 4, 1803-October 23, 1834).

Q: Who was the first woman to vote for her son for president?

A: Sara Delano Roosevelt in 1932. Although the 19th Amendment granting women the right to vote became law twelve years earlier, the mothers of the intervening presidents, Warren Harding, Calvin Coolidge and Herbert Hoover all died before their sons ran for president.

Q: Which president's wife was a widow with two children from a prior marriage?

A: George Washington's wife Martha.

Q: Which presidents fathered children after leaving office?

A: John Tyler had seven children after his term ended in 1845 (in addition to the eight he had before that). See chart above. **Grover Cleveland** had three daughters after his first term ended but before his second term ended. He then had two sons after both terms ended. Finally, **Benjamin Harrison** had a daughter with his second wife in 1897. His term ended in 1893.

Q: Who was the first president whose daughter was married in the White House?

A: James Monroe. Maria Hester Monroe Gouverneur (1803-1850) married her cousin Samuel L. Gouverneur on March 8, 1820.[6]

Q: Who were the only presidents who had a child born in the White House?

A: First was **Grover Cleveland**, whose wife gave birth to daughter Esther on September 9, 1893, during Cleveland's second term in the White House. Patrick Bouvier Kennedy, son of **John F. Kennedy**, was the only other child of a United States president to be born during his father's time in office. He was born on August 7, 1963 and only lived two days. He was born five and a half weeks prematurely by emergency caesarean section at the Otis Air Force Base Hospital in Bourne, Massachusetts. A funeral mass was held on August 10, 1963 and his body was laid to rest at Arlington National Cemetery. The first child born in the White House was James Madison Randolph, son of Martha Jefferson Randolph, daughter of **Thomas Jefferson**. The first girl born in the White House was **John Tyler**'s granddaughter Letitia.

Q: What president's wife and mother died on the same day?

A: Theodore Roosevelt's. Alice Hathaway Lee (July 29, 1861-February 14, 1884) was the first wife of Roosevelt and mother of their child, Alice. Roosevelt's wife died of an undiagnosed (since it was camouflaged by her pregnancy) case of kidney failure (in those days called Bright's disease) two days after Alice Lee was born. Theodore Roosevelt's mother had died of typhoid fever in the same house, on the same day, at three o'clock a.m., some eleven hours earlier. After the near simultaneous deaths of his mother and wife, Roosevelt left his daughter in the care of his sister, Anna "Bamie/Bye" in New York City. In his diary he wrote a large "X" on the page and wrote "the light has gone out of my life."

Q: Which president had a daughter who married Jefferson Davis, who was later to become the president of the Confederate States of America?

A: Zachary Taylor. In 1835, one of Taylor's daughters, Sarah Knox Taylor, decided to marry Jefferson Davis, the future president of the Confederate States of America, who at that time was a lieutenant. Taylor did not wish Sarah to marry him, and Taylor and Davis would not be reconciled until 1847 at the Battle of Buena Vista, where Davis distinguished himself as a colonel. Sarah died only three months into the marriage.

Q: What well-known candy bar may have been named for the daughter of a president?

A: The Baby Ruth candy bar. Grover Cleveland's daughter was named Ruth Cleveland. As for whether or not the candy bar was actually named after Ruth's daughter has always been a matter of controversy. It was made by Chicago's Curtiss Candy Company in 1921. The company has always claimed that it was named after Cleveland's daughter. In fact, this assertion continues to be made today on the company's website babyruth.com, which adds that "the trademark was patterned after the engraved lettering used on a medallion struck for the 1893 Chicago World's Colombian Exposition. The image pictured the president, his wife, and young daughter Baby Ruth."

However, to name the candy bar after Ruth Cleveland would have been a very odd marketing decision. Grover Cleveland had been out of office since 1897 (twenty-four years earlier) and Ruth Cleveland had died of diphtheria at age thirteen in 1904. Her name was hardly high on the national consciousness. Babe Ruth on the other hand was a nationally famous baseball player by 1921 and had astonished the country by hitting 54 home runs in 1920, smashing his own record of 29, set the year before. Therefore, the timing of the name choice seems like a striking coincidence if in fact the candy bar was named after Cleveland's daughter.

Claiming that the bar was named after Ruth Cleveland gave

Curtiss a plausible basis to fight off competing products (as well as to avoid paying royalties to Babe Ruth himself). Indeed, in 1926, the George H. Ruth Candy Company sought to register its own trademark confections with the United States Patent and Trademark Office, called "Ruth's Home Run Bar" and "Babe Ruth's Own Candy." (Babe Ruth's real name was George Herman Ruth.) The Commissioner of Patents spurned the registration, saying "Babe" was too close to "Baby," particularly as it related to "Ruth." In 1931, the Court of Customs and Patent Appeals upheld the ruling, saying that there would be confusion if "Babe" and "Baby" competed for the same market.

Today, the Baby Ruth bar is owned by Nestlé, and has been since 1990 (the fourth owner after Curtiss, Standard Brands (1963) and Nabisco (1981).[7]

Q: Which early president's son is believed to have committed suicide?

A: John Quincy Adams' first son, George Washington Adams. He disappeared from the ship *Benjamin Franklin* on April 30, 1829, on its way from Providence, RI to New York. The June 13, 1829 *New York Herald* reported his body washing up on shore.[8]

Q: Which 20th-century president's son died between the convention and the general election?

A: Calvin Coolidge's. In 1924, Calvin, Jr., developed a blister from playing tennis on the White House courts. The blister became infected, and within days, he developed sepsis and died. He was sixteen years old. Coolidge later said that "when he died, the power and glory of the presidency went with him."[9]

Q: Which president had two sons to whom he gave the exact same name?

A: Franklin Roosevelt. Two of his sons were named Franklin Delano Roosevelt, Jr. The first died in 1909 at less than a year of age. The second was born in 1914 and died in 1988 at age 74.

Q: Incredibly, a president who was born in 1790, shortly after George Washington became president, had two grandchildren still alive in 2014? Which one?

A: John Tyler. Harrison Ruffin Tyler (born 1928) and Lyon Gardiner Tyler, Jr. (born 1824) are the sons of Lyon Gardiner Tyler, Sr. (August 24, 1853-February 12, 1935) and Sue Ruffin (1889-1953). The father of Lyon Tyler, Sr. was president Tyler. Lyon Gardiner Tyler, Sr. was born when president Tyler was 63 years old. Lyon Gardiner Tyler, Jr. was born when his father was 71 years old. Harrison Tyler was born when he father was 75.

In other words, these three generations of Tyler's have a life span which covers 223 years so far. To put that remarkable fact in perspective, Tyler was our 10th president. The next President who has a living grandchild in 2013 in William Howard Taft, our 27th President (Seth Chase Taft, born in 1922) and there are no others after that until our 32nd president, Franklin Roosevelt who has several living grandchildren. The oldest living child of a President as of 2013 is John Sheldon Doud Eisenhower, born in 1922.

President John Tyler's grandson, Harrison Tyler, made news during the 2012 presidential campaign. He called Republican candidate Newt Gingrich a "big jerk" for his three marriages. Harrison said he doesn't spend much time focusing on the 2012 presidential race—"I can't stand watching television"—but considers himself a conservative. His big problem, he said, is with the candidates. "I don't really like any of them," he said in an interview. "[Gingrich] needs to stick with the same wife, that's what my mother taught me," Tyler said. "But that doesn't seem to happen much today."[10]

Q: Who was the only president whose parents were both born abroad?

A: Andrew Jackson. Both of his parents were born in Ireland. The presidents who had one parent born abroad are as follows:

James Buchanan's father was born in Ireland.
Chester Arthur's father was born in Ireland
Thomas Jefferson's mother was born in England
Woodrow Wilson's mother was born in England
Herbert Hoover's mother born in Ontario, Canada
Barack Obama's father was born in Kenya.[11]

Q: Which future president had a child when he was only nineteen years old?

A: Andrew Johnson. His daughter was Martha.

CHAPTER TEN NOTES:

1) http://www.laughtergenealogy.com/bin/histprof/misc/olio/family.html
2) *Has That Corsage Been Cleared? Susan Ford Holds Her Prom in the White House*, People Magazine, June 16, 1975
3) Quinn-Musgrove, Sandra; Kanter, Sanford. *America's Royalty: All the President's Children.* Greenwood Publishing (1995)
   http://www.nhhistory.org/libraryexhibits/manuscriptcollection/mom/501
   janepierce/janepierce3.html
4) http://en.wikipedia.org/wiki/List_of_children_of_the_Presidents_of_the_
   United_States
   Wead, Doug, A*ll the Presidents' Children: Triumph and Tragedy in the Lives of America's First Families*, Atria (2004)
5) Moore, Chieko and Hale, Hester Anne, *Benjamin Harrison: Centennial President*, Nova Publishers (2006).
6) *White House History web site*. The White House Historical Association. http://www.whitehousehistory.org/whha_history/history_faqs-06.html. Retrieved March 13, 2011.
(7) Sandomir, Richard. *Baseball adopts a candy, whatever it's named for.* The *New York Times*, 06-06-2006.
   http://www.diningchicago.com/blog/2011/06/27/chicagos-baby-ruth
   http://www.snopes.com/business/names/babyruth.asp
   http://www.babyruth.com
   Feldman, David. *How Do Astronauts Scratch an Itch?*, Putnam (1996).

(8) Shepherd, Jack, *Cannibals of the Heart: A Personal Biography of Louisa Catherine and John Quincy Adams*, McGraw-Hill (1980)
(9) Sobel, Robert. *Coolidge: An American Enigma*. Regnery (1998). Coolidge, Calvin. *The Autobiography of Calvin Coolidge*. Cosmopolitan Book Corp. (1929).
(10) http://www.politico.com/news/stories/0112/72089.html
(11) http://presidentsparents.com/ancestry.html

CHAPTER 10

General

Q: Who was the last president who was never photographed?

A: Surprisingly, it was **James Monroe,** who was only our fifth president and who died in 1831. Every president from John Quincy Adams onwards has been photographed at some point in their lives. [1]

Q: What were the two years in which there were three presidents?

A: 1841 (Martin Van Buren, William Henry Harrison and John Tyler) and 1881 (Rutherford B. Hayes, James Garfield and Chester Arthur).

Q: Which president originated the custom of shaking hands with the president?

A: Thomas Jefferson. Before Jefferson, people bowed to the president.

Q: *Washington Crossing the Delaware* is an iconic 1851 oil-on-canvas painting by German-American artist Emanuel Gottlieb Leutze. It commemorates General George Washington's crossing of the Delaware River on December 25, 1776, during the American Revolutionary War. **Immediately to the right of General Washington is a future president. Who is it?**

A: James Monroe. He was a lieutenant at the time and is seen holding the American flag, as designed by Betsy Ross. However, this is a historical anachronism. That flag had not yet been designed and did not fly until September 3, 1777, well after the scene depicted. The historically accurate flag would have been the Grand Union Flag, which was the first national flag. That flag resembles our national flag today except that, instead of the 50 stars, the upper left resembles a squared-off Union Jack, without the red diagonal lines. [2]

Q: Which president was the primary draftsman of the Monroe Doctrine?

A: John Quincy Adams, who was the Monroe's Secretary of State at the time. Generally speaking, the Monroe Doctrine called for the establishment of separate spheres of influence for the United States and Europe, a call for an end to European colonization in the "New World," and a demand for nonintervention by Europe in the affairs of the Western Hemisphere. Thus, notwithstanding its name, Monroe was not the primary draftsman of the Monroe Doctrine, which was delivered to Congress on December 2, 1823. Its essence is expressed in the introductory statement: "The occasion has been judged proper for asserting, as a principle in which the rights and interests of the United States are involved, that the American continents, by the free and independent condition which they have assumed and maintain, are henceforth not to be considered as subjects for future colonization by any European powers." [3]

Q: What is the only non-American capital city named after a U.S. president, and who is that president?

A: James Monroe. The city of Monrovia, capital and most populous city in Liberia, was named after him in 1824, because he was a prominent supporter of the colonization of Liberia. [4]

Q: One would think that the phrase "founding fathers" has been around forever, but that is not the case. In fact it was coined by a 20th-century president. Which one?

A: Warren Harding. He used it a number of times between 1912 and 1921, but most notably in his keynote address to the 1916 Republican National Convention and in his 1921 inaugural address as president. In the beginning of the latter speech, he stated: "Standing in this presence, mindful of the solemnity of this occasion, feeling the emotions which no one may know until he senses the great weight of responsibility for himself, I must utter my belief in the divine inspiration of the founding fathers." [5]

Q: Which president is credited, perhaps apocryphally, with popularizing Maxwell House Coffee Company's advertising slogan "Good to the last drop"?

A: Theodore Roosevelt. He drank coffee at the Hermitage, the home of Andrew Jackson in Nashville, Tennessee, and supposedly said it "was good to the last drop." The coffee served to him was from the Maxwell House (Hotel) in Nashville, a regional brand of coffee, marketed by the Cheek family. The Cheek family sold the brand to General Foods in New York, which in the 1920s made wide use of the slogan. Maxwell House became a national brand name and product in that decade. The Hermitage origin was attested to by a college student who witnessed it, and who went on to become president of the Tennessee Historical Society. [6]

Q: Which president met with Adolf Hitler in Berlin?

A: Herbert Hoover. The International News Service reported that: "For the first time in his career, Reichsfuehrer Adolf Hitler today heard from an American statesman a forthright denunciation of Nazism as a practical and enduring force in world affairs. The detractor, speaking straight from the shoulder, was Herbert Clark Hoover, who spent 40 minutes in private with the Fuehrer ..."[7]

Q: Which president who was never elected served the longest?

A: John Tyler, who served out William Henry Harrison's term after Harrison died one month after being elected in 1841. There were other vice presidents who became president due to the premature ending of their predecessor's term who served longer than Tyler, such as Theodore Roosevelt, Calvin Coolidge and Lyndon Johnson, but they were later elected to office.

Q: When was the only time we had three consecutive presidents who each served two full terms?

A: From 1801-1825, our third, fourth and fifth presidents (Thomas Jefferson, James Madison and James Monroe) each served two full terms. That was the last time. One might think that the threesome of Franklin Roosevelt, Harry Truman and Dwight Eisenhower might be another answer to this question, but Truman did not serve a full first term. Rather he became president three months into Franklin Roosevelt's fourth term. Thus his first term was only three years and nine months. In addition, when Barack Obama serves out his second term in 2017, we will have had three consecutive two-term presidents from 1993-2017, including Bill Clinton and George W. Bush. These are also the only times we have had two consecutive presidents who each served two full terms.

Q: When was the only time there were three consecutive presidents who served exactly one full term?

A: Between 1885 and 1897, when Grover Cleveland served two full nonconsecutive four-year terms and Benjamin Harrison served one in between.

Q: When was the only time there were four consecutive presidents, none of whom served exactly one term or exactly two terms and who were the presidents?

A: From 1961-1977. The four presidents were **John F. Kennedy** (between two and three years), **Lyndon Johnson** (between five and six years), **Richard Nixon** (between five and six years) and **Gerald Ford** (between two and three years).

Q: Which president's cabinet, except one member, resigned en masse shortly after he assumed office?

A: John Tyler's in 1841. His cabinet was angry that he had twice vetoed Henry Clay's legislation for a national banking act following the Panic of 1837. Although Tyler was a Whig, it was felt by his cabinet (which of course was William Henry Harrison's cabinet before he died one month into his term) that he was not supportive of the Whig agenda. On September 11, 1841, they all resigned except for Daniel Webster, his Secretary of State. Two days later, Tyler was expelled from the Whig Party.[8]

Q: Which president popularized the term "silent majority" and in what context?

A: Richard Nixon, when calling on Americans to support the administration's Vietnam War policy. In a November 3, 1969 speech he said, "And so tonight—to you, the great silent majority of my fellow Americans—I ask for your support." He was referring to Americans who did not join in the demonstrations against the Vietnam War at the time, who did not join in the counterculture, and who did not participate in public discourse. Earlier in the speech, he had stated: "If a vocal minority, however fervent its cause, prevails over reason and the will of the majority, this nation has no future as a free society."[9]

Q: Which president's entire cabinet was age 46 or less when appointed, including a secretary of the treasury who was only 32 (or 34)?

A: George Washington's. Of course, there were only four cabinet positions in his two terms, namely state, war, treasury and attorney general. Secretary of State Thomas Jefferson was the oldest, at 46. The reason for the uncertainty of Hamilton's age is because there has always been uncertainty about his birth date-1755 or 1757. Biographer Ron Chernow has written that "few questions bedevil Hamilton biographers more than the baffling matter of the year of his birth." As treasury secretary, Hamilton earned $3,500 a year, far less than he was making as a lawyer.[10]

Q: Although it is likely a false legend, which president has long been reputed to have been playing marbles when informed that he had become president as a result of the death of his predecessor?

A: John Tyler. However, Edward Crapol, a noted authority on Tyler, states:

> "Another tale about that momentous day, delightful for its rustic simplicity and republican innocence, had the fifty-one-year-old aristocratic Virginian playing marbles with his sons in front of his home when the young Webster (the son of the Secretary of State who notified Tyler of Harrison's death) arrived from Washington.

Tyler initially may have been startled by the dispatch from Harrison's cabinet announcing the president's death, but surely the marbles tale is apocryphal. It surfaced decades later in the early twentieth century, long after the principal parties involved had died, in a breezy and unreliable collection of personal reminiscences about former presidents."

There is also no reference to the incident in the U.S. Senate history of Tyler. [11]

Q: Which president had an operation for removal of urinary stones when he was seventeen years old, which may have left him sterile or impotent?

A: James Polk. [12]

Q: Five of our first seven presidents served exactly two full consecutive terms. Of our next 36 presidents (i.e. through George W. Bush), how many did the same?

A: Only six: **Ulysses Grant, Woodrow Wilson, Dwight Eisenhower, Ronald Reagan, Bill Clinton** and **George W. Bush**. This means that between 1837, when Andrew Jackson's term ended, and 1980, when Reagan's began, only three presidents served exactly two full terms in that 143 year span. Barack Obama will have served two full terms when he serves out his second term.

Q: During a presidential campaign, accusations began surfacing that this man (a 20th-century former president) was a drunkard. He decided that if this was ever printed, he would file a lawsuit. A newspaper called *Iron Ore* did print that he was a heavy drinker and that he frequently issued torrents of "lies and curses" when drunk. He filed a lawsuit against the paper's editor. During the trial, many witnesses testified that he abstained from heavy liquor and beer and drank only an occasional glass of wine with meals. The newspaper editor was unable to produce a single witness to support his article's claim, and he offered a retraction and apology. Having proven his point (and won a great deal of free publicity), the man generously asked the judge to award him the lowest amount which the law would allow: six cents. The judge agreed. **Who was this man?**

A: Theodore Roosevelt. This occurred in 1913.[13]

Q: Which president attempted to relieve his crushing debt burden by conducting a lottery, the winning prize for which would be his house?

A: Thomas Jefferson. The house in question was of course Monticello, in Virginia. Jefferson referred to his straitened circumstances and his plans to alleviate them in a January 20, 1826 letter to a friend: "My application to the Legislature is for permission to dispose of property . . . in a way which, bringing a fair price for it, may pay my debts, and leave a living for myself in my old age, and leave something for my family. . . To me it is almost a question of life and death."

When the law authorizing the lottery was passed, a prospectus was published, advertising that the winning combination would be drawn from 11,477 tickets at $10.00 each, a rather high figure for that day. Ultimately the lottery never took place because it was decided that the needed money could be raised by voluntary public contribution in a dignified manner and at less expense and trouble to Jefferson. However when Jefferson died on July 4, 1826, he still was in debt over $100,000.[14]

Q: Who was the first president to be subject to a serious impeachment attempt?

A: John Tyler. Tyler had been a Democrat but he left that Party in 1836 for the Whig Party because he opposed the power wielded by president Andrew Jackson. However, he continued to have more in common with the States' rights and limited government approach of Jacksonian Democrats than the more nationally-minded Whigs. Still, he was added to the Whig ticket as a vice presidential candidate because of his appeal to Southern voters as a Virginian. Tyler became Vice President when William Henry Harrison was inaugurated in 1841, then succeeded to the presidency when Harrison died less than a month later. Whigs believed Tyler would follow the Party's congressional leadership and platform.

Tyler proved to be more independent. He vetoed two bills to create a new national bank. Following the second veto, his cabinet resigned with the exception of Secretary of State Daniel Webster. When Tyler quickly appointed a new cabinet, Whigs kicked him out of the Party. In 1842, Tyler vetoed a tariff bill which would have raised tariffs and which was supported by the Whigs. The Whigs in Congress were outraged. They began exploring grounds for impeaching the president, and they overrode Tyler's veto, the first time Congress had ever overridden a presidential veto. The House adopted a resolution charging him with offenses justifying impeachment. However, the resolution to begin impeachment hearings failed 127 to 83.[15]

Q: Which president appeared on the cover of the *Spider Man* comic book?

A: Barack Obama. Just before the 2008 election, one of Obama's advisers gave an interview to journalist Jon Swaine of *The Daily Telegraph* and the accompanying article was titled, "Barack Obama: The 50 facts you might not know." In the interview, it was mentioned that Obama collects *Spider-Man* and *Conan the Barbarian*. When Marvel Comics, the publishers of the comic book, discovered this, they decided to have Obama, drawn as a comic book character, put on the cover of their *Amazing Spider-*

Man No. 583 issue (January 2009), for the story "Spidey Meets the president!" There were ultimately five variations of the comic book. The first variant, which came out on Inauguration Day in 2009, sells for over $200 on Ebay.[16]

Q: Which president's wife hosted the first Thanksgiving dinner?

A: James K. Polk's wife Sarah.

Q: Lyndon's Johnson's campaign was under investigation by the Internal Revenue Service for tax fraud. However, according to his biographer Robert Caro and based on papers which were turned over to Princeton University in 2011, a president stepped in and caused the investigation to be quashed. Who was it?

A: **Franklin Roosevelt.** In 1944, the IRS was investigating contributions to Johnson's failed 1941 Senate campaign. It is believed that Roosevelt stepped in and caused the investigation to be halted because he did not want to derail Johnson's budding political-career.[17]

Q: Which president distrusted banks and paper currency and thus kept all his money in gold and silver?

A: **James K. Polk.** However, Polk's wife Sarah disagreed with Polk's stance against the use of paper money, pointing out how difficult it was for a woman to carry gold or silver on her person.[18]

Q: Which president did not become immediately aware that he had been nominated for president because he refused all postage due correspondence?

A: **Zachary Taylor.**[19]

Q: One president removed another (future) president, from his position as collector of the Port of New York because he was a spoils system appointee and he refused to resign voluntarily? Who were the two presidents?

A: Rutherford Hayes and **Chester Arthur**. This occurred in July, 1878 when Hayes fired Arthur during a Congressional recess after he refused to resign. [20]

Q: In what may be the only photograph of its kind, a sixteen-year old member of Boys Nation is shown shaking hands with the president (to whom he is not related). The boy grew up to be president himself. Who are these two people?

A: Bill Clinton and **John F. Kennedy.** The photo was taken at the Rose Garden on July 24, 1963. A video of the scene can be seen on YouTube.

Q: When this vice president assumed office before his predecessor's term was finished, the entire cabinet of his predecessor resigned due to differences over slavery. Who was he?

A: Millard Fillmore. Fillmore's views on slavery were markedly different from his predecessor Zachary Taylor's, and everyone in Taylor's cabinet knew it. Taylor wanted the new states to be free states, while Fillmore supported slavery in those states to appease the South. In his own words: "God knows that I detest slavery, but it is an existing evil ... and we must endure it and give it such protection as is guaranteed by the Constitution." Days before Taylors' death, Fillmore told him that if the Compromise of 1850 (which created the possibility of slavery in the Southwest) came to a vote in the Senate, he would cast his vice presidential tie-breaking vote to pass it if necessary. Members of the cabinet, who had barely spoken to Fillmore up to this point, saw the writing on the wall and unanimously resigned; the new president curtly accepted them all. [21]

Q: True or false: There have never been more than five former presidents living at the same time.

A: True. However, there have been three occasions when there have been five former presidents living at the same time. From March 4, 1861-January 18, 1862, Martin Van Buren, John Tyler, Millard Fillmore, Franklin Pierce and James Buchanan were all alive during the Lincoln administration until Tyler died. From January 20, 1993-April 22, 1994, Richard Nixon, Gerald Ford, Jimmy Carter, Ronald Reagan and George H.W. Bush were all alive until Nixon died. From January 20, 2001-June 5, 2004, Gerald Ford, Jimmy Carter, Ronald Reagan George H.W. Bush and Bill Clinton were alive until Reagan died.

Q: True or false: There has never been a time when the only president alive was the sitting president.

A: False. It has happened on three occasions. In 1875, after the death of Andrew Johnson, Ulysses Grant was the only president alive. In February, 1933, after the death of Calvin Coolidge and before the swearing in of Franklin Roosevelt, Herbert Hoover was the only president alive. Finally, in 1973, after Harry Truman and Lyndon Johnson died, Richard Nixon was the only president alive.

Q: Which former president was sued by an insurance agent for alleged injury to reputation in an insurance commercial?

A: Calvin Coolidge. In 1930, an insurance agent named Lewis Tebbetts was listening to the radio and heard former president Coolidge delivering a radio advertisement. At the time, Tebbets was a director for New York Life Insurance, Coolidge said: "Beware of the so-called 'twister' and 'abstractor' or any agent who offers to save money for you by replacing your policy in another company." Believing that his reputation was injured, agent Tebbetts filed a $100,000 libel suit against the former president. In response, Coolidge wrote Mr. Tebbetts a letter of apology, assuring him "no personal offense was intended." His attorney, Everett Sanders, sent Mr. Tebbetts a check for $2,500 to cover legal expenses, and the case was dropped.[22]

Q: Which president had no credentials as a major political figure or statesman, was not a military hero, and had not held elective office for the last ten years before being nominated by his party?

A: Franklin Pierce.

Q: Which president had 56% of his vetoes overridden, the most of any president?

A: Franklin Pierce.

Q: Of the presidents who had at least one veto overridden, which president had the fewest percentage of votes overridden?

A: Grover Cleveland. Only two of his 414 vetoes, or less than 0.5%, were overridden.

President	No. of vetoes	Vetoes Overridden	Percentage of Vetoes Overridden
George Washington	2	0	0
John Adams	0	0	0
Thomas Jefferson	0	0	0
James Madison	7	0	0
James Monroe	1	0	0
John Quincy Adams	0	0	0
Andrew Jackson	12	0	0
Martin Van Buren	1	0	0
William Henry Harrison	0	0	0
John Tyler	10	1	10

President	No. of vetoes	Vetoes Overridden	Percentage of Vetoes Overridden
James Polk	3	0	0
Zachary Taylor	0	0	0
Millard Fillmore	0	0	0
Franklin Pierce	9	5	56
James Buchanan	7	0	0
Abraham Lincoln	7	0	0
Andrew Johnson	29	15	52
Ulysses S. Grant	93	4	5
Rutherford Hayes	13	1	7
James Garfield	0	0	0
Chester Arthur	12	1	8
Grover Cleveland	414	2	0.5
Benjamin Harrison	44	1	2
William McKinley	42	0	0
Theodore Roosevelt	82	1	0
William Taft	39	1	3
Woodrow Wilson	44	6	14
Warren Harding	6	0	0
Calvin Coolidge	50	4	8
Herbert Hoover	37	3	8
Franklin Roosevelt	635	9	1
Harry Truman	250	12	5
Dwight Eisenhower	181	2	1
John Kennedy	21	0	0
Lyndon Johnson	30	0	0
Richard Nixon	43	7	16
Gerald Ford	66	12	18
Jimmy Carter	31	2	6
Ronald Reagan	78	9	12
George H. W. Bush	44	1	2
Bill Clinton	37	2	5
George W. Bush	12	4	33

Q: True or false: The secession of Southern States started after Lincoln was elected the first time.

A: False. Seven States, over half of the thirteen which eventually seceded, did so while James Buchanan was president. His term lasted until March 3, 1861.

DATES OF SOUTHERN SECESSION

State	Date
Alabama	2/4/1861
Florida	2/4/1861
Georgia	2/4/1861
Louisiana	2/4/1861
Mississippi	2/4/1861
South Carolina	2/4/1861
Texas	3/2/1861
Virginia	5/7/1861
North Carolina	5/16/1861
Tennessee	5/16/1861
Arkansas	5/18/1861
Missouri	8/19/1861
Kentucky	12/10/1862

Q: Which presidents were also intended victims of the plot to assassinate president Lincoln?

A: Andrew Johnson and **Ulysses Grant**. Lincoln's assassin, John Wilkes Booth, had assigned George Atzerodt to kill vice president Andrew Johnson, who was staying at the Kirkwood Hotel in Washington. Atzerodt was to go to the Vice President's room at 10:15 p.m. on the evening of April 14, 1865 and shoot him. This was about the time that Booth was at Ford's Theatre, carrying out his plan to kill Lincoln. That day, Atzerodt rented room 126 at the Kirkwood, directly above the room where Johnson was staying. He arrived at the Kirkwood shortly before the appointed time and went to the bar downstairs. He was carrying a gun and a knife. Atzerodt asked the bartender, Michael Henry, about the vice president's character and behavior. After spending some time at the hotel saloon, Atzerodt got drunk and wandered away down the streets of Washington. Nervous, he tossed his knife away in the street. He made his way to the Pennsylvania House Hotel by 2 a.m., where he checked into a room and went to sleep. Atzerodt was later executed by hanging for his role in the Lincoln assassination.

As for Grant, Booth had read that he and his wife would be accompanying Lincoln to watch *Our American Cousin* at Ford's Theatre that night. Booth planned to shoot Lincoln with his single-shot Philadelphia derringer and then stab Grant with a knife. However, contrary to the information Booth had read in the newspaper, General and Mrs. Grant had declined the invitation to see the play with the Lincolns, as Mrs. Lincoln and Mrs. Grant were not on good terms with each other. [23]

Q: True or false: president Andrew Johnson gave unconditional amnesty to all Confederates.

A: True. He did so on Christmas Day, 1868, after Ulysses Grant had already been elected to succeed him.

Q: A man named Benjamin Wade was never vice president and was never Speaker of the House and yet he came within one vote of being president of the United States. How did this happen?

A: When Andrew Johnson was president, he had no Vice President. Therefore, in the Andrew Johnson impeachment proceedings, the first in line of succession was Benjamin Wade, the president pro tempore of the Senate at the time. The result of the initial impeachment vote was 35 to 19, one vote short of the required two-thirds majority for conviction. The editor of *The Detroit Post* wrote that "Andrew Johnson is innocent because Ben Wade is guilty of being his successor." Indeed, several moderate and conservative Republicans resisted the movement to impeach and remove Johnson because they considered Wade to be a dangerous demagogue and opposed his stance on other issues, especially his support of "soft money." [24]

Q: The Congressional Gold Medal is an award bestowed by the United States Congress and is, along with the Presidential Medal of Freedom, the highest civilian award in the United States. It is awarded to an individual who performs an achievement likely to have an impact on American history and culture.

The first recipient was George Washington in 1776. Despite the civilian nature of the award, most presidents who have won it were famous for their military exploits before becoming president, including Andrew Jackson, William Henry Harrison, Zachary Taylor and Ulysses Grant. It was not until 1984 that a president won the award who was not known for heroic military exploits. Since then, three presidents and three first ladies have won. On two occasions, a husband and wife won the award together. On another occasion, a president won and first lady won but they were not married to each other. The awards were bestowed in 1984 (the solo president and the solo first lady), 1998 and 2000 (the two married couples). Bear in mind however that the Medal is often awarded many years after the act occurred so that is not necessarily a clue. **Who are the six Gold Medal winners?**

A: 1984—Harry Truman and Lady Bird Johnson
1998—Gerald and Betty Ford
2000—Ronald and Nancy Reagan. [25]

Q: Who was the last secretary of state to become president?

A: James Buchanan, who was secretary of state under James

Polk. Interestingly, before that, five of our first eight Presidents had previously been secretaries of state, namely, Jefferson, Madison, Monroe, John Quincy Adams and Van Buren.

Q: The first trans-Atlantic cable was sent by Queen Victoria to this president. Who was he?

A: James Buchanan.

Q: Who wrote the first presidential autobiography?

A: James Buchanan. Surprisingly, of our first seventeen presidents, he was the only one to write an autobiography.

Q: Which presidents wrote the following autobiographies?:

1. *Years of Trial and Hope*
2. *My Life*
3. *Waging Peace*
4. *The Vantage Point*
5. *Decision Points*
6. *Mr. [_]'s Administration on the Eve of the Rebellion*
7. *An American Life*
8. *Keeping Faith*
9. *Where's the Rest of Me?*
10. *[Initials of President's first and last names]*

Answers:	1.	**Harry Truman**
	2.	**Bill Clinton**
	3.	**Dwight Eisenhower**
	4.	**Lyndon Johnson**
	5.	**George W. Bush**
	6.	**James Buchanan**
	7.	**Ronald Reagan**
	8.	**Jimmy Carter**

9.   **Ronald Reagan (again)**
10.   **Richard Nixon [RN]**

Q: Which president was arrested for speeding while driving a horse and buggy in Washington, D.C.?

A: **Ulysses Grant,** who had to pay a fine of $20.00 and walk back to the White House. [26]

Q: What man went from working at his family's leather store to president in seven years?

A: **Ulysses Grant.** In 1860, after many failed business pursuits, Grant was given a job as an assistant in his father's tannery in Galena, Illinois. The leather shop, "Grant & Perkins" sold harnesses, saddles, and other leather goods and purchased hides from farmers in the Galena area. He continued working at the store in the early years of the Civil War. [27]

Q: What president was also a senator-elect at the time he was sworn in?

A: **James Garfield.**

Q: Which president was ambidextrous and could hear a question in English and write the answer simultaneously in Latin with one hand and in Greek with the other?

A: **James Garfield.** It was said that one could ask him a question in English and he could simultaneously write the answer in Latin with one hand, and Ancient Greek with the other. [28]

It is difficult to establish the handedness of Presidents with any certainty before recent decades. However, from Hoover forward, their handedness is as follows:

President	Term	Handedness
Herbert Hoover	1929-1933	Left-handed
Franklin D. Roosevelt	1933-1945	Right-handed
Harry S Truman	1945-1953	Ambidextrous
Dwight D. Eisenhower	1953-1961	Right-handed
John F. Kennedy	1961-1963	Right-handed
Lyndon B. Johnson	1963-1969	Right-handed
Richard Nixon	1969-1974	Right-handed
Gerald Ford	1974-1977	Left-handed
Jimmy Carter	1977-1981	Right-handed
Ronald Reagan	1981-1989	Ambidextrous
George H. W. Bush	1989-1993	Left-handed
Bill Clinton	1993-2001	Left-handed
George W. Bush	2001-2009	Right-handed
Barack Obama	2009-now	Left-handed [29]

Q: Which president secretly had surgery on a yacht to remove a cancerous tumor, during which parts of his upper left jaw and hard palate were removed?

A: Grover Cleveland. On July 1, 1893, Cleveland and his surgeons left for New York. The surgeons operated aboard the yacht *Oneida* as it sailed off Long Island. Cleveland was out of public sight for four days. The surgery was conducted through the president's mouth to avoid any scars or other signs of surgery.

The reason for the secrecy was that the country was in the middle of a financial crisis caused by the inflationary Sherman Silver Purchase Act of 1890. Cleveland had been elected to a second term on a platform that called for repeal of the Act and he felt that his leadership was essential to that process, which was to begin at a special session of Congress on August 7, 1893. His vice president, Adlai Stevenson, was a "silver man" and opposed to the repeal. Feeling that any sign of ill health might be interpreted as weakness and throw support to the pro-silver side, Cleveland decided to keep the operation secret.

Dr. Keen, one of the doctors, wrote that, "The entire operation was done within the mouth, without any external incision, by means of a cheek retractor, the most useful instrument I have ever seen for such operations, which I had brought back from Paris in 1866." Dr. Kasson C. Gibson, a New York prosthodontist, was later called up to the president's summer home to make a vulcanized rubber prosthesis to fill in the large defect in the president's palate and restore his speech to normal.

In a letter to Dr. Gibson written in October 1893, Cleveland stated: "My dear Doctor, I hasten to announce that you have scored another dental victory and a greater one than has before attended your manipulation of my corpus. The new plate came last night ... I have worn it all day with the utmost ease and comfort ... my wife says that my voice and articulation are now much better than they have been for a number of days. If I could only regain my strength and hearing I should feel quite like myself."

The Silver Purchase Act was repealed in August, 1893.

In 2011, an entire book was written about the secret Cleveland surgery entitled *The President Is a Sick Man: Wherein the Supposedly Virtuous Grover Cleveland Survives a Secret Surgery at Sea and Vilifies the Courageous Newspaperman Who Dared Expose the Truth*, by Matthew Algeo, Chicago Review Press (2011).

Was the attempt to keep the surgery secret a success? No and yes. Two months after the president's "fishing trip," *Philadelphia Press* reporter E.J. Edwards published a story about the surgery which he had confirmed with one of Cleveland's doctors. However, the President flatly denied Edwards' story and no one believed Edwards. According to Algeo, "Twenty-four years after the operation—when all the other principals were dead—there were only three witnesses left to the operation. Keen decided it would be the right thing to do to publish an article to explain what really happened and to vindicate E.J. Edwards." The closest Cleveland ever came to confessing to the surgery was in a letter he wrote to a friend after one of the doctors talked to Edwards. It reads, "The report you saw regarding my health resulted from a most astounding breach of professional duty on the part of a medical man ... I tell you this in strict confidence for the policy here has been to deny and discredit this story."[30]

Q: A 19th-century man named John Harrison is unique in American history. Why?

A: He is the only man whose father and son were both presidents.

Q: What is the longest period of time between presidents who served exactly one full term?

A: 48 years, from 1933 (the end of Herbert Hoover's term) until 1981 (the end of Jimmy Carter's term). Every president between them served more or less than four years: Franklin Roosevelt-twelve years; Harry Truman—eight years; Dwight Eisenhower—eight years; John Kennedy-two and a half years; Lyndon Johnson-five and a half years; Richard Nixon—five and a half years; and Gerald Ford—two and a half years.

Q: Which president was known as the "Centennial President"?

A: Benjamin Harrison because he was inaugurated 100 years after George Washington.

Q: Which president was the son of a signer of the Declaration of Independence?

A: William Henry Harrison. The signer's name was Benjamin, the same name as his great grandson (and William Henry Harrison's grandson) who was our 23rd president.

Q: Which president's father's body was stolen from his grave?

A: Benjamin Harrison's. His father's body was stolen from an Ohio cemetery after his death in 1878 and sold to the Ohio Medical College of Cincinnati for dissection. In a public letter, Harrison described how he was horrified when his father's body was discovered "hanging by the neck...in the pit of a medical college." [31]

Q: Which president personally answered the White House phone?

A: Grover Cleveland.

Q: Which president is mentioned in the theme song to the hit 1970's TV show, *All in the Family*?

A: Herbert Hoover—"Mister, we could use a man like Herbert Hoover again."

Q: Which president was the first to refer to his residence as the White House?

A: Theodore Roosevelt. The building was originally referred to variously as the "President's Palace," "Presidential Mansion," or "President's House." The name "Executive Mansion" was used in official contexts until President Roosevelt established the formal name by having "White House-Washington" engraved on the stationery in 1901.[32]

Q: Zachary Taylor from Kentucky was elected president in 1848. Who was the next Southerner to be elected president and when?

A: Woodrow Wilson in 1912. He was born in Virginia and raised in Georgia. The next Southerner elected was Lyndon Johnson in 1964.

Q: John Adams personally delivered the "State of the Union" address to Congress in 1799. Who was the next president to do so?

A: Woodrow Wilson. Thomas Jefferson discontinued the practice because he was concerned that the practice of appearing before the representatives of the people was too similar to the British monarch's ritual of addressing the opening of each new Parliament with a list of policy mandates, rather than "recommendations." Therefore, from 1801-1912, the address was sent to Congress as a written report. Wilson believed that the presidency was more than an impersonal institution, and that instead it is dynamic and alive. He therefore delivered the address personally in 1913.

For the most part, State of the Union messages have been delivered in person since then but there have been exceptions. The last time a written message was sent was in 1981 when Jimmy Carter delivered his message very close to the end of his presidency. Calvin Coolidge's 1923 speech was the first to be broadcast on radio. Harry S Truman's 1947 address was the first to be broadcast on television. Lyndon B. Johnson's address in 1965 was the first delivered in the evening.

For many years, the speech was referred to as "The President's Annual Message to Congress." The actual term "State of the Union" first emerged in 1934 when Franklin D. Roosevelt used the phrase.

Customarily, one member of the president's cabinet does not

attend. This precaution is taken in order to provide continuity in the presidency in the event a catastrophe were to result in the death or disablement of the president, the vice president, and other officials in the line of presidential succession gathered in the House chamber. [33]

Q: What president suffered a serious stroke that almost totally incapacitated him, leaving him paralyzed on his left side and blind in his left eye?

A: **Woodrow Wilson** in 1919. This was one of the most serious cases of presidential disability in American history and was later cited as an argument for the 25th Amendment, which relates to the inability of the president to perform his duties (and is discussed more fully below under vice presidents). For the remainder of his presidency, his wife Edith Wilson played a substantial role in secretly fulfilling his duties. Although she referred to her own role as a "stewardship" in her memoirs, others have called her "the Secret President," "the first woman to run the government" and "the first female president of the United States." The full extent of Wilson's disability was kept from the public until after his death on February 3, 1924.[34]

Q: Samuel Byck was a man who planned to kill a president by crashing a commercial airliner into the White House. Once he had hijacked the plane, while it was still on the ground, he was informed that it could not take off with the wheel blocks still in place. He shot the pilot and co-pilot, then was shot by an officer through the plane's door window before killing himself. Which president was his target?

A: **Richard Nixon.** The events surrounding this assassination attempt were depicted in the film *The Assassination of Richard Nixon* starring Sean Penn. The event took place on February 22, 1974.

Q: Which post-Civil War president did not learn to read until he was ten?

A: Woodrow Wilson.[35]

Q: Sigmund Freud wrote a psychological study in which he asserted that this president unconsciously identified himself with Jesus Christ. Who was the president?

A: Woodrow Wilson. Freud never met Wilson. The book, entitled *Woodrow Wilson: A Psychological Study*, was not published until 1967.[36]

Q: In which presidential race did one of the candidates receive over 3% of the popular vote even though he was in prison at the time?

A: 1920. The candidate was Eugene V. Debs. He had been found guilty of violating the Espionage Act of 1917 based on a speech he made in Canton, Ohio criticizing the Wilson administration and urging resistance to the military draft of World War I. After his arrest and trial, he was sentenced to 10 years imprisonment. In the 1920 election, he received nearly one million votes, or about 3.4% of the vote, running as a member of the Socialist party. On December 23, 1921, President Harding commuted Debs' sentence to time served, effective Christmas Day. He did not issue a pardon.

Q: What president served copious amounts of alcohol to guests at the White House during Prohibition?

A: Warren Harding. He allowed bootleg whiskey to be freely given to his guests during after dinner parties, at a time when the president was supposed to be enforcing Prohibition. One witness, Alice Longworth, daughter of President Theodore Roosevelt, once described the scene that she encountered at one of Harding's card games: "the air heavy with tobacco smoke, trays with bottles containing every imaginable brand of whiskey, cards and poker chips ready at hand—a general atmosphere of waistcoat unbuttoned, feet on the desk, and spittoons alongside."

Some of this alcohol had been directly confiscated from the Prohibition department by Jess Smith, assistant to U.S. Attorney General Harry Daugherty.[37]

Q: Which president had more average press conferences per year than any other?

A: Calvin Coolidge, which is ironic since his nickname was "Silent Cal." He gave about 73 per year, just ahead of Franklin Roosevelt. The fewest was Ronald Reagan, who gave only 46 over 8 years, or an average of 5.75 per year. Before Woodrow Wilson, there were no press conferences, so it is difficult to know how many prior presidents might have given if they had the opportunity.

Until Franklin Roosevelt became president, reporters would submit their questions in writing and the president would choose those which he wished to answer. There is a story about Coolidge and the press which may be apocryphal because the details change from one telling to the next, including the year and the questions asked, but the common thread is that reporters were asking whether Coolidge had anything to say about various issues of the day and he kept replying "no." As the disappointed reporters were preparing to leave, Coolidge yelled out "Don't quote me on that!"[38]

Q: In 1964 the School of Engineering and Applied Science of Columbia University named Thomas Edison and which president as the two greatest engineers in U. S. History?

A: Herbert Hoover. [39]

Q: Which presidents donated their entire salary to charity?

A: Herbert Hoover and **John F. Kennedy.** [40]

Q: Which president created the Secret Service and what was he trying to prevent against?

A: Abraham Lincoln created the Secret Service in 1865 to combat counterfeiting. It was established on April 14, 1865, the same day he was assassinated. One-third of the currency in circulation was counterfeit at the time. It was commissioned on July 5, 1865 as the "Secret Service Division" of the Department of the Treasury. [41]

Q: During their first three years in the White House, this 20th-century president and his wife dined alone only three times, each time on their wedding anniversary. Who were they?

A: Herbert Hoover and **Lou Hoover.**

Q: Which president once chased William Crawford, his Secretary of the Treasury, from the White House, while brandishing a pair of fire tongs?

A: James Monroe. [42]

Q: Which president's wife graduated from Stanford as the only woman in her class, with a degree in geology?

A: Herbert Hoover's wife Lou.

Q: Which president, formerly a lawyer, would not work on divorce cases because he was "severely embarrassed by women's confessions of sexual misconduct?"

A: Richard Nixon. [43]

Q: Which president has had the longest retirement period?

A: As of September 8, 2012, it was **Jimmy Carter** at 11,554 days, beating by one day, **Herbert Hoover**'s retirement of 11,553 days. Both retirement periods are over 31 and 1/2 years.

Q: Which president had the shortest retirement of all presidents before his death?

A: James Polk—103 days. This may be attributed to Polk's workaholic habits. In his diary entry of December 29, 1848, he stated: "No president who performs his duties faithfully and conscientiously can have any leisure. If he entrusts the details and smaller matters to subordinates, constant errors will occur. I prefer to supervise the whole operations of the government myself rather than entrust the public business to subordinates, and this makes my duties very great." [44]

Of the presidents who have died, the length of their retirement (obviously excluding presidents who died in office) is as follows:

President	Length of Retirement
Herbert Hoover	31.65 years
Gerald Ford	29.95 years
John Adams	25.35 years
Martin Van Buren	21.4 years
Millard Fillmore	21.02 years
Harry Truman	19.95 years
Richard Nixon	19.72 years
James Madison	19.33 years
John Quincy Adams	18.99 years
Thomas Jefferson	17.34 years
William Howard Taft	17.02 years
John Tyler	16.88 years
Ronald Reagan	15.38 years

Grover Cleveland	15.32 years
Franklin Pierce	12.61 years
Rutherford Hayes	11.88 years
Theodore Roosevelt	9.85 years
Ulysses Grant	8.32 years
Andrew Jackson	8.27 years
Dwight Eisenhower	8.19 years
Benjamin Harrison	8.03 years
James Buchanan	7.25 years
Andrew Johnson	6.41 years
James Monroe	6.34 years
Lyndon Johnson	4.01 years
Calvin Coolidge	3.84 years
Woodrow Wilson	2.92 years
George Washington	2.78 years
Chester Arthur	1.7 years
James K. Polk	103 days [45]

Q: Which president frequently wore a dress until he was five?

A: Franklin Roosevelt. In writing about the photo in this book, Smithsonian Magazine wrote:

> "Little Franklin Delano Roosevelt sits primly on a stool, his white skirt spread smoothly over his lap, his hands clasping a hat trimmed with a marabou feather. Shoulder-length hair and patent leather party shoes complete the ensemble.
>
> We find the look unsettling today, yet social convention of 1884, when FDR was photographed at age 2 1/2, dictated that boys wore dresses until age 6 or 7, also the time of their first haircut. Franklin's outfit was considered gender-neutral." [46]

Q: Which president was the first to name a woman to his cabinet?

A: Franklin Roosevelt. Frances Perkins was his Secretary of Labor.

Q: Who was the last cabinet secretary who was directly elected president of the United States?

A: Herbert Hoover. He was Secretary of Commerce under Warren Harding.

Q: Which president served on the Warren Commission investigating the assassination of president Kennedy?

A: Gerald Ford.

Q: What is another name for Naval Support Facility Thurmont?

A: Camp David, first known as Hi-Catoctin (because it is located in Catoctin Mountain Park) and then as Shangri-la, based on the fictional Himalayan paradise in James Hilton's 1933 novel, *Lost Horizon*. It received its present name from Dwight Eisenhower in honor of his father and grandson, both named David. The first President to go there was Franklin Roosevelt in 1943 after it had been converted to a presidential retreat in 1942. Although its exact location is kept secret from the public, Google does list an address for it: 14900 Park Central Road, Sabillasville, MD. [47]

Q: Two Puerto Rican pro-independence activists, Oscar Collazo and Griselio Torresola, attempted to assassinate which President?

A: Harry Truman in 1950. Their story is discussed in the Pardons chapter. Collazo was pardoned by Jimmy Carter in 1979.

Q: Which president's mother was briefly locked up in a Union internment camp during the Civil War?

A: Harry Truman's. His mother Martha, the daughter of an old-line Confederate family, was a Confederate sympathizer through and through. As a result of her treatment during the Civil War, she never forgave either President Lincoln or the U.S. government. Many years later, when she came to visit her son in the White House and was offered accommodations in the Lincoln bedroom, she refused to sleep there. At the age of 92, back in Independence, Missouri, Mrs. Truman broke her hip when she tripped in her kitchen. The president flew out to see her. Looking up at him from her bed as he walked into the room she said: "I don't want any smart cracks out of you. I saw your picture in the paper last week putting a wreath at the Lincoln Memorial."[48]

Q: Which presidents held no political office other than President?

A: Zachary Taylor, Ulysses Grant and **Dwight Eisenhower.**

Q: Which president has a tree named after him at the Augusta National Golf Course, home of the Masters?

A: Dwight Eisenhower. A tree overhanging the seventeenth hole that always gave him trouble at Augusta, where he was a member, is named the Eisenhower Tree in his honor.

Q: Which president was given $1,000,000 when he turned twenty-one?

A: John F. Kennedy.[49]

Q: Which president never owned a home before turning age sixty?

A: Dwight Eisenhower. When the Eisenhower's bought a farm in Gettysburg, PA in 1950, it was the first permanent home they owned. [50]

Q: What tragic event befell president Kennedy less than 100 days before he was assassinated?

A: His son, Patrick Bouvier Kennedy, died on August 9, 1963 after being alive only two days. He died from hyaline membrane disease, now more commonly called respiratory distress syndrome.

Q: Which president ran for governor of California and lost?

A: Richard Nixon. He lost to Pat Brown in the 1962 election. It was on the morning after that election that he famously said: "You won't have Nixon to kick around anymore because, gentlemen, this is my last press conference." [51]

Q: Only one vice president who later became president was under forty years old when elected vice president. Who was it?

A: Richard Nixon. He was thirty-nine when elected Vice president in November of 1952.

Q: Who lived longer than any other president?

A: Gerald Ford, who died at age 93 years and 165 days.

Q: Which president's parents separated when he was only sixteen days old?

A: Gerald Ford's. [52]

Q: Which president was vice president for the shortest period of time, excluding cases where their predecessors died in office?

A: **Gerald Ford** was vice president for 246 days when Nixon resigned on August 9, 1974. He had become vice president on December 6, 1973, about two months after vice president Spiro Agnew resigned and then pleaded no contest to criminal charges of tax evasion and money laundering.

Q: **Which president had been, at age 44, the youngest senate minority leader in history?**

A: **Lyndon Johnson.**

Q: **Which president, when he entered his party's presidential primary, had a name recognition factor of only 2%?**

A: **Jimmy Carter.** When he told his mother Lillian that he was running for president, she said, "president of what?"[53]

Q: **Which president was derisively mentioned in pre-song banter during the 1969 Woodstock rock festival? The speaker was Jeffrey Shurtleff, who was about to perform *Drug Store Truck Drivin' Man*, by Roger McGuinn and Gram Parsons, as a duet with Joan Baez.**

A: **Ronald Reagan.** Shurtleff said: "Hello to all the friends of the draft resistance revolution in America. Good evening. I hope it stops raining. One thing about the draft resistance that's different from other movements and revolutions in this country is that we have no enemies, and that's one of the beautiful things about it. And to show that our hearts are in the right place, we'd like to sing a song for the governor of California, Ronald Ray-Gun...Zap!" The video can be seen on YouTube.

Q: **Who was the last president to have served in World War II?**

A: **George H.W. Bush.**

Q: Who are the only presidents who have lived past ninety years of age?

A: As of 2013, **John Adams, Herbert Hoover, Gerald Ford** and **Ronald Reagan.**

Q: Who was the oldest president inaugurated?

A: **Ronald Reagan**—age sixty-nine.

Q: Who was the youngest president inaugurated?

A: **John Kennedy**—age forty-three.

Q: Who was the youngest man to become president?

A: **Teddy Roosevelt**, after the assassination of William McKinley. He was forty-two years, 322 days old. Kennedy, when elected, was forty-three years, 236 days.

Q: Which president's wife was known as Lemonade Lucy because she did not serve alcohol in the White House?

A: **Rutherford Hayes'.**

Q: Which president had all of his personal papers destroyed before he died?

A: **Chester Arthur.** [54]

Q: Which president's wife was the youngest first lady ever?

A: **Grover Cleveland**'s wife, Frances Folsom, age twenty-one when they married. He was forty-nine when they married.

Q: Which president sometimes conversed with his wife in Chinese when they wanted to speak confidentially while in the presence of White House guests?

A: Herbert Hoover [55]

Q: Only one president's native tongue was not English. Which president and what was the language?

A: Martin Van Buren's native language was Dutch. Ironically, he was also the first president born as a United States citizen. [56]

Q: More than half of our presidents through Franklin Roosevelt were fluent in writing or speaking at least one language besides English. How many presidents since FDR were fluent in writing or speaking at least one language besides English?

A: None.

In the following table, ✓̄ denotes native tongue, ✓ denotes fluency is speaking or writing, and **X** denotes some familiarity with the language.

	President					
2	John Adams	French ✓	Greek ✓	Hebrew ✓	Latin ✓	
3	Thomas Jefferson	French ✓	Greek ✓	Italian ✓	Latin ✓	Spanish ✓
4	James Madison	Greek ✓	Hebrew ✓	Latin ✓		
5	James Monroe	French ✓				

6	John Quincy Adams	Dutch	French	German	Greek	Latin
		Dutch ✗	French ✓	German ✓	Greek ✗	Latin ✓

8	Martin Van Buren	Dutch ✓

9	William Henry Harrison	French ✗	Latin ✓

10	John Tyler	Greek ✓	Latin ✓

11	James K. Polk	Greek ✓	Latin ✓

15	James Buchanan	Greek ✓	Latin ✓

19	Rutherford B. Hayes	Greek ✓	Latin ✓

20	James A. Garfield	Greek ✓	Latin ✓

21	Chester A. Arthur	Greek ✓	Latin ✓

26	Theodore Roosevelt	French ✓	German ✓	Italian ✗

28	Woodrow Wilson	German ✓

31	Herbert Hoover	Latin ✓	Mandarin Chinese ✓

32	Franklin D. Roosevelt	French ✓	German ✓

39	Jimmy Carter	Spanish ✗

42	Bill Clinton	German X
43	George W. Bush	Spanish X
44	Barack Obama	Indonesian X

Q: Which president was deemed not qualified for the Army for medical reasons?

A: **John F. Kennedy**, in September 1941, was medically disqualified by the Army for his chronic lower back problems. As discussed in *War and Peace* below, he did serve in the Navy.

Q: Which president had to wear corrective shoes because his left leg was 3/4" shorter than his right?

A: **John F. Kennedy.** [58]

Q: Who was the last president to fight in the War of Independence?

A: **James Monroe.**

Q: This president was born when George Washington was president and had a child who died when Harry Truman was president, a span of 32 presidents and 157 years. Who was he?

A: **John Tyler.** Tyler was born in 1790, during Washington's first term. The last of his fifteen children, Pearl, was born in 1860 when Tyler was seventy, and she died in 1947.

Q: Who is the first president who was the subject of an assassination attempt?

A: Andrew Jackson. In 1835, Richard Lawrence, an unemployed house painter, approached Jackson as he left a congressional funeral held in the House chamber of the Capitol and shot at him. The gun misfired. A delusional Lawrence later told his interrogators that the U.S. government owed him a large sum that Jackson was keeping from him and he believed that release of the funds would allow him to take his rightful place as King Richard III of England. Richard III had been dead since 1485. Lawrence was deemed insane and institutionalized. Jackson, who was 67 at the time, repeatedly clubbed Lawrence with his walking cane. During the ensuing scuffle, Lawrence took another pistol out of his pocket and pulled the trigger. But that gun also misfired. Bystanders joined in, wrestling Lawrence to the ground and disarming him. One of them was Rep. Davy Crockett of Tennessee. Afterward, due to public curiosity concerning the double misfires, the pistols were tested and retested. Each time they performed perfectly. [59]

CHAPTER ELEVEN NOTES:

1) http://www.ipl.org/div/potus/jqadams.html
2) Anne Hawkes Hutton, *Portrait of Patriotism: Washington Crossing the Delaware.* Chilton Book Company, 1975.
   David Hackett Fischer, *Washington's Crossing.* Oxford University Press, 2004
3) Tremblay, Rodrigue, *The New American Empire*, Infinity Publishing (2004).
   Herring, George C., *From Colony to Superpower: U.S. Foreign Relations Since 1776*, Oxford University Press, (2008)
   Dozer, Donald, *The Monroe Doctrine: Its Modern Significance*, Knopf (1965).
   http://usinfo.org/PUBS/LivingDoc_e/monroe.htm
4) http://goafrica.about.com/od/africatraveltips/ig/Africa-s-Capital-Cities/Monrovia--Liberia-s-capital-ci.htm
6) Bernstein, Richard B., *The Founding Fathers Reconsidered*, Oxford University Press (2009). http://www.famousquotes.me.uk/speeches/presidential-speeches/presidential-speech-warren-harding.htm
7) http://www.theodoreroosevelt.org/life/Maxwell.htm
8) http://www.americanthinker.com/2008/02/a_tribute_to_herbert_hoover_th.html
   http://millercenter.org/president/hoover/essays/biography/6
9) Crapol, Edward. *John Tyler, the Accidental President*, University of North Carolina Press (2006).
   Chitwood, Oliver Perry, *John Tyler, Champion of the Old South.* Russell & Russell (1964).

10) http://www.watergate.info/nixon/silent-majority-speech-1969.shtml
11) Crapol, Edward P., *John Tyler, the Accidental President.* University of North Carolina Press (2006).
https://www.senate.gov/artandhistory/history/common/generic/VP_John_Tyler.htm
11) Chernow, Ron. *Alexander Hamilton,* Penguin Press (2004)
12) http://www.theamericanpresidents.net/polk.html
Seigenthaler, *John, James K. Polk: 1845-1849: The American Presidents Series,* Times Books (2004).
13) http://www.sparknotes.com/biography/troosevelt/section12.rhtml
http://www.anecdotage.com/index.php?aid=17153
14) http://www.monticello.org/site/research-and-collections/jefferson-lottery
15) May, Gary. *John Tyler (The American Presidents Series: The 10th President, 1841-1845),* Times Books (2008).
Crapol, Edward. *John Tyler, the Accidental President,* University of North Carolina Press (2006).
16) http://www.telegraph.co.uk/news/worldnews/barackobama/3401168/Barack-Obama-The-50-facts-you-might-not-know.html
17) http://www.nj.com/news/index.ssf/2011/05/princeton_university_receives_1.html
Starkman, Jay, *The Sex of a Hippopotamus: A Unique History of Taxes and Accounting,* Twinset, Inc. (2008).
18) National first ladies biography. firstladies.org
19) http://www.potus.com/ztaylor.html
Zachary Taylor by John Eisenhower,
http://allthepresidentsbooks.com/2009/05/22/zachary-taylor/
20) Hoogenboom, Ari. *Rutherford Hayes: Warrior and President.* Lawrence, Kansas: University Press of Kansas (1995)
Trefousse, Hans L. *Rutherford B. Hayes.* Times Books (2002)
21) http://millercenter.org/academic/americanpresident/fillmore/essays/biography/4
http://en.wikipedia.org/wiki/Millard_Fillmore
Bahles, Gerald. "Millard Fillmore: Domestic Affairs." American President: Miller Center of Public Affairs (2010)
22) *Time* magazine, Business: *The Man Who Sued Coolidge,* April 11, 1932
23) Goodwin, Doris Kearns. *Team of Rivals: The Political Genius of Abraham Lincoln.* Simon and Schuster, New York, 2005. Kunhardt Jr., Phillip B., Kunhardt III, Phillip, and Kunhardt, Peter W. *Lincoln: An Illustrated Biography.* Gramercy Books, New York, 1992
Steers, Edward. *Blood on the Moon: The Assassination of Abraham Lincoln.* University Press of Kentucky, 2001.
Sandburg, *Carl. Abraham Lincoln: The War Years IV.* Harcourt, Brace & World (1936)
Vowell, Sarah. *Assassination Vacation.* (Simon and Schuster, 2005)
24) http://law2.umkc.edu/faculty/projects/ftrials/impeach/imp_account2.html
25) http://en.wikipedia.org/wiki/List_of_Congressional_Gold_Medal_recipients
26) http://www.presidentialmuseums.com/Presidents/18.htm

27) McFeely, William S. *Grant: A Biography*. Norton (1981).
28) http://www.academickids.com/encyclopedia/index.php/James_Garfield
29) http://en.wikipedia.org/wiki/Handedness_of_Presidents_of_the_United_States
30) http://www.healthmedialab.com/html/president/cleveland.html
    http://www.npr.org/2011/07/06/137621988/a-yacht-a-mustache-how-a-president-hid-his-tumor
    http://www.doctorsreview.com/history/the-presidents-secret-surgery
    Algeo, Matthew, *The President Is a Sick Man: Wherein the Supposedly Virtuous Grover Cleveland Survives a Secret Surgery at Sea and Vilifies the Courageous Newspaperman Who Dared Expose the Truth*, by Matthew Algeo (Chicago Review Press (2011).
31) http://mcgady.net/ms/dpotus/p23/23bh.html
    indiana-fda.org/pdf/harrison_horror.doc
32) Seale, William. *The President's House, A History. Volume I and Volume II*. White House Historical Association (1986)
    Seale, William. *The White House, The History of an American Idea*. The American Institute of Architects Press (1986)
33) http://www.presidency.ucsb.edu/sou.php#ixzz1ye8xqZF8
    http://www.senate.gov/artandhistory/history/resources/pdf/stateoftheunion.pdf
34) Lamb, Brian. *Who's Buried in Grant's Tomb?: A Tour of Presidential Gravesites*. Public Affairs, (2010).
    Wilson, Edith Bolling Galt. *My Memoir*. The Bobbs-Merrill Company (1939).
    Young, Dwight and Johnson, Margaret. *Dear First Lady: Letters to the White House: From the Collections of the Library of Congress & National Archives*. National Geographic (2008).
    Hoover, Herbert, *The Ordeal of Woodrow Wilson*. (Johns Hopkins University Press, 1958)
35) "Wilson: A Portrait." American Experience, PBS Television. 2001.
    http://www.pbs.org/wgbh/amex/wilson/portrait/wp_wilson.html.
36) http://www.nybooks.com/articles/archives/1967/feb/09/the-strange-case-of-freud-bullitt-and-woodrow-wilson
37) http://www.ohiohistorycentral.org/entry.php?rec=199
    http://millercenter.org/president/harding/essays/biography/4
    Behr, Edward. *Prohibition: Thirteen Years That Changed America*, Skyhorse Publishing (2011).
38) Kane, Gregory, *When Silent Cal spoke, a few words were golden*, *The Baltimore Sun*, 07-06-1996.
    http://www.presidency.ucsb.edu/data/newsconferences.php
    http://www.presidentprofiles.com/General-Information/A-History-of-the-Presidency-Presidents-and-the-press.html
    http://www.calvincoolidge.us/
    http://new.yankeemagazine.com/article/funniest-preside
39) http://www.uspresidents.org/category/31-herbert-hoover.htm
40) http://www.orwelltoday.com/jfksalary.shtml
    http://hoover.archives.gov/education/hooverbio.html

www.therichest.org/nation/richest-american-presidents

41) http://clinton2.nara.gov/WH/kids/inside/html/spring98-2.html
http://www.secretservice.gov/history.shtml
Petro, Joseph; Robinson, Jeffrey. *Standing Next to History, An Agent's Life Inside the Secret Service*. St. Martin's Press (2005).

42) http://www.independent.co.uk/news/presidents/james-monroe-1391113.html

43) http://www.independent.co.uk/news/presidents/richard-m-nixon-1451817.html

44) http://www.questia.com/read/3453762/polk-the-diary-of-a-president-1845-1849

45) http://en.wikipedia.org/wiki/List_of_Presidents_of_the_United_States_by_age

46) http://www.smithsonianmag.com/arts-culture/When-Did-Girls-Start-Wearing-Pink.html#ixzz24ymKp83E

47) http://www.nps.gov/cato/historyculture/retreat.htm
http://www.whitehouse.gov/about/camp-david/
http://www.fas.org/nuke/guide/usa/c3i/campdavid.htm
Eisenhower, David; Eisenhower, Julie Nixon, *Going Home to Glory: A Memoir of Life with Dwight David Eisenhower, 1961-1969*. Simon and Schuster (2010).

48) Geselbracht, Raymond (ed.). *The Civil Rights Legacy of Harry S. Truman*. Truman State University Press (2007).
William E. Leuchtenburg, *Franklin D. Roosevelt and the New Deal: 1932-1940*, Harper Perennial (2009)
http://www.trivia-library.com/a/president-harry-s-truman-little-known-facts-and-trivia.htm

49) http://www.presidentialpetmuseum.com/presidents/35JK.htm

50) http://www.whitehouse.gov/about/first-ladies/mamieeisenhower

51) Aitken, Jonathan. *Nixon: A Life. Regnery* (1996)

52) http://www.fordlibrarymuseum.gov/grf/genealog.asp

53) http://www.guardian.co.uk/world/2011/sep/11/president-jimmy-carter-interview
http://www.scribd.com/doc/19654/Paper-on-Jimmy-Carter
Muschiano, Joe. *100 Grass Roots Campaign Strategies*, Trafford (2010).
http://www.kingstreenews.com/story/-And-the-Winner-is

54) http://dmna.ny.gov/historic/reghist/civil/arthur/arthurIdex.htm
Reeves, Thomas C. *Gentleman Boss: The Life of Chester A. Arthur*. Knopf (1975).

55) Sturgis, Amy H. *The Trail of Tears and Indian Removal*, Greenwood Publishing (2007)

56) King, David. Herbert Hoover. Marshall Cavendish (2009).

57) http://en.wikipedia.org/wiki/List_of_Presidents_of_the_United_States_who_knew_a_foreign_language

58) Schlesinger, Arthur, Sobel, David. *A Thousand Days: John F. Kennedy in the White House* Black Dog (2005).

59) http://www.politico.com/news/stories/0108/8184.html

CHAPTER 12

Inauguration

Q: Who are the only presidents who were alive at the time who did not attend their successor's inaugurations?

A: There were four. The first two were **John Adams** and his son **John Quincy Adams,** both of whom had poor relations with their successors (Thomas Jefferson and Andrew Jackson respectively) at the time they left office. Although John Adams later reconciled with Jefferson, the same cannot be said of his son and Jackson. Also, **Andrew Johnson** did not attend Ulysses Grant's inauguration and **Woodrow Wilson** did not attend Warren Harding's inauguration.[1]

Q: Which president's inaugural address was the shortest in history, at only 135 words?

A: George Washington's second inaugural address, delivered on March 4, 1797, which was as follows:

Fellow Citizens:
"I am again called upon by the voice of my country to execute the functions of its Chief Magistrate. When the occa-

sion is proper, for it shall arrive, I shall endeavor to express the high sense I entertain of this distinguished honor, and of the confidence which has been reposed in me by the people of united America.

Previous to the execution of any official act of the president the Constitution requires an oath of office. This oath I am now about to take, and in your presence: That if it shall be found during my administration of the Government I have in any instance violated willingly or knowingly the injunctions thereof, I may (besides incurring constitutional punishment) be subject to the upbraidings of all who are now witnesses of the present solemn ceremony." [2]

Q: Which president gave the longest inaugural address (1 hour, 45 minutes)?

A: William Henry Harrison.

Q: Which president gave his 3,319 word inaugural address entirely from memory?

A: Franklin Pierce. [3]

Q: The oath of office of the president of the United States is an oath or affirmation required by the United States Constitution before the president begins the execution of the office. The wording is specified in Article Two, Section One, Clause Eight:

> "I do solemnly swear (or affirm) that I will faithfully execute the Office of President of the United States, and will to the best of my ability, preserve, protect and defend the Constitution of the United States."

Who is the only president to use the word "affirm" rather than "swear" in the oath of office?

A: Franklin Pierce. He felt God had passed his judgment with the death of his son Bennie, one month before Pierce was inaugurated. Instead he "affirmed" the oath of office.[4]

Q: Which two-term president holds the records for both the coldest and warmest inaugurations?

A: Ronald Reagan. At 55 degrees, his first inauguration in 1981 was the warmest January inauguration in history. To balance things out, Mother Nature made his second inauguration, in 1985, the coldest. The frigid seven-degree temperature forced the ceremony inside the Capitol Rotunda.[5]

Q: During whose inauguration ceremony did a Supreme Court clerk drop the Bible?

A: Franklin D. Roosevelt's. In 1941, Charles Elmore Cropley, the Supreme Court clerk who held the Bible for Roosevelt's third inauguration, dropped the Bible after the oath was given. Photos detailing the mishap filled a full page of *Life* magazine the next week.[6]

On a few other occasions there have been "oath mishaps" including:

- In 1909, when President William Howard Taft was sworn in, Chief Justice Melville Fuller misquoted the oath, but the error was not publicized at the time.
- In 1929, William Howard Taft, then the Chief Justice, garbled the oath when he swore in President Herbert Hoover, using the words "preserve, *maintain*, and defend the Constitution," instead of "preserve, *protect*, and defend." The error was picked up by a schoolgirl on the radio. Taft later acknowledged his error, but did not think it was important, and Hoover did not retake the oath. Recalling the 1909 incident, Taft wrote, "When I was sworn in as President by Chief

Justice Fuller, he made a similar slip," and added, "but in those days when there was no radio, it was observed only in the Senate chamber where I took the oath." [7]

- The S in Harry Truman's middle name does not stand for anything. Thus, in 1945, when Chief Justice Harlan Stone began reading the oath by saying "I, Harry Shipp Truman...," Truman responded: "I, Harry S Truman... ." As to why Stone may have thought that Truman's middle name was Shipp, chapter below on "Names." [8]

- In 1965, Chief Justice Earl Warren prompted Lyndon Johnson to say, "the Office of *the Presidency* of the United States."

- In 2009, Chief Justice John G. Roberts, while administering the oath to Barack Obama, incorrectly recited part of the oath. Roberts said, "That I will execute the Office of President *to* the United States *faithfully*." Obama stopped at "execute," and waited for Roberts to correct himself. Roberts, after a false start, then followed Obama's "execute" with "faithfully," which results in "execute faithfully," which is also incorrect. Obama then repeated Roberts' initial, incorrect prompt, with the word "faithfully" after "United States." The correct oath was re-administered the next day by Roberts at the White House. [9]

Q: Who is the only president who promised not to run for re-election in his inauguration speech, stating: "Having determined not to become a candidate for re-election, I shall have no motive to influence my conduct in administering the Government except the desire ably and faithfully to serve my country and to live in grateful memory of my countrymen?"

A: James Buchanan. Given that his presidency did not go so well, it is not likely he would have won anyway. Buchanan's inauguration in 1857 is the first one to have been photographed. [10]

Q: Who was the first president whose mother appeared at his inauguration?

A: James Garfield. [11]

Q: Which president held an umbrella over his successor's head during the inauguration speech?

A: Grover Cleveland over Benjamin Harrison's in 1889.

Q: Which president's inauguration was the first to be filmed?

A: William McKinley's in 1897. [12]

Q: Who was the first president whose parents were both alive at his inauguration?

A: Ulysses Grant. However neither parent attended.

Q: Which president gave the first presidential inauguration broadcast on radio?

A: Calvin Coolidge in 1925.

Q: Which president's inauguration was the first televised nationally?

A: Harry Truman in 1949.

Q: Who was the only president inaugurated in two cities?

A: George Washington was inaugurated in New York and Philadelphia.

Q: Which president took the oath of office on a book of laws, instead of the more traditional Bible, to preserve the separation of church and state?

A: John Quincy Adams.[13]

Q: Who is the only president who administered the oath of office to another president?

A: William Howard Taft did it twice when he was Chief Justice of the Supreme Court. In 1925, he administered the oath to Calvin Coolidge and in 1929, he administered the oath to Herbert Hoover.

Q: Which president received the oath of office from his father, a notary public?

A: Calvin Coolidge, when he first became president in 1923 after Warren Harding died. It took several hours for the news of President Harding's death in California to reach Vermont, where Coolidge was at the time. Traditionally, the Chief Justice of the Supreme Court (then Taft) swears in the president, but he was 500 miles away, so at 2:30 a.m., Coolidge's father, a notary republic, administered the oath of office to his son by the light of a kerosene lamp.

Q: Which president did not take the oath of office at all, but merely "affirmed" his presidency because of religious beliefs?

A: Herbert Hoover, a Quaker.

Q: Who was the only president to take the oath of office from a female official?

A: Lyndon Johnson, by Judge Sarah T. Hughes.

Q: Who was the only president to take the oath of office on a plane?

A: Lyndon Johnson, on November 22, 1963, the day Kennedy was shot.

Q: Who are the only presidents who used no book or Bible at their inaugurations?

A: Chester Arthur was sworn in at his home in 1881 following the assassination of James Garfield and there was no Bible in the house. Similarly, **Theodore Roosevelt** was sworn in at a friend's house in 1901 after the assassination of William McKinley and again there was no Bible available. Finally, in 1923, **Calvin Coolidge** was sworn in at his father's house upon the death of Warren Harding. Although a Bible was in the house it was not used for the swearing-in.[14]

Q: Who was the only president who used two Bibles at his inauguration?

A: Barack Obama during his second inauguration on January 21, 2013. One was Martin Luther King's "traveling Bible." It is heavily annotated and was used by Dr. King in preparing sermons and speeches. It had never been used previously in a presidential inauguration. The public portion of Obama's second inauguration was on Martin Luther King Day in 2013. (His actual inauguration was the day before, since all presidents are sworn into office on January 20.)

The other Bible used by Obama was the Lincoln Bible. The Lincoln Bible, also used during Lincoln's first inauguration, had not been used again until Obama chose it for his first inaugural. Lincoln had no previous ties to the book. Facing assassination threats, Lincoln entered the capital for his first inaugural in secret and in haste, under the guard of Pinkerton detectives. His luggage, including the family Bible, had not yet caught up with him en route from Springfield, Illinois. The faded burgundy velvet Bible was one of several like it on hand at the U.S. Supreme Court for use on such occasions. Lincoln opened this Bible, at random, for the swearing in at his first inauguration. Obama did not open this Bible for the oath, because it is too fragile to open easily or to lay flat. The two Bibles were placed one on top of the other. [15]

CHAPTER TWELVE NOTES:

1) Nagel, Paul C. *John Quincy Adams: A Public Life, a Private Life* (1999).

2) http://www.bartleby.com/124/pres14.html
http://inaugural.senate.gov/history/factsandfirsts/index.cfm

3) www.potus.com/fpierce.html. The text of Pierce's speech may be found at www.bartleby.com

4) http://www.npr.org/templates/story/story.php?storyId=99539230
http://inaugural.senate.gov/history/chronology/fpierce1853.cfm

5) http://abcnews.go.com/Politics/Inauguration/story?id=393117&page=2

6) http://www.icollector.com/Franklin-D-Roosevelt_i11898366
http://www.law.com/jsp/law/LawArticleFriendly.jsp?id=1202427189694&slreturn=1

7) *An Old Man's Memory, Time* magazine, March 25, 1929

8) McCullough, David. *Truman*. Simon and Schuster (1992).
http://www.trumanlibrary.org/speriod.htm

9) http://www.youtube.com/watch?v=3PuHGKnboNY

10) http://inaugural.senate.gov/history/chronology/jbuchanan1857.cfm
http://www.bartleby.com/124/pres30.html

11) http://www.ipl.org/div/potus/jagarfield.html

12) http://www.youtube.com/watch?v=F4uOmSEw5-U

13) Bendat, Jim. *Democracy's Big Day: The Inauguration of Our President*, iUniverse, available online at Googlebooks.com.

14) Bendat, Jim. *Democracy's Big Day: The Inauguration of Our President*, iUniverse, available online at Googlebooks.com.

15) Chaddock, Gail. *Inauguration Day Bibles: How Presidents Choose, and What That Reveals, Christian Science Monitor*, 1-21-2013

CHAPTER 13

Marriage

Q: **Which president's wife died within a month of his leaving office?**

A: **Millard Fillmore.** Abigail Fillmore died of pneumonia at age 55 in 1853. She had the shortest post-presidential life of any former first lady.

Q: **Which 20th-century president's wife's maiden name was Claudia Alta Taylor?**

A: **Lyndon Johnson**'s wife, better known as Lady Bird Johnson.

Q: **Which president gave away a future first lady at her wedding?**

A: **Theodore Roosevelt** gave away Eleanor Roosevelt at her wedding to Franklin.[1]

Q: **Who was the first president to marry while in office?**

A: **John Tyler.** He married his second wife Julia in 1844.

Q: Which president's wedding was delayed until after he won his party's nomination for Congress because he "wasn't sure how voters might feel about his marrying a divorced ex-dancer?"

A: Gerald Ford. His wife Betty ran the *Betty Bloomer Dance School* in Grand Rapids from approximately 1935-1937 (Betty Bloomer being her maiden name). She then spent two summers (1937-1938) studying modern dance at Bennington College, where she met Martha Graham. She was a dancer with the *Martha Graham Auxiliary Dance Company* in 1940-1941. Although she did not tour the country with the main Graham dance company, she made numerous appearances in New York, including at least one at Carnegie Hall.

Her first marriage was to William Warren, an insurance and furniture salesman. They married on April 23, 1942 in Grand Rapids, Michigan. Warren suffered from diabetes and was ineligible for the draft. He was also an alcoholic. Just as she was intending to file for divorce from Warren due to "extensive repeated cruelty," she received word that he had suffered a coma in Boston. Living there to care for him as he began to recover, the couple then relocated to his parents' home in Grand Rapids. For two years, Betty Warren lived in the home of her in-laws in an upstairs room while her semi-invalid husband was cared for on a lower floor. Once he was able to recover and return to full employment, the divorce proceeded and was completed on December 15, 1947.

Betty met Gerald in 1947 before her divorce was finalized. He proposed to her in late 1947 or early 1948, but told her they could not marry until the fall because he had a secret regarding "something he had to do first." She accepted, only to soon be told by him that he was planning to run for the Republican nomination for the local seat to the U.S. Congress. Ford had practical concerns that the morally conservative district in Grand Rapids might not support his marriage to a divorced woman who had a career in modern dance. The wedding was announced in June of that year —after he had won the Republican nomination. They married on October 15, 1948.[2]

Q: Who was the only president to marry his wife twice?

A: **Andrew Jackson** married his wife Rachel twice. When he married her the first time in 1790, her divorce from her previous husband was not completed, which made making her marriage to Jackson technically bigamous and therefore invalid. He therefore married her again in 1794.[3]

Q: Which president married his wife with a $2.50 wedding ring bought at Sears & Roebuck?

A: **Lyndon Johnson.** Lyndon and Lady Bird met in 1934 when he was 26 and she was 21. Their first date alone was the day after they met. Johnson proposed marriage that same day but Lady Bird said she wanted to wait a year. After about 7 weeks of trying to persuade her to marry him, on November 17, 1934, Johnson said, "We either do it now, or we never will. And if you say goodbye to me, it just proves to me that you don't love me enough to dare to. And I just can't bear to go and keep on wondering if it will ever happen." She finally said yes. Although they remained married until his death in 1973, Lyndon was demanding and ordered Lady Bird around. He would embarrass her in public by making negative comments about how she dressed.

It has been written that he was unfaithful throughout their marriage and in fact was a competitive womanizer. When people mentioned President Kennedy's many affairs, Johnson would bang the table and declare that he had more women by accident than Kennedy ever had on purpose.[4]

Q: Who is the only president whose wedding ceremony was held in the White House?

A: Grover Cleveland. On June 2, 1886, at age forty-nine, he married Frances Folsom, age 21, in the Blue Room of the White House.

Q: Who was the youngest president to be married?

A: Andrew Johnson. He was eighteen on May 5, 1827 and Eliza McCardle was sixteen.

Q: This president's wife was married at age eighteen, widowed at age twenty-six and married her future president husband at age twenty-eight. Who was she?

A: Martha Dandridge Custis, wife of George Washington.

Q: Which presidents' wives died while they were president?

A: John Tyler's, Benjamin Harrison's and Woodrow Wilson's. Tyler's first wife, Letitia Christian Tyler, died after he had been president for one year. Caroline Harrison died of tuberculosis in 1892 at age 60. Woodrow Wilson's first wife, Ellen Louise Axson Wilson, died of Bright's Disease on August 6, 1914, during Wilson's second year in office.[5]

Q: It is reasonably well known that James Buchanan was our only bachelor president. What is less well known is that there were four presidents whose wives died before they were elected president and thus were not married during their term in office. Who were they?

A: Thomas Jefferson, Andrew Jackson, Martin Van Buren and **Chester Arthur.** Martha Wayles Skelton Jefferson died in 1782, nineteen years before Thomas Jefferson became president. Their daughter Martha Jefferson Randolph assumed the role of White

House hostess and unofficial first lady during his incumbency. When she was unavailable, Jefferson called upon Dolley Madison, wife of his Secretary of State, James Madison.

Rachel Jackson died in December, 1828, three months before Andrew Jackson became president. Rachel's niece, Emily Donelson, assumed the role of White House hostess and unofficial first lady until her death on December 19, 1836. Jackson's daughter-in-law, Sarah Yorke Jackson, served as White House hostess and unofficial first lady. She remained at the White House until Jackson's term expired on March 4, 1837.

Hannah Van Buren died on February 5, 1819, eighteen years before Martin Van Buren became president. Angelica Singleton Van Buren, Martin's daughter-in-law, assumed the role of White House hostess and unofficial first lady during his incumbency.

Ellen Arthur died in 1880. When Chester Arthur became president after James Garfield died, he asked his sister, Mary Arthur McElroy, to be the White House hostess.[6]

Q: Who were the only presidents to remarry in office?

A: John Tyler, Grover Cleveland and **Woodrow Wilson.** John Tyler married Julia Gardiner on June 26, 1844. Cleveland married Frances Folsom on June 2, 1886. Wilson married Edith Galt on December 18, 1915.

Q: Which president was engaged to a woman who broke off the engagement and died a week later, likely by suicide?

A: James Buchanan. He was engaged to Anne Caroline Coleman. Just before they were to get married, she broke off the engagement and died one week later.

Q: Which president's father-in-law was incensed by his daughter's decision to marry this man, prohibited his wife

from attending the wedding (she snuck in long enough to see the vows exchanged), and refused to speak to his daughter or son-in-law for eight years?

A: Warren Harding.[7]

Q: Which president's wife was the first to graduate from college?

A: Rutherford Hayes' wife Lucy. She enrolled at Wesleyan Women's College (now Ohio Wesleyan University), was a member of the class of 1850 and was a member of the Kappa Kappa Gamma sorority.[8]

Q: Which president's wife considered sex "an ordeal to be endured," although she had six children with her husband?

A: Franklin Roosevelt's wife Eleanor.

Q: Which president and his wife were both models before they got married?

A: Gerald and **Betty Ford.**

Q: Who was the only divorced president?

A: Ronald Reagan. He was married to Jane Wyman from 1940 to 1949, before marrying Nancy Davis.

Q: Which president's wife became an invalid before he became president, and never left the upstairs living quarters, except for one occasion, before dying during her husband's term in office?

A: John Tyler's. In 1839, his wife Letitia suffered a paralytic stroke that left her an invalid. In 1841, Tyler was vice president but became president after William Henry Harrison died after just one month in office. As first lady, Letitia remained in the upstairs living quarters of the White House; she came down just once, to attend the wedding of her daughter Elizabeth in January 1842. She died later that year after 29 years of marriage.[9]

Q: Which president's wife said: "His nomination is a plot to deprive me of his society and to shorten his life by unnecessary care and responsibility."

A: Zachary Taylor's wife, Margaret.

Q: Who was the only president whose wife's maiden name was the same as his?

A: Franklin Roosevelt. His wife Eleanor was distantly related to him. Theodore Roosevelt was his uncle.

Q: Which president's wife suffered from severe epilepsy?

A: William McKinley's wife Ida.

Q: Who is the only president whose wife was foreign-born?

A: John Quincy Adams. His wife, Louisa Catherine Johnson (February 12, 1775-May 15, 1852), was born in London. However, of the first nine presidents beside Adams, all but one of their wives was born before 1776 and thus would be considered British subjects, though born on American soil.

Q: Who was the only president married to one woman when his term began and married to another when it finished (i.e. two first ladies)?

A: John Tyler (Letitia Christian Tyler and Julia Gardiner Tyler). Letitia died in 1842 and he married Julia in 1844.

Q: Which first lady was committed to an insane asylum?

A: Mary Todd Lincoln, by her son Robert. After the death of her son Tad (which occurred after the death of her son Willie and the assassination of her husband), Robert believed that she was showing signs of mental instability and he successfully had her tried for insanity.

In 1875, she was committed to the Bellevue Insane Asylum, in Batavia, Illinois. She twice attempted suicide by taking what she believed to be the drugs laudanum and camphor—which the suspicious druggist had replaced with a sugar substance. One of the nation's first women lawyers, Myra Bradwell, believed Mrs. Lincoln was not insane and being held against her will. She filed an appeal on Mrs. Lincoln's behalf and after four months of confinement, the former first lady was released to the care of her sister Elizabeth Edwards in Springfield. In a second trial on June 19, 1876, she was declared sane, after which she moved to France.[10]

Q: How many presidents were younger than their wives?

A: There were six. Of these, only two, Millard Fillmore and Warren Harding were more than one year older. Martha Washington was on June 2, 1731 and her husband George on February 22, 1732, making her 265 days older then her husband. Abigail Fillmore was born on March 13, 1798 and her husband Millard on January 7, 1800, making her one year, 301 days older then her husband. Caroline Harrison was born on October 1, 1832 and her husband Benjamin on August 20, 1833, making her 323 days older then her husband. Florence Harding was born on August 15, 1860 and her husband Warren on November 2, 1865, making her five years, 79 days older then her husband. Lou Henry Hoover was born on March 29, 1874 and her husband Herbert on August 10, 1874, making her 134 days older then her husband. Pat Nixon was born on March 16, 1912 and her husband Richard on January 9, 1913, making her 299 days older then her husband.

CHAPTER THIRTEEN NOTES:

1) http://www.gwu.edu/~erpapers/teachinger/q-and-a/q8-newsarticle.cfm (*New York Times* article from March 18, 2005).
2) Howard, Jane (December 8, 1974). *"The 38th First Lady: Not a Robot At All."* *The New York Times*
   Ford, Betty, *The Times of My Life*, Harper & Row (1978)
   Greene, John Robert, *Betty Ford: Candor and Courage in the White House*, University Press of Kansas, 2004)
   http://www.firstladies.org/biographies/firstladies.aspx?biography=39
3) Robert Remini: *Andrew Jackson: The Course of American Empire, 1767-1821*, *Vol. 1* (Johns Hopkins University Press)
4) Dallek, Robert, *Flawed Giant: Lyndon Johnson and His Times, 1961-1973*, Oxford University Press (1998)
   Anderson, Alice and Baxendale, Hadley. *Behind Every Successful President: The Hidden Power and Influence of America's First Ladies*. S.P. I. Books (1992)
   Goldberg, Wendy and Goodwin, Betty, *Marry Me! Courtships and Proposals of Legendary Couples*. Angel City Press (1994).
   Joe Holley, *Champion of Conservation, Loyal Force Behind LBJ*, The Washington Post, July 12, 2007
   http://marriage.about.com/od/presidentialmarriages/p/ljohnson.htm
   http://www.pbs.org/ladybird/earlyyears/earlyyears_report.html
5) Slovick, Matt. *"The American President." The Washington Post*. 7-23-1997.
6) Black, Allida. *The First Ladies of the United States of America*, White House Historical Association (2009).
   http://www.whitehouse.gov/about/first-ladies/marthajefferson
   http://www.whitehouse.gov/about/first-ladies/racheljackson/
   http://www.whitehouse.gov/about/first-ladies/hannahvanburen/
   http://www.whitehouse.gov/about/first-ladies/ellenarthur
7) Russell, Francis *The Shadow of Blooming Grove—Warren G. Harding In His Times*. Easton Press (1962)
   http://www.americanheritage.com/content/four-mysteries-warren-harding
8) http://www.firstladies.org/biographies/firstladies.aspx?biography=20
9) http://www.whitehouse.gov/about/first-ladies/letitiatyler
   Black, Allida. *The First Ladies of the United States of America*, White House Historical Association (2009).
10) http://www.firstladies.org/biographies/firstladies.aspx?biography=17
    http://showcase.netins.net/web/creative/lincoln/sites/bellevue.htm

CHAPTER 14

Media—
TV, Radio,
Magazines, Music

Q: Which president's image has been on the cover of *Time* magazine the most frequently since its inception in 1923?

A: Richard Nixon—51 times.

Q: Which president appeared on the *Time* magazine cover the most frequently after his term was over?

A: Ronald Reagan—7 times.

Q: Who is the only president since 1923 who was never on *Time*'s cover while president, although he did appear both before and after being president?

A: Herbert Hoover.

Q: Besides Herbert Hoover, three presidents appeared on

the *Time* magazine cover more frequently before they were president than during. Who are they?

A: **Dwight Eisenhower** (9 before, 7 during), **John F. Kennedy** (5 before 3 during) and **George H.W. Bush** (10 before and 9 during).

Q: Besides Herbert Hoover, only one president appeared on the *Time* magazine cover more frequently after he was president than during. Who is he?

A: **John F. Kennedy** (3 during and 5 after).

Q: Since Herbert Hoover, who is the only president to have never appeared on the cover of *Time* after his term was over?

A: **Gerald Ford**. Presidents typically appear on the cover after their presidency for various reasons. Sometimes this is for actions they have taken post-presidency, but more frequently it is due to their historical legacy and connections which may exist between that legacy and the current White House occupant.

The ranking of the presidents in terms of *Time* magazine covers follows. In this chart, "F" means future meaning they were not yet president, "C" means current, meaning that that they were in office at the time, and "P" means past, meaning they had already been president:

	F	C	P	Total
George Washington			5	5
Thomas Jefferson			2	2
James Monroe			1	1
Abraham Lincoln			5	5
Theodore Roosevelt			3	3
William Taft			2	2

	F	C	P	Total
Woodrow Wilson			1	1
Warren Harding		1		1
Calvin Coolidge		1		1
Herbert Hoover	2		2	4
Franklin Roosevelt	3	4	4	11
Harry Truman	1	5	1	7
Dwight Eisenhower	9	7	2	18
John Kennedy	5	3	5	13
Lyndon Johnson	6	14	1	21
Richard Nixon	14	33	4	51
Gerald Ford	2	17		19
Jimmy Carter	10	17	2	29
Ronald Reagan	13	25	7	45
George H. W. Bush	10	9	1	20
Bill Clinton	9	22	5	36
George W. Bush	12	20	2	34
Barack Obama	18	11		29 [1]

Q: The first two presidents who were on the cover of *Sports Illustrated* were actually not yet president when they appeared. Who were they?

A: John F. Kennedy was on the cover as president-elect on December 26, 1960 with his wife Jacqueline. **Gerald Ford** was on the cover on July 8, 1974, one month before Nixon resigned the presidency.

Q: Two presidents have been featured on the cover of *Sports Illustrated* while president, one twice. Who are they?

A: Ronald Reagan (twice) and **Bill Clinton**. Reagan was on the cover on November 26, 1984 with Georgetown Hoyas basketball coach John Thompson and Patrick Ewing, and again on February 16, 1987 with America's Cup champion Dennis Conner. Clinton was on the cover on March 21, 1994 regarding an article about the Arkansas Razorbacks basketball team. The only time a president was on the cover but not featured was when George H.W. Bush appeared on a small inset photo ("the Prez at play") on August 19, 1991. The featured person on the cover was golfer John Daly, who had just won the PGA Championship. [2]

Q: Who is the only president interviewed by *Playboy* magazine?

A: Jimmy Carter. This was the controversial interview given just before the election in November, 1976 in which Carter admitted to having committed "adultery in my heart many times." Carter took a hit in the polls as a result of the interview and frequently lamented his remarks for years thereafter, especially given that the remark was unsolicited and had nothing to do with the question asked. Nevertheless, he won the election over Gerald Ford by a narrow margin. The key exchange with interviewer Robert Scheer was as follows:

> Scheer: Do you feel you've reassured people with this interview, people who are uneasy about your religious beliefs, who wonder if you're going to make a rigid, unbending president?

> Carter: I don't know if you've been to Sunday school here yet. But we had a good class last Sunday. It's a good way to learn what I believe and what the Baptists believe. What Christ taught about most was pride, that one person should never think he was any better than anybody else. The thing that's drummed into us all the time is not to be proud, not to be better than anyone else, not to look down on people, but to make ourselves acceptable in God's eyes through our own actions and recognize the simple truth that we're saved by grace. I'm not trying to commit a deliberate sin. I recognize that I'm going to do it anyhow,

because I'm human and I'm tempted. And Christ set some almost impossible standards for us. Christ said, I tell you that anyone who looks on a woman with lust has in his heart already committed adultery. I've looked on a lot of women with lust. I've committed adultery in my heart many times. This is something that God recognizes I will do—and I have done it—and God forgives me for it.[3]

Q: Who is the only president to have appeared on the television show *Laugh-In* (though he was not president at the time he appeared)?

A: Richard Nixon. It was the 15th episode of the show and aired on September 16, 1968 in the midst of the campaign. Nixon's opponent was Hubert Humphrey. It was the first appearance by a President on a comedy show in American history. By way of background, one of the many catch-phrases of the show was "sock it to me." Commenting about the event in *The New Yorker*, Elizabeth Kolbert wrote:

> "Judy Carne [a show regular] answers a phone, and on the other end (ostensibly) is Governor Nelson Rockefeller. "Oh, no, I don't think we could get Mr. Nixon to stand still for a 'Sock it to me,'" she chirps, at which point the show cuts away to Richard Nixon. Nixon's appearance on *Laugh-In* lasts four seconds. At first, he is looking stage right; then he turns toward the camera. He widens his eyes in what seems to be an effort at feigned surprise but comes off looking more like mock dismay. "Sock it to me?" he asks, drawing out the "me?" in a way that suggests he has perhaps never heard the line before. ..."
>
> George Schlatter [the creator of *Laugh-In*], told me that Nixon had been extremely reluctant to be on the show; although the producers had repeatedly entreated him to appear, his campaign aides had even more insistently urged him not to. It took about six takes because it sounded

angry. Then, realizing what we had done—because he did come out looking like a nice guy—we pursued Humphrey all over the country, trying to get him to say, 'I'll sock it to you, Dick!'" Schlatter went on. "And Humphrey later said that not doing it may have cost him the election.

"Nixon on *Laugh-In* is often cited as a watershed moment in the history of television. [However] as president, he never went near *Laugh-In*, or anything like it. Indeed, according to Schlatter, he became critical of the show and eventually pressured NBC into muffling its politics." [4]

Q: Who is the only sitting president to have appeared on *The Tonight Show*?

A: Barack Obama. He appeared for the first time on March 19, 2009, just two months into his presidency. He has also appeared a number of times since. John Kennedy appeared as a candidate on the show in 1960, when Jack Paar was the host.

Q: Who is the only president to have visited a daytime talk show?

A: Barack Obama was on *The View* on July 29, 2010 and has appeared several times since. George W. Bush appeared on *Dr. Phil* on September 29, 2004 but that was filmed at Bush's ranch, not at the *Dr. Phil* studio.

Q: Who was the only president who said, "Live from New York!" to open *Saturday Night Live*?

A: Gerald Ford on April 17, 1976. Ford's press secretary Ron Nessen was the host. George H.W. Bush appeared in a cameo in 1994 after he was president and Barack Obama appeared in a cameo on the show as a candidate in 2007. [5]

Q: Which past or future president appeared on the TV game

show *What's My Line?* not as a mystery guest (i.e. the pan-elists were not blindfolded)?

A: **Jimmy Carter.** He appeared while he was governor of Georgia in December, 1973. He signed his name with a large "X", indicating that the producers felt that he might be recognized by name though not by sight. One of the early exchanges that threw off the panel was when he was asked if his service "has to do with women" and his answer was, "Yes, it certainly does … but not enough." Although the panel eventually determined that he was a governor, none of them knew who he was and it was the host who had to identify him as "Jimmy Carter, Governor of Georgia." A clip of the show can be seen on YouTube.

Q: Besides Jimmy Carter, which president or presidents appeared on *What's My Line?* as mystery guests?

A: **Ronald Reagan** while he was still an actor and **Gerald Ford** while he was House Minority Leader. The panel was able to guess Reagan but not Ford.

There is only one first lady who has ever appeared on *What's My Line?* and that is Eleanor Roosevelt, who appeared in 1953.

Q: Which past, sitting or future president appeared (by pre-recorded video) on the television game show *Deal or No Deal*?

A: **George W. Bush** in 2008. The 43rd president thanked con-testant Joseph Kobes, a Purple Heart and Bronze Star recipient and a three-time Iraq veteran, for his service and wished him luck on the show. Bush, who struggled with low approval ratings, also joked that he was thrilled to be on *Deal or No Deal*, or "anywhere with high ratings these days."[6]

Q: Which president is mentioned in the theme song to the hit 1970's TV show, *All in the Family*?

A: **Herbert Hoover**—"Mister, we could use a man like Herbert Hoover again."

Q: **Which president appeared on the television show, *Mythbusters*?**

A: **Barack Obama** on December 8, 2010. His "viewer challenge" was to examine the ancient legend of Archimedes' solar death ray. Supposedly, the Greek scientist used giant mirrors to reflect sunlight towards attacking Roman ships around 212 B.C., setting them aflame. The Obama twist was to use hundreds of mirrors, held by hundreds of San Francisco-area students, to try and light a mock trireme on fire. It didn't work, though. The mirrors couldn't combine into one ray that was focused enough to sufficiently heat up the fake ship's sail. [7]

Q: **Which president was asked on live television: "Mr. President, the world's dying to know: Is it boxers or briefs?"**

A: **Bill Clinton** was asked that question at an MTV's *Enough is Enough* town forum on April 19, 2004. He laughed and answered "usually briefs." In 2008, before Barack Obama was the Democratic nominee for president, *US* magazine asked him the same question. He answered: "I don't answer those humiliating questions." That response may have given the impression that he was annoyed by the question, but the very next thing he said was "But whichever one it is, I look good in 'em!" [8]

Q: **Who was the first president to deliver a speech on television?**

A: **Franklin Roosevelt** in 1939. The setting was the 1939 World's Fair in New York. The appearance was broadcast to a handful of TV sets in the New York area. The outbreak of World War II temporarily halted the development of television, and it would be more than a decade before the new medium became popular. [9]

Q: There have been relatively few well-known rock songs which have mentioned presidents by name in their lyrics, and even fewer that mention any in the title. Can you identify any presidents mentioned? Although my list is obviously not exclusive, the GOLD medal answer is to do so without benefit of the artist or the title. The SILVER medal answer is with the benefit of the artist only and the BRONZE medal answer is to do so with benefit of both artist and title. So don't peek.

Silver medal hints:

Neil Young
Rolling Stones
David Bowie
Billy Joel
Queen
Chicago
John Lennon
Randy Newman
Gil Scott Heron
The Dream Academy
Beastie Boys
Dion
Elvis Costello
James Taylor
Sting
Prince
Elton John
Bob Dylan
They Might be Giants
Johnny Horton (mentioning a future President)

Bronze medal hints:

Neil Young—*Ohio*

Rolling Stones—*Sympathy For the Devil*
David Bowie—*Young Americans*
Billy Joel—*We Didn't Start the Fire* (more than one president)
Queen—*Killer Queen*
Chicago—*Harry Truman*
John Lennon—*"God"*
Randy Newman—*Louisiana 1927*
Gil Scott Heron—*The Revolution Will Not Be Televised*
The Dream Academy—*Life In a Northern Town*
Beastie Boys—*Shadrach*
Dion—*Abraham, Martin and John*
Elvis Costello—*Eisenhower Blues*
James Taylor—*Line 'em Up*
Sting—*Russians*
Prince—*Ronnie Talks to Russia*
Elton John—*Postcards From Richard Nixon*
They Might be Giants—*James K. Polk*
Bob Dylan—*Talkin World War III Blues*
Johnny Horton (mentioning a future president)—*Battle of New Orleans*

Answers:

Neil Young—*Ohio* (Nixon)
Rolling Stones—*Sympathy For the Devil* (Kennedy)
David Bowie—*Young Americans* (Nixon)
Billy Joel—*We Didn't Start the Fire* (Truman, Eisenhower, Kennedy and Nixon)
Queen—*Killer Queen* (Kennedy)
Chicago—*Harry Truman*
John Lennon—*"God"* (Kennedy)
Randy Newman—*Louisiana 1927* (Coolidge)
Gil Scott Heron—*The Revolution Will Not Be Televised* (Nixon)
The Dream Academy—*Life In a Northern Town* (Kennedy)

Beastie Boys—*Shadrach* (Truman)

Dion—*Abraham, Martin and John* (Lincoln and Kennedy)

Elvis Costello—*Eisenhower Blues*

James Taylor—*Line 'em Up* (Nixon)

Sting—*Russians* (Reagan)

Prince—*Ronnie, Talk to Russia* (Reagan)

Elton John—*Postcards From Richard Nixon*

They Might be Giants—*James K. Polk* (Polk, Van Buren and Buchanan)

Bob Dylan—*Talkin World War III Blues* (Lincoln)

Johnny Horton—*Battle of New Orleans* (Andrew Jackson)

Q: How many fireside chats were given by Franklin Roosevelt during his twelve-year presidency?
   a. 30
   b. 129 (roughly one per month with some months missed)
   c. 576 (roughly one per week with some weeks missed)
   d. 879 (roughly one per week but with multiple chats frequently given during some weeks)

A: The answer is a. He only gave thirty fireside chats, which is likely far fewer than many people imagine. Of those thirty, four were given in 1933, the first year of his presidency (starting March 12, 1933 after he had been in office only eight days). Another fourteen were given between 1941 and 1945. Only twelve were given in the seven year period between 1934 and 1940 inclusive. The term "fireside chat" was not coined by Roosevelt, but by Harry C. Butcher of CBS, who used the phrase in a press release before Roosevelt's second speech of May 7, 1933. The term was quickly adopted by press and public, and the president himself later used it.[10]

Q: Way before Ronald Reagan (in fact before the 20th-century), there was a president who "acted" in a motion picture while president, although it was called a "picture play" or "photo play" at the time. Who was the president?

A: Grover Cleveland. In 1895, Alexander Black came to Washington and asked Cleveland to appear in "A Capital Courtship," his new picture play. He agreed to be filmed while signing a bill into law. Black had a difficult time trying to explain to Cleveland what a picture play was. When Cleveland at last comprehended that the idea was to show him signing a bill, he searched his desk for an actual bill which awaited signature. The picture play was presented at a rate of only four frames per minute, so that each image lasted for fifteen seconds. By contrast, motion pictures today are filmed at the rate of twenty-four frames per second.[11]

CHAPTER FOURTEEN NOTES:

1) http://www.time.com/time/coversearch
2) http://sportsillustrated.cnn.com/multimedia/photo_gallery/0811/presidents.on.si. covers/content.2.html
3) Scheer, Robert. *Playing President: My Close Encounters with Nixon, Carter, Bush I, Reagan, and Clinton—and How They Did Not Prepare Me for George W. Bush.* Akashir Books (2006). http://www.truthdig.com/report/item/20060622_classic_scheer_carter
4) Kolbert, Elizabeth, *Stooping to Conquer, The New Yorker,* 04-19-2004.
5) http://www.saturday-night-live.com/qanda/guests.html http://www.youtube.com/watch?v=5jbdBfBlJes
6) http://blog.starcam.com/post/5-presidential-cameos.aspx
7) http://www.csmonitor.com/USA/Politics/The-Vote/2010/1209/Obama-on-Mythbusters-What-happened-with-his-death-ray
8) http://www.aoltv.com/2011/08/01/30-years-of-mtv-early-show-video/ http://latimesblogs.latimes.com/washington/2008/03/barack-obama-ge.html
9) http://timelines.com/1939/4/30/franklin-d-roosevelt-becomes-first-president-to-appear-on-tv
10) http://www.mhric.org/fdr/fdr.html
    Buhite, Russell D. and Levy, David W. *FDR's Fireside Chats.* University of Oklahoma (1992)
    FDR's first fireside chat on March 12, 1933 can be heard at: http://www.museum.tv/exhibitionssection.php?page=79
11) http://www.alexanderblack.com/millionandonenights.htm http://www.ipl.org/div/potus/gcleveland.html

Names and Named After

Q: Who is the only president whose first and last names at birth are different from the name by which he became known?

A: Gerald Ford. He was born Leslie Lynch King, Jr. Ford said that his biological father Leslie Lynch King, Sr. had a history of hitting his mother Dorothy. James M. Cannon, a member of the Ford administration, wrote in a Ford biography that the Kings' separation and divorce were sparked when, a few days after Ford's birth, Leslie King threatened Dorothy with a butcher knife and threatened to kill her, Ford, and Ford's nursemaid. On February 1, 1916, Dorothy married Gerald Rudolff Ford, a salesman in a family-owned paint and varnish company. They then began calling her son Gerald Rudolff Ford, Jr. The future president was never formally adopted, however, and he did not legally change his name until December 3, 1935; he also used a more conventional spelling of his middle name (Rudolph). [1]

Q: Besides Gerald Ford, who was the only president whose last name at birth was different than the name by which he became known?

A: Bill Clinton. Clinton was born William Jefferson Blythe, III. His father, William Jefferson Blythe, Jr., was a traveling salesman who died in an automobile accident three months before Bill was born. In 1950, Bill's mother married Roger Clinton. Although he assumed use of his stepfather's surname, it was not until Billy (as he was known then) turned fourteen that he formally adopted the surname Clinton as a gesture toward his stepfather. Not withstanding that gesture, Clinton says he remembers his stepfather as a gambler and an alcoholic who regularly abused his mother and half-brother Roger Clinton, Jr., to the point where he intervened multiple times with the threat of violence to protect them.[2]

Q: Andrew Jackson's well-known nickname was Old Hickory. Whose nickname was "Young Hickory"?

A: James Polk.

Q: Which president was nicknamed "Old Rough and Ready"?

A: Zachary Taylor.

Q: What president was referred to by his friends as "Rud"?

A: Rutherford Hayes.

Q: Which president reversed his first and middle names?

A: Dwight David Eisenhower was born David Dwight Eisenhower.

Q: Who was the only president sworn in to office using his nickname?

A: Jimmy Carter.

Q: Which presidents have the same full name as their fathers?

A: John Adams, James Madison, John Tyler, James Buchanan, William McKinley, Theodore Roosevelt, Gerald Ford (born Leslie Lynch King, Jr.), Jimmy Carter and Barack Obama.

Q: Which president's first name was Stephen?

A: Grover Cleveland.

Q: Which president detested his nickname, calling it vulgar and "an outrageous impertinence"?

A: Theodore Roosevelt. [3]

Q: Who is the only president with two middle names?

A: George Herbert Walker Bush.

Q: Which presidents had the following middle names: Gamaliel, Rudolph and Birchard?

A: Warren Harding, Gerald Ford and Rutherford Hayes respectively.

Q: Who are the only presidents having the same last names who are unrelated?

A: Andrew Johnson and Lyndon Johnson.

Q. Which consecutive presidents have the same first names?

A. James Madison and James Monroe.

Q: Who is the only president whose last name has four syllables?

A: Dwight Eisenhower.

Q: Are there any presidents whose first and last names have more than two syllables?

A: Two. **Benjamin Harrison** and **Theodore Roosevelt**.

Q: Are there any presidents whose first and last names are one syllable only?

A: Three. **James Polk, George H.W. Bush** and **George W. Bush.**

Q: Who is the only president whose last name begins and ends with a vowel?

A: **Barack Obama.**

Q: Who is the only president whose first name begins with a vowel other than A?

A: **Ulysses Grant.**

Q: Only one president's name (including middle name) contains a letter that is found in no other president's names. Which president and which letter?

A: **John Quincy Adams**—the letter Q.

Q: Who are the only presidents whose names (including middle names) contain the letter X?

A: **Richard Nixon** and **James Knox Polk.**

Q: Who are the only presidents whose names (including middle names) contain the letter Z?

A: **Zachary Taylor** and **John Fitzgerald Kennedy.**

Q: Only one president has two consecutive vowels in his first name. Who is he?

A: Woodrow Wilson.

Q: Only one president has two consecutive consonants in his first name other than L. Who is he?

A: Ulysses Grant.

Q: Only one president has a capital letter in his name which is not the initial letter. Who is he?

A: William McKinley.

Q: What did the S in Harry S Truman stand for?

A: Nothing. His parents chose "S" as his "middle name" in an attempt to please both of Harry's grandfathers, Anderson Shipp (or Shippe) Truman and Solomon Young. Having an initial which does not actually stand for anything is a common practice among the Scots-Irish.

Q: Only two presidents have their first, middle and last names are in alphabetical order (excluding Harry Truman who did not have a middle name). Who are they?

A: James Knox Polk and **Barack Hussein Obama.**

Q: Which presidents' names, if any, contain every vowel in their names?

A: One is **Rutherford Birchard Hayes**. A possible additional correct answer is Ulysses Simpson Grant. However, there is dispute as to whether his middle name was actually Simpson. His birth name was Hiram Ulysses Grant. Beyond this however, there is discrepancy among historians as to when and why his name came to be changed and even what his name was after it was changed. What is generally agreed upon is that his name changed just after or just before he enrolled at West Point. It is not agreed as to whether this was intentional on Grant's part or due to an error by the Congressman who nominated him for West Point. It is also not agreed whether his name became Ulysses S. Grant (with the S standing for nothing) or whether it stood for Simpson, which was his mother's maiden name. Grant's own memoirs are silent on this issue. [4]

Q: Which presidents, if any, have repeating letters in both their first and last names?

A: Millard Fillmore and **William Harrison.**

Q: Which president's surname is most frequently thought of as a first name?

A: Chester Arthur.

Q: Which two letters of the alphabet appear, with respect to one or both letters, in the first or last names of every president but four, with both letters appearing in the in the first or last names more than half of the presidents.

A: N and O. The only four presidents who do not have either of these letters in their first or last names are James Garfield, Chester Arthur, William Taft and Jimmy Carter.

Q: Who is the only president whose first name contains, in consecutive, non-rearranged order, the last name of another president?

A: Rutherford Hayes (Gerald Ford)

Q: Which presidents have identical initials for their first and last names?

A: Woodrow Wilson, Calvin Coolidge, Herbert Hoover and **Ronald Reagan.**

Q: Which presidents, if any, have names for which the last letters of their first and last names are identical?

A: Martin Van Buren and **Gerald Ford.**

Q: Which three presidents used their middle names instead of their first names while president?

A: Stephen Grover Cleveland, John Calvin Coolidge, and **Thomas Woodrow Wilson.**

Q: Of the first seventeen presidents, who are the only three with middle names?

A: John Quincy Adams, James Knox Polk and **William Henry Harrison.** Adams is therefore also the answer to another question: Who was the first president to have a middle name?

Q: Who are the only presidents whose middle names were also the last names of presidents?

A: Ronald Wilson Reagan and **William Jefferson Clinton.**

Q: Putting aside Harry Truman, who was the last president who had no middle name?

A: Theodore Roosevelt.

Q: What do these three presidents—and only these three Presidents—have in common: Pierce, Grant, and Ford?

A: They are the only presidents whose last names are also verbs in

American english. Ford can be a verb meaning to cross a shallow body of water by wading. In Great Britain, "hoover" means to clean with a vacuum.

Q: Which eight presidents' names end with the same three letters in order?

A: Thomas Jefferson, James Madison, Andrew Jackson, William Henry Harrison, Andrew Johnson, Benjamin Harrison, Woodrow Wilson and **Lyndon Johnson.**

Q: True or false: There has been no president since Theodore Roosevelt (president from 1901-1909) who has had a county named after him?

A: True. This means that no counties have been named after presidents such as Woodrow Wilson, Franklin Roosevelt, Harry Truman, Dwight Eisenhower or John Kennedy.

Q: There are only two presidents before Theodore Roosevelt who do not have counties named after them. Who are they?

A: Benjamin Harrison and **Andrew Johnson.** This is somewhat of an ignominious distinction since even William Henry Harrison (who served one month) has four counties named after him and James Garfield (who served less than seven months) has six counties named after him!

Q: True or false: Besides George Washington, no New England States have counties named for presidents.

A: True.

Q: Which president after the second most counties named for him after George Washington (who has thirty-one)?

A: Thomas Jefferson, with twenty-four.

Q: Only one county in the United States is named after the first name of a president. Which one?

A: Millard County, Utah is named in honor of Millard Fillmore. The complete list of counties named after presidents, in descending order, is as follows (Louisiana, which has parishes, is counted as having counties for purposes of this list):

1. **George Washington** (31): AL, AR, CO, FL, GA, ID, IL, IN, IO, KS, KY, LA, ME, MD, MN, MS, MO, NE, NY, NC, OH, OK, OR, PA, RI, TN, TX, UT, VT, VI, WI

2. **Thomas Jefferson** (24): AL, AR. FL, GA, ID, IL, IN, IO, KS, KY, LA, MS, MO, NE, NY, OR, OH, OK, PA, TN, TX, WA, WV, WI. Also Jefferson County, Colorado is named for the Territory of Jefferson, which in turn is named for Thomas Jefferson.

3. **Andrew Jackson** (21): AL, AR, CO, FL, IL, IN, IO, KS, KY, LA, MI, MS, MO, NC, OH, OR, SD, TN, TX, WV, WI

4. **James Madison** (19): AL, AR, FL, GA, ID, IL, IN, IO, KY, LA. MS, MO, NY, NC, OH, TN, TX, VA.

5. **Abraham Lincoln** (17): AR, CO, ID, KS, LA, MN, MS, MO, NE, NM, NV, OK, OR, WA, WV, WI.WY

6. **James Monroe** (17): AL, AR, FL, GA, IL, IN, IO, KY, MI, MS, MO, NY, OH, PA, TN, WV, WI

7. **Ulysses Grant** (12): AR, KS, LA, MN, NE, NM, ND, OK, OR, SD, WA, WV

8. **James Polk** (11): AR, FL, GA, IA, MN, MO, NE, OR, TN, TX, WI

9   **James Garfield** (6): CO, MN, NE, OK, UT, WA

10. **John Adams** (6): ID, MS, NE, OH, PA, WA

11. **William Henry Harrison** (4): IN, IO, MS, OH

12. **Franklin Pierce** (4): GA, NE, WA, WI

13. **Zachary Taylor** (4): FL, GA, IO, KY

14. **Martin Van Buren** (4): AR, IO, MI, TN

15. **John Quincy Adams** (4): IL, IO, IN, WI. Since John Quincy Adams is named for his father, these counties can also be considered to be named for John Adams. Also, sources differ as to whether Adams County, Iowa is named for the son or the father, although the original county seat was Quincy.

16. **James Buchanan** (3): IO, MO, VA

17. **Millard Fillmore** (3): MN, NE, UT (Millard County)

18. **Grover Cleveland** (2) AR, OK

19. **Theodore Roosevelt** (2): MN,NM

20. **John Tyler** (2): TX, WV

21. **Chester Arthur** (1): NE

22. **Warren Harding** (1): NM

23. **Rutherford Hayes** (1): NE

24. **William McKinley** (1): NM

Note that some states have counties having the same name as presidents which were not necessarily named after presidents. [5]

Q: Who was the relatively unpopular vice president under Martin Van Buren who has five counties named after him?

A: Richard Mentor Johnson, vice president from 1837-1841 under Martin Van Buren. The counties are located in Illinois, Iowa, Kentucky, Missouri and Nebraska. What makes this particularly odd is that this vice president's term was unremarkable and he was considered to have so little influence with his president that he was not nominated to run as vice president when his president ran a second time.

The vice president with the most counties named after him is John C. Calhoun with eleven, mostly in the Deep South: Alabama, Arkansas, Florida, Georgia, Illinois, Iowa, Michigan, Mississippi, South Carolina, Texas, and West Virginia. He was vice president under John Quincy Adams and Andrew Jackson, the only vice president to serve under two different presidents.[6]

Q: Which four states have capitals named after presidents?

A: Mississippi (Jackson), Missouri (Jefferson City), Nebraska (Lincoln) and Wisconsin (Madison).

Q: What is the highest number of consecutive presidents whose last names are in alphabetical order?

A: Five. Grover Cleveland, William McKinley, Theodore Roosevelt, William Howard Taft and Woodrow Wilson.

Q: Between (but excluding) Herbert Hoover and Barack Obama, every president but two has a United States military vessel (U.S.S.—) named after them which has either been built or is in construction as of 2014. Which two?

A: Richard Nixon and **George W. Bush.**[7]

Q. Which two consecutive presidents have the same initials?

A. James Madison and **James Monroe.**

SECRET SERVICE CODE NAMES

The United States Secret Service uses code names for U.S. presidents, first ladies, and other prominent persons and locations.

This was originally for security purposes and dates to a time when sensitive electronic communications were not routinely encrypted. Today, the names simply serve for purposes of brevity, clarity, and tradition. Therefore, the idea of secret code names is something of a misnomer these days. "There's nothing Top Secret about them," Secret Service spokesman Eric Zahren said. "It has no operational security significance anymore because of encrypted communication capabilities." Nowadays, code names are more about ease in radio communication when tracking the subjects' movements.

The Secret Service does not choose code names however. The White House Communications Agency assigns them. Good code names are unambiguous words that can be easily pronounced and readily understood by those who transmit and receive voice messages by radio or telephone regardless of their native language. However, the subjects do have some say in the names they will be known by, and some have been given more leeway than others. Which is not always a good thing. Al Gore's oldest daughter, Karenna, was 19 when her father became vice president in 1993. In 1997, she wrote: "Ever since, four years ago, when I was put on the spot and told 'two syllables' and 'It has to start with an s,' I have been cringing in the back seat when identified as 'Smurfette'."

When John Kerry was running for president, his daughter Vanessa joked that if her father beat George W. Bush she wanted her Secret Service code name to be "the hot one."

Traditionally, all family members' code names start with the same letter.

Code names provide never-ending fodder for comics and politicians looking for a laugh. As vice president, Gore repeatedly told crowds that he is so boring, his code name is . . . Al Gore.

During the 2008 campaign, Jay Leno mocked some of Sarah Palin's foot-in-mouth moments by saying: "It's gotten so bad her

Secret Service code name is now 'Joe Biden.'" (Palin's code name actually was "Denali.") And Conan O'Brien said about Barack Obama: "They say that Barack Obama has been successful in politics because he's a black man who doesn't make white people feel threatened. Yeah, which explains Obama's Secret Service code name: Al Roker."

In the 2012 election, Mitt and Ann Romney had the names Javelin and Jockey respectively. When a presidential candidate loses an election, the secret service detail is lost almost immediately. The same night that Romney lost the 2012 election, a quiet call went out on the radio channel used by his Secret Service agents: "Javelin, Jockey details, all posts, discontinue." One of the indignities involved in losing a presidential race is the sudden emptiness of the entourage. The Secret Service detail guarding Governor Romney since February 1 stood down quickly. He had ridden in a 15-car motorcade to the Intercontinental Hotel in Boston for his concession speech. He rode in a single-car motorcade back across the Charles River to Belmont. His son Tagg did the driving.

Over the years, some code names have seemed fairly random while others seemed tailor-made for their subjects.

The first President to have a Secret Service code name was Harry Truman and his was "General."

Q: Match the Secret Service code name with the president and first lady

1. Dwight and Mamie Eisenhower
2. John and Jacqueline Kennedy
3. Lyndon and Lady Bird Johnson
4. Richard and Pat Nixon
5. Gerald and Betty Ford
6. Jimmy and Rosalynn Carter
7. Ronald and Nancy Reagan

a. Volunteer and Victoria
b. Deacon and Dancer
c. Searchlight and Starlight
d. Timberwolf and Tranquility
e. Renegade and Renaissance
f. Scorecard and Springtime
g. Lancer and Lace

8. George and Barbara Bush

9. Bill and Hillary Clinton

10. George and Laura Bush

11. Barack and Michelle Obama

h. Rawhide and Rainbow

i. Tumbler or Trailblazer and Tempo

j. Eagle and Evergreen

k. Passkey and Pinafore [8]

Answers:
1. f; 2. g; 3. a; 4. c; 5. k; 6. b; 7. h; 8. d; 9. j; 10. i; 11. e.

CHAPTER FIFTEEN NOTES:

1) Ford, Gerald R. *A Time to Heal: The Autobiography of Gerald R. Ford*. Harper & Row (1979).
   Funk, Josh (December 27, 2006). *"Nebraska-born Ford Left State as Infant."* Associated Press
   http://www.foxnews.com/wires/2006Dec27/0,4670,FordNebraska,00.html
   Cannon, James. "Gerald R. Ford." *Character Above All*. Public Broadcasting System. http://www.pbs.org/newshour/character/essays/ford.html.
2) "Biography of William J. Clinton." The White House.
   http://www.whitehouse.gov/about/presidents/williamjclinton/
   Clinton, Bill. *My Life*. Random House, Inc. (2004)
   Maraniss, David. *First In His Class: A Biography Of Bill Clinton*. Touchstone (1996)
3) http://www.public.navy.mil/airfor/cvn71/Pages/THENAMESAKE.aspx
4) McFeely, William S. *Grant: A Biography*. Norton (1981)
   http://www.ohiohistorycentral.org/entry.php?rec=155
   http://civilwar.bluegrass.net/OfficersAndEnlistedMen/hiramulyssesgrant.html
5) http://en.wikipedia.org/wiki/List_of_U.S._counties_named_after_U.S._Presidents
6) http://millercenter.org/academic/americanpresident/vanburen/essays/vicepresident/1862
7) http://en.wikipedia.org/wiki/List_of_U.S._military_vessels_named_after_Presidents
8) http://www.cbsnews.com/stories/2008/09/16/earlyshow/main4452073.shtml
   http://www.chicagotribune.com/news/local/chi-secret-service-code-names-obama
   http://www.dailymail.co.uk/news/article-1085316
   http://www.washingtonpost.com/wpdyn/content/article/2007/06/16/AR2007061601079.html
   http://www.gq.com/news-politics/blogs/death-race/2012/11

The first American postage stamp was issued in 1847 and was a comparatively expensive 10-cent stamp bearing the image of—who else?—George Washington.

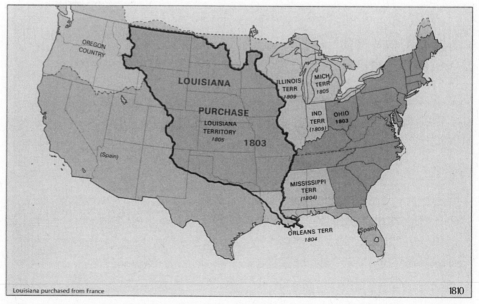

Louisiana purchased from France

1810

The Louisiana Purchase more than doubled the size of the United States. Which president actually negotiated the purchase?

"HERE WAS BURIED
THOMAS JEFFERSON
AUTHOR OF THE
DECLARATION
OF
AMERICAN INDEPENDENCE
OF THE
STATUTE OF VIRGINIA
FOR
RELIGIOUS FREEDOM
AND FATHER OF THE
UNIVERSITY OF VIRGINIA."

BORN APRIL 2, 1743, O.S.
DIED JULY 4, 1826.

Thomas Jefferson's epitaph made no mention of the fact that he was
President of the United States.

This President was the only one whose native language was not English. Who is the president and what was the language?

Amazingly, only five of our presidents were never photographed at some point in their lives. Here is an 1843 Daguerreotype of the sixth president, John Quincy Adams.

This image is of the first president who was the subject of an assassination attempt. Who was it?

The death of William Henry Harrison only one month into his term—the first president not to complete his term in office—raised important Constitutional questions about the laws of presidential succession. Here, vice president John Tyler is being handed the news of Harrison's death in 1841.

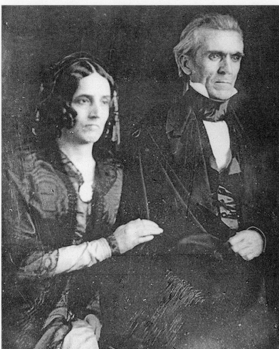

James Polk—"our least known consequential president"—was the only one who wore his hair in a 1980's style mullet. Here he is pictured with his beloved wife Sarah.

In their official portraits, every president but one is portrayed wearing either a suit or the equivalent of a suit given the era in which the president served. The exception is Zachary Taylor, who wore full military garb.

In a list of the sexiest presidents, it was said of Pierce: "There's not much to say about this obscure president, except that he's gorgeous."
Historian Michael Holt's book on Pierce begins with: "Franklin Pierce was arguably the most handsome man ever to serve as president of the United States." Here is a photo of "Handsome Frank," as he was known.

One of our presidents conducted a good portion of his campaign from the front porch of his house in Ohio shown here. Which president was it?

This is known as Grant's Tomb, in New York City. As the famous question goes: "Who is buried in Grant's Tomb?" The answer is not what you may think.

The only president to receive a patent was Abraham Lincoln. On May 22, 1849, he received Patent No. 6469 for a device to lift boats over shoals. The intent was to help larger ships navigate in shallow waters. The invention was never manufactured.

Presidents as a whole have had unusual misfortune when it comes to the premature death of their children. While mortality rates in the 1800's were much higher than they are now, the early deaths of presidential children has been unusual and tragic by any measure. President Lincoln's sons Edward, Willie and Tad died at ages 3, 11 and 18 respectively. His son Robert died in 1926, at age 82. Here he is pictured with his son Tad in 1864, when he was nine.

President Garfield is at center right, leaning after being shot. He is supported by Secretary of State James G. Blaine. To the left, the shooter, Charles Guiteau, is restrained by members of the crowd, one of whom is about to strike him with a cane.

President Chester Arthur, was known not only for his muttonchop sideburns but also as a dapper dresser. For his official portrait, he chose to wear a luxuriant knee-length coat with fur on the lapels and sleeves.

President Woodrow Wilson suffered a serious stroke that almost totally incapacitated him, leaving him paralyzed on his left side and blind in his left eye. For the remainder of his presidency, his wife Edith Wilson played a substantial role in secretly fulfilling his duties. Although she referred to her own role as a "stewardship" in her memoirs, others have called her "the Secret President," "the first woman to run the government" and "the first female president of the United States." Here she holds a document steady so he can sign it in June of 1920.

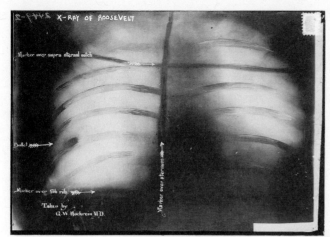

One president was shot in the chest while campaigning, and nevertheless proceeded to speak for ninety minutes with blood on his shirt. This is a x-ray showing the bullet. Which president was it?

One president's wife and mother died on the same day, February 14, 1884. In his diary he wrote a large X on the page and wrote "the light has gone out of my life." Which president was it?

This is Pauline, owned by the last president to have a cow grazing on the White House lawn. Here she is in front of the Navy Building, known today as the Eisenhower Executive Office Building. Who was this milk-loving president?

The president pictured here frequently wore dresses until he was five years old. In analyzing this photo, the Smithsonian stated: "[He] sits primly on a stool, his white skirt spread smoothly over his lap, his hands clasping a hat trimmed with a marabou feather. Shoulder-length hair and patent leather party shoes complete the ensemble. We find the look unsettling today, yet social convention [of the time] dictated that boys wore dresses until age six or seven, also the time of their first haircut." Which President is pictured here?

This 1938 photo shows the only occasion that Adolf Hitler ever met with an American president. Which one?

President Lyndon Johnson, when trying to obtain support from members of Congress for particular pieces of legislation, would often subject them to "the Treatment." As one writer said: "The Treatment could last ten minutes or four hours. ... Its tone could be supplication, accusation, cajolery, exuberance, scorn, tears, complaint and the hint of threat. 'The Treatment' [was] an almost hypnotic experience and rendered the target stunned and helpless." Here he is giving "the Treatment" to Senator Richard Russell.

Harry Truman was the first president, and in fact the first American, to have a Medicare card. The Social Security Act of 1965 included the establishing of the Medicare program. At the bill-signing ceremony photographed here, President Lyndon Johnson enrolled Truman as the first Medicare beneficiary and presented him with the first Medicare card, and Truman's wife Bess, the second. Lady Bird Johnson stands behind the president and Bess Truman stands behind former President Truman.

Three of our presidents were actually wounded in war. One of them, pictured on the far right in this photo, was honored by the military for heroism in combat. Which president was it?

Richard Nixon, a reasonably accomplished piano player also composed pieces of his own. A 1961 clip of Nixon playing one of his own pieces on *The Jack Paar Show* can be seen on You Tube. Here he is playing in Beverly Hills, California in 1962.

Gerald Ford was the only president to become an Eagle Scout. Scouting was so important to him that his family asked that Scouts participate in his funeral.

Ronald Reagan was credited with saving 77 lives during the seven summers he worked as a lifeguard at Lowell Park, near Dixon, Illinois, from 1926-1932. Here he is pictured in 1927.

George H. W. Bush played in the first two baseball college World Series. In the 1948 Series, he got to meet Babe Ruth, who was presenting a manuscript of his autobiography, which he was giving to Yale University. Of the meeting, Bush said, "I was the captain of the ball club, so I got to receive him there. He was dying. He was hoarse and could hardly talk." Ruth did in fact die later that year.

There have been only three occasions when five former presidents were alive at the same time. Although George H.W. Bush was president when this picture was taken at the dedication of the Ronald Reagan Presidential Library in 1991, all five were still alive in 1993 when Bill Clinton became president. When were the other two occasions?

Barack Obama was the only president to be sworn in using two Bibles, one of which was Martin Luther King's traveling Bible and the other was used by Abraham Lincoln during his first inauguration. Here he is being sworn in for his second term on January 21, 2013.

CHAPTER 16

Pardons

Q: Who was the only president since John Adams who pardoned, commuted, or rescinded the convictions of less than 100 people?

A: George H. W. Bush—77 people. [1]

Q: Which president pardoned, commuted or rescinded the convictions of the most people?

A: Franklin D. Roosevelt—3,687 people.

LIST OF PRESIDENTIAL PARDONS, COMMUTATIONS
AND CONVICTION RESCISSIONS:

President	Acts of clemency
Franklin Roosevelt	3,687

Notables: Roy Olmstead. Roy Olmstead, nicknamed the "King of the Puget Sound Bootleggers," was a lieutenant on the Seattle police force when he was caught bootlegging whiskey and was fired from the police. He then turned himself into a professional bootlegger and soon was making more in one week then he would have earned in twenty years as a policeman. He was eventually caught by evidence obtained through wiretapping in 1924 and sentenced to four years hard labor. He appealed on the grounds that the wiretapping evidence used against him constituted a violation of his constitutional rights to privacy and against self-incrimination. However, in 1928, the U.S. Supreme Court ruled five to four to uphold the conviction in the landmark case of *Olmstead v. United States*. Justice Louis Brandeis asserted that there was a right to privacy embedded in the American Constitution. On Christmas day, 1935, he was pardoned by Roosevelt but by then he had served his sentence. [1] The *Olmstead* decision was overturned in the case of *Katz v. United States* in 1935.

Woodrow Wilson   2,480

Notables: George Burdick was a New York newspaper editor, who in 1913 had refused to testify in federal court regarding the sources used in his article concerning the collection of customs duties. He pled the 5th Amendment. President Wilson granted him a full pardon for any offenses he may have committed, but Burdick refused it. He continued to plead the 5th Amendment, for which he was sentenced by a federal judge for contempt. The case went up to the Supreme Court which in 1915 held that a pardon must be accepted in order to be valid. A pardon carries an 'imputation of guilt,' and accepting a pardon is 'an admission of guilt.' [2]

Frederick Krafft was twice nominated by the Socialist Party of America as its candidate for Governor of New Jersey and twice a candidate for United States Congress. He was convicted for alleged violations of the Espionage Act of 1917. He was the only person convicted under this law to receive a full executive pardon.

Harry Truman   2,044

Notables: Oscar Collazo. Collazo was one of two Puerto Ricans who attempted to assassinate Truman. Collazo and Torresola Griselio were strong supporters of Puerto Rican independence. On November 1, 1950, with guns in hand, they attempted to enter the Blair House with the intention of assassinating the president, who was residing there while the White House was being renovated. During the attack, one White House police officer, Private Leslie Coffelt, was killed and multiple others were wounded. Torresola was killed by the mortally wounded Coffelt, and Collazo was shot in the chest and arrested.

In prison, Collazo was asked why he had targeted Truman, who was in favor of self-determination for Puerto Rico and who had appointed the first native-born Puerto Rican governor. Collazo replied that he had nothing against Truman, saying that he was "a symbol of the system. You don't attack the man, you attack the system." Collazo was sentenced to death, but President Truman commuted his sentence to life imprisonment. Collazo's sentence was commuted to time served by President Jimmy Carter on September 6, 1979, after spending 29 years in jail. Collazo is the only person who assassinated or attempted to assassinate a president who has received a pardon.[3]

Calvin Coolidge   1,545

Herbert Hoover   1,385

Notables: Warren McCray was the Governor of Indiana from 1921 to 1924. He came into conflict with the growing influence of the Indiana Ku Klux Klan after vetoing legislation they supported. A case was brought against him in federal court alleging that he had fraudulently solicited private loans. He was convicted of mail fraud, resigned from office and served three years in federal prison. He was paroled in 1927 and pardoned by Hoover in 1930 as a result of the Klan's involvement in his prosecution.[4]

Ulysses Grant   1,332

Notables: All but 500 top Confederate leaders were pardoned when President Grant signed the Amnesty Act of 1872.

Lyndon Johnson   1,184

Dwight Eisenhower   1,157

Grover Cleveland   1,107 (in two terms combined)

Theodore Roosevelt   981

Richard Nixon   926

Notables: Jimmy Hoffa. In 1964, Hoffa was convicted of attempted bribery of a grand juror and was sentenced to eight years in prison. He also received a five-year sentence for fraud that same year that was to run consecutively with the bribery sentence. Hoffa spent the next three years unsuccessfully appealing his 1964 convictions. He did not begin serving his sentence until March 1967 at the Lewisburg Federal Penitentiary in Pennsylvania.

On December 23, 1971, less than five years into his thirteen-year sentence, Hoffa was released from the Lewisburg, Pennsylvania prison, when President Richard Nixon commuted his sentence to time served. Hoffa had served nearly 58 months, or just over one-third of his original sentence.

William McKinley   918

Rutherford B. Hayes   893

Warren Harding   800

Notables: Eugene V. Debs, who was the candidate of the Socialist Party of America for President of the United States on several occasions. He was convicted of sedition under the Espionage Act of 1917 but his sentence was commuted.

William Howard Taft   758

Andrew Johnson   654

Notables: All soldiers who were Confederates in the Civil War. Samuel Arnold, Dr. Samuel Mudd and Edmund Spangler, all of whom were charged with conspiring to murder Lincoln.

Robert E. Lee. On December 25, 1868, Johnson gave an unconditional pardon to those who "directly or indirectly" rebelled against the United States. Although this did not mention Lee by name, he was covered by it. However full citizenship was not restored until Gerald Ford did so posthumously in 1975. See Gerald Ford below for more.

John F. Kennedy   575

Notables: First-time offenders convicted of crimes under the Narcotics Control Act of 1956.

Jimmy Carter   556

Notables: Oscar Collazo—Attempted assassination of President Harry S. Truman. See Harry Truman above.

G. Gordon Liddy—Watergate figure, convicted for twenty years, commuted after serving four and one half years for conspiracy, burglary and illegal wiretapping.

Peter Yarrow—Singer-songwriter of Peter, Paul and Mary. In 1970, Yarrow was convicted of, and served three months in prison for, taking "improper liberties" with a fourteen-year-old female fan. He later apologized for the incident: "In that time, it was common practice, unfortunately — the whole groupie thing."

Vietnam draft dodgers—Unconditional amnesty issued in the form of a pardon.

Jefferson Davis—President of the Confederate States of America.

Patty Hearst—Hearst was convicted of bank robbery on March 20, 1976. She was sentenced to 35 years' imprisonment, but her sentence was later shortened to seven years. Her prison term was eventually commuted by President Carter, and Hearst was released from prison on February 1, 1979, having served twenty-two months. She was granted a full pardon by President Bill Clinton on January 20, 2001.

Bill Clinton   459

Notables: Roger Clinton, Jr.—Clinton's brother was pardoned after serving a year in federal prison for cocaine possession.

Patty Hearst—See Jimmy Carter above.

Marc Rich, Pincus Green—Business partners with Clinton. They were indicted on charges of tax evasion and illegal trading with Iran and pardoned at the request of three Republicans, including Lewis Libby.

Dan Rostenkowski—Democrat from Illinois. He served his entire seventeen-month sentence for mail fraud, and was then pardoned.

Fife Symington III—The Republican Governor of Arizona was convicted of bank fraud. He was pardoned by Clinton whom Symington had once saved from a rip current off of Cape Cod, Massachusetts near the end of his presidency in January 2001.

Susan McDougal—She was a partner with Clinton and Hillary Rodham Clinton in the failed Whitewater deal. Guilty of contempt of court, she served her entire eighteen-month sentence and was then pardoned.

Henry Cisneros—Clinton's Secretary of Housing and Urban Development. He pleaded guilty to a misdemeanor count for lying to the FBI, and was fined $10,000.

Henry O. Flipper—The first black West Point cadet was found guilty of "conduct unbecoming an officer" in 1882. In 1881,

Lieutenant Flipper's commanding officer accused him of "embezzling funds and of conduct unbecoming an officer and a gentleman." Some suspected that he had been framed. As a result of these charges, he was court-martialed. He was acquitted of the embezzlement charge but was found guilty, by general court martial, of conduct unbecoming an officer. On June 30, 1882, he was dismissed from the Army as required by this conviction.

In 1976, Flipper's descendants and supporters applied to the Army Board for the Correction of Military Records on his behalf. The Board, after stating that it did not have the authority to overturn his court-martial conviction, concluded that the conviction and punishment were "unduly harsh and unjust" and recommended that Lieutenant Flipper's dismissal commuted to a good conduct discharge. He was eventually pardoned by Clinton in 1999. A bust of Flipper is now at West Point and an annual Henry O. Flipper Award is awarded to graduating cadets at the Academy who exhibit "leadership, self-discipline, and perseverance in the face of unusual difficulties."[5]

John Deutch—Director of Central Intelligence, former Provost and University Professor at MIT. Deutch had admitted to mishandling sensitive data while heading the CIA, and was investigated by the Defense Department for similar incidents. Defense Department documents alleged that Deutch used unsecured computers at home and his America Online account to access classified defense information in the early to mid-1990s when he held high-ranking jobs at the Pentagon. [6]

Rick Hendrick—NASCAR team owner. In 1997, Hendrick pled guilty to mail fraud. In the 1980s, Honda automobiles were in high demand and Honda executives allegedly solicited bribes from dealers for larger product disbursements. Hendrick admitted to giving hundreds of thousands of dollars, BMW automobiles, and houses to American Honda Motor Company executives. Hendrick was sentenced in December 1997 to a $250,000 fine, and twelve months home confinement. In December 2000, Hendrick received a full pardon from Clinton. [7]

James Monroe 419

Gerald Ford 409

Notables: Richard Nixon—He was granted a full and unconditional pardon just before he could be indicted.

Iva Toguri D'Aquino—"Tokyo Rose." She was the only U.S. citizen convicted of treason to be pardoned.

Vietnam draft dodgers—Ford offered conditional amnesty to over 50,000 draft dodgers.

Robert E. Lee—Lee had no rights of citizenship between the Civil War and 1975. Why? On May 29, 1865, less than two months after the end of the Civil War, President Andrew Johnson issued a Proclamation of Amnesty and Pardon to persons who had participated in the rebellion against the United States. There were fourteen excepted classes, though, and members of those classes had to make special application to the president. Lee wrote an amnesty application to President Johnson on June 13, 1865:

> *Being excluded from the provisions of amnesty & pardon contained in the proclamation of the 29th Ulto; I hereby apply for the benefits, & full restoration of all rights & privileges extended to those included in its terms. I graduated at the Mil. Academy at West Point in June 1829, resigned from the U.S. Army April '61, was a General in the Confederate Army, & included in the surrender of the Army of N. Va. 9 April '65.*

This application was followed up by an amnesty oath which Lee signed on October 2, 1865. However, Lee's amnesty oath was given to Secretary of State William H. Seward who gave it to a friend as a souvenir. The application never made its way to President Johnson.

On December 25, 1868, President Johnson issued a second broader pardon "unconditionally, and without reservation, to all and every person who directly or indirectly participated in the late insurrection or rebellion, a full pardon and amnesty for the offense of treason against the United States, or of adhering to their enemies during the late civil war, with restoration of all rights, privileges, and immunities under the Constitution and the laws which have been made in pursuance thereof." This did not require an application to the president and thus Lee's pardon was in place.

However, Lee was still not considered a citizen of the United States and until 1970, this was not even known. In 1970, an archivist at the National Archives discovered Lee's original Amnesty Oath among State Department records. In 1975, President Ford, posthumously reinstated Lee as a United States citizen. He acknowledged the discovery of Lee's Oath of Allegiance in the National Archives and remarked: "General Lee's character has been an example to succeeding generations, making the restoration of his citizenship an event in which every American can take pride." [8]

Ronald Reagan   406

Notables: W. Mark Felt and Edward S. Miller—FBI officials convicted of authorizing illegal break-ins. Felt later in life admitted to being *Deep Throat*, the informant during the Watergate affair.

George Steinbrenner—He was convicted of illegal campaign contributions to Richard Nixon and obstruction of justice.

Andrew Jackson   386

Notables: George Wilson—convicted of robbing the United States mails. Strangely, Wilson refused to accept the pardon. The case went before the Supreme Court, and in *United States v. Wilson* (1833) the court stated: "A pardon is a deed, to the validity of which delivery is essential, and delivery is not complete without acceptance. It may then be rejected by the person to whom it is tendered; and if it is rejected, we have discovered no power in this court to force it upon him." As such, Wilson was not released from prison early. As we saw earlier, the Court reaffirmed this principle 82 years later with respect to George Burdick, who was pardoned by President Wilson.

Chester Arthur   337

Abraham Lincoln   343

Notables: Pardoned 264 of 303 Dakota Indians who attacked White settlers in the Great Sioux Uprising of 1862.

James Polk   268

Notables: John C. Frémont—convicted by court martial of mutiny. Frémont later became the 1856 Republican candidate for the presidency of the United States.

John Tyler   209

George W. Bush   200

Notables: Lewis "Scooter" Libby—The Assistant to President Bush and Chief of Staff to Dick Cheney was convicted of perjury in connection with the CIA leak scandal involving members of Bush's administration who 'outed' CIA agent Valerie Plame. Libby received commutation, not a full pardon.

Charles Winters—Posthumous pardon for smuggling three B-17 Flying Fortress heavy bombers to Israel in the late 1940s. Winters was not Jewish but he was said to have decided to help supply the Israeli forces as a favor to his Jewish friends. He received no monetary compensation for the work. His efforts gained him the nickname "The Godfather of the Israeli Airforce." [9]

James Madison   196

Notables: Jean Lafitte and Pierre Lafitte and the Baratarian Pirates were pardoned on February 6, 1815 due to their assistance to America during the War of 1812.

John Quincy Adams   183

Millard Fillmore   170

Martin Van Buren   168

James Buchanan   150

Notables: Brigham Young. Members of The Church of Jesus Christ of Latter-Day Saints began settling in what is now Utah in the summer of 1847. The U.S. Congress created the Utah Territory as part of the Compromise of 1850. President Millard Fillmore selected Brigham Young, President of the LDS Church, as the first Governor of the Territory. However, many politicians, such as President Buchanan, were alarmed by the semi-theocratic dominance of the Utah Territory under Young. This resulted in an armed confrontation between LDS settlers and armed forces of the United States government which lasted from May 1857 until July 1858, now known as the Utah War. In November, 1857, Young was indicted for treason. However, as part of the resolution, Young was pardoned and Utah's governorship was transferred from Church President Young to non-Mormon Alfred Cumming. [10]

Franklin Pierce   142

Thomas Jefferson   119

Notables: Jefferson pardoned those found guilty of violating the Sedition Act of 1798, which had been designed to prevent criticism of the federal government.

George H.W. Bush   77

Notables: Armand Hammer—CEO of the Occidental Petroleum Company. He contributed $110,000 to the Republican National Committee just prior to his pardon. He was pardoned for illegally contributing $54,000 to Richard Nixon's presidential campaign in 1972.

Caspar Weinberger—Republican Secretary of Defense under President Ronald Reagan for his role in the Iran-Contra Affair. Others pardoned by Bush for their roles in the Iran-Contra Affair include Robert C. McFarlane, Elliott Abrams and Duane Clarridge.

Zachary Taylor   38

John Adams   21

Notables: John Scotchlar, for stealing rigging from the new USS Constitution.

George Washington   16

William Henry Harrison 0

James Garfield   0

CHAPTER SIXTEEN NOTES:

1) http://www.pbs.org/kenburns/prohibition/media_detail/2082733861-olmstead
   Olmstead v. United States, 277 U.S. 438 (1928)
2) http://www.justice.gov/pardon/actions_administration.htm
3) McCullough, David. *Truman*. Simon and Schuster (1992).
   http://www.trumanlibrary.org/trivia/assassin.htm
   http://www.presidency.ucsb.edu/ws/index.php
4) http://downfalldictionary.blogspot.com/2010/05/warren-t-mccray-signing-off.html
5) http://www.history.army.mil/html/topics/afam/flipper.html
   Eppinga, Jane, *Henry Ossian Flipper, West Point's First Black Graduate* (Republic of Texas Press, 1996).
6) http://www.apfn.org/apfn/deutch.htm
7) http://www.cbc.ca/sports/story/2000/12/22/hendrick001222.html
8) http://www.archives.gov/publications/prologue/2005/spring/piece-lee.html

http://www.ford.utexas.edu/library/speeches/750473.htm
http://www.freerepublic.com/focus/f-news/1503932/posts
9) http://www.jta.org/news/article/2008/12/23/1001785/pardon-granted-to-man-who-flew-planes-to-israel
10) http://www.pbs.org/weta/thewest/people/s_z/young.htm

CHAPTER 17

Pets

Q: Who was the last president to have a cow grazing on the White House lawn?

A: William Howard Taft. Taft liked milk so much that he brought his own cow to the White House. The cows name was Mooly Wooly. Mooly was replaced by another cow called Pauline Wayne. Pauline Wayne was the last cow to graze on the White House lawn.

Q: Which president had a dog that "wrote" a book, "as dictated to" the first lady?

A: George H.W. Bush. The book was *Millie's Book: As Dictated to Barbara Bush*, published in 1990.

Q: Which president had a pet that was the puppy of one of the Soviet space dogs?

A: John F. Kennedy. Soviet Premier Kruschev gave Kennedy a dog named Pushinka who was the offspring of the Russian space dog Strelka. Pushinka had four puppies of her own who JFK called "pupniks."

Q: Who delivered the "Checkers speech", why, and why is it so named?

A: It was delivered by Richard Nixon in the midst of the 1952 campaign in which he was running on the Republican ticket as Dwight Eisenhower's running mate. He had been accused of accepting illegal gifts, and specifically an $18,000 campaign contribution that he allegedly, used for personal expenses. On September 23, 1952, he appeared on live television to deny the allegations. The speech lasted about 30 minutes and was heard by 60 million Americans. After outlining his personal financial circumstances in rather painstaking detail, including all of his assets and liabilities, he stated:

"Well, that's about it. That's what we have. And that's what we owe. It isn't very much. But Pat and I have the satisfaction that every dime that we've got is honestly ours. I should say this, that Pat doesn't have a mink coat. But she does have a respectable Republican cloth coat, and I always tell her she'd look good in anything.

One other thing I probably should tell you, because if I don't they'll probably be saying this about me, too. We did get something, a gift, after the election. A man down in Texas heard Pat on the radio mention the fact that our two youngsters would like to have a dog. And believe it or not, the day before we left on this campaign trip, we got a message from Union Station in Baltimore, saying they had a package for us. We went down to get it. You know what it was? It was a little cocker spaniel dog in a crate that he'd sent all the way from Texas, black and white, spotted. And our little girl Tricia, the six year old, named it 'Checkers.' And you know, the kids, like all kids, love the dog, and I just want to say this, right now, that regardless of what they say about it, we're gonna keep it."

The speech was a success (at least with the public) as millions of supportive letters, telegrams, postcards came in to Republican National Committee headquarters. Many letters included contributions to help pay for the $75,000 cost of the broadcast. Eisenhower and Nixon handily won the 1952 election. The media reaction was more mixed.[1]

Q: Which two 20th-century presidents owned more pets than any others?

A: Calvin Coolidge and Theodore Roosevelt.

Q: Match the president with the well-known dog(s) he owned.

1.	Warren Harding	a.	Bo
2.	Herbert Hoover	b.	Buddy
3.	Franklin Roosevelt	c.	Laddie Boy
4.	Lyndon Johnson	d.	King Tut
5.	Gerald Ford	e.	Liberty
6.	Ronald Reagan	f.	Him and Her
7.	Bill Clinton	g.	Falla
8.	George W. Bush	h.	Rex
9.	Barack Obama	i.	Barney

A: 1.c; 2.d; 3.g; 4.f; 5.e; 6.h; 7.b; 8.i; 9.a

A list of Presidents' pets follows:

President	Pet(s)
Barack Obama	• Bo–Portuguese Water Dog. Popularly known as the First Dog of the United States.
George W. Bush	• Spot "Spotty" Fetcher (1989-2004)–female English Springer Spaniel named after Scott Fletcher, a Texas Rangers baseball player; Puppy of Millie who belonged to George H.W. Bush; Euthanized after suffering a series of strokes.

	• Barney–Scottish Terrier. First Dog of the United States.
	• Miss Beazley (b. October 28, 2004)–Scottish Terrier;
	  Nicknamed "Beazley Weazley"; 2005 birthday gift
	  from George to his wife.
	• India "Willie"–cat (1990-2009)

Bill Clinton	• Socks–Chelsea's cat (1989-2009) • Buddy–Bill's chocolate Labrador Retriever (1997-2002). First Dog of the United States.
George H.W. Bush	• Millie–Springer Spaniel. First Dog of the United States. • Ranger–one of Millie's puppies
Ronald Reagan	• Lucky–Bouvier des Flandres • Rex–Cavalier King Charles Spaniel. First Dog of the United States. • Victory–Golden Retriever • Peggy–Irish Setter • Taca–Siberian Husky • Fuzzy–Belgian Sheepdog

Jimmy Carter	• Grits–Border Collie; Given to his daughter Amy by
	  her teacher, but quickly returned.
	• Lewis Brown–Afghan Hound
	• Misty Malarky Ying Yang, daughter Amy
	  Carter's pet–Siamese cat

Gerald Ford	• Liberty–Golden Retriever • Misty–(Liberty's puppy born in the White House) • Shan–Siamese cat
Richard Nixon	• Vicki–Poodle • Pasha–Terrier • King Timahoe–Irish Setter • Checkers–Cocker Spaniel (note: Checkers died while Nixon was Vice President, before becoming President)
Lyndon B. Johnson	• Him and Her–Beagles • Edgar–Beagle • Blanco–white Collie • Freckles–Beagle • Yuki–Mongrel • Hamsters and lovebirds

John F. Kennedy	• Gaullie–Poodle • Charlie–Welsh Terrier • Tom Kitten–cat • Robin–canary • Bluebell and Marybelle–parakeets • Macaroni–pony • Tex and Leprechaun–ponies • Debbie and Billie–hamsters • Pushinka–mutt (gift of Russian premier, puppy of Soviet space dog Strelka) • Shannon–Irish Cocker Spaniel • Wolf–(mutt, possibly part Wolfhound and Schnauzer) • Clipper–German Shepherd • Butterfly, White Tips, Blackie, and Streaker–(offspring of Pushinka and Charlie) • Zsa Zsa–a rabbit • Sardar–horse
Dwight D. Eisenhower	• Heidi–Weimaraner
Harry S. Truman	• Feller–Cocker Spaniel • Mike–Irish Setter
Franklin D. Roosevelt	• Fala–Scottish Terrier • Majora–German Shepherd • Meggie–Scottish Terrier • Winks–Llewellyn Setter • Tiny–Old English Sheepdog • President–Great Dane • Blaze–Bullmastiff
Herbert Hoover	• King Tut Belgian Shepherd • Pat–German Shepherd • Big Ben and Sonnie–Fox Terriers • Glen–Scotch Collie • Yukonan–Eskimo dog • Patrick–Irish Wolfhound • Eaglehurst Gillette–Setter • Weejie–Norwegian Elkhound • 2 crocodiles

Calvin Coolidge	• Rob Roy and Prudence Prim–White collies • Peter Pan–Terrier • Paul Pry–Airedale Terrier • Calamity Jane–Shetland Sheepdog • Tiny Tim and Blackberry–Chow Chows • Ruby Rouch–Collie • Boston Beans–Bulldog • King Cole–German shepherd • Palo Alto–Bird dog • Bessie–Collie • Rebecca and Horace–Raccoons • Ebeneezer–Donkcy • Nip and Tuck–Canaries • Enoch–Goose • Smoky–Bobcat • Tiger–cat • Tax Reduction and Budget Bureau–lion cubs • Billy–Pygmy hippo • A Wallaby • A Duiker (a very small antelope) • A black bear
Warren G. Harding	• Laddie Boy–Airedale Terrier • Old Boy–Bulldog
William Howard Taft	• Davie–Airedale Terrier • Old Ike–Ram • Puffins–Cat • Mountain Boy–Greyhound • Bruce–Bull Terrier • songbirds • sheep
Theodore Roosevelt	• Pete–Bull Terrier • Skip–Rat Terrier • Jack and Peter–Terriers • Blackjack–Manchester Terrier • Manchu–Pekingese • Rollo–Saint Bernard • Sailor Boy–Chesapeake Bay Retriever

	• Tom Quartz and Slippers–Cats • Emily Spinach–Garter snake • Algonquin–Pony • Maude–Pig • Josiah–Badger • Jonathan–Piebald rat • Dr. Johnson, Bishop Doane, Fighting Bob Evans, and • Father O'Grady–Guinea pigs • Baron Spreckle–Hen • Eli Yale–Macaw • Fedelity–Pony • Gem and Susan–Dogs • A one-legged rooster
William McKinley	• Washington Post–Yellow-headed Mexican parrot • Valeriano Weyler and Enrique DeLome–Angora kittens • Roosters
Benjamin Harrison	• Whiskers–Goat • Dash–Collie • Mr. Reciprocity and Mr. Protection–Opossums
Grover Cleveland	• Hector-Japanese Poodle • mockingbirds
Chester A. Arthur	• Three horses
James A. Garfield	• Kit–Horse • Veto–Dog
Rutherford B. Hayes	• Dot–Cocker Spaniel • Hector–Newfoundland • Duke–English Mastiff • Grim–Greyhound • Otis–Miniature Schnauzer • Juno and Shep–Hunting dogs • Jet–Dog • Piccolomini–Cat • Siam–First Siamese Cat in the United States • Miss Pussy–Siamese Cat

Ulysses S. Grant	• Butcher Boy, Cincinnatus (a gift from the citizens of • Cincinnati, Ohio), Egypt, Jeff Davis (his wartime • mount), Jennie, Julia, Mary and St. Louis–Horses • Billy Button and Reb–Ponies Faithful–Newfoundland Rosie–Dog
Andrew Johnson	• Fed white mice he found in his bedroom
Abraham Lincoln	• Nanny and Nanko–goats • Jack–Turkey • Fido–Dog • Jip–Dog • Horse • Rabbit
James Buchanan	• Lara–Newfoundland • Punch–Toy Terrier • Eagle
Franklin Pierce	• Seven miniature Oriental dogs • Two birds from Japan
Millard Fillmore	• Mason and Dixon–Ponies
Zachary Taylor	• Old Whitey–Horse
James K. Polk	• Horse
John Tyler	• Le Beau–Italian Greyhound • Johnny Ty–Canary • The General–Horse
William Henry Harrison	• Sukey–Cow • Goat
Martin Van Buren	• Briefly owned two tiger cubs

Andrew Jackson	• Pol–parrot (taught to swear) • Fighting cocks • Bolivia, Emily, Lady Nashville, Sam Patches and Truxton–Horses
John Quincy Adams	• American Alligator • Silkworms
James Monroe	• Spaniel
James Madison	• Macaw–Parrot
Thomas Jefferson	• Dick–Mockingbird • Buzzy and unknown–Briards (dogs) • 2 Bear Cubs • Caractacus–Horse
John Adams	• Juno, Mark, and Satan–Dogs • Cleopatra–Horse
George Washington	• Sweet Lips, Scentwell and Vulcan–American Staghounds • Drunkard, Taster, Tipler and Tipsy–Black and Tan • Coonhounds • Royal Gift–Donkey • Nelson–Horse [2]

CHAPTER SEVENTEEN NOTES:

1) http://www.americanrhetoric.com/speeches/richardnixoncheckers.html
   http://watergate.info/1952/09/23/nixon-checkers-speech.html
   Morris, Roger. *Richard Milhous Nixon: The Rise of an American Politician.*
   Henry Holt and Company (1990).
2) Choron, Sandra, *Planet Dog: A Doglopedia*, Houghton Mifflin Harcourt (2005)
   Ruth, Amy, *Herbert Hoover*, Twenty-First Century Books (2004)
   Smith, Sally Bedell, *Grace And Power*, Random House, Inc. (2006)
   Taraborrelli, J. Randy, *Jackie, Ethel, Joan: The Women of Camelot*, Warner Books (2000)
   http://www.jfklibrary.org/Historical+Resources/Archives/Reference+Desk/Pets.htm
   Lyndon B. Johnson Library and Museum President Johnson's Dogs Bryant,
   Traphes, *Dog Days at the White House: The Outrageous Memoirs of the Presidential*

Kennel Keeper, Macmillan Publishing (1975).
Bauer, Stephen, *At Ease in the White House: Social Life as Seen by a Presidential Military Aide*, Taylor Trade Publications (2004)
Ford Presidential Library and Museum, Ford Family White House and Pets
http://famouspets.freebase.com/view/base/famouspets/pets
http://www.reagan.utexas.edu/archives/reference/pets.html
http://www.highland-ohio.com/presidential_dog.htm
http://www.presidentialpetmuseum.com/whitehousepets-1.htm
http://www.animalshelter.org/education/newsletter/feb2007-the-first-dogs.asp
http://en.wikipedia.org/wiki/United_States_presidential_pets

CHAPTER 18

Political Parties

Q: Who was the last member from the Whig Party to be president?

A: Millard Fillmore.

Q: What was the only time when a major political party intentionally ran more than one candidate?

A: The Whig party ran William Henry Harrison and others in 1836 in a failed effort to defeat Democratic candidate Martin Van Buren.

Q: Who were the only presidents whose terms ended without them being a member of a political party?

A: There were three. The first was **George Washington** since he did not have an endorsement by a political party to begin with. The second was **John Tyler**. Tyler was formerly a Democrat (and before that a Democrat-Republican), but he was nonetheless elected vice president on the Whig ticket, when William Henry

Harrison won the presidency. However, after Tyler became president, he vetoed most of their entire agenda, including most significantly Henry Clay's legislation for a national banking act following the Panic of 1837. On September 11, 1841, most members of the cabinet entered Tyler's office one by one and resigned. Two days later, the Whigs in Congress officially expelled Tyler from the party, leaving him without a party.

The third president whose term ended with him not being a member of a party was **Andrew Johnson**. Johnson was nominated as the vice presidential candidate in 1864 on the National Union Party ticket. He and Lincoln were elected in November, 1864 and inaugurated on March 4, 1865. Johnson succeeded to the presidency upon Lincoln's assassination on April 14, 1865. Johnson's party status was ambiguous during his presidency. As president, he did not identify with the two main parties, though he did try for the Democratic nomination in 1868. While president, he attempted to build a party of loyalists under the National Union label.

Asked in 1868 why he did not become a Democrat, he said, "It is true I am asked, why don't I join the Democratic Party. Why don't they join me ... if I have administered the office of president so well?" His failure to make the National Union brand an actual party made Johnson effectively an independent during his presidency, though he was supported by Democrats and later rejoined the party as a Democratic Senator from Tennessee from 1875 until his death.[1]

Q: Which presidents were members of the Whig party?

A: William Henry Harrison, John Tyler, Zachary Taylor and **Millard Fillmore.** In other words, every president from 1841-1853 except for James K. Polk, who served from 1845-1849, was a member of the Whig party. Tyler was eventually expelled from the Whig party however. Taylor was the last Whig to win a presidential election. However he died after just sixteen months in office.

Q: Who was the only president elected from the Federalist Party?

A: John Adams. The party was formed in 1790. Although George Washington was broadly sympathetic to their policies, he remained an independent while president. [2]

Q: Which presidents were elected as members of the Democratic—Republican Party?

A: Thomas Jefferson, James Madison, James Monroe and **John Quincy Adams.**

Q: What former president later ran for office as a member of the Know Nothing Party, which was known for its anti-Catholic views?

A: Millard Fillmore. The Know Nothing Party was mainly active from 1854 to 1856, and was based on fears that the country was being overwhelmed by German and Irish Catholic immigrants, who were often regarded as hostile to Anglo-Saxon Protestant values and controlled by the Pope in Rome. It wanted only American-born Protestants elected to public office. It was thus considered to be the anti-Catholic party. In the 1856 election, Fillmore carried only one State, Maryland. [3]

Q: Which president was the first Republican to ever carry Texas?

A: Herbert Hoover in 1928.

Q: Excluding men who were formerly military generals (i.e. Grant and Eisenhower) who was the first Republican ever to serve two full terms in office?

A: Believe it or not, it was **Ronald Reagan.**

Q: Which president formally requested Nixon to resign from office?

A: George H.W. Bush in 1974. He was Chairman of the Republican Party at the time.

Q: Which president joined "Democrats for Eisenhower" in 1952?

A: Ronald Reagan.

Q: When Lincoln was elected president for a second term in 1864, what party did he belong to?

A: The National Union Party.

Q: Which former or future president is the only third party candidate to come in second place?

A: Theodore Roosevelt, running as the Bull Moose candidate in the 1912 election.

Q: True or false: There have never been four consecutive presidents from the same political party.

A: False. In fact it has happened twice (sort of). Thomas Jefferson, James Madison, James Monroe and John Quincy Adams were all members of the Democratic-Republican party. However, in the election of 1824, the Democratic-Republican caucus system broke down, even though John Quincy Adams won that election and he was a member of that party. Certain factions of the party, including Adams, became members of the short-lived National Republican Party which later became the Whig Party. Also, Ulysses Grant, Rutherford Hayes, James Garfield and Chester Arthur were all Republicans. However Arthur became president because of the assassination of Garfield and not because he was elected.

Q: True or false: No political party has ever won five consecutive elections.

A: False. Franklin Roosevelt won four and Harry Truman won one. The run of twenty years (1933-1953) marks the longest period in which one party was in power.

Q: Between and including Abraham Lincoln (the first Republican president) and Barack Obama, what percentage of those men elected president have been Democrats?

A.   36% B.   43% C.   48% D.   53%

A: The correct answer is A. Only ten of the twenty-eight presidents in that interval have been Democrats (and that counts Grover Cleveland twice).

Q. In the 52-year span between 1861-1913, how many Democrats were elected presidents?

A. One. **Grover Cleveland**, although he won twice.

CHAPTER EIGHTEEN NOTES:

1) Graff, Henry (ed.), *The Presidents: A Reference History*, Scribner (1997) (essay by Richard P. McCormick)
Roseboom, Eugene, *A History of Presidential Elections*, Collier (1970)
Trefousse, Hans Louis. *Andrew Johnson: A Biography* (American Political Biography Press 1998)
Trefousse, Hans Louis, *Andrew Johnson: A Biography* (W. W. Norton, 1989)
http://www.whitehouse.gov/about/presidents/johntyler
http://www.newworldencyclopedia/org/entry/Whig_Party_(United_States)
http://en.wikipedia.org/wiki/Andrew_Johnson
2) Levine, Bruce. "Conservatism, Nativism, and Slavery: Thomas R. Whitney and the Origins of the Know Nothing Party" *Journal of American History* 2001 p. 455-488

CHAPTER 19

Quotes About Presidents

Q: In paying tribute to this multi-talented president while welcoming 49 Nobel Prize winners to the White House in 1962, John F. Kennedy stated: "I think this is the most extraordinary collection of talent and of human knowledge that has ever been gathered together at the White House—with the possible exception of when [this president] dined alone." Who was Kennedy referring to?

A: Thomas Jefferson, who achieved distinction as, among other things, a horticulturist, political leader, architect, archaeologist, paleontologist, musician, inventor, and founder of the University of Virginia.[1]

Q: To whom was he referring when General George McClellan said that this president was an "idiot," a "well-meaning baboon," and "the original gorilla?"

A: Abraham Lincoln.[2]

Q: Of which early president was it said, after he was decisively defeated in his bid for re-election: "Seldom has the public mind been so successfully poisoned against an honest and high-minded man?"

A: John Quincy Adams.[3]

Q: Of which post-Civil War president was it said: "No man ever entered the presidency so profoundly and widely distrusted, and no one ever retired ... more generally respected?"

A: Chester Arthur.[4]

Q: An article in a newspaper stated: "Give him a barrel of hard (alcoholic) cider and settle a pension of two thousand a year on him, and take my word for it, he will sit the remainder of his days in his log cabin." What future president was this article referring to?

A: William Henry Harrison. This quote appeared in a newspaper editorial in 1840. While of course it was meant to be derogatory, the Whig party chose to embrace this notion of Harrison as a man of the people, in touch with the needs and concerns of common folk, while depicting his opponent, Martin Van Buren as a wealthy elitist. This become known as the Log Cabin Campaign. This message, combined with the snappy slogan of "Tippecanoe and Tyler too" helped propel Harrison to the White House. Ironically, Van Buren was the one born into a working class family, while Harrison was from a wealthy political family, his father being one of the original signers of the Declaration of Independence.[5]

Q: About which pre-Civil War president was it said: "With the possible exception of Lyndon B. Johnson, [he was] America's most unhappy vice-president"?

A: Millard Fillmore.   One historian wrote: "Fillmore was far from the 'executive' vice-president that Jimmy Carter and Walter Mondale would later help create. When the Whigs nominated Zachary Taylor as their candidate, they decided on a northern vice president to balance out their slave holding southerner. Ironically, the massive issue of slavery was left out of the Whig's main platform. Even after winning the election of 1848 with 163 electoral votes, Fillmore had yet to meet Taylor. They first met in passing just one week prior to being sworn in. It was soon made clear that Fillmore's counsel 'was not welcomed by the Taylor administration, leaving him as, with the possible exception of Lyndon B. Johnson, America's most unhappy vice-president.'" [6]

Q: Walt Whitman wrote a famous poem which begins:

O Captain! My Captain! our fearful trip is done;
The ship has weathered every rack, the prize we sought is won;
The port is near, the bells I hear, the people all exulting,
While follow eyes the steady keel, the vessel grim and daring.

Which president is this poem about?

A: Abraham Lincoln. It was written in 1865, just after the Civil War ended and Lincoln had been assassinated. Whitman was mourning his death. The last verse reads:

My Captain does not answer, his lips are pale and still;
My father does not feel my arm, he has no pulse nor will;
The ship is anchored safe and sound, its voyage closed and done;
From fearful trip, the victor ship, comes in with object won;
Exult, O shores, and ring, O bells!
But I, with mournful tread,
Walk the deck my Captain lies,
Fallen cold and dead. [7]

Q: A Chicago newspaper panned a presidential speech by writing: "The cheek of every American must tingle with shame as he reads the silly, flat and dishwatery utterances of the man who has to be pointed out to intelligent foreigners as the president of the United States." Who was the president and what was the speech?

A: Abraham Lincoln. The speech was his Gettysburg Address. The piece appeared in the November 20, 1863 edition of the *Chicago Times*. Speaking of the Gettysburg Address, historian James Humes writes that the phrase "that these dead shall not have died in vain" was not original to Lincoln:

> "The ten-year-old Lincoln taught himself by borrowing books. Someone in his church loaned him Mason Weems' *Life of General Washington*. He read and re-read it by candlelight in the cabin loft. One morning he woke to find the book destroyed by spring rains that seeped through the logs. He had to repay the farmer by pulling stumps from his fields. The ruined book was now his only possession.
>
> One part of the book, however, remained intact. It contained a picture of a kneeling General Washington in front of a stone memorial entitled, 'Valley Forge.' Below it was the sentence, 'That these dead shall not have died in vain.' Those nine words remained forever etched in the boy's heart. And forty years later he would recite them before the graves at Gettysburg." [8]

Q: In the following passage, X is a president. Who is he?

"No president had more 'women scrapes,' as his attorney general put it, than [X]. His first affair, three years into his marriage to [his wife], was with Susie Hodder—his wife's best friend from childhood—resulting in the birth of a daughter. His second affair was with [his wife's] closest adult friend, Carrie Fulton Phillips. It lasted fifteen years. His third enduring mistress was his Senate aide, Grace Cross. Number four was the most infamous and the first presidential mistress to write a memoir. In the large Oval Office closet, the president had at least one tryst with Nan Britton, a campaign volunteer who had started having sex with [X] when he was fifty-one and she was twenty-two. Their assignations, facilitated by Secret Service agents James Sloan and Walter Ferguson, ('[X hated to have them around, for he despised being watched,' reported the chief usher), came to an abrupt stop when another agent, Harry Barker, tipped Florence off, and she ran down for a confrontation.

Britton claimed she conceived their daughter, Elizabeth Ann. They disrobed because [X] wanted to "visualize" her while he worked there during the day. Britton worried that they lacked the "usual paraphernalia which we always took to the hotels . . . and of course, the Senate offices do not provide preventive facilities for use in such emergencies."

A: Warren Harding. His wife is Florence. Carl Sferrazza Anthony, an authority on the political and social power of presidential wives and families, and the author of a dozen books, wrote the above passage. The memoir to which Anthony is referring and which is indeed the first known memoir by a presidential mistress is *The President's Daughter* published in 1927, four years after Harding's death. In the book, Britton claimed that Harding was the father of her daughter, Elizabeth Ann (1919-2005), a position she maintained her entire life until her death at age 94 in 1991.[9]

Q: Historian John Alcott Carpenter wrote: "His success stemmed from a complicated set of circumstances which worked in his favor, but also from specific traits within his own character which only needed the right conditions to reveal themselves, conditions which had been present during the Mexican War, and on the isthmus, but which were singularly lacking on the West Coast, in Missouri, and at the leather store in Galena. These traits were determination, mental acuteness, excellent memory, ability to look into the minds of others, and a willingness to subordinate self to a cause." **Of whom was he speaking?**

A: Ulysses Grant.[10]

Q: Aaron Burr, who was Jefferson's vice president, called this president: "naturally dull and stupid; extremely illiterate; indecisive to a degree that would be incredible to one who did not know him; pusillanimous, and of course hypocritical; has no opinion on any subject, and will always be under the government of the worst men." **Of whom was he speaking?**

A: James Monroe. [11]

Q: When this president died, Dorothy Parker remarked: "How could they tell?" Of whom was she speaking?

A: Calvin Coolidge.

Q: In 1835, Davy Crockett wrote a biography of a man who later became president. Crockett didn't care for the man. He wrote: "[This future president] is as opposite to General [Andrew] Jackson as dung is to a diamond ... He travels about the country and through the cities in an English coach; has English servants, dressed in uniform— I think they call it livery. . . . When he enters the Senate chamber in the morning, he struts and swaggers like a crow in a gutter. He is laced up in corsets, such as women in a town wear, and, if possible, tighter than the best of them. It would be difficult to say, from his personal appearance, whether he was a man or woman, but for his large red and gray whiskers." **Who was this future president?**

A: Martin Van Buren, who became president two years later in 1837, shortly after Crockett was killed in the Battle of the Alamo.

Crockett's book, available as a free download from Google Books, was called *Life of Martin Van Buren*, and the subtitle is hilarious: *Heir-Apparent to the "Government," and the Appointed Successor to General Andrew Jackson, Containing Every Authentic Particular By Which His Extraordinary Character Has Been Formed, With a Concise History of the Events That Have Occasioned His Unparalleled Elevation; Together with a Review of His Policy as a Statesmen.*[12]

Q: Which president said: "Richard Nixon is a no-good lying bastard. He can lie out of both sides of his mouth at the same time, and if he ever caught himself telling the truth, he'd lie just to keep his hand in … Nixon has never told the truth in his life"?

A: Harry Truman. [13]

Q: A biographer of this president stated that his "ambition was uncommon—in the degree to which it was unencumbered by even the slightest excess weight of ideology, of philosophy, of principles, of beliefs." To whom was he referring?

A: Lyndon Johnson. His biographer is Robert Caro. [14]

Q: One man, both while in Congress and later as president, when trying to obtain supporting votes for particular pieces of legislation, would often subject members of Congress to what famously became known as "the treatment." One journalist described it as follows:

> "The Treatment could last ten minutes or four hours. … Its tone could be supplication, accusation, cajolery, exuberance, scorn, tears, complaint and the hint of threat. It was all of these together. It ran the gamut of human emotions. Its velocity was breathtaking, and it was all in one direc-

tion. Interjections from the target were rare. [He] antici- pated them before they could be spoken. He moved in close, his face a scant millimeter from his target, his eyes widening and narrowing, his eyebrows rising and falling. From his pockets poured clippings, memos, statistics. Mimicry, humor, and the genius of analogy made 'The Treatment' an almost hypnotic experience and rendered the target stunned and helpless."

Another biographer wrote: "He could get up every day and learn what their fears, their desires, their wishes, their wants were and he could then manipulate, dominate, persuade and cajole them."

A third described it as follows: "It was an incredible blend of badg- ering, cajolery, reminders of past favors, promises of future favors, predictions of gloom if something doesn't happen. When that man started to work on you, all of a sudden, you just felt that you were standing under a waterfall and the stuff was pouring on you."

Which president were these writers referring to?

A: Lyndon Johnson. [15]

Q: Which early president was described as follows: "He is polite with dignity, affable without formality, distant without haughtiness, grave without austerity; modest, wise and good"?

A: George Washington. [16]

Q: Thomas Jefferson wrote a letter to James Madison about another president. It said: "He is vain, irritable, and a bad calcu- lator of the force and probable effect of the motives which govern men. This is all the ill which can possibly be said of him. He is as disinterested as the Being who made him. He is profound in his views and accurate in his judgment, except where knowledge of the world is necessary to form a judgment. He is so amiable that I pronounce you will love him, if ever you become acquainted with him. He would be, as he was, a great man in Congress." **To which president was Jefferson referring?**

A: John Adams. [17]

Q: While this man was president, he and his wife banned dancing, card playing, liquor and tobacco, leading one man to remark: "The trouble with [this president] is that he drank too much water." Who was he?

A: James Polk. [18]

Q: Which president, though having spent twenty-five years in Congress, did not, according to *The New York Times*, **"write a single piece of major legislation in his entire career"?**

A: Gerald Ford. [19]

Q: Senator Charles Sumner said that this post-Civil War president was "an insolent, drunken brute, in comparison with which Caligula's horse was respectable." To whom was he referring?

A: Andrew Johnson. [20]

Q: Biographer Allan Nevins wrote that, in this post-Civil War president "the greatness lies in typical rather than unusual qualities. He had no endowments that thousands of men do not have. He possessed honesty, courage, firmness, independence, and common sense. But he possessed them to a degree other men do not." **Of which president was he speaking?**

A: Grover Cleveland. [21]

Q: Which pre-Civil War president, generally considered to

be among the bottom tier of presidents, was lampooned in the following passage for a series of "magnificent" proposals which all failed ?

> "We must retrench the extravagant list of magnificent schemes which received the sanction of the Executive ... the great Napoleon himself, with all the resources of an empire at his sole command, never ventured the simultaneous accomplishments of so many daring projects. The acquisition of Cuba . . . ; the construction of a Pacific Railroad . . . ; a Mexican protectorate, the international preponderance in Central America, in spite of all the powers of Europe; the submission of distant South American states; . . . the enlargement of the Navy; a largely increased standing Army . . . what government on earth could possibly meet all the exigencies of such a flood of innovations?"

A: James Buchanan. [22]

Q: Which president was Theodore Roosevelt referring to when he called him "a cold-blooded, narrow-minded, prejudiced, obstinate, timid old psalm-singing Indianapolis politician"?

A: Benjamin Harrison.

Q: Of which president was historian Doris Kearns Goodwin referring to when she wrote the following:

> "I was told that [he] had always been a generous and demanding giver, but before his White House days he had never been able to distribute so dazzling an assortment of presents. Every White House budget includes an allocation for gifts. Numberless trinkets—ranging from booklets, bracelets, and bowls to charms and certificates—are

distributed in the name of the president. At no time before, however had the budget been as large or as personally managed as it was under [this president].

For most presidents, the distribution of gifts is a routine function handled mechanically by the staff. For [this president], the giving of gifts was a personal task, 'a great opportunity,' he said, 'for engraving my spirit on the minds and hearts of my people.' In the first year of his presidency, the stock of presidential gifts more than tripled. To the traditional bowls, lighters, tie clasps, and cufflinks he added electric toothbrushes, engraved with the presidential seal; waterproof watches, inscribed with [his] initials and the Biblical injunction: 'Do unto others as you would have others do unto you'. . . .

There was often a ritual connected with the giving of the gifts. [He] often gave the same person the same gift again and again; the giver decided what he wanted to give, not what the recipient wanted to receive. 'I give these toothbrushes to friends,' [He] explained to me, 'for then I know that from now until the end of their days they will think of me the first thing in the morning and the last at night.' In the last month of [his] presidency, I received my first electric toothbrush. 'Open it,' [He] said to me as I awkwardly held the gift unopened in my hands, 'open it and tell me, have you ever seen anything like that in your entire life? Tell me now, what do you think?' I didn't tell him what I thought, for, in truth, I didn't know what to think. But I had to thank him, so I did.

Several weeks later he handed me another package, still another toothbrush. When he noticed that I was perplexed, he glowered and said, 'Why the hell should I give anything to anyone who is not grateful for my gift?' There was, as [he] saw it, an ethic to the charitable act, an expectation of gratefulness, a ritual that demanded the proper completion. So it happened that over time I was given, and with a measure of good grace accepted, no less than twelve electric toothbrushes!"

A: Lyndon B. Johnson. [23]

Q: Which president, besides Barack Obama, was rumored to be partially of African-American lineage, causing his campaign manager to state: "No family in the state has a clearer, a more honorable record than [this president's], a blue-eyed stock from New England and Pennsylvania, the finest pioneer blood."

A: Warren Harding. [24]

Q: Which president did Fidel Castro refer to as "a madman, an imbecile and a bum"?

A: Ronald Reagan. [25]

Q: Will Rogers, the widely popular comedian, said of this president that, "he didn't do anything, but that's what the people wanted done." To whom was he referring?

A: Warren Harding. [26]

CHAPTER NINETEEN NOTES:

1) John F. Kennedy, in an address at a White House dinner honoring Nobel Prize winners (April 29, 1962), quoted in *The White House Diary*, at the JFK Library.
2) William Lee Miller, President Lincoln: *The Duty of a Statesman*. Knopf.
3) Bailey, Thomas. *The American Pageant, A History of the Republic*. Vol.1, 4th Edition. Lexington, Massachusetts: D.C. Heath and Company (1971)
4) http://www.whitehouse.gov/about/presidents/chesterarthur
5) http://www.life123.com/parenting/education/american-history/meaning-of-tippecanoe-and-tyler-too.shtml?White House.
6) http://www.sacredheart.edu/pages/32940_millard_fillmore_inspired_life_uninspired_presidency_michael_fazzino.cfm (quoting from: Moore, Kathryn, *The American President* (Barnes and Noble, 2007)(first quote) and Smith, Elbert B.,

The Presidencies of Zachary Taylor & Millard Fillmore, University Press of Kansas (1988)(second quote)).

7) Reef, Catherine,. *Walt Whitman*. Houghton Mifflin Harcourt (2002). p. 100
   Kaplan, Justin. *Walt Whitman: A Life*. New York: Simon and Schuster (1979). p. 309

8) Humes, James, *Gettysburg Address still cherished on Nov. 19, the 147th anniversary*, 11-14-2010
   (http://www.chieftain.com/opinion/ideas/article_1467a2da-ef81-11df-bfd7001cc4c002e0.html
   http://civilwar.bluegrass.net/PoliticsAndPoliticians/thegettysburgaddress.html
   http://www.newsmax.com/US/gettysburg-address-abraham-lincoln/2010/11/18/id/377520

9) Britton, Nan. *The President's Daughter*. Elizabeth Ann Guild, New York City, 1928 (reprinted 1973),
   Dean, John; Schlesinger, Arthur M. *Warren Harding (The American President Series)*, Times Books, (2004)
   Ferrell, Robert H. *The Strange Deaths of President Harding*, University of Missouri Press (1996)
   Anthony, Carl Sferrazza, *Florence Harding: The First Lady, The Jazz Age, And The Death Of America's Most Scandalous President* (Harper, 1999).
   Anthony, Carl Sferrazza. *Florence Harding*, Morrow (1998)
   http://www.washingtonpost.com/wp-srv/style/features/harding.htm

10) http://faculty.css.edu/mkelsey/usgrant/quotes.html
11) http://www.independent.co.uk/news/presidents/james-monroe-1391113.html
12) http://americantalleyrand.com/?p=126
    http://books.google.com/books/life+of+martin+van+buren
13) Margaret Truman (editor). *Where the Buck Stops: The Personal and Private Writings of Harry S. Truman*, Warner Books (1989).
14) Caro, Robert A. *The Years of Lyndon Johnson: The path to power*. Knopf (1982).
15) First quote: Evans, Rowland; Novak, Robert. Lyndon B. Johnson: *The Exercise of Power* (1966).
    Second quote: Goodwin, Doris Kearns, *Lyndon Johnson and the American Dream*, St. Martin's Press (1991)
    Third quote: George Reedy, Johnson Press Secretary, quoted in http://www.pbs.org/wgbh/americanexperience/features/transcript/lbj-transcript/
16) quote from Abigail Adams, in a letter to John Adams, 1789; from Alexander Hamilton, by Ron Chernow (2004)
17) John Adams, quote from Thomas Jefferson in a letter to James Madison (January 30, 1787)
18) quote from Sam Houston. Combs, Gerald. *The History of American Foreign Policy to 1920*. M.E. Sharpe (2008)
19) http://www.nytimes.com/2006/12/28/opinion/28thur1.html
20) http://www.time.com/time/magazine/article/0,9171,890792,00.html#ixzz1bNOFKrwZ
21) Nevins, Allan. *Grover Cleveland: A Study in Courage* (1932)

22) http://pediaview.com/openpedia/James_Buchanan#cite_note-76

23) Goodwin, Doris Kearns, *Lyndon Johnson and the American Dream*, St. Martin's Press (1991)

24) http://www.usa-presidents.info/harding.htm

25) http://www.independent.co.uk/news/presidents/ronald-reagan-1482923.html

26) http://www.u-s-history.com/pages/h1385.html

CHAPTER 20

Quotes by Presidents

Q: Which president said: "I have opinions of my own—strong opinions—but I don't always agree with them"?

A: George H.W. Bush. [1]

Q: Which pre-Civil War president said: "It is a national disgrace that our presidents, after having occupied the highest position in the country, should be cast adrift, and, perhaps, be compelled to keep a corner grocery for subsistence"?

A: Millard Fillmore. [2]

Q: Which president has a plaque outside his home which contains one of his more famous quotes and one of his core beliefs, namely that what is important is what we can do for our country, not what our country can do for us?

A: Not John Kennedy but **Warren Harding**. His actual quote was, "In the great fulfillment, we must have a citizenship less concerned about what the government can do for it and more anxious about what it can do for the nation." He made this remark in his address at the Republican Convention on June 7, 1916 in Chicago. The plaque is outside his home in Marion, Ohio.

The concept did not originate with Harding either. In a Memorial Day speech in Keene, New Hampshire on May 30, 1884, Oliver Wendell Holmes, Jr., stated: "It is now the moment when by common consent we pause to become conscious of our national life and to rejoice in it, to recall what our country has done for each of us, and to ask ourselves what we can do for our country in return." [3]

Q: Which president shot a hole-in-one (not necessarily while president) and later called it "the greatest thrill of my life- even better than being elected"?

A: Richard Nixon. The September 5, 1961, issue of *Golf Digest* includes the Official Hole-in-One Clearinghouse Application Form filled out and sent in by Richard Nixon after he aced the 2nd hole at the Bel Air Country Club. on September 4: "Age: 44. Address: Los Angeles. Handicap: 18. Right-handed. Spalding club, five-iron; Spalding ball."

Dwight Eisenhower also shot a hole in one. On February 6th, 1968, in Palm Springs, California, the 77-year-old former president achieved every golfer's dream on the par three, thirteenth hole at the Seven Lakes Country Club. An aide to President Lyndon Johnson stated that Eisenhower himself referred to this hole-in-one while golfing with Johnson twelve days later. In the February 18, 1968 entry of Johnson's daily diary, it states:

1:30p Mrs. Eisenhower directed the president to a room to change for golf session.

1:35p President General Eisenhower proceeded to Seven Lakes

Country Club where they played 18 holes of golf.

1:45p Teed off!

Hole 9–they had fresh orange juice

Hole 11–they met up with Mr. Dan Kimball–former Secretary of Navy.

Hole 13–the general told the president that the last time he played this hole—he shot a hole in one.

Hole 18–The president shot a 122 yd. drive down the green and parred the shot. General Eisenhower also parred the hole.[4]

Q: Which president said at the Gridiron Dinner in Washington, D.C.: "I just received the following wire from my generous daddy: 'Don't buy a single vote more than is necessary. I'll be damned if I'm going to pay for a landslide'"?

A: John Kennedy.[5]

Q: Which president said he knew only two songs: "One was Yankee Doodle and the other wasn't"?

A: Ulysses Grant.[6]

Q: Which 20th-century president wrote the following poem to his mistress? For extra credit, what was the name of his mistress?

I love your back, I love your breasts
Darling to feel, where my face rests,
I love your skin, so soft and white,
So dear to feel and sweet to bite. . . .
I love your poise of perfect thighs,
When they hold me in paradise. . . .

A: Warren Harding to Carrie Phillips. Harding also wrote to Phillips: "Honestly I hurt with insatiate longing until I feel there will never be relief until I take a long deep wild draught on your lips and then bury my face on your pillowy breasts." There are over 800 pages of correspondence between the two of them.

While on the subject of presidents and sex, in 1915, *The Washington Post* contained an article describing an evening at the theater attended by President Wilson and his fiancé Edith Galt. A reporter wrote that instead of watching the performance, "the president spent most of his time entering Mrs. Galt." After a White House aide detected the error and placed a desperate phone call to the managing editor, this edition was hastily retrieved from newsstands. Later editions used the corrected word "entertaining." [7]

Q: Which president said the following?

"Bill Rogers has got—to his credit it's a decent feeling— but somewhat sort of a blind spot on the black thing because he's been in New York. He says well, 'They are coming along, and that after all they are going to strengthen our country in the end because they are strong physically and some of them are smart.' So forth and so on.

My own view is I think he's right if you're talking in terms of 500 years. I think it's wrong if you're talking in terms of 50 years. What has to happen is they have to be, frankly, inbred. And, you just, that's the only thing that's going to do it, Rose."

A: Richard Nixon. Bill Rogers refers to Nixon's Secretary of State. "Rose" is Nixon's secretary Rose Mary Woods. The remarks were recorded as part of a conversation between Nixon and Woods on February 13, 1973 that veered from whom to invite to a state dinner to whether Ms. Woods should get her hair done. [8]

Q: Which president said: "This administration is going to be cussed and discussed for years to come"?

A: Harry Truman.

Q: Which president said on *60 Minutes*: "I would put our legislative and foreign policy accomplishments in our first two years against any president—with the possible exceptions of Johnson, F.D.R., and Lincoln—just in terms of what we've gotten done in modern history"?

A: Barack Obama. This statement was edited out of the on-air broadcast but could be heard online on *60 Minutes Overtime.*

Q: Which president's last words were: "I love you Sarah. For all eternity, I love you"?

A: James K. Polk.

Q: Which president said, "There is no Soviet domination of Eastern Europe and there never will be under [my] administration"?

A: Gerald Ford in his second debate with Jimmy Carter in 1976. This remark is considered to have substantially damaged Ford's hopes for election in 1976. It was said in answer to a comment by Max Frankel of the *The New York Times:*

> MAX FRANKEL: Mr. President, I'd like to explore a little more deeply our relationship with the Russians. Our allies in France and Italy are now flirting with Communism. We've recognized the permanent Communist regime in East Germany. We've virtually signed, in Helsinki, an agreement that the Russians have dominance in Eastern Europe.
>
> PRESIDENT FORD: I'm glad you raised it, Mr. Frankel. In

the case of Helsinki, thirty-five nations signed an agreement, including the secretary of state for the Vatican. I can't under any circumstances believe that the—His Holiness, the Pope would agree by signing that agreement that the thirty-five nations have turned over to the Warsaw Pact nations the domination of the—Eastern Europe. It just isn't true. There is no Soviet domination of Eastern Europe and there never will be under a Ford administration.

MR. FRANKEL: I'm sorry, I—could I just follow—did I understand you to say, sir, that the Russians are not using Eastern Europe as their own sphere of influence in occupying most of the countries there and making sure with their troops that it's a Communist zone?

PRESIDENT FORD: I don't believe, Mr. Frankel, that the Yugoslavians consider themselves dominated by the Soviet Union. I don't believe that the Romanians consider themselves dominated by the Soviet Union. I don't believe that the Poles consider themselves dominated by the Soviet Union.[9]

Q: Which president said: "Some folks are silly enough to have formed a plan to make a president of the U.S. out of this Clerk and Clod Hopper"?

A: William Henry Harrison. He said it to his friend Solomon Van Ransellaer in 1836. He was at the time the Clerk of the Court of Common Pleas of Hamilton County, Ohio.

Take this job and shove it—

A surprising number of presidents did not care at all either for their time as president and/or the frustration of the experiences. However perhaps the job is getting better. Only three of the presidents who made the following quotes served after 1900 and only two served after World War II.

Q: Which presidents said the following?

1. "I can say with truth mine is a situation of dignified slavery."
2. "Make no mistake about it, the four most miserable years of my life were my four years in the presidency."
3. "The second office in the government [vice president] is honorable and easy; the first [president] is but a splendid misery."
4. "Being president is like being a jackass in a hailstorm. There's nothing to do but to stand there and take it."
5. "It's a nice prison but a prison nevertheless. No man in his right mind would want to come here of his own accord."
6. "No man who ever held the office of president would congratulate a friend on obtaining it. He will make one man ungrateful, and a hundred men his enemies, for every office he can bestow."
7. "If you are as happy on entering the White House as I on leaving, you are a very happy man indeed."
8. "It is my wish that you may never be president of the United States."
9. "I'll be damned if I am not getting tired of this. It seems to be the profession of a President simply to hear other people talk."
10. "I was called from my farm to undertake the administration of public affairs and I foresaw that I was called to a bed of thorns. I now leave that bed which has afforded me little rest, and eagerly seek repose in the quiet enjoyments of rural life."

Answers:
1. **Andrew Jackson**
2. **John Quincy Adams**
3. **Thomas Jefferson**
4. **Lyndon Johnson**
5. **Harry Truman**, in a 1946 letter to his daughter
6. **John Adams**

7.   **James Buchanan**
8.   **Grover Cleveland**
9.   **William Howard Taft**
10.   **John Tyler.**[10]

Q: Which 19th-century President said: "I may be President of the United States, but my private life is my own damn business"?

A: Chester Arthur.

Q: Which President stated, with respect to the issue of whether women should have the right to vote, "Sensible and responsible women do not want to vote. The relative positions to be assumed by men and women in the working out of our civilization were assigned long ago by a higher intelligence"?

A: Grover Cleveland in a 1905 article in *The Ladies Home Journal*.[11]

Q: Which President said: "I don't go so far as to think that the only good Indians are dead Indians, but I believe nine out of ten are, and I shouldn't like to inquire too closely into the case of the tenth"?

A: Theodore Roosevelt. [12]

Q: Which President said: "Mr. Nixon in the last seven days has called me an economic ignoramus, a Pied Piper, and all the rest. I've just confined myself to calling him a Republican, but he says that is getting low"?

A: John Kennedy. [13]

Q: Which President said: "I have not been able to think out any solution of the terrible problem offered by the presence

of the Negro on this continent, but of one thing I am sure, and that is that inasmuch as he is here and can neither be killed nor driven away, the only wise and honorable and Christian thing to do is to treat each black man and each white man strictly on his merits as a man, giving him no more and no less that he shows himself worthy to have"?

A: Theodore Roosevelt.

Q: Which president said: "I have no trouble with my enemies. I can take care of my enemies all right. But my damn friends, my god-damned friends, White, they're the ones who keep me walking the floor nights"?

A: Warren Harding.[14]

Q: Which president, as nominee, stated: "We in America today are nearer to the final triumph over poverty than ever before in the history of any land"?

A: Herbert Hoover, shortly before the stock market crash of 1929.[15]

Q: What president stated, the day after the Nazis attacked the Soviet Union in 1941: "If we see that Germany is winning we ought to help Russia and if Russia is winning we ought to help Germany, and that way let them kill as many as possible, although I don't want to see Hitler victorious under any circumstances. Neither of them thinks anything of their pledged word"?

A: Harry Truman.

Q: In response to a critical review of a vocal concert by his daughter, a president wrote the following letter to the reviewer: "I've just read your lousy review of [my daughter's] concert. I've come to the conclusion that you are an 'eight ulcer man on four ulcer pay.' It seems to me that you are a frustrated old man who wishes he could have been successful. When you write such poppy-cock as was in the back section of the paper you work for, it shows conclusively that you're off the beam and at least four of your ulcers are at work. Some day I hope to meet you. When that happens you'll need a new nose, a lot of beefsteak for black eyes, and perhaps a supporter below! Pegler, a gutter snipe, is a gentleman alongside you. I hope you'll accept that statement as a worse insult than a reflection on your ancestry." **Which president was it?**

A: Harry Truman, writing about a review of his daughter Margaret's concert. He was responding to a review written by *The Washington Post* music critic Paul Hume who wrote about a December 5, 1950 concert given by Truman at Constitution Hall in Washington as follows: "Miss Truman is a unique American phenomenon with a pleasant voice of little size and fair quality. She is extremely attractive on stage. Yet Miss Truman cannot sing very well. She is flat a good deal of the time—more so last night than at any time we have heard her in past years."[16]

Q: Which president wrote the following speech, to be used in the event a planned military attack did not work: "My decision to attack at this time and place was based on the best information available. The troops, the air and the Navy did all that bravery and devotion to duty could do. If any blame or fault attaches to the attempt, it is mine alone"?

A: Dwight Eisenhower. It was never certain that Operation Overlord would succeed. Long after the successful landings on D-Day, the above never-used speech was found in a shirt pocket by an aide. The previous sentence stated: "Our landings in the Cherbourg-Havre area have failed to gain a satisfactory foothold and I have withdrawn the troops."[17]

Q: Author James Michener was invited to a dinner at the White House. He declined, saying: "Dear Mr. President: I received your invitation three days after I had agreed to speak a few words at a dinner honoring the wonderful high school teacher who taught me how to write. I know you will not miss me at your dinner, but she might at hers."

A week later, Michener received a handwritten reply from the president: "In his lifetime a man lives under fifteen or sixteen presidents, but a really fine teacher comes into his life but rarely. Go and speak at your teacher's dinner."[18] **Who was this president?**

A: Dwight Eisenhower.

Q: Which president rejected his official portrait painting, saying it was "the ugliest thing I ever saw"?

A: Lyndon Johnson. It was painted by Peter Hurd. The portrait was to have been hung in the White House, but is now at the Smithsonian's National Portrait Gallery. Shortly after the unveiling of the portrait in 1967, the pun was making the rounds in Washington that "artists should be seen around the White House—but not Hurd." Johnson's wife Lady Bird was upset that Johnson didn't like the portrait.[19]

Q: Which 20th-century president stated: "I was never popular. The popular boys were the ones who were good at games and had big, tight fists. I was never like that. Without my glasses I was blind as a bat, and to tell the truth, I was kind of a sissy. If there was any danger of getting into a fight, I always ran. I guess that's why I'm here today"?

A: Harry Truman. [20]

Q: Which president said: "It's a good thing I am not a woman. I would always be pregnant. I can't say no"?

A: **Warren Harding.** [21]

Q: **Which president asked not to be awarded the Congressional Medal of Honor, stating: "I don't consider what I've done to be a reason for any award, Congressional or otherwise"?**

A: **Harry Truman.** This occurred in 1971 on his 87th birthday. [22]

Q: **Which president was tape-recorded ordering several pairs of pants from the Haggar Pants Company?**

A: **Lyndon Johnson.** The conversation with Joe Haggar (son of the founder) included the following dialogue:

LBJ: I want them half a inch larger in the waist than they were before except I want two or three inches of stuff left back in there so I can take them up. I vary ten or 15 pounds a month.

JH: Alright sir.

LBJ: So leave me at least two and a half, three inches in the back where I can let them out or take them up. And make these a half an inch bigger in the waist. Make the pockets at least an inch longer. My money and my knife and everything falls out—wait just a minute.

Operator: Would you hold on a minute please?
[conversation on hold for two minutes]

LBJ: Now the pockets, when you sit down in a chair, the knife and your money comes out, so I need at least another inch in the pockets. And another thing—the crotch, down where your nuts hang— is always a little too tight. So when you make them up, give me an inch that I can let out there, uh because they cut me. It's just like riding a wire fence. These are almost, these are the best I've had anywhere in the United States.

JH: Fine.

LBJ: But, uh when I gain a little weight they cut me under there. So, leave me, you never do have much margin there. See if you can't leave me an inch from where the zipper (burps) ends, round, under my, back to my bunghole, so I can let it out there if I need to.

JH: Alright, sir.

LBJ: Now be sure you have the best zippers in them. These are good that I have. If you get those to me I would sure be grateful.

JH: Fine. Now where would you like them sent please?

LBJ: White House.

The president ordered these pants on August 9, 1964 at 1:17 p.m. [23]

Q: Which president, in a letter to his wife wrote the following, which is now lettered in gold in the White House State Dining Room: "I pray Heaven to bestow the best of Blessings on this House and all that shall hereafter inhabit it. May none but honest and wise men ever rule under this roof"?

A: John Adams, who at the time was spending his second night at the White House, while the paint was still wet.

Q: Which president said: "They misunderestimated me"?

A: George W. Bush in a speech in Bentonville, Arkansas on November 6, 2000.

Q: Which president said, "There's an old saying in Tennessee—I know it's in Texas, probably in Tennessee—that says, fool me once, shame on—shame on you. Fool me—you can't get fooled again"?

A: George W. Bush on September 17, 2002.[24]

Q: Which president said, "Our enemies are innovative and resourceful, and so are we. They never stop thinking about new ways to harm our country and our people, and neither do we"?

A: George W. Bush, on August 5, 2004.[25]

Q: Which president said, "Facts are stupid things"?

A: Ronald Reagan, at the 1988 Republican National Convention, attempting to quote John Adams, who said, "Facts are stubborn things; and whatever may be our wishes, our inclinations, or the dictates of our passion, they cannot alter the state of facts and evidence." Argument in Defense of the British Soldiers in the Boston Massacre Trials (4 December 1770).

Q: Which president said, "If I were a single man, I might ask that mummy out. That's a good-looking mummy"?

A: Bill Clinton, on "Juanita," a newly discovered Incan mummy on display at the National Geographic Museum.[26]

Q: After campaigning hard in Alaska and losing, and not visiting Hawaii at all, and winning easily, this president stated: "Just think what my margin might have been if I had never left home at all?" Who was he?

A: John F. Kennedy.

Q: Which president said, "Whenever you are asked if you can do a job, tell 'em, 'Certainly, I can!' Then get busy and find out how to do it?"

A: Theodore Roosevelt.

Q: Which president said, "I'm a conservative, but I'm not a nut about it"?

A: George H. W. Bush. [27]

Q: Which president said, "If one morning I walked on top of the water across the Potomac River, the headline that afternoon would read: 'President Can't Swim'"?

A: Lyndon Johnson.

Q: Which president said, "Well, I learned a lot ... I went down to (Latin America) to find out from them and (learn) their views. You'd be surprised. They're all individual countries"?

A: Ronald Reagan.

Q: Which president said, "An atheist is a guy who watches a Notre Dame-SMU football game and doesn't care who wins"?

A: Dwight D. Eisenhower.

Q: Which president said, "Golf is a game in which one endeavors to control a ball with implements ill adapted for the purpose"?

A: Woodrow Wilson.

Q: Which president said, "Banking establishments are more dangerous than standing armies"?

A: Thomas Jefferson. [28]

Q: Which president said, "Democracy never lasts long. It soon wastes, exhausts, and murders itself. There never was a democracy yet that did not commit suicide"?

A: John Adams. [29]

Q: Which president said, "Popularity, I have always thought, may aptly be compared to a coquette-the more you woo her, the more apt is she to elude your embrace"?

A: John Tyler. Message to the House (December 18, 1816)

Q: Which president said, "Blessed are the young, for they will inherit the national debt"?

A: Herbert Hoover.

Q: A young woman sitting next to this president at a dinner party confided to him she had bet she could get at least three words of conversation from him. Without looking at her he quietly responded, "You lose." Who was he?

A: Calvin Coolidge .[30]

Q: Which president said, "I would have made a good Pope"?

A: Richard M. Nixon.

Q: Which president said, "If you want a friend in Washington, get a dog"?

A: Harry Truman.

Q: Which president said, "The people can never understand why the president does not use his powers to make them behave. Well all the president is, is a glorified public relations man who spends his time flattering, kissing, and kicking people to get them to do what they are supposed to do anyway"?

A: Harry Truman, Letter to Mary Jane Truman (November 14, 1947).

Q: Which 19th-century president said, "Whatever you do, tell the truth"?

A: Grover Cleveland. Telegram to his friend Charles W. Goodyear (July 23, 1884), in response to a query as to what the Democratic Party should say about reports that he fathered a child out of wedlock. [31]

Q: Which pre-Civil War president said, "The legitimate powers of government extend to such acts only as are injurious to others. But it does me no injury for my neighbour to say there are twenty gods, or no god. It neither picks my pocket nor breaks my leg"?

A: Thomas Jefferson, Notes on the State of Virginia, Query XVII. [32]

Q: Which president said, "If men were angels, no government would be necessary"?

A: James Madison, Federalist No. 51.[33]

Q: Which president said, "Politics is supposed to be the second oldest profession. I have come to realize that it bears a very close resemblance to the first"?

A: Ronald Reagan.

Q: Which president said, "I got my middle name from somebody who obviously didn't think I'd ever run for president"?

A: Barack Hussein Obama. His follow-up line was, "If I had to name my greatest strength, I guess it would be my humility. Greatest weakness? It's possible that I'm a little too awesome."[34]

Q: In speaking about FBI director J. Edgar Hoover, this president stated: "It's probably better to have him inside the tent pissing out, than outside the tent pissing in." Who was he?

A: Lyndon Johnson. [35]

Q: Which future president, asked by friends to leave the Army to campaign for Congress, refused, saying that an "officer fit for duty who at this crisis would abandon his post to electioneer for a seat in Congress ought to be scalped"?

A: Rutherford Hayes.

Q: What president stated: "Free government cannot long endure if property is largely in a few hands and large masses of people are unable to earn homes, education, and a support in old age"?

A: Rutherford Hayes.

Q: To what five-year old visitor to the White House did Grover Cleveland say: "My little man, I am making a strange wish for you. It is that you may never be president of the United States"?

A: Franklin Roosevelt. [36]

Q: When advised of his nomination, this pre-Civil War president replied: "It has been well observed that the office of President of the United States should neither be sought nor declined. I have never sought it, nor should I feel at liberty to decline it, if conferred upon me by the voluntary suffrages of my fellow citizens." Who was he?

A: James Polk.

Q: Julian Assange, founder of Wikileaks, in his 2006 manifesto, quoted from a president who said: "Behind the ostensible government sits enthroned an invisible government, owing no allegiance and acknowledging no responsibility to the people. To destroy this invisible government, to dissolve the unholy alliance between corrupt business and corrupt politics is the first task of the statesmanship of the day." **Which president was he quoting?**

A: Theodore Roosevelt. Roosevelt was actually quoting (with approval) from the Progressive platform. This is taken from his 1913 autobiography. [37]

Q: While a number of presidents were heavy drinkers, which pre-Civil War one said, after losing his party's nomination for re-election, "There's nothing left to do but get drunk"?

A: Franklin Pierce.

Q: Which president said, "Rarely is the question asked: Is our children learning"?

A: George W. Bush. [38]

Q: Which president said, "When the president does it, that means it's not illegal"?

A: Richard Nixon, in a televised 1977 interview with David Frost.[39]

Q: Which president said, "I've now been in 57 states—I think one left to go"?

A: Barack Obama, at a campaign event in Beaverton, Oregon, May 9, 2008. [40]

CHAPTER TWENTY NOTES:

1) http://www.quotationspage.com/quote/759.html
2) *Millard Fillmore Papers Volume II*, (New York: Buffalo Historical Society, 1907)
3) http://ohsweb.ohiohistory.org/places/c03/index.shtml
    http://ricochet.com/main-feed/Reevaluating-Warren-G.-Harding http://news
    blogs.chicagotribune.com/vox_pop/2009/01/president-obama.html
4) http://www.accuracyproject.org/cbe-Eisenhower,DwightD.html http://www.

lbjli brary.org/collections/daily-diary.html

Jack McCallum, *Ace Venture, Sports Illustrated*, 6/17/96. http://sportsillustrated. cnn.com/vault/article/magazine/MAG1008266/5/index.htm

5) http://home.comcast.net/~ceoverfield/humor.html

6) http://www.pbs.org/civilwar/war/facts.html

7) http://abluteau.wordpress.com/2009/10/10/president-warren-hardings-lover-carrie-phillips-spied-for-kaiser/
http://www.washingtonpost.com/wp-srv/style/features/harding.htm
http://thehardingaffair.com/the-letters
http://www.forbes.com/forbes-life-magazine/1998/0504/031_print.html

8) Nagourney, Adam. *In Tapes, Nixon Rails About Jews and Blacks. The New York Times*, December 10, 2010.

9) http://www.pbs.org/newshour/debatingourdestiny/dod/1976-broadcast.htmlhe Soviet Union.

10) http://americanhistory.about.com/cs/andrewjackson/a/quotejackson.htm
http://www.presidentprofiles.com/Washington-Johnson/Andrew-Jackson-Administration-and-appointments.html
http://www.pbs.org/wnet/historyofus/web12/segment3.html http://ourwhite-house.org/prespgs/jqadams.html
Time magazine: *The Presidency: Splendid Misery*, July 27, 1959
http://www.quoteworld.org/quotes/7305
http://en.wikiquote.org/wiki/John_Adams
http://www.trivia-library.com/a/president-harry-s-truman-ghosts-in-the-white-house.htm   http://www.quoteworld.org/quotes/10277
http://www.brainyquote.com/quotes/authors/w/william_howard_taft.html

11) http://public.wsu.edu/~campbelld/amlit/1900.html

12) http://www.historytoday.com/tim-stanley/contrarian-teddy-roosevelt-laid-bare

13) http://home.comcast.net/~ceoverfield/humor.html

14) Remark to editor William Alan White. Russell, Francis. *The Shadow of Blooming Grove-Warren G. Harding In His Times.* Easton Press. (1962).

15) http://www.whitehouse.gov/about/presidents/herberthoover

16) Bret Barnes, *Margaret Truman Daniel Dies at Age 83, The Washington Post*, 1/29/2008 http://ireport.cnn.com/docs/DOC-530565

17) Safire, William, *Lend Me Your Ears: Great Speeches in History*, Norton (2004)
http://languagemagazine.com/?page_id=2110
http://suzyred.com/teacher.html
http://pawprints.kashalinka.com/anecdotes/michener.shtml

19) http://www.texasarchive.org/library/index.php/Presidential_Painting_-_Portrait_Rejected_as_'Ugly'
http://www.npg.si.edu/exh/hall2/lbjs.htm

20) Alonzo Hamby, *Man of the People*, http://www.washingtonpost.com/wp-srv/style/longterm/books/chap1/man_of.htm

21) http://articles.sun-sentinel.com/2010-12-05/news/fl-rwcol-harding-oped1205-20101205_1_attorney-general-harry-daugherty-naval-oil-reserves-mistresses
http://potus-geeks.livejournal.com/99260.html

22) http://www.snopes.com/quotes/truman/truman.asp

23) http://whitehousetapes.net/clip/lyndon-johnson-joe-haggar-lbj-orders-some-new-haggar-pants

24) The clip can be seen on YouTube.
http://www.youtube.com/watch?v=eKgPY1adc0A

25) The clip can be seen on YouTube.
http://www.youtube.com/watch?v=1PTiMKsTo-o

26) The clip can be seen on YouTube.
http://www.youtube.com/watch?v=ZkDoCU09V74

27) http://www.theamericanconservative.com/article/2009/nov/01/00018/

28) Thomas Jefferson to John Taylor, Monticello, May 28, 1816. Ford, Paul Leicester, ed. *The Writings of Thomas Jefferson* (1892-1899). Cornell University Library (1999)
http://www.monticello.org/site/jefferson/private-banks-quotation#footnote3_myau26h

29 Letter to John Taylor in 1814. http://compuball.com/Inquisition/democracyevil.htm

30) http://www.whitehouse.gov/about/presidents/calvincoolidge

31) Jeffers, H. Paul, *An Honest President* (Harper, 2002)

32) http://churchstatelaw.com/historicalmaterials/8_8_1.asp

33) http://www.constitution.org/fed/federa51.htm

34) The clip can be seenonYouTube.http://www.youtube.com/watch?v=6SkFjTCscM4

35) http://observer.com/2008/11/idaily-showis-lbj-piss-take; *The New York Times* (October 31, 1971)

36) http://www.pbs.org/wnet/historyofus/web12/segment3.html

37) http://www.bartleby.com/55/15b.html.

38) The clip can be seen on YouTube. http://www.youtube.com/watch?v=-ej7ZEnjSeA

39) The clip can be seen on YouTube. http://www.youtube.com/watch?v=ejvyDn1TPr8

40) The clip can be seen on YouTube. http://www.youtube.com/watch?v=OrsBKGpwi58

CHAPTER 21

Quotes by Presidents About Presidents

These days, it is fairly unusual for one president to criticize another personally, especially when the two men do not even know each other. However, that was not always the case and even if there was ever an unwritten rule to this effect, it has long been honored in the breach. Often the president doing the talking (or writing) is criticizing a president of a different political party, but not always: The following passages—usually but not always non-complimentary—are all by presidents about other presidents. Either the speaker or the subject is identified. Try and guess the other.

Q: **This 20th-century president called Thomas Jefferson "perhaps the most incapable executive that ever filled the presidential chair," Andrew Jackson "not more than half civilized," John Tyler "a politician of monumental littleness," [a** great oxymoron], William McKinley "[a man with] no more backbone than a chocolate éclair" and Woodrow Wilson "rotten through and through." Who was the president?

A: Theodore Roosevelt. [1]

Q: Which president stated of Abraham Lincoln: "[Lincoln] is to the extent of his limited ability and narrow intelligence the willing instrument [of the Abolitionists] for all the woe which [has] thus far been brought upon the country and for all the degradation, all the atrocity, all the desolation and ruin"?

A: Franklin Pierce. [2]

Q: John Adams once wrote: "That [this man] was not a scholar is certain. That he was too illiterate, unlearned, unread for his station is equally past dispute." To whom was he referring?

A: George Washington. [3]

Q: Woodrow Wilson called this president "a nonentity with side whiskers." Who was he?

A: Chester Arthur. [4]

Q: Who said of Eisenhower: "Why, this fellow don't know any more about politics than a pig knows about Sunday. ... A glamorous military hero, glorified by the press. ... If Eisenhower should become president, his administration would make Grant's look like a model of perfection"?

A: Harry Truman. [5]

Q: Which president said of John F. Kennedy in 1960: "He leaves little doubt that his idea of the 'challenging new world' is one in which the Federal Government will grow bigger and do more and of course spend more. . . . Under the tousled boyish haircut it is still old Karl Marx"?

A: Ronald Reagan. [6]

Q: Which president said of Ronald Reagan: "Reagan is not one that wears well. Reagan on a personal basis, is terrible. He just isn't pleasant to be around. Maybe he's different with others. No, he's just an uncomfortable man to be around-strange"?

A: Fellow Republican **Richard Nixon**. This was recorded as part of a discussion with H.R. Haldeman in 1972 as part of the Nixon Tapes. [7]

Q: Harvard-educated John Quincy Adams called this man, "a barbarian who could not write a sentence of grammar and hardly could spell his own name." To whom was he referring?

A: Andrew Jackson. [8]

Q: Lyndon Johnson said that this president, "is so dumb he can't fart and chew gum at the same time. . . . He's a nice guy but he spent too much time playing football without a helmet." To whom was he referring?

A: Gerald Ford. [9]

Q: Dwight Eisenhower praised this president as "a good soldier. There is no man in the history of America who has had such careful preparation as has [Mr. X] for carrying out the duties of the presidency. [He is] a man of great reading, a man of great intelligence and a man of great decisiveness." Of whom was he speaking?

A: Richard Nixon. [10]

Q: Lyndon Johnson said: "Boys, I may not know much, but I know the difference between chicken shit and chicken salad. . . . He's like a Spanish horse, who runs faster than anyone for the first nine lengths and then turns around and runs backward. You'll see, he'll do something wrong in the end. He always does." Of whom was he speaking?

A: Richard Nixon, less flatteringly than Eisenhower had. [11]

Q: Warren Harding said: "Well, the mad [president] has a new achievement to his credit. He succeeded in defeating the party that furnished him a job for nearly all of his manhood days after leaving the ranch, and showed his gratitude for the presidency, at that party's hands. The eminent fakir can now turn to raising hell, his specialty, along other lines." Of whom was he speaking?

A: Theodore Roosevelt. Harding made the comment in 1912, when Roosevelt decided to run for president as a member of the Bull Moose Party rather than the Republican Party. [12]

* * *

It seems that the president has commented in writing on his fellow presidents more than any other. That is Harry Truman. Sometimes he was very complimentary but more frequently that was not the case. Of the presidents he opined on, eight were rated great or nearly great, five were mixed and eighteen were mediocre or worse. Not too surprisingly, the Democratic presidents fared better than the Republicans, especially after 1900. Try to guess which former president he was writing about in each of the following quotes. Some hints are provided along the way.

Great or close to it:

Q: "He was a great man, a truly great man. ... In many ways [he] was the greatest of the greats. He was obviously and vis-

ibly one of the smartest people in the country and possibly in the world. [He] had the idea that he was the smartest man in the United States, and . . . of course people associated with him didn't like that attitude, but it's probably the truth." (Hint: 20th-century president)

A: Woodrow Wilson

Q: "The next man on my list of great presidents, a man who isn't much thought of these days, is [this president]. ... He exercised his powers of the presidency as I think they should be exercised. [He] was living in an age when the terrible burden of making decisions in a war was entirely in the hands of the president. And when that came about, he decided that that was much more important than going to parties and shaking hands with people. I know exactly how he felt, but in my time there were more able and informed people who were helping the president, and that made a difference. [He was] a great president. Said what he intended to do and did it." (Hint: pre-Civil War President)

A: James Polk

Q: "[He] is my next choice as a great president after Jefferson, the next president who really did things." (Hint: pre-Civil War president)

A: Andrew Jackson

Q: "He was a great president in his first term; in his second term, he wasn't the same [man] he was to begin with. ... [He] reestablished the presidency by being not only a chief executive but a leader." (Hint: post-Civil War president)

A: Grover Cleveland

Q: "[This president] was just as important [as Washington and Lincoln] because he was working continuously for the preservation of free government as established by the Constitution."

A: Thomas Jefferson.

Q: "He was a great, great president. He had the ability to make people believe he was right and go along with the things he wanted to do, and he was also very daring in his actions. ... He had defects, of course. ... For one thing, he was a first-rate executive, never afraid to make those decisions he made, but he wasn't a good administrator because he just wasn't able to delegate authority to anybody else. It goes without saying that I am highly impressed by him for a thousand reasons." (Hint: 20th-century president)

A: Franklin Roosevelt.

Q: "In my view, he missed being a great president, though only by a narrow margin. The trouble with [him] is that, though he was the president who finally awakened to the fact that the welfare of the country was wrapped up in the forests and the mines and the other things the country owned ..., he had his troubles with Congress and he had his troubles with the trusts, and he didn't get a heck of a lot done. ... He ended up adding up to more talk than achievement."

A: Theodore Roosevelt. Truman added: "He finally got to be called a trustbuster, but he didn't bust very many of them."

Q: "My people didn't think much of [him], but I thought he was wonderful. It took me a long time to come to that realization, however, because my family were all against him and all thought it was a fine thing he got assassinated. (Well, that's an exaggeration, but not by much.) I began to feel just the opposite after I'd studied the history of the country. ..."

A: **Abraham Lincoln.** By "my people," Truman was referring to members of his family. As noted earlier, Truman's mother in particular was a full-fledged Confederate sympathizer during and after the Civil War.

<u>Mixed:</u>

Q: "[He] wasn't too bad, but he was overwhelmed by a hostile Congress." (Hint: post-Civil War president who Truman rated more generously than most historians).

A: **Andrew Johnson.**

Q: "Despite his unimpressive appearance and manner, he was a brilliant fellow with a crystal-clear mind.... It was just that, when it came time for him to act like an executive, he was like a great many other people; when the time comes to make decisions, they have difficulty doing it." (Hint: pre-Civil War president who Truman rated less generously than most historians).

A: **James Madison**

Q: "I happen to be in the minority in my opinion of [this man]. I know most people think he was a poor president ... but I think he was actually a president who tried hard and did the best he possibly could and was faced with difficulties he wasn't able to overcome at the time. ... You see, he'd been out of the country for quite a while." (Hint: 20th-century president)

A: **Herbert Hoover.**

Q: "Elected by a fluke and knew it, and he did his level best to do a good job."

A: Rutherford Hayes

Q: "One of the presidents we could have done without.... There are some things I admire about [him], but there were also plenty of things that weren't so admirable. ... The reason I have a certain amount of grudging respect for [him] is that he knew his own mind and stuck to his decisions." (Hint: pre-Civil War president)

A: John Tyler

Medicore ... or worse:

Q: "I consider [this man] a pretty minor president. In spite of [a foreign policy adopted during his administration]. That's the only important thing he ever did more or less on his own, when you really get down to it."

A: James Monroe. The policy in question was the Monroe Doctrine, though it was primarily authored by John Quincy Adams.

Q: "He was a conscientious and well-meaning man, and I wish I could say more about his achievements. . . . Practically nothing was accomplished in his administration. I just don't think there were any events in [his] administration that were very outstanding." (Hint: early president)

A: John Quincy Adams. Truman added: "The single really interesting thing about Adams, I'm afraid, is that he was the only son of a president in our history to become president himself." Of course, after George H. W. Bush and George W. Bush that is no longer true.

Q: "I've got to say that our country would have done just as well not to have had [him] as president.... My particular reason for not thinking much of him is that he was just too timid and indecisive. I don't know whether or not he even had any personal philosophy on the role of government; I think he was a man who was always worrying about what might happen if he did this or that, and always keeping his ear to the ground to the point where he couldn't act as the chief executive, and for that reason he was just a politician and nothing more, a politician who was out of his depth." (Hint: This president and the five which follow are all Pre-Civil War presidents generally rated as mediocre by most historians).

A: Martin Van Buren

Q: "[He] didn't accomplish a thing [while] he was in office. He made no contribution whatsoever. He had no policy. He didn't know what the government was about, to tell the truth. About the only thing he did during that brief period was see friends and friends of friends, because he was such an easy mark that he couldn't say no to anybody, and everybody and his brother was beseeching him for jobs."

A: **William Henry Harrison.** Instead of "while," he actually said "during the month," but that would have given the answer away.

Q: "[This man] was one of the do-nothing presidents.... When [he] became president of the United States, I don't think he knew what to do. I can't be charitable and say that he failed to carry out his program; he didn't have any program to carry out, so he couldn't fail because he had no program. ... [A president] must have ideas and imagination as to what's needed for the good of the country, and he can create conditions that will make him great, or he can take things as they are and do nothing, like [this man]. [He] certainly became expert at doing nothing." (Hint: pre-Civil War president).

A: Zachary Taylor

Q: "Another of those detached, do-nothing presidents. ... He had no regular viewpoint on anything. ... He was a man who changed with the wind, and as president of the United States he didn't do anything that's worth pointing out." (Hint: pre-Civil War president).

A: Millard Fillmore

Q: "[He] was a nincompoop. ... It was [his] foolish notion that he could cool down the slavery question and make people forget about it by doing two things: filling his cabinet with people of different viewpoints, and concentrating almost entirely on foreign policy and territorial expansion instead of slavery problems. But the net result was that his cabinet members kept bickering with each other and didn't accomplish much, and [his] moves in other directions didn't distract people's attention from the slavery problems for a minute."

A: Franklin Pierce (As discussed in the "appearance" chapter, while Truman had no high regard for Pierce's abilities as president, he certainly was impressed by his handsome appearance.)

Q: "[He] hesitated and backtracked and felt that his constitutional prerogative didn't allow him to do things, and he ended up doing absolutely nothing and threw everything into [his successor's] lap."

A: James Buchanan.   His successor was of course Abraham Lincoln.

Q: "[His] period in office seems to prove the theory that we can coast along for eight years without a president. ... [His] period as president was one of the low points in our history. ... I don't think [he] knew very much about what the president's job was except that he was commander in chief of the armed forces. That was the thing, I think, that impressed him more than anything, and he was pretty naïve or ignorant about everything else. ... He wasn't even a chief executive; he was another sleepwalker whose administration was even more crooked than Warren Harding's, if that's possible."

A: Ulysses Grant.

Q: "The only thing that stands out about [him] is that he took all the wonderful furniture that had been brought to this country by Jefferson, Monroe, and several of the other presidents of that period and sold it in an auction for about $6,500." (Hint: post-Civil War president)

A: Chester Arthur.

Q: "I tend to pair up [these two men] because they're the two presidents I can think of who most preferred laziness to labor. ... There's not much else you can say about [this man] except that he was president of the United States." (Hint: the first was a 19th-century post-Civil War president and the second was a 20th-century president).

A: **Benjamin Harrison** and **Dwight Eisenhower** (first sentence); Benjamin Harrison (second sentence).

Q: "A fat, jolly, likeable, mediocre man."

A: William Howard Taft.

Q: "In our own days, he is probably the nearest example of a sit-still president we've ever had, except possibly Dwight Eisenhower. He believed that the less a president did, the better for his country, and I don't agree with that at all. He sat with his feet in his desk drawer and did nothing. He just sat there and signed bills and vetoed a few and that's all there was to it." (Hint: 20th-century president)

A: Calvin Coolidge.

Q: "All I'll say now is that when the people elect a man to the presidency who doesn't take care of the job, they've got nobody to blame but themselves.... The trouble with [him] is he's just a coward. He hasn't got any backbone at all.... [He] didn't know anything, and all the time he was in office he didn't learn a thing. ..." (Hint: 20th-century president who served after Truman)

A: Dwight Eisenhower.

Q: "I wonder how many people remember our history and realize how close Jefferson came to losing the election in 1800, and how close Aaron Burr came to being our third president, which would have been as bad as electing [this man] today. ... You don't set a fox to watching the chickens just because he has a lot of experience in the henhouse ..." (Hint: 20th-century president).

A: Richard Nixon (As noted above, Truman also called Nixon a "no-good lying bastard.") [13]

CHAPTER TWENTY-ONE NOTES:

1) http://www.federalobserver.com/archive.php?aid=10258
    Ruddy, Daniel, *Theodore Roosevelt's History of the United States* (Harper, 2010).
2) http://www.huffingtonpost.com/seth-swirsky/lincoln-lied-and-thousand
    _b_28920.html

    http://www.diplom.org/manus/Presidents/ratings/prez.html

3) http://gwpapers.virginia.edu/articles/warren.html

4) http://www.americanheritage.com/content/presidents-presidents

5) http://www.pbs.org/wgbh/amex/presidents/34_eisenhower/filmmore/
filmscript.html http://ww2db.com/person_bio.php?person_id=105

6) http://www.time.com/time/specials/packages/article/0,28804,1894529_1894528
_1894518,00.html   http://en.wikiquote.org/wiki/Ronald_Reagan

7) http://www.cbsnews.com/stories/2003/11/13/politics/main583368.shtml

8) H. W. Brands, *Andrew Jackson: His Life and Times* (Doubleday)

9) http://www.independent.co.uk/news/presidents/gerald-r-ford-1451818.html
http://www.huffingtonpost.com/joe-lapointe/football-helmets-as-weapo_b_
768004.html
Ralph Keyes, *The Quote Verifier: Who said what, where, and when*, St. Martin's
Press 2006, p. 24

10) http://www.diplom.org/manus/Presidents/ratings/prez.html

11) http://www.trivia-library.com/b/u-s-president-lyndon-b-johnson-quotes-from-
johnson-part-2.htm
http://www.barrypopik.com/index.php/new_york_city/entry/you_cant_make_
chicken_salad_out_of_chicken_shit/

12) http://www.diplom.org/manus/Presidents/ratings/prez.html

13) Margaret Truman (editor). *Where the Buck Stops: The Personal and Private
Writings of Harry S. Truma*n, Warner Books (1989).

CHAPTER 22

Rankings and Approval Ratings

The ranking of presidents is obviously a subjective enterprise. Nevertheless, based on multiple ranking of the presidents over the years, certain trends emerge. The first major ranking of the presidents was performed by historian Arthur M. Schlesinger in 1948. A Wikipedia analysis shows the results of seventeen major surveys of the rankings of presidents done between 1948 and 2011. The seventeen polls are as follows:

Schlesinger 1948 poll. Harry Truman was president at the time.
Schlesinger 1962 poll. This was a survey of 75 historians. John Kennedy was president at the time.
1982 Murray-Blessing survey. Murray, Robert K.; Blessing, Tim H. (1994). *Greatness in the White House: Rating the Presidents, from Washington Through Ronald Reagan.* Pennsylvania State University Press.

***Chicago Tribune* 1982 poll.** This was a survey of 49 historians conducted by the *Chicago Tribune*. See DeGregorio, William A. *The Complete Book of U.S. Presidents, 4th ed.* Barricade Books, 1993

Siena polls, 1982, 1990, 1994, 2002, 2010. These were conducted by the Siena Research Institute of Siena College.

Ridings-McIver 1996 poll. This is a poll conducted by William J. Ridings, Jr. and Stuart B. McIver, and published in their book *Rating the Presidents: A Ranking of U.S. leaders, from the Great and Honorable to the Dishonest and Incompetent.* Carol Publishing (1997). More than 719 people took part in the poll, primarily academic historians and political scientists, although some politicians and celebrities also took part.

Schlesinger 1996 poll. *"Rating the Presidents: Washington to Clinton."* http://www.pbs.org/wgbh/pages/frontline/shows/choice 2004/leadership/schlesinger.html#chart. Retrieved 2010-03-25.

CSPAN 1999 poll. The C-SPAN Survey of Presidential Leadership consists of rankings from a group of presidential historians and "professional observers of the presidency." Survey Participants, C-Span 2009 Historians Presidential Leadership Survey.

***Wall Street Journal* 2000 poll.** This survey by The *Wall Street Journal* consisted of an "ideologically balanced group of 132 prominent professors of history, law, and political science." This poll sought to include an equal number of liberals and conservatives in the survey, as the editors argued that previous polls were dominated by either one group or the other, but were never balanced.

***Wall Street Journal* 2005 poll** Presidential Leadership; *The Rankings, Wall Street Journal Online*, September 12, 2005.

***Times* 2008 poll.** The *Times*, a British newspaper, asked eight of its own "top international and political commentators" to rank all 42 U.S. presidents "in order of greatness." Griffin, Jeremy; Nico Hines. "Who's the greatest? The *Times US presidential rankings*." The *Times* London. http://www.timesonline.co.uk/tol/ news/world/us_and_americas/us_elections/article5030539.ece. Retrieved 2010-03-24.

CSPAN 2009 poll. "CSPAN Survey of Presidential Leadership." http://www.c-span.org/PresidentialSurvey/Overall-Ranking.aspx. **USPC 2011 poll.** In 2011, through the agency of its United States presidency Centre [USPC], the Institute for the Study of the Americas (located in the University of London's School of Advanced Study) released the first ever U.K. academic survey to rate U.S. presidents. This polled the opinion of U.K. specialists in U.S. history and political studies to assess presidential performance and produced an overall rating on the basis of the responses. [1]

Q: Who are the only five presidents who appear in the top quartile of all seventeen surveys?

A: George Washington, Thomas Jefferson, Abraham Lincoln, Theodore Roosevelt and **Franklin Roosevelt.**

Q: Of these five, who are the only ones who have never been ranked as the best president?

A: Thomas Jefferson and **Theodore Roosevelt.**

Q: Which president is ranked as the best based on an aggregate ranking of all presidents?

A: Abraham Lincoln.

Q: Who is the only president besides Lincoln who never ranks lower than third?

A: Franklin Roosevelt.

Q: Which president is ranked as the worst based on an aggregate ranking of all Presidents?

A: James Buchanan. The second worst is Andrew Johnson. Interestingly, the two lowest-ranked presidents are sandwiched around the highest-ranked.

Q: Who are the only four presidents who appear in the bottom quartile of all seventeen surveys?

A: Millard Fillmore, Franklin Pierce, James Buchanan and **Warren Harding.**

Q: Since John F. Kennedy, only one president appears in the top quartile in one out of fifteen surveys and one appears in the top quartile in four out of thirteen surveys. None of the other presidents since that time appear at all in the top quartile. Who are the two presidents?

A: Lyndon Johnson and **Ronald Reagan** respectively. Johnson, Richard Nixon, Gerald Ford and Jimmy Carter were reviewed fifteen times, Ronald Reagan thirteen times, George H.W. Bush twelve times, Bill Clinton eleven times, George W. Bush six times and Barack Obama one time.

Q: Only one president appears in three different quartiles at least three times. Who is he?

A: Ronald Reagan, who appears in the first quartile five times, the second five times and the third three times.

Q: Besides Reagan, only one president appears in three different quartiles at least twice. Who is he?

A: Jimmy Carter, who appears in the second quartile in the Ridings-McIver 1996 poll and in the 2011 USPC poll. However, he appears in the fourth quartile in the 1982 Siena poll and the 2005 *Wall Street Journal* poll. He appears in the third quartile in all of the remaining polls.

Q: Who is the only president who served exactly one term whose aggregate ranking is in the top quartile?

A: James Polk.

Q: Prior to George W. Bush, who is the only president who served more than four years whose aggregate ranking is in the bottom quartile?

A: Ulysses Grant.

Q: Only once have three consecutive presidents averaged in the top quartile. Who are they?

A: Franklin Roosevelt, Harry Truman and Dwight Eisenhower.

Q: Only once have four consecutive presidents averaged in the bottom quartile. Who are they?

A: Zachary Taylor, Millard Fillmore, Franklin Pierce and James Buchanan.

The chart starting on the following page summarizes the 17 rankings of all the presidents and also includes an aggregate ranking.

No.	President	Political party	Schlesinger 1948 poll rank	Schlesinger 1962 poll rank	1982 Murray-Blessing survey	Chicago Tribune 1982 poll rank	Siena 1982 poll rank	Siena 1990 poll rank	Siena 1994 poll rank
1	George Washington	None	02	02	03	03	04	04	04
2	John Adams	Federalist	09	10	09	14 (tie)	10	14	12
3	Thomas Jefferson	Dem-Repub	05	05	04	05	02	03	05
4	James Madison	Dem-Repub	14	12	14	17	09	08	09
5	James Monroe	Dem-Repub	12	18	15	16	15	11	15
6	John Quincy Adams	Dem-Repub	11	13	16	19	17	16	17
7	Andrew Jackson	Democratic	06	06	07	06	13	09	11
8	Martin Van Buren	Democratic	15	17	20	18	21	21	22
9	William Henry Harrison	Whig	–	–	–	38	26	35	28
10	John Tyler	Whig	22	25	28	29	34	33	34
11	James K. Polk	Democratic	10	08	12	11	12	13	14
12	Zachary Taylor	Whig	25	24	27	28	29	34	33
13	Millard Fillmore	Whig	24	26	29	31	32	32	35
14	Franklin Pierce	Democratic	27	28	31	35	35	36	37
15	James Buchanan	Democratic	26	29	33	36	37	38	39
16	AbrahamLincoln	Rep./National Union	01	01	01	01	03	02	02
17	Andrew Johnson	Dem./National Union	19	23	32	32	38	39	40
18	Ulysses Grant	Republican	28	30	35	30	36	37	38
19	Rutherford Hayes	Republican	13	14	22	22	22	23	24
20	James Garfield	Republican	–	–	–	33	25	30	26
21	Chester A. Arthur	Republican	17	21	26	24	24	26	27
22/24	Grover Cleveland	Democratic	08	11	17	13	18	17	19
23	Benjamin Harrison	Republican	21	20	23	25	31	29	30
25	William McKinley	Republican	18	15	18	10	19	19	18
26	Theodore Roosevelt	Republican	07	07	05	04	05	05	03
27	William Howard Taft	Republican	16	16	19	20	20	20	21
28	Woodrow Wilson	Democratic	04	04	06	07	06	06	06
29	Warren G. Harding	Republican	29	31	36	37	39	40	41
30	Calvin Coolidge	Republican	23	27	30	27	30	31	36
31	Herbert Hoover	Republican	20	19	21	21	27	28	29
32	Franklin D. Roosevelt	Democratic	03	03	02	02	01	01	01
33	Harry S. Truman	Democratic	–	09	08	08	07	07	07

Ridings-McIver 1996 poll rank	Schlesinger 1996 poll rank	CSPAN 1999 poll rank	Wall Street Journal 2000 poll rank	Siena 2002 poll rank	Wall Street Journal 2005 poll rank	Times 2008 poll rank	CSPAN 2009 poll rank	Siena 2010 poll rank	USPC 2011 poll rank	Aggregate ranking
03	02	03	01	04	01	02	02	04	03	03
14	11	16	13	12	13	13	17	17	12	12
04	04	07	04	05	04	04	07	05	04	04
10	17	18	15	09	17	15	20	06	14	13
13	15	14	16	08	16	21	14	07	13	14 (tie)
18	18	19	20	17	25	16	19	19	20	18
08	05	13	06	13	10	14	13	14	09	08 (tie)
21	21	30	23	24	27	40	31	23	27	24
35	–	37	–	36	–	39	39	35	–	38 (tie)
34	32	36	34	37	35	31	35	37	37	36
11	09	12	10	11	09	09	12	12	16	10
29	29	28	31	34	33	28	29	33	33	35
36	31	35	35	38	36	33	37	38	35	38 (tie)
37	33	39	37	39	38	41	40	40	39	40
40	38	41	39	41	40	42	42	42	40	42
01	01	01	02	02	02	01	01	03	02	01
39	37	40	36	42	37	24	41	43	36	41
38	34	33	32	35	29	18	23	26	29	37
25	23	26	22	27	24	27	33	31	30	25
30	–	29	–	33	–	34	28	27	–	29 (tie)
28	26	32	26	30	26	22	32	25	32	28
16	13	17	12	20	12	19	21	20	21	19
31	19	31	27	32	30	30	30	34	34	33
17	16	15	14	19	14	17	16	21	17	20 (tie)
05	06	04	05	03	05	05	04	02	05	05
20	22	24	19	21	20	23	24	24	25	22 (tie)
06	07	06	11	06	11	10	09	08	06	06
41	39	38	37	40	39	35	38	41	38	43
33	30	27	25	29	23	26	26	29	28	31
24	35	34	29	31	31	38	34	36	26	29 (tie)
02	03	02	03	01	03	03	03	01	01	02
07	08	05	07	07	07	07	05	09	07	07

No.	President	Political party	Schlesinger 1948 poll rank	Schlesinger 1962 poll rank	1982 Murray-Blessing survey	Chicago Tribune 1982 poll rank	Siena 1982 poll rank	Siena 1990 poll rank	Siena 1994 poll rank
34	Dwight D. Eisenhower	Republican	-	22	11	09	11	12	08
35	John F. Kennedy	Democratic	-	-	13	14 (tie)	08	10	10
36	Lyndon B. Johnson	Democratic	-	-	10	12	14	15	13
37	Richard Nixon	Republican	-	-	34	34	28	25	23
38	Gerald Ford	Republican	-	-	24	23	23	27	32
39	Jimmy Carter	Democratic	-	-	25	26	33	24	25
40	Ronald Reagan	Republican	-	-	--	--	16 *	22	20
41	George H. W. Bush	Republican	-	-	--	--	-	18 *	31
42	Bill Clinton	Democratic	-	-	--	--	-	-	16 *
43	George W. Bush	Republican	-	-	--	--	-	-	-
44	Barack Obama	Democratic	-	-	--	--	-	-	-
Total in Survey			29	31	36	38	39	40	41

The above rankings are an after-the-fact analysis by various organizations as to how a particular president performed during his term relative to the others. Approval ratings are a current analysis of how a president is performing at any point in time according to the American public. The Gallup Organization has been providing approval ratings for every president since Franklin Roosevelt. The Gallup Organization also creates disapproval ratings. While there is obviously some correlation between disapproval and lack of approval, that correlation is not precise. Thus, approval plus disapproval does not equal 100%.[2]

The following questions are based on those polls and therefore only apply to presidents from Franklin Roosevelt onwards:

Q: Which president has had the highest approval rating?

A: **George W. Bush**: 90%, on September 21, 2001, shortly after the 9/11 attacks. The second highest, 89%, was attained by his father George H.W. Bush on February 28, 1991, which was the last day of the Persian Gulf War.

Ridings-McIver 1996 poll rank	Schlesinger 1996 poll rank	CSPAN 1999 poll rank	Wall Street Journal 2000 poll rank	Siena 2002 poll rank	Wall Street Journal 2005 poll rank	Times 2008 poll rank	CSPAN 2009 poll rank	Siena 2010 poll rank	USPC 2011 poll rank	Aggregate ranking
09	10	09	09	10	08	06	08	10	10	08 (tie)
15	12	08	18	14	15	11	06	11	15	11
12	14	10	17	15	18	12	11	16	11	14 (tie)
32	36	25	33	26	32	38	27	30	23	32
27	28	23	28	28	28	25	22	28	24	26
19	27	22	30	25	34	32	25	32	18	27
26	25	11	08	16	06	08	10	18	08	17
22	24	20	21	22	21	20	18	22	22	22 (tie)
23 *	20 *	21 *	24 *	18	22	23	15	13	19	20 (tie)
-	-	-	-	23 *	19 *	37 *	36	39	31	34
-	-	-	-	-	-	-	-	15 *	-	14 (tie) *
41	39	41	39	42	40	42	42	43	40	43

Q: Which president has had the lowest approval rating?

A: Harry Truman: 22%, on February 9, 1952. This was likely due to a combination of factors including the threat of Communism, the Korean War and alleged corruption in the Truman cabinet. Surprisingly, this was 2% lower than Richard Nixon's approval rating on August 2, 1974, just days before he resigned from office.

Q: Which president had the highest average approval rating over his term?

A: John F. Kennedy: 70.1%. Next is Dwight Eisenhower at 65%.

Q: Which president had the lowest average approval rating over his term?

A: Harry Truman: 45.4%. Next is Jimmy Carter at 45.5%

Q: Which two presidents had the widest variation between their highest and lowest approval ratings?

A: Interestingly, it was the same two presidents who had the highest and lowest one-time approval differentials, **George W. Bush** and **Harry Truman**, 65% for each. Bush fell from his high of 90% just after 9/11 to 25% in October, 2008 (inconveniently for John McCain, who was the Republican nominee in the 2008 election). Truman was at 87% on June 1, 1945, which was just before V-E Day and 22% seven years later.

Q: Which president had the lowest variation between his highest and lowest approval ratings?

A: **John F. Kennedy**: 27% (83% high on March 8, 1962 to 56% low on September 12, 1963). Kennedy is also the only president who never dropped below a 50% approval rating.

Q: Who are the only presidents whose approval ratings never reached 70% at any time?

A: **Richard Nixon, Ronald Reagan** and **Barack Obama.**

Order	President	Highest Approval	Lowest Approval	High-Low	Highest Disapproval	Approval Average
44	Obama	**69** (1/22/09)	**38** (8/22/11, 8/27/11, 8/29/11, 10/6/11, 10/13/11, 10/17/11)	**31**	**55** (8/27/11, 8/29/11)	**49**
43	George W. Bush	**90** (9/21/01)	**25** (10/3/08, 10/10/08, 10/31/08)	**65**	**71** (10/10/08)	**49.4**
42	Clinton	**73** (12/19/98)	**37** (5/26/93)	**36**	**54** (9/6/94)	**55.1**
41	George H. W. Bush	**89** (2/28/91)	**29** (7/31/92) **5** (1/28/83)	**60**	**60** (7/31/92) **60** (7/31/92)	**60.9**
40	Reagan	**68** (5/16/86)		**33**		**52.8**

Order	President	Highest Approval	Lowest Approval	High-Low	Highest Disapproval	Approval Average
39	Carter	**75** (3/18/77)	**28** (6/29/79)	**47**	**59** (6/29/79)	**45.5**
38	Ford	**71** (8/16/74)	**37** (3/28/75)	**34**	**46** (4/18/75)	**47.2**
37	Nixon	**67** (1/26/73)	**24** (8/2/74)	**43**	**66** (8/2/74)	**49.1**
36	Johnson	**79** (2/28/64)	**35** (8/7/68)	**44**	**52** (8/7/68, 3/10/68)	**55.1**
35	Kennedy	**83** (3/8/62)	**56** (9/12/63)	**27**	**30** (9/12/63, 11/8/63)	**70.1**
34	Eisenhower	**79** (12/14/56)	**48** (3/27/58)	**31**	36 (3/27/58)	**60.5**
33	Truman	**87** (6/1/45)	**22** (2/9/52)	**65**	**67** (1/6/52)	**45.4**
32	Roosevelt	**84** (1/8/42)	**48** (8/18/39)	**36**	**46** (5/22/38, 5/29/38, 11/7/38)	

How important is it to win a second term to be considered a great president? Nate Silver, who writes the 538.com blog for *TheNew York Times* suggests that the answer is: very. [3] Taking the average of the four most recent surveys, Silver found that nine of the top ten ranked presidents (**John Kennedy** being the exception) were elected to two terms. The only three ranked 27 or below were **Calvin Coolidge** (27), **Richard Nixon** (29) and **George W. Bush** (38).

Another 10 presidents were nominated by their parties for a second term but lost in the general election. This group tends to be bunched in the middle, ranging from a high of **John Adams** (16) to a low of **Benjamin Harrison** (34).

The worst-rated presidents are those who didn't even try to win a second term or were disallowed the opportunity to do so. With the exception of **James Polk** (11) who had a one-term pledge, the seven other presidents in this group range from a high of **Chester Arthur** (28) to a low of **James Buchanan** (43).

Interestingly, all presidents in this group served within a narrow 44 year range lasting from 1841-1885. Of course, as Silver points out, so did **Lincoln**, the top-ranked president.

Five presidents died during their first terms, and except for **Kennedy** (9), the other four are lowly ranked (**Garfield**-30, **Taylor**-33, **William Henry Harrison**-40 and **Warren Harding**-41). Whether or not this is fair is hard to say.

CHAPTER TWENTY-TWO NOTES:

1) http://americas.sas.ac.uk/research/survey/pdf/analysis.pdf;
   http://americas.sas.ac.uk/research/survey/index.html)
   http://en.wikipedia.org/wiki/Historical_rankings_of_Presidents_of_the_United_States
   http://history-world.org/pres.pdf
2) http://www.gallup.com/poll/116677/Presidential-Approval-Ratings-Gallup-Historical-Statistics-Trends.aspx
   http://en.wikipedia.org/wiki/United_States_presidential_approval_rating
3) http://fivethirtyeight.blogs.nytimes.com/2013/01/23/contemplating-obamas-place-in-history-statistically/#more-38340

CHAPTER 23

Religion

Q: Which president's wife banned all Jewish visitors from their home and which president himself, based in diary entries, held anti-Semitic views?

A: Harry Truman and his wife Bess. According to historian David Beschloss, when talk show host David Susskind asked the ex-president, in 1953, why he had never been invited to the Truman home in Independence Missouri despite their many interviews, Truman replied: "You're a Jew, David, and no Jew has ever been in the house. Bess runs it, and there's never been a Jew inside the house in her or her mother's lifetime."

There is also evidence that Truman himself held anti-Semitic views. For example, Beschloss also wrote that in a private letter to his wife in 1957, Truman referred to New York City as "the U.S. capital of Israel." In addition, in 2003, researchers found a Truman diary entry from 1947 which declared:

"The Jews, I find, are very, very selfish. They care not how many Estonians, Latvians, Finns, Poles, Yugoslavs or

Greeks get murdered or mistreated as [Displaced Persons] as long as the Jews get special treatment. Yet when they have power, physical, financial or political, neither Hitler nor Stalin has anything on them for cruelty or mistreatment to the underdog. Put an underdog on top and it makes no difference whether his name is Russian, Jewish, Negro, Management, Labor, Mormon, Baptist, he goes haywire. I've found very, very few who remember their past condition when prosperity comes."

Professor Michael Cohen's book, *Truman and Israel*, stated that Truman called New York City "kike town," referred to his Jewish friend and business partner, Eddie Jacobson, as his "Jew clerk," and wrote to his wife about someone in a poker game who had "screamed like a Jewish merchant." Truman's diary entries startled historian scholars since Truman is credited with helping bring about the creation of the State of Israel in 1948, despite opposition from his own Department of State.[1]

Q: Which president made the following remarks?

"I've just recognized that, you know, all people have certain traits. The Jews have certain traits. The Irish have certain—for example, the Irish can't drink. What you always have to remember with the Irish is they get mean. Virtually every Irish I've known gets mean when he drinks. Particularly the real Irish. . . . The Jews are just a very aggressive and abrasive and obnoxious personality."

A: Richard Nixon. The remarks were recorded as part of a conversation on February 13, 1973, with Charles W. Colson, a senior adviser who had just told Nixon that he had always had "a little prejudice." In a separately recorded conversation with his secretary Rose Mary Woods, Nixon laid down clear rules about who would be permitted to attend the state dinner for Israeli Prime Minister Golda Meir—he called it "the Jewish dinner"—after learning that the White House was being besieged with requests to attend.

"I don't want any Jew at that dinner who didn't support us in that campaign," he said. "Is that clear? No Jew who did not support us." Nixon listed many of his top Jewish advisers—among them, Mr. Kissinger and William Safire, who went on to become a columnist at *The New York Times*—and argued that they shared a common trait, of needing to compensate for an inferiority complex. "What it is, is it's the insecurity," he said. "It's the latent insecurity. Most Jewish people are insecure. And that's why they have to prove things."

Nixon also strongly hinted to Colson that his reluctance to even consider amnesty for young Americans who went to Canada to avoid being drafted during the Vietnam War was because so many of them were Jewish. "I didn't notice many Jewish names coming back from Vietnam on any of those lists; I don't know how the hell they avoid it," he said, adding: "If you look at the Canadian-Swedish contingent, they were very disproportionately Jewish. The deserters."

In one of the "Nixon tapes", the following conversation took place between Nixon and Bob Haldeman on July 3, 1971.

> **President Nixon:** All right. I want a look at any sensitive areas around where Jews are involved, Bob. See, the Jews are all through the government, and we have got to get in those areas. We've got to get a man in charge who is not Jewish to control the Jewish . . . do you understand?
>
> **Haldeman:** I sure do.
>
> **President Nixon:** The government is full of Jews.
>
> **Haldeman:** I sure do.

President Nixon: Second, most Jews are disloyal. You know what I mean? You have a—you have a [White House Consultant Leonard] Garment and a [National Security Adviser Henry] Kissinger and, frankly, a [White House Speechwriter William] Safire, and, by God, they're exceptions. But, Bob, generally speaking, you can't trust the bastards. They turn on you. Correct? Am I wrong or right?

Haldeman: Sure, and their whole orientation is against this administration anyway or against you.

President Nixon: They have this arrogant attitude, too.

Haldeman: That's right.

President Nixon: So.

Haldeman: And they're smart. They have the ability to do what they want to do, which is to hurt us.[2]

Q: Which two presidents were Quaker?

A: Richard Nixon and **Herbert Hoover.**

Q: How many Catholic presidents have there been?

A: One—John F. Kennedy.

Q: Which president, prior to becoming president, issued an order expelling all Jews from Kentucky, Tennessee and Mississippi?

A: Ulysses S. Grant. In December, 1862, in the heat of the Civil War, Grant issued his General Order No. 11, which expelled all Jews from those three States:

> "The Jews, as a class violating every regulation of trade established by the Treasury Department and also department orders, are hereby expelled from the department [the

'Department of the Tennessee,' an administrative district of the Union Army of occupation composed of Kentucky, Tennessee and Mississippi] within twenty-four hours from the receipt of this order.

Post commanders will see to it that all of this class of people be furnished passes and required to leave, and any one returning after such notification will be arrested and held in confinement until an opportunity occurs of sending them out as prisoners, unless furnished with permit from headquarters. No passes will be given these people to visit headquarters for the purpose of making personal application of trade permits."

Because Northern textile mills needed Southern cotton and because the Union Army used Southern cotton in its tents and uniforms, President Lincoln decided to allow limited trade in Southern cotton. To control that trade, Lincoln insisted it be licensed by the Treasury Department and the army. As commander of the Department of the Tennessee, Grant was charged with issuing trade licenses in his area.

In the fall of 1862, Grant's headquarters were besieged by merchants seeking trade permits. When Grant's own father appeared one day seeking trade licenses for a group of Cincinnati merchants, some of whom were Jews, Grant's frustration overflowed. In November 1862, convinced that the black market in cotton was organized "mostly by Jews and other unprincipled traders," Grant ordered that, "no Jews are to be permitted to travel on the railroad southward [into the Department of the Tennessee] from any point," nor were they to be granted trade licenses. When illegal trading continued, Grant issued Order No. 11 on December 17, 1862.

In a letter of the same date sent to Christopher Wolcott, the assistant United States Secretary of War, Grant explained his reasoning:

"[The Jews] come in with their Carpet sacks in spite of all that can be done to prevent it. The Jews seem to be a privileged class that can travel anywhere. They will land at any wood yard or landing on the river and make their way through the country. If not permitted to buy cotton themselves they will act as agents for someone else who will be at a Military post, with a Treasury permit to receive cotton and pay for it in Treasury notes which the Jew will buy up at an agreed rate, paying gold."

Subordinates enforced the order at once. In Paducah, Kentucky, military officials gave the town's thirty Jewish families twenty-four hours to leave. A group of Paducah's Jewish merchants sent a telegram to President Lincoln, condemning Grant's order as an "enormous outrage on all laws and humanity, . . . the grossest violation of the Constitution and our rights as good citizens under it."

In January, 1863, shortly after issuance of the Emancipation Proclamation, the president told General Henry Halleck to have Grant revoke General Order No. 11, which Halleck did in the following message: "A paper purporting to be General Order, No. 11, issued by you December 17, has been presented here. By its terms, it expells (sic) all Jews from your department. If such an order has been issued, it will be immediately revoked." Grant revoked the Order three days later. Grant carried the Jewish vote in the presidential election of 1868 and named several Jews to high office.[3]

Q: How many presidents have had no known denominational affiliation and who are they?

A: Thomas Jefferson, Abraham Lincoln, Andrew Johnson, Rutherford Hayes and Barack Obama (though he was previously with the United church of Christ)

In a letter to Benjamin Rush prefacing his *"Syllabus of an Estimate of the Merit of the Doctrines of Jesus,"* Jefferson wrote:

"In some of the delightful conversations with you, in the evenings of 1798-99, and which served as an anodyne to the afflictions of the crisis through which our country was then laboring, the Christian religion was sometimes our topic; and I then promised you, that one day or other, I would give you my views of it. They are the result of a life of inquiry & reflection, and very different from that anti-Christian system imputed to me by those who know nothing of my opinions. To the corruptions of Christianity I am indeed opposed; but not to the genuine precepts of Jesus himself. I am a Christian, in the only sense he wished any one to be; sincerely attached to his doctrines, in preference to all others; ascribing to himself every human excellence; & believing he never claimed any other."

Of course, having no commonly recognized religious affiliation is not necessarily the same thing as not being a religious person. Such is the case with Lincoln. One of his early biographers, Colonel Ward Lamon, intimately acquainted with him in Illinois, and during the years that he lived in Washington, says: "Never in all that time did he let fall from his lips or his pen an expression which remotely implied the slightest faith in Jesus as the son of God and the Savior of men." However, in an 1874 letter to Henry Beecher, Lamon wrote: "Speaking of Mr. Lincoln in reference to this feature of his character, I express the decided opinion that he was an eminently moral man. Regarding him as a moral man, with my views upon the relations existing between the two characteristics, I have no difficulty in believing him a religious man! Yet he was not a Christian. He possessed, it is true, a system of faith and worship, but it was one which Orthodox Christianity stigmatizes as a false religion." [4]

Identifying presidential religious affiliations can be a hazardous enterprise because the historical records are sometimes silent or contradictory. With that caveat, the presidential religious affiliations are as follows:

Baptist
    Warren Harding
    Harry Truman
    Jimmy Carter (Southern Baptist)
    Bill Clinton (Southern Baptist)

Congregationalist
    Calvin Coolidge
    John Adams (later Unitarian)

Disciples of Christ
    James Garfield
    Lyndon Johnson
    Ronald Reagan (also Presbyterian)

Dutch Reformed
    Martin Van Buren
    Theodore Roosevelt

Episcopalian
    George Washington
    James Madison
    James Monroe
    William Henry Harrison
    John Tyler
    Zachary Taylor
    Franklin Pierce
    Chester A. Arthur
    Franklin D. Roosevelt
    Gerald Ford
    George H. W. Bush
    George W. Bush (later Methodist)

Methodist
    James Polk (originally Presbyterian)
    William McKinley

George W. Bush (originally Episcopalian)

Presbyterian
Andrew Jackson
James Polk (later Methodist)
James Buchanan
Grover Cleveland
Benjamin Harrison
Woodrow Wilson
Dwight D. Eisenhower
Ronald Reagan (also Disciples of Christ)

Quaker
Herbert Hoover
Richard Nixon

Roman Catholic
John F. Kennedy

Unitarian
John Adams
John Quincy Adams
Millard Fillmore
William Howard Taft

United Church of Christ
Barack Obama (later no affiliation)

Note that the 1957 merger which formed the U.C.C. included the Congregational Christian Churches.[5]

Q: Which president wrote a book called *Life and Morals of Jesus of Nazareth* in which he took a razor blade and went through the New Testament, cutting and pasting so as to delete all references to miracles or supernatural events depicted in the New Testament and leave only the teachings of Jesus?

A: Thomas Jefferson. Jefferson did not believe Jesus was divine. He also dismissed traditional Judaism as "the fumes of the most disordered imaginations." In an 1820 letter, he wrote: "Jesus did not mean to impose himself on mankind as the Son of God, physically speaking, I have been convinced by the writings of men more learned than myself in that lore. But that he might conscientiously believe himself inspired from above, is very possible. The whole religion of the Jews, inculcated on him from his infancy, was founded in the belief of divine inspiration. The fumes of the most disordered imaginations were recorded in their religious code, as special communications of the Deity."

What we now know as the Jefferson Bible was written in 1820. Jefferson had written an earlier version of the book in 1804 entitled *"The Philosophy of Jesus of Nazareth extracted from the account of his life and doctrines as given by Matthew, Mark, Luke, and John. Being an abridgement of the New Testament for the use of the Indians unembarrassed with matters of fact or faith beyond the level of their comprehensions."* [5]

CHAPTER TWENTY-THREE NOTES:

1) Beschloss, Michael. *Presidential Courage: Brave Leaders and How They Changed America 1789-1989*, Simon & Schuster (2007).
Cohen, Michael Joseph. *Truman and Israel*, University of California Press. (1990)
Medoff, Rachel, *Was Truman Antisemitic—and Does it Matter?* The David S. Wyman Institute for Holocaust Studies, July, 2007 reprinted at
http://www.wymaninstitute.org/articles/2007-7-truman-antisemitic.php
http://news.bbc.co.uk/2/hi/americas/3059087.stm
2) Nagourney, Adam. *In Tapes, Nixon Rails About Jews and Blacks*. The *New York Times*, December 10, 2010.
http://whitehousetapes.net/transcript/nixon/536-016
3) http://www.jewishvirtuallibrary.org/jsource/anti-semitism/grant.html
Karp, Abraham. *From the Ends of the Earth: Judaic Treasures of the Library of Congress*, Rizzoli (1991).
Jacob Rader Marcus, The Jew in the American World: A Source Book, Wayne State University Press (1996).
Brooks D. Simpson, Ulysses S. Grant: Triumph Over Adversity, 1822-1865 Houghton Mifflin Books, (2000).
4) *Recollections of Abraham Lincoln 1847-1865*, by Ward Hill Lamon.

See http://www.gutenberg.org/files/39630/39630-h/39630-h.htm
5) http://www.beliefnet.com/Faiths/Faith-Tools/The-Founding-Faith-Archive/
The-Pious-Infidel.aspx
http://www.positiveatheism.org/hist/jeff1435.htm
http://www.theology.edu/journal/volume2/ushistor.htmhttp://en.wikipedia.org/
wiki/Religious_affiliations_of_Presidents_of_the_United_States
http://www.adherents.com/adh_presidents.html
http://yamaguchy.com/library/jefferson/benrush.html
http://www.tutorgig.info/ed/Jefferson_Bible#_note-7

CHAPTER 24

Slavery/Race Relations

Q: Which president made the following remarks?

"I will say then that I am not, nor ever have been in favor of bringing about in any way the social and political equality of the white and black races—that I am not nor ever have been in favor of making voters or jurors of Negroes, nor of qualifying them to hold office, nor to intermarry with white people; and I will say in addition to this that there is a physical difference between the white and black races which I believe will forever forbid the two races living together on terms of social and political equality. And inasmuch as they cannot so live, while they do remain together there must be the position of superior and inferior, and I as much as any other man am in favor of having the superior position assigned to the white race. I say upon this occasion I do not perceive that because the white man is to have the superior position, the Negro should be denied everything."

A: Abraham Lincoln. The occasion was the fourth debate with Stephen A. Douglas at Charleston, Illinois, September 18, 1858. Just before making the above remarks, Lincoln started his speech by saying: "While I was at the hotel today, an elderly gentleman called upon me to know whether I was really in favor of producing a perfect equality between the Negroes and white people." This remark prompted "great laughter" among the 12,000 in attendance. He also drew laughs when he stated shortly thereafter, "I do not understand that because I do not want a Negro woman for a slave I must necessarily want her for a wife."

According to Randall Kennedy, who wrote *"Nigger: The Strange Career of a Troublesome Word,"* several presidents are known to have used the n-word. Harry Truman referred to Congressman Adam Clayton Powell as "that damned nigger preacher." Early in his political career, Lyndon Johnson once said, "I talk everything over with [my wife]. [Of course] I have a nigger maid, and I talk my problems over with her, too." [1]

Q: In the infamous *Dred Scott* case, the Supreme Court held that Congress had no right to prohibit slavery in the territories, that slaves were property, and that slave owners could not be deprived of their property without due process. Which president wrote to a Supreme Court Justice before the decision was handed down, urging him to adopt the result it eventually did, and then expressed satisfaction over the result?

A: James Buchanan. Buchanan not only wanted the *Dred Scott* case to be decided quickly, but he also wanted the Supreme Court to affirm the right of each State to decide the slavery issue for itself. As it happened, both of his wishes were granted, as the Supreme Court decision was handed down on March 6, 1857, only two days after his inauguration. Moreover, historians later discovered that he had actually lobbied for the result by contacting

Northern Supreme Court Justice Robert Grier and soliciting his support.

In his inauguration address, Buchanan stated:

"What a happy conception, then, was it for Congress to apply this simple rule, that the will of the majority shall govern, to the settlement of the question of domestic slavery in the territories. Congress is neither 'to legislate slavery into any territory or state nor to exclude it therefrom, but to leave the people thereof perfectly free to form and regulate their domestic institutions in their own way, subject only to the Constitution of the United States.'. . .

[It] is the imperative and indispensable duty of the Government of the United States to secure to every resident inhabitant the free and independent expression of his opinion by his vote. This sacred right of each individual must be preserved. That being accomplished, nothing can be fairer than to leave the people of a Territory free from all foreign interference to decide their own destiny for themselves, subject only to the Constitution of the United States.

The whole Territorial question being thus settled upon the principle of popular sovereignty—a principle as ancient as free government itself—everything of a practical nature has been decided. No other question remains for adjustment, because all agree that under the Constitution slavery in the States is beyond the reach of any human power except that of the respective States themselves wherein it exists." [2]

Q: How many of our presidents owned slaves while president?

A: Eight—George Washington, Thomas Jefferson, James Madison, James Monroe, Andrew Jackson, John Tyler, James Polk and Zachary Taylor.

Q: How many presidents owned slaves but not as president?

A: Three-Martin Van Buren, William Henry Harrison and Ulysses Grant.

Q: Of our first twelve presidents, who were the only ones who never owned slaves?

A: John Adams and his son, **John Quincy Adams**.

Q: Who was the last president to own slaves while president?

A: Zachary Taylor in 1850.

Q: Who was the last president to own slaves whether in office or prior to holding the office?

A: Ulysses Grant.

President	Quotations regarding slavery [3]
1. George Washington—Yes	1786: "I can only say that there is not a man living wishes more sincerely than I do to see (the abolition of slavery)... But, when slaves who are happy & content to remain with their present masters, are tampered with & seduced to leave them... it introduces more evils than it can cure." [4]
2. John Adams—No	1820: "I shudder when I think of the calamities which slavery is likely to produce in this country. You would think me mad if I were to describe my anticipations. If the gangrene is not stopped I can see nothing but insurrection of the blacks against the whites." [5]
3. Thomas Jefferson—Yes	An early draft of the Declaration of Independence drafted by Jefferson contains language that specifically condemns slavery in

	forceful language: "(King George III) has waged cruel war against human nature itself, violating its most sacred rights of life and liberty in the persons of a distant people who never offended him, captivating & carrying them into slavery in another hemisphere, or to incur miserable death in their transportation thither. This piratical warfare, the opprobrium of infidel powers, is the warfare of the CHRISTIAN king of Great Britain. Determined to keep open a market where MEN should be bought and sold, he has prostituted his negative for suppressing every legislative attempt to prohibit or to restrain this execrable commerce: and that this assemblage of horrors might want no fact of distinguished die, he is now exciting those very people to rise in arms against us, and to purchase that liberty of which he has deprived them, by murdering the people upon whom he also obtruded them thus paying off former crimes committed against the liberties of one people, with crimes which he urges them to commit against the lives of another." —from Thomas Jefferson's draft of the Declaration of Independence. This paragraph was voted down by the Congressional Congress. [6]
4. James Madison—Yes	1819: "A general emancipation of slaves ought to be 1. gradual. 2. equitable & satisfactory to the individuals immediately concerned. 3. consistent with the existing & durable prejudices of the nation ... To be consistent with existing and probably unalterable prejudices in the U.S. freed blacks ought to be permanently removed beyond the region occupied by or allotted to a White population."[7]

5. James Monroe—Yes	1801: "We perceive an existing evil which commenced under our Colonial System, with which we are not properly chargeable, or if at all not in the present degree, and we acknowledge the extreme difficulty of remedying it."[8]
6. John Quincy Adams—No	1841: "What can I do for the cause of God and man, for the progress of human emancipation, for the suppression of the African slave-trade? Yet my conscience presses me on; let me but die upon the breach."[9]
7. Andrew Jackson—Yes	1822: "As far as lenity can be extended to these unfortunate creatures I wish you to do so; subordination must be obtained first, and then good treatment."[10]
8. Martin Van Buren—yes, but not while President	1837: "I must go into the Presidential chair the inflexible and uncompromising opponent of every attempt on the part of Congress to abolish slavery in the District of Columbia against the wishes of the slaveholding States, and also with a determination equally decided to resist the slightest interference with it in the States where it exists"[11]
9. William Henry Harrison—Yes, but not while President	1820: "We cannot emancipate the slaves of the other states without their consent... (except) by producing a convulsion which would undo us all. We must wait the slow but certain progress of those good principles which are everywhere gaining ground, and which assuredly will ultimately prevail."[12]
10. John Tyler—Yes	1838: "(God) works most inscrutably to the understandings of men; - the negro is torn from Africa, a barbarian, ignorant and idolatrous; he is restored civilized, enlightened, and a Christian."[13]

11. James K. Polk—Yes	1830: "A slave dreads the punishment of stripes (i.e. whipping) more than he does imprisonment, and that description of punishment has, besides, a beneficial effect upon his fellow-slaves." [14]
12. Zachary Taylor—Yes	1847: "So far as slavery is concerned, we of the south must throw ourselves on the constitution and defend our rights under it to the last, and when arguments will no longer suffice, we will appeal to the sword, if necessary." [15]
13. Millard Fillmore-No	1850: "God knows that I detest slavery, but it is an existing evil, for which we are not responsible, and we must endure it, and give it such protection as is guaranteed by the constitution, till we can get rid of it without destroying the last hope of free government in the world. [16]
14. Franklin Pierce—No	1838: "The citizen of New Hampshire is no more responsible, morally or politically for the existence and continuance of this domestic institution (slavery) in Virginia or Maryland, than he would be for the existence of any similar institutions in France or Persia. Why? Because these are matters over which the States ... retained the sole and exclusive control, and for which they are alone responsible ... It is admitted that domestic slavery exists here (Washington, DC) in its mildest form. That part of the population are bound together by friendship and the nearer relations of life. They are attached to the families in which they have lived from childhood. They are comfortably provided for, and apparently contented." [17]

15. James Buchanan—No	1836: "The natural tendency of their publications is to produce dissatisfaction and revolt among the slaves, and to incite their wild passions to vengeance ... Many a mother clasps her infant to her bosom when she retires to rest, under dreadful apprehensions that she may be aroused from her slumbers by the savage yells of the slaves by whom she is surrounded. These are the works of the abolitionists." [18]
16. Abraham Lincoln—No	1865: "I have always thought that all men should be free; but if any should be slaves it should be first those who desire it for themselves, and secondly those who desire it for others. Whenever I hear any one arguing for slavery I feel a strong impulse to see it tried on him personally." [19]
17. Andrew Johnson—Yes, but not while president	1865: "You tell me, friends, of the liberation of the colored people of the South. But have you thought of the millions of Southern white people who have been liberated by the war?" [20]
18. Ulysses S. Grant—Yes, but not while president	1885: "The (South) was burdened with an institution abhorrent to all civilized people not brought up under it, and one which degraded labor, kept it in ignorance and enervated the governing class... Soon the slaves would have outnumbered the masters, and, not being in sympathy with them, would have risen in their might and exterminated them. The war was expensive to the South, as well as to the North, both in blood and treasure, but it was worth all it cost." [21]

CHAPTER TWENTY-FOUR NOTES:

1) Neely, Mark E. Jr. *The Abraham Lincoln Encyclopedia.* Da Capo Press, Inc. (1982). Basler, Roy. *The Collected Works of Abraham Lincoln.* Rutgers University Press (1953).
   http://www.nps.gov/liho/historyculture/debate4.htm
   Kennedy, Randall. *Nigger: The Strange Career of a Troublesome Word,* Pantheon (2001).
2) http://www.re-quest.net/history/inaugurals/buchanan/index.htm
3) http://www.nathanielturner.com/whichpresidentsownedslaves.htm
   http://home.nas.com/lopresti/ps.htm
4) Hirschfield, Fritz, *George Washington and Slavery: A documentary portrayal,* University of Missouri Press (1997)
5) Smith, Page. *John Adams.* (Doubleday, 1962)
6) Jefferson, Thomas. *Writings.* Library of America, 1984
7) Madison, James. *Writings.* The Library of America. 1999.
   Madison, James. *The Papers of James Madison.* (University of Chicago, 1967)
   http://press-pubs.uchicago.edu/founders/documents/v1ch15s65.html
8) Monroe, James. *The Writings of James Monroe.* Knickerbocker Press, 1903. v3.
   http://thisisreno.com/2012/02/celebrating-the-emancipation-proclamation-madison-and-monroe
9) Adams, John Quincy. *The Diary of John Quincy Adams.* (Scribner's Sons, 1951)
   http://ourwhitehouse.org/prespgs/jqadams.html
10) James, Marquis. *Andrew Jackson: Portrait of a President.* (Grosset & Dunlap, 1971)
11) "Martin Van Buren: Inaugural Address, Saturday, March 4, 1837";
    http://www.bartleby.com/124/pres25.html
12) Cleaves, Freeman. *Old Tippecanoe: William Henry Harrison and His Time.* Kenninat Press, (1939).
13) Tyler, Lyon G. *The Letters and Times of the Tylers.* Whittet and Shepperson, 1884
14) Sellers, Charles Grier, Jr. James K. Polk, Jacksonian, 1795-1843. (Princeton University Press, 1957)
15) Hamilton, Holman. *Zachary Taylor: Soldier in the White House.* (Bobbs Merrill,. 1951)
16) Rayback, Robert J. *Millard Fillmore.* (Eastman, 1989).
17) http://thisisreno.com/2012/06/celebrating-the-emancipation-proclamation-franklin-pierce
18) Curtis, George Ticknor. *Life of James Buchanan.* (Harper and Brothers, 1883)
    http://books.google.com/books?id=0i8OAAAAIAAJ&pg=PA315&source=gbs_toc_r&cad=4#v=onepage&q&f=false
19) Lincoln, Abraham. *The Collected Works of Abraham Lincoln.* (Rutgers University Press, 1953)
20) Lately, Thomas. *The first President Johnson;: The three lives of the seventeenth President of the United States of America,* (Morrow, 1968)
21) Grant, Ulysses S. *Personal Memoirs of U.S. Grant.* (Century Co, 1885); http://www.bartleby.com/1011/41.html

CHAPTER 25

Subjective/Whimsical

Q: Which president is sometimes referred to as "our least known consequential president?"

A: James Polk. Polk fought the Mexican War, expanded the Union by settling claims to Texas and the Oregon Territory and by acquiring California and the Southwest, and solidified national economic policy, all in one term. [1]

Q: Besides John F. Kennedy, which president was well-known for his handsomeness?

A: Franklin Pierce, whose nickname was "Handsome Frank." In a list of the sexiest presidents it, was said of Pierce: "There's not much to say about this obscure president, except that he's gorgeous." Similarly, historian Michael Holt's book on Pierce begins with: "Franklin Pierce was arguably the most handsome man ever to serve as president of the United States." Harry Truman once remarked that Pierce was "the best looking president the White House ever had." [2]

Q: Which president was sometimes derisively referred to by his opponents as "His Fraudulency"?

A: Rutherford Hayes. In the 1876 election, Samuel J. Tilden of New York outpolled Hayes in the popular vote, and had 184 electoral votes to Hayes's 165, with twenty votes uncounted. These twenty electoral votes were in dispute in three states: Florida, Louisiana, and South Carolina. An informal deal was struck to resolve the dispute: the Compromise of 1877. In return for the Democrats' acquiescence to Hayes's election, the Republicans agreed to withdraw federal troops from the South, ending Reconstruction. The twenty disputed electoral votes were thus ultimately awarded to Hayes, giving him the victory.

Many of Tilden's supporters believed that he had been cheated out of victory. Hayes was variously dubbed "Rutherfraud," "His Fraudulency," and "His Accidency." On March 3, 1877, the House of Representatives passed a resolution declaring its opinion that Tilden had been "duly elected president of the United States." Hayes was peacefully sworn in as president on March 5, 1877.[4]

Q: As to which president was there a hair controversy—more specifically, did he truly have a head full of "curly black hair" or had he simply perfected the comb-over?

A: Franklin Pierce. David Holzel writes: "Pierce had some of the finest hair of any U.S. president. One witness described it approvingly as a 'mass of curly black hair . . . combed on a deep slant over his wide forehead.' And that was after viewing Pierce's body in state after his death in 1869. Yet that mass of curls may have been an act of misdirection away from the truth that deep slant hinted at. In an 1862 photograph, Pierce's hair in profile appears to exist on two levels—above, the hair combed on a deep slant, and below, a small patch at the front and center of his wide forehead. Pierce's hair unquestionably is a subject for future historians to wrestle with." In other words, he may have been combing over his hair to hide male pattern baldness. [3]

Q: Which president played more golf than any other?

A: Woodrow Wilson. [5]

Q: Which president was sometimes referred to as the Human Iceberg as a result of his frosty personality?

A: Benjamin Harrison.[6]

Q: Which president may have been homosexual?

A: James Buchanan. Buchanan was the only president who never married (which by itself of course proves little). However, for fifteen years before his presidency, Buchanan lived with his close friend, Alabama Senator William Rufus King, who later became vice president under Franklin Pierce. King became ill and died shortly after Pierce's inauguration, four years before Buchanan became president. Buchanan's and King's close relationship prompted Andrew Jackson to call King "Miss Nancy" and "Aunt Fancy," while Aaron V. Brown spoke of the two as "Buchanan and his wife."

In May 1844, during one of King's absences that resulted from King's appointment as minister to France, Buchanan wrote, "I am now solitary and alone, having no companion in the house with me. I have gone a wooing to several gentlemen, but have not succeeded with any one of them. I feel that it is not good for man to be alone, and [I] should not be astonished to find myself married to some old maid who can nurse me when I am sick, provide good dinners for me when I am well, and not expect from me any very ardent or romantic affection."

As has been noted in connection with the relationship between Abraham Lincoln and Joshua Speed, in that era, sharing a bed and other forms of intimacy between men was not uncommon and did not necessarily equate to homosexuality. Jonathan Katz wrote: "At the start of the twenty-first century it may even be difficult to imagine a man, especially a bachelor, offering another a place in his bed without some conscious fear or desire that the proposition will be understood as a come-on. In the nineteenth century, Speed was probably not conscious of any such erotic possibility. His immediate, casual offer, and his later report of it, suggests that men's bed sharing was not then often explicitly understood as con-ducive to forbidden sexual experiments." [7]

Q: Who is considered to be our best golf-playing president?

A: John F. Kennedy. The ranking of the presidential golfers by *Golf Digest* as of 2009 (including their comments) is as follows:

1. John F. Kennedy. Despite chronic back pain, averaged 80.
2. Dwight D. Eisenhower. Had a green outside the Oval Office.
3. Gerald R. Ford. Clumsy, but was a legitimate 80s-shooter.
4. Franklin D. Roosevelt. At 39, polio robbed him of a powerful golf swing.
5. George H.W. Bush. Once got his handicap down to 11.
6. George W. Bush. Outgoing prez is a capable 15-handicapper.
7. Bill Clinton. Can break 90, especially using his "Billigans."
8. Barack Obama. The lefty plays more hoops than golf.
9. Ronald Reagan. Didn't play often or well (best was low 90s).
10. Warren G. Harding. Struggled to break 95.
11. William Howard Taft. As hapless a golfer as he was a chief executive.
12. Woodrow Wilson. Played more than Ike but almost never broke 100.

13. Richard M. Nixon. He shot 79 once and quit the game.
14. Lyndon B. Johnson. Played with senators to secure votes for the Civil Rights Act of 1964.
15. Calvin Coolidge. When he vacated the White House, he left his clubs behind.[8]

Q: While many presidents are obscure, which one is specifically often referred to as "America's most obscure president?"

A: Franklin Pierce.[9]

CHAPTER TWENTY-FIVE NOTES:

1) Merry, Robert W. *A Country of Vast Designs, James K. Polk, the Mexican War, and the Conquest of the American Continent.* Simon & Schuster (2009).
   http://www.thedailybeast.com/newsweek/2009/11/12/the-overlooked-president.html (Donald Graham).
   http://www.lessonsonamericanpresidents.com/james_k_polk.html
2) http://www.nerve.com/dispatches/the-top-43-sexiest-us-presidents?page=1
   Holt, Michael. *Franklin Pierce: The American Presidents Series: The 14th President, 1853-1857,* Times Books (2010).
   http://www.mindspring.com/~dbholzel/pierce/triviality.html
3) http://www.mentalfloss.com/blogs/archives/9778
4) Holt, Michael, *By One Vote: The Disputed Presidential Election of 1876*, Univ. Press of Kansas (2008).
   Morris, Roy, Jr. *Fraud Of The Century. Rutherford B. Hayes, Samuel Tilden and the Stolen Election of 1876.*
5) http://www.metronc.com/article/?id=672 (Presidents and Golf by Arch Allen)
6) http://millercenter.org/president/bharrison/essays/biography/print
7) Klein, Philip S., *President James Buchanan: A Biography*, American Political Biography Press (1995 ed.).
   Katz, Jonathan, *Gay American History: Lesbians and Gay Men in the U.S.A.: A Documentary.* Crowell (1976).
   James W. Loewen. *Lies across America*, (The New Press. 1999)
   http://en.wikipedia.org/wiki/James_Buchanan
8) http://www.golfdigest.com/magazine/2009-02/presidentsranking
   See also Don Van Natta Jr., *First Off the Tee: Presidential Hackers, Duffers, and Cheaters from Taft to Bush.*
9) Wallner, Peter, *Franklin Pierce: New Hampshire's Favorite Son.* Plaidswede Publishing (2004).
   http://www.ipl.org/div/potus/fpierce.html
   http://www.mindspring.com/~dbholzel/pierce/pierce.html

CHAPTER 26

Supreme Court

Q: Of the two-term presidents, only one was able to appoint but a single Supreme Court Justice. Who was it?

A: James Monroe, whose only appointment was Smith Thompson of New York, who served from 1823-1843.

Q: One president was able to appoint three Supreme Court Chief Justices. Who was he?

A: George Washington. The appointments were John Jay (1789-1795), John Rutledge (1795) and Oliver Ellsworth (1796-1800).

Q: Aside from George Washington and excluding "acting" Chief Justices (i.e. those who temporarily occupied the position until a successor could be appointed), only one president was able to appoint both a Chief Justice and another Justice who later became Chief Justice. Who was he?

A: Grover Cleveland. He appointed Melville Fuller, who served as Chief Justice from 1888-1910 and then appointed Edward Douglas White as an Associate Justice, until he was made Chief Justice by Taft. He served in the latter position from 1910-1921.

Q: Which president had the highest number of unsuccessful Supreme Court nominees, with four?

A: John Tyler. John C. Spencer was nominated on January 9, 1844 and his nomination was defeated by the Senate. Reuben H. Walworth was nominated on March 13, 1844, and a resolution to table the nomination passed on June 15, 1844. The nomination was later withdrawn from the Senate on June 17, 1844. Edward King was nominated on June 5, 1844. A resolution to table the nomination passed by a vote of 29-18 on June 15, 1844. No other action was taken on this nomination. All three men were later re-nominated but their nominations were later withdrawn or tabled. Finally, John M. Read was nominated on February 8, 1845 and there was a motion to consider the nomination in the Senate on January 21, 1845, but the motion was unsuccessful and no other action was taken. [1]

Q: Who is the only president who unsuccessfully nominated a female for the Supreme Court, and who was that woman?

A: George W. Bush. Harriet Miers was nominated on October 3, 2005 but was widely perceived to be unqualified for the position on both sides of the political spectrum. Her nomination was withdrawn on October 27, 2005. [2]

Q: Besides Miers, there have been only two occasions since 1875 where a Supreme Court nominee was withdrawn prior to a vote by the Senate. Which presidents made these nominations? For extra credit, name the nominees. As a hint, one occurred since 2000 and the other occurred since 1950 and the latter case involved nominating a sitting Supreme Court Associate Justice for Chief Justice.

A: **George W. Bush** and **Lyndon Johnson.** Johnson's nomination of Abe Fortas was withdrawn on October 4, 1968 when it became apparent that he did not have the votes to become Chief Justice. Bush's nomination of John Roberts was withdrawn because, while his nomination was pending to fill the vacancy that would be created by the retirement of Justice Sandra Day O'Connor, Chief Justice William H. Rehnquist died on September 3, 2005. Shortly thereafter, on September 5, Bush withdrew Roberts's nomination as O'Connor's successor and announced Roberts's new nomination for the position of Chief Justice.[3]

Q: Who was the only president who was also Chief Justice of the U.S. Supreme Court?

A: **William Howard Taft.** Taft enjoyed his years on the court and was respected by his peers. Justice Felix Frankfurter once remarked to Justice Louis Brandeis that it was "difficult for me to understand why a man who is so good a Chief Justice ... could have been so bad as president." Taft remains the only person to have led both the Executive and Judicial branches of the United States government. He considered his time as Chief Justice to be the highest point of his career. Allegedly, he once remarked, "I do not remember that I was ever president."[4]

Q: Since 1900, there have been only four occasions where a Supreme Court nominee was rejected by the Senate. Two of these were the nominees of one president. Who were the three presidents who made the nominations. For extra credit, name the nominees. As a hint, three of these occurred after 1950 and one before.

A: **The presidents were Herbert Hoover, Richard Nixon** and **Ronald Reagan.** In 1930, Hoover's nominee John Parker was rejected by a 41-39 vote. In 1969, Nixon's nominee Clement

Haynsworth, Jr. was rejected by a 55-45 vote. The following year, Nixon's nominee G. Harrold Carswell was rejected by a 51-45 vote. Most recently, in 1987, Reagan's nominee Robert C. Bork was rejected by a 58-42 vote. [5]

Q: This president made six Supreme Court appointments (five new appointees and one elevation to Chief Justice), more than any president other than Washington (who of course had to appoint the entire Court) and Franklin Roosevelt. Who was he?

A: William Howard Taft. During his presidency, Taft appointed the following Justices to the Supreme Court of the United States:

- Horace Harmon Lurton—1910
  Lurton had served on the United States Court of Appeals for the Sixth Circuit with Taft, and Taft's attorney general said that at 66 he was too old to become a Supreme Court justice. However, Taft had always admired Lurton. According to the *Complete Book of U.S. Presidents* (2001 edition), Taft later said that "the chief pleasure of my administration" was the appointment of Lurton.

- Charles Evans Hughes—1910
  Even though Hughes resigned in 1916 to run in the presidential election that year, he became Taft's successor as Chief Justice.

- Edward Douglass White—Chief Justice—1910
  Already on the Court as an associate justice since 1894, White was the first Chief Justice to be elevated from an associate justiceship since President George Washington appointed John Rutledge to Chief Justice in 1795. Taft succeeded White as Chief Justice in 1921.

- Willis Van Devanter—1911

- Joseph Rucker Lamar—1911
- Mahlon Pitney—1912

Q: Who was the only president who served at least one full term who did not nominate anyone for the Supreme Court?

A: Jimmy Carter.

Q: Besides Jimmy Carter, who were the only presidents not to appoint any justices to the Supreme Court?

A: William Henry Harrison, Zachary Taylor, and **Andrew Johnson.**

Q: Which president appointed the first Jewish person to the Supreme Court?

A: Woodrow Wilson, who appointed Louis Brandeis in 1916.

Jewish Justices of the Supreme Court of the United States			
	Active service	Appointed by	Status
1 Louis Brandeis	1916-1939	Wilson	Retirement
2 Benjamin N. Cardozo	1932-1938	Hoover	Death
3 Felix Frankfurter	1939-1962	F. Roosevelt	Retirement
4 Arthur Goldberg	1962-1965	Kennedy	Resignation
5 Abe Fortas	1965-1969	Johnson	Resignation
6 Ruth Bader Ginsburg	1993-present	Clinton	Currently serving
7 Stephen Breyer	1994-present	Clinton	Currently serving
8 Elena Kagan	2010-present	Obama	Currently serving

Q: Which president nominated the first female Supreme Court Justice?

A: Ronald Reagan nominated Sandra Day O'Connor.

Q: Which president, besides George Washington, was able to appoint the highest percentage of justices sitting on the Supreme Court at any one time?

A: Franklin Roosevelt, who appointed seven of the nine justices.

Q: Besides, George Washington, William Taft and Franklin Roosevelt, who were the only presidents who were able to appoint more than a majority of the Supreme Court justices during their term?

A: Andrew Jackson and **Dwight Eisenhower**, both with five.

Q: Which president declined a nomination to the Supreme Court?

A: James Buchanan by James Polk.

Q: Of the presidents, which one argued by far the most cases before the Supreme Court?

A: William Howard Taft. He was appointed as Solicitor General by Benjamin Harrison in 1890 and served in that a position for two years. In that position, he won sixteen of the eighteen cases he argued before the Supreme Court. In 1892, Harrison appointed him to the U.S. Court of Appeals for the Sixth Circuit. [6]

Q: Which president argued a case before the Supreme Court which was made into a movie directed by Steven Spielberg?

A: John Quincy Adams. Adams argued the case of *United States v. The Libellants and Claimants of the Schooner Amistad, Her Tackle, Apparel, and Furniture, Together with Her Cargo, and the Africans Mentioned and Described in the Several Libels and Claims* before the Supreme Court in 1841. On July 1, 1839, fifty-three Africans, recently kidnapped into slavery in Sierra Leone and sold at a Havana slave market, revolted on the schooner *Amistad*. They killed the captain and other crew and ordered the two Spaniards who had purchased them to sail them back to Africa. Instead, the ship was seized off Long Island by a U.S. revenue cutter on August 24, 1839. The *Amistad* then landed in New London, Connecticut, where the American captain filed for salvage rights to the *Amistad*'s cargo of Africans. The two Spaniards claimed ownership themselves, while Spanish authorities demanded the Africans be extradited to Cuba and tried for murder.

Connecticut officials jailed the Africans and charged them with murder. The slave trade had been outlawed in the U.S. since 1808, but the institution of slavery itself still thrived in the South when the *Amistad* case entered the federal courts and caught the nation's attention. The murder charges against the *Amistad* captives were quickly dropped, but they remained in custody as the legal focus turned to the property rights claimed by various parties.

Abolitionists raised money for the *Amistad* captives' defense, arguing that the Africans had always been and remained free, and had acted in self-defense. Abolitionists enlisted Adams to represent the *Amistad* captives' petition for freedom before the Supreme Court. Adams, then a 73-year-old U.S. Congressman from Massachusetts, spoke before the Court for nine hours and succeeded in moving the majority to decide in favor of freeing the captives. The Court did however order the thirty surviving captives (the others had died at sea or in jail) returned to their home in Sierra Leone.

A movie based on the facts of the case, *Amistad*, directed by Steven Spielberg, was released in 1997. It starred Anthony Hopkins as John Quincy Adams, and Morgan Freeman as one of the abolitionists.[7]

Q: Which president argued an important libel case in front of the Supreme Court which stemmed from a home invasion that lasted nineteen hours which then became the basis for a novel called *The Desperate Hours*?

A: Richard Nixon. In the case of *Time, Inc. v. Hill*, 385 US 374 (1967), Nixon represented the respondent James Hill. The case resulted from a 1953 *Life* magazine article about a book and a play partially inspired by an actual event in which three escaped convicts held Hill, his wife and five children hostage in their home. The family was released unharmed nineteen hours later, and the episode was widely reported in the press. Joseph Hays subsequently wrote a novel, *The Desperate Hours*, about a fictional family of four who were held hostage in their home.

Life magazine wrote an article about a play adaptation of *The Desperate Hours*. Through a series of editorial missteps, the *Life* article mistakenly claimed the play was based on the Hills' ordeal. James Hill and his wife sued Time, Inc., *Life*'s parent company, for deliberate misrepresentation and unauthorized use of the family's name to advance advertising objectives. The family claimed *Life* knew that Hays' work was fictional and sensationalized, but nevertheless published an article presenting the material as fact. For example, right after the event, Hill had told the press the family had not been molested or harmed, and in fact had been treated courteously. The *Life* magazine article, however, stated that some family members had been assaulted, profanity was used, and in other ways differed from the account Hill had given.

Time, Inc. acknowledged that the article was in error, but claimed that the mistake was honest, not calculated. The lower courts awarded the Hills damages, and Time, Inc. appealed the decision. The question before the Supreme Court involved the scope of liability and First Amendment protections involving freedom of the press arising from the article. In a 5-4 decision, the Warren Court reversed the lower court rulings, finding no cause of action against the magazine or its publisher because there was no evidence that the publisher knew of the falsity of the article or acted in reckless disregard of the truth. Although Hill lost the Supreme Court case, Justice Brennan later remarked that Nixon was an excellent advocate for his clients. [8]

Q: What other presidents argued cases before the Supreme Court?

A: One was **James Garfield**. He argued the case of *Ex parte Milligan*, 71 U.S. 2 (1866), that ruled that the application of military tribunals to citizens when civilian courts are still operating is unconstitutional. Lambdin P. Milligan and four others were accused of planning to steal Union weapons and invade Union prisoner-of-war camps. Once the first prisoner of war camp was liberated, they planned to use the liberated soldiers to help fight against the Government of Indiana and free other camps of Confederate soldiers. They also planned to take over the state governments of Indiana, Ohio, and Michigan. When the plan leaked, they were charged, found guilty, and sentenced to hang by a military court in 1864. However, their execution was not set until May 1865, so they were able to argue the case after the Civil War ended.

Garfield represented Milligan against the United States. The Supreme Court ruled, in a 9-0 decision, that military tribunals did not apply to citizens in states that had upheld the authority of the Constitution and where civilian courts were still operating, even when the military had been authorized to detain individuals without trial. Despite many years of practicing law, this was Garfield's first court appearance.[9]

Other presidents to argue cases before the Supreme Court include **Abraham Lincoln** (*Lewis v. Lewis* (48 U.S. 776, (1849)) and **Grover Cleveland** (*Peake v. City of New Orleans*, 139 U.S. 342, (1891)). The Lewis case concerned the interpretation of the Illinois statute of limitations in its application to a suit brought by a non-resident plaintiff. Lincoln argued on behalf of Thomas Lewis. The court decided against Lincoln and his client, and the majority opinion was rendered by Chief Justice Roger B. Taney, who later authored the infamous *Dred Scott* opinion. Justice John McLean wrote a long dissenting opinion in which he opined in accordance with Lincoln's contention.[10]

CHAPTER TWENTY-SIX NOTES:

1) http://www.senate.gov/pagelayout/reference/nominations/nominations.htm
2) Greenburg, Jan Crawford. *Supreme Conflict: The Inside Story of the Struggle for Control of the United States Supreme Court.* Penguin Books (2007)
3) http://www.senate.gov/pagelayout/reference/nominations/Nominations. htm#result
4) Schwartz, Bernard, *A History of the Supreme Court*, Oxford University Press (1993). http://www.let.rug.nl/usa/P/wt27/about/taftbio.htm
5) http://www.senate.gov/pagelayout/reference/nominations/Nominations.htm#result
6) http://lawbrain.com/wiki/William_Howard_Taft
7) http://www.gilderlehrman.org/collection/doc_print.php?doc_id=81
   Davis, David. *Inhuman Bondage:The Rise and Fall of Slavery in the New World.* (Oxford University Press, 2006).
   http://www.law.cornell.edu/supct/html/historics/USSC_CR_0040_0518_ZS.html
8) Lewis, Anthony,. *Freedom for the Thought That We Hate: A Biography of the First Amendment.* Basic Books (2007)
   http://supreme.justia.com/us/385/374/case.html (text of Justice Brennan's opinion)
   http://www.oyez.org/cases/1960-1969/1965/1965_22 (audio of oral argument in the original case and on reargument)
9) Klaus, Samuel. *The Milligan Case.* (Da Capo Press, 1970)
   Rehnquist, William H.. *All the Laws but One: Civil Liberties in Wartime.* William Morrow & Co (1998)
   Peskin, Allan. Garfield: *A Biography.* Kent State University Press. (1978)
   http://www.oyez.org/cases/1851-1900/1865/1865_0/
10) http://blog.nixonfoundation.org/2010/08/nixon-lincoln-et-al-before-the-high-court/

CHAPTER 27

Vice Presidents As They Relate to Presidents

Q: When this vice president was running for president, the sitting president was asked at a televised press conference whether he could name a "major idea" of the vice president which was adopted by the president. The president's response was, "If you give me a week, I might think of one." Who were these two men?

A: Dwight Eisenhower and **Richard Nixon.** This occurred in August, 1960. Nixon, then the sitting Vice President, lost the race to John Kennedy. Although both Eisenhower and Nixon later claimed that Ike was merely joking with the reporter, the remark hurt Nixon, as it undercut his claims of having greater decision-making experience than John Kennedy. The Democrats turned Eisenhower's statement into a television commercial against Nixon, which can be seen on YouTube. [1]

Q: Who were the only two presidents who served exactly one full term as vice president?

A: Thomas Jefferson (to John Adams) and **Martin Van Buren** (to Andrew Jackson).

Q: Who were the only two presidents who served two full terms as vice presidents?

A: Richard Nixon (to Dwight Eisenhower) and **George H. W. Bush** (to Ronald Reagan). John Adams served two terms to George Washington, but the first term inaugural was postponed because the U.S. Congress had not properly convened.

Q: The first two vice presidents, John Adams and Thomas Jefferson, were both elected president. After that, only two sitting vice presidents have ever been elected president. Who are they?

A: Martin Van Buren and **George H.W. Bush.**

VICE PRESIDENTS WHO RAN FOR PRESIDENT

Vice President	President	Result
John Adams	George Washington	Won in 1796
Thomas Jefferson	John Adams	Won in 1800
Martin Van Buren	Andrew Jackson	Won in 1836
Henry A. Wallace	Franklin Roosevelt	Lost in 1948
Richard Nixon	Dwight Eisenhower	Lost in 1960
(Nixon won in 1968 but was not Vice President at the time)		
Hubert Humphrey	Lyndon Johnson's	Lost in 1968
Walter Mondale	Jimmy Carter	Lost in 1984
George HW Bush	Ronald Reagan	Won in 1988
Al Gore	Bill Clinton	Lost in 2000

Q: Who were the only vice presidents elected president who did not seek a full second term?

A: Calvin Coolidge, Harry Truman and **Lyndon Johnson.**

Q: True or false: No vice president who became vice president because his predecessor died in office has ever been elected twice?

A: True.

Q: Calvin Coolidge's vice president accomplished two feats as to which it is safe to say will never again be accomplished by a vice president or likely any other person. He won a Nobel Peace Prize and he was a co-writer of a song which reached number one on the *Billboard* pop chart. Who was this man?

A: Charles Dawes. He won the Nobel Peace Prize in 1925 for his work on the Dawes Plan, a program to enable Germany to restore and stabilize its economy after World War I. Unfortunately, the Dawes Plan proved unworkable and was replaced with a different plan in 1929.

The song was called *It's All in the Game.* Dawes, an amateur pianist, composed the tune in 1911. It was entitled *Melody in A Major.* In 1951, the year Dawes died, songwriter Carl Sigman added lyrics to it (although the tune was popular before then, so much so that Dawes grew to detest hearing it wherever he appeared). In 1958, it was recorded by Tommy Edwards. It reached number one on the *Billboard* pop chart on September 29, 1958, and stayed there for six weeks. Edwards' song ranked at #38 on *Billboard's All Time Top 100*, one ahead of *I Want to Hold your Hand,* by the Beatles. It has been recorded by Dinah Shore, Sammy Kaye, Louis Armstrong, Nat King Cole, Andy Williams, Robert Goulet, Cliff Richard, The Lettermen, Jackie DeShannon, The Four Tops, Cass Elliott, Van

Morrison, Neil Sedaka, Merle Haggard and Johnny Mathis, among others. Imagine how tired Dawes would have become of the song if he had lived a few more years. [2]

Q: Two vice presidents shot people while in office. Who are they?

A: Aaron Burr shot and killed Alexander Hamilton in their famous duel in Weehawken, New Jersey on July 11, 1804. More recently, on February 11, 2006, Richard Cheney accidentally shot Harry Whittington, a 78-year-old Texas attorney, in the face, neck, and upper torso with birdshot pellets when he turned to shoot a quail while hunting on a Texas ranch. Whittington suffered a mild heart attack and atrial fibrillation due to a pellet that embedded in the outer layers of his heart. Whittington was discharged from the hospital on February 17, 2006. Later, Whittington stated, "My family and I are deeply sorry for all that vice president Cheney has had to go through this past week." [3]

Q: Which presidents did not have a vice president at any point during their terms?

A: John Tyler, Millard Fillmore, Andrew Johnson and **Chester Arthur.** Of course, these were the only "one term or less" presidents whose predecessors died while they were in office.

Q: Which was the only president/vice president team not elected by the people?

A: Gerald Ford and **Nelson Rockefeller** after Richard Nixon resigned.

Q: Who are the only vice presidents to be elected to two terms as president?

A: Thomas Jefferson and Richard Nixon.

Q: Who are the only two vice presidents who served under two different presidents?

A: George Clinton served under both Thomas Jefferson and James Madison, and John Calhoun served under both John Quincy Adams and Andrew Jackson.

Q: Which presidential nominee (who was later elected president), when advised who had been nominated as his vice presidential nominee, remarked: "I am ashamed to say: Who is [he]?"

A: Rutherford B. Hayes. The vice presidential candidate, who later became vice president, was William A. Wheeler. [4]

Q: Which president had his former vice president arrested?

A: Thomas Jefferson had Aaron Burr arrested on February 19, 1807 on charges that Burr was plotting to annex Spanish territory in Louisiana and Mexico to be used toward the establishment of an independent republic. He was sent to Richmond, Virginia, to be tried. On September 1, 1807, he was acquitted on the grounds that, although he had conspired against the United States, he was not guilty of treason because he had not engaged in an "overt act," a requirement of treason as specified by the U.S. Constitution. [5]

Q: Which president did not meet his vice president until just prior to being sworn in?

A: Zachary Taylor. His Vice President was Millard Fillmore. [6]

Q: Who was the only elected president who had no vice president except for the first six weeks of his term?

A: Franklin Pierce. His vice president, William King, died of tuberculosis after only six weeks. King holds the distinction of being the only vice president who was not inaugurated in the United States. He took the oath of office on March 24, 1853, in Cuba (twenty days after President Pierce was inaugurated). He had gone there due to his ill health. This unusual inauguration took place because it was believed that King, who was terminally ill with tuberculosis, would not live much longer. The privilege of taking the oath on foreign soil was extended by a special act of Congress for his long and distinguished service to the government of the United States. Even though he took the oath twenty days after the inauguration day, he was still vice president during those three weeks. [7]

Interestingly however, presidents have been without vice presidents more frequently than most people would probably imagine. In many cases this has occurred where the prior president did not finish out his term and there was no new vice president selected, unless the successor was re-elected in his own right.

President	Vacancy period
James Madison	4/20/1812-3/4/1813 and 11/23/1814-3/4/1817
Andrew Jackson	12/28/1832-3/4/1833
John Tyler	Entire term but replaced William Henry Harrison
Millard Fillmore	Entire term but replaced Zachary Taylor
Franklin Pierce	4/18/1853-3/4/1857
Andrew Johnson	Entire term but replaced Abraham Lincoln
Ulysses Grant	11/22/1875-3/4/1877
Chester Arthur	Entire term but replaced James Garfield
William McKinley	11/21/1899-3/4/1901
Theodore Roosevelt	Vacant for first term but replaced William McKinley

Calvin Coolidge	Vacant for first term but replaced Warren Harding
Harry Truman	Vacant for first term but replaced Franklin Roosevelt
Lyndon Johnson	Vacant for first term but replaced John Kennedy
Richard Nixon	10/10/1973-12/6/1973
Gerald Ford	8/9/1974-12/19/1974

Q: At age thirty-six, John C. Breckinridge was, by over five years, the youngest vice president ever sworn in. Who was his president?

A: James Buchanan.

Q: Which of the following statements is accurate, in terms of the date of swearing in?

(1) We had a vice president before we ever had a president.

(2) We had a president before ever we had a vice president.

(3) Both the initial president and vice president were sworn in on the same day.

A: (1). John Adams was sworn in on April 21, 1789, nine days before George Washington was sworn in on April 30, 1789.

Q: Which president was the oldest vice president to succeed to the presidency?

A: Harry Truman at age sixty.

Q: Who is the only president who had two vice presidents die while in office?

A: James Madison. George Clinton was vice president from March 4, 1809-April 20, 1812 and Elbridge Gerry was vice president from March 4, 1813-November 23, 1814.

Q: True or false: No vice president has ever been assassinated.

A: True.

Q: Four presidents have died in office other than by assassination. However, seven vice presidents have died in office. Match the vice president who died with the president they served with:

1. William Rufus DeVane King   a. Franklin Pierce
2. Henry Wilson   b. Ulysses Grant
3. Thomas Hendricks   c. Grover Cleveland
4. Garret Hobart   d. William McKinley
5. George Clinton   e. James Madison
6. Elbridge Gerry   f. James Madison
7. James Sherman   g. William Howard Taft

Answer: All of them are correctly aligned with the men who served as president while they were vice president.

Q: Excluding vice presidents who died or resigned while their president was in office, only three presidents have run for re-election and won with different vice presidential running mates than they had when they first won the office. Who are they?

A: Thomas Jefferson replaced Aaron Burr with George Clinton in the 1804 election. **Ulysses Grant** replaced Schuyler Colfax with Henry Wilson in the 1872 election. **Franklin Roosevelt** did it twice. He replaced John Nance Garner with Henry Wilson in the 1940 election and he replaced Wilson with Truman in the 1944 election. That is the last time it has happened.

Q: Who was the only non-elected president who ever appointed a vice president?

A: Gerald Ford. Nelson Rockefeller was his vice president from December 19, 1974 to January 20, 1977.

Q: Excluding George Washington (who belonged to no political party), who was the only president who had a vice president who was of a different party?

A: Abraham Lincoln. His vice president in his second term, Andrew Johnson, was a Democrat.

Q: Which president and vice president have lived the longest after their term was over?

A: Jimmy Carter and Walter Mondale. On December 1, 2012, they had been out of office for over thirty-two years, surpassing the former record of twenty-five years established by President John Adams and Vice President Thomas Jefferson, who both died on July 4, 1826.

Q: True or false: The nine vice presidents who have become presidents after the death or resignation of the sitting presidents at the time have done so via the authority granted by Article II, Section 1 of the Constitution, which provides that:

> "In case of the removal of the president from office, or of his death, resignation, or inability to discharge the powers and duties of the said office, the same shall devolve on the vice president, and the Congress may by law provide for the case of removal, death, resignation or inability, both of the president and vice president, declaring what officer shall then act as president, and such officer shall act accordingly, until the disability be removed, or a president shall be elected."

A: False. The wording of this portion of the Constitution led to the question of whether the office of the presidency itself "devolved" upon the vice president (in which case he would be an "acting president"), or merely its powers and duties. Further, the Constitution did not stipulate whether the vice president could serve the remainder of the president's term, until the next election, or if emergency elections should be held.

These questions were first put to the test upon the death of William Henry Harrison in 1841, the first president to die in office. There was substantial disagreement among members of Congress as to how to deal with the situation. Eventually, on June 1, 1841, both houses of Congress passed resolutions declaring Vice President John Tyler the tenth president of the United States, although Harrison had died almost two months earlier, on April 4, 1841.

Even so however, it was not concluded that the wording of Article II, Section 1 of the Constitution put the matter to rest, which is why the Twenty-fifth Amendment was eventually adopted, although not until 1967. It provides in part: "In case of the removal of the president from office or of his death or resignation, the vice president shall become president."

Although Tyler's accession was given approval by both the Cabinet, and later, the Senate and House, his detractors never fully accepted him as president. He was referred to by many nicknames, including "His Accidency," a reference to his having become president, not through election, but by the accidental circumstances regarding his nomination and Harrison's death. However, Tyler never wavered from his conviction that he was the rightful president. When his political opponents sent correspondence to the White House addressed to the "vice president" or "acting president," Tyler had it returned unopened. [8]

Q: Aside from John Tyler, who ascended to the presidency after only thirty days, who had the second shortest vice presidency?

A: Andrew Johnson—forty-two days. Some may forget that Johnson was not Lincoln's vice president in his first term.

Q: Aside from vice presidents who became presidents, which three vice presidents have last names which are the same as last names of people who became president?

A: Richard Mentor Johnson (Van Buren), Henry Wilson (Grant), George Clinton (Jefferson and Madison).

Q: Which vice presidents succeeded to the office after the death or resignation of their predecessors and then won re-election?

Answers:
   Theodore Roosevelt, 1904
   Calvin Coolidge, 1924
   Harry Truman, 1948
   Lyndon Johnson, 1964

Q: Which vice presidents were directly elected president?

A: There have been only four: **John Adams**, 1796; **Thomas Jefferson**; 1800, **Martin Van Buren**; 1836, **George Bush**; 1988. When Richard Nixon was elected president, he was not Vice president at the time.

Q: Section three of the Twenty-fifth Amendment, which was ratified in 1967, provides: "Whenever the president transmits to the President pro tempore of the Senate and the Speaker of the House of Representatives his written declaration that he is unable to discharge the powers and duties of his office, and until he transmits to them a written declaration to the contrary, such powers and duties shall be discharged by the Vice President as Acting President." **When were the three times in American history**

that Section three of the Twenty-fifth Amendment has been invoked? As a hint, they have all occurred since 1980.

Answers:
1.) July 13, 1985: Acting President George Herbert Walker Bush. On July 12, 1985, President Ronald Reagan underwent a colonoscopy procedure. Having been prepared for potential emergency surgery as part of the colonoscopy procedure and not wanting to undergo the regimen a second time, Reagan elected to undergo the operation the following day.

A decision was made to invoke Section three of the Twenty-fifth Amendment. That evening, Reagan consulted with White House Chief of Staff Donald Regan, Attorney General Edwin Meese, Vice President George H.W. Bush, and White House counsel Fred Fielding as to whether or not the provisions of Section three should be invoked. At 10:32 a.m. on July 13, 1985, Reagan signed a letter drafted by White House counsel Fred Fielding and ordered its transmission to House Speaker Thomas P. "Tip" O'Neill and Senate President Pro Tempore J. Strom Thurmond, which occurred at 11:28 a.m., whereupon Vice President George H.W. Bush became the first "Acting President of the United States" in the nation's history. The letter read as follows:

July 13, 1985

Dear Mr. Speaker (Dear Mr. President):

"I am about to undergo surgery during which time I will be briefly and temporarily incapable of discharging the constitutional powers and duties of the office of President of the United States.

"After consultation with my counsel and the Attorney General, I am mindful of the provisions of Section 3 of the 25th Amendment to the Constitution and of the uncertainties of its application to such brief and temporary periods of incapacity. I do not believe that the drafters of this

Amendment intended its application to situations such as the instant one.

"Nevertheless, consistent with my long-standing arrangement with Vice President George Bush, and not intending to set a precedent binding anyone privileged to hold this office in the future, I have determined and it is my intention and direction that Vice President George Bush shall discharge those powers and duties in my stead commencing with the administration of anesthesia to me in this instance.

"I shall advise you and the Vice President when I determine that I am able to resume the discharge of the constitutional powers and duties of this office."
May God bless this Nation and us all.
Sincerely,
Ronald Reagan"

The follow-up later, in which Reagan resumed the powers and duties of the presidency, would be transmitted at 7:22 p.m., just eight hours and fifty minutes later. It read as follows:

July 13, 1985

Dear Mr. Speaker (Dear Mr. President):

"Following up on my letter to you of this date, please be advised that I am able to resume the discharge of the constitutional powers and duties of the office of the President of the United States. I have informed the Vice President of my determination and my resumption of those powers and duties."
Sincerely,
Ronald Reagan

2.) June 29, 2002: Acting President Richard Bruce Cheney. Like Reagan, George W. Bush was scheduled to undergo a colonoscopy procedure, which required sedation. At 7:09 a.m. on June 29th, he signed a letter transferring executive authority to Vice President

Dick Cheney. Cheney acted as President for just under two and a half hours. Bush's procedure found no abnormalities and at 9:24 a.m., he transmitted a second, one-paragraph letter, declaring himself once again capable of resuming his powers and duties.

3.) July 21, 2007: Acting President Richard Bruce Cheney (second occurrence). Once again, Bush had to undergo a colonoscopy procedure. As was the case in 2002, Bush opted to invoke Section three of the twenty-fifth Amendment, and at 7:16 a.m. on July 21 he signed a letter transferring executive authority to Cheney. Vice President Cheney acted as President for all of 125 minutes, and, unlike the previous two times the nation had an Acting President, Cheney actually did something. Perhaps somewhat aware of the fleeting and footnote-like historical situation he was in, Acting President Cheney took at least a portion of his time as our nation's acting commander-in-chief to write a letter to his grandchildren. He asked them to "always strive in your lives to do what is right" and signed it "Richard B. Cheney, Acting President of the United States (Grandpa Cheney)."

Section four of the Twenty-fifth Amendment provides: "Whenever the Vice President and a majority of either the principal officers of the executive departments or of such other body as Congress may by law provide, transmit to the President pro tempore of the Senate and the Speaker of the House of Representatives their written declaration that the President is unable to discharge the powers and duties of his office, the Vice President shall immediately assume the powers and duties of the office as Acting President." In other words, it is intended to address emergencies which have already occurred. It has never been invoked. The one logical time it might have been was when Ronald Reagan was shot by John Hinckley on March 30, 1981. Following the assassination attempt, Reagan immediately went into surgery and thus was unable to invoke Section three. Vice

President George H. W. Bush did not assume the role of Acting President under Section four. In 1995, Birch Bayh, the primary sponsor of the Amendment in the Senate, wrote that Section four should have been invoked. However, Bush was on a plane returning from Texas. By the time Bush had arrived in Washington, Reagan was out of surgery. [9]

Q: Who said: "Look at all the vice presidents in history. Where are they? They were about as useful as a cow's fifth teat?"

A: Harry Truman. [10]

Q: This man, when advised that Franklin Roosevelt wanted him to be his vice president, said: "Tell him to go to hell; I'm for Jimmy Byrnes." Who was he?

A: Harry Truman again. This occurred at the 1944 Democratic convention. Of course, notwithstanding his comment above that vice presidents are "about as useful as a cow's fifth teat," Truman eventually accepted the nomination. His acceptance speech in Chicago on July 21, 1944 lasted less than one minute:

> "You won't know how very much I appreciate the very great honor which has come to the State of Missouri. It is also a great responsibility which I am perfectly willing to assume. Nine years and five months ago I came to the Senate. I expect to continue the efforts I have made there to help shorten the war and to win the peace under the great leader, Franklin D. Roosevelt. I don't know what else I can say, except that I accept this great honor with all humility. I thank you."

Of course Truman became president himself within the year as a result of Roosevelt's death in April, 1945. [11]

CHAPTER TWENTY-SEVEN NOTES:

1) http://www.youtube.com/watch (Ike Knocks Nixon Commercial: John F. Kennedy 1960 Presidential Campaign Election Ad)
2) Schuker, Stephen A., *The End of French Predominance in Europe: The Financial Crisis of 1924 and the Adoption of the Dawes Plan.* Chapel Hill: University of North Carolina Press (1976).
   http://en.wikipedia.org/wiki/Its_All_in_the_Game_(song)
3) Dana Bash, Cheney *Accidentally Shoots Fellow Hunter*; 2-13-2006. cnn.com
   http://articles.cnn.com/2006-02-12/politics/cheney_1_katharine-armstrong-bird-shot-saturday-afternoon-armstrong-ranch?_s=PM:POLITICS
   http://msnbc.msn.com/id/11409731
4) Barzman, Sol. *Madmen and Geniuses.* Follett Books (1974).
   Hoogenboom, Ari. *Rutherford Hayes: Warrior and President.* University Press of Kansas (1995).
5) Melton, Buckner, *Aaron Burr, Conspiracy to Treason*, 2002
   http://www.history.com/this-day-in-history/aaron-burr-arrested-for-treason
6) http://www.sacredheart.edu/pages/32940_millard_fillmore_inspired_life_uninspired_presidency_michael_fazzino.cfm
7) Brooks, Daniel Fate, *The Face of William R. King*, Alabama Heritage (2003).
8) Chitwood, Oliver Perry, *John Tyler, Champion of the Old South.* Russell & Russell (1964).
   Crapol, Edward P., *John Tyler, the Accidental President.* University of North Carolina Press (2006).
9) http://www.amendment25.com/invocations.html
   http://transcripts.cnn.com/TRANSCRIPTS/0103/30/lkl.00.html
   http://www.nytimes.com/1995/04/08/opinion/the-white-house-safety-net.html
10) http://boingboing.net/2009/01/19/veeps-profiles-in-in.html
11) http://www.u-s-history.com/pages/h897.html
    http://partners.nytimes.com/library/politics/camp/440722convention-dem-ra.html

CHAPTER 28

War and Peace

Q: Which two presidents who never served in the military presided over major overseas American armed conflicts?

A: **Woodrow Wilson** (World War I) and **Franklin Roosevelt** (World War II).

Q: Only two presidents since Franklin Roosevelt have had no military experience. Who are they?

A: **Bill Clinton** and **Barack Obama**.

Q: There were six consecutive presidents with no military experience. Who were they?

A: **William Howard Taft, Woodrow Wilson, Warren Harding, Calvin Coolidge, Herbert Hoover,** and **Franklin Roosevelt.**

Q: Who was the first president who served in the Navy?

A: **John F. Kennedy**

Q: There were six presidents who served in the military in some capacity but never in a war. Who are they?

A: James Madison, James Polk, Millard Fillmore, Jimmy Carter, Ronald Reagan and **George W. Bush.** James Madison was a colonel in the Virginia Militia, James Polk was a colonel in his local militia, Millard Fillmore was in the New York militia, Jimmy Carter was a lieutenant in the Navy, Ronald Reagan was a captain in the Army during World War II but did not face combat due to poor eyesight, and George W. Bush was a First Lieutenant in the Texas Air National Guard. [1]

Q: Which three presidents were wounded in war?

A: James Monroe, Rutherford Hayes, and **John Kennedy.** In the Battle of Trenton on December 26, 1776, Monroe was struck in the left shoulder by a musket ball, which severed an artery. Doctor John Riker clamped the artery, preventing him from bleeding to death.

As for Hayes, he sustained several injuries during the Civil War, including an injury to his knee, a bone fracture after being shot through the left arm at the Battle of South Mountain (Maryland) on September 14, 1862, a shoulder injury resulting from a bullet wound at the Battle of Kernstown (Virginia) on July 24, 1864 and a sprained ankle after being thrown from a horse at the Battle of Cedar Creek (Virginia) on October 19, 1864.

As for Kennedy, on August 2, 1943, his boat, PT-109, was on nighttime patrol near New Georgia in the Solomon Islands, when it was rammed by the Japanese destroyer Amagiri, knocking the men overboard. Deciding not to surrender, the men swam towards a small island. Kennedy, whose back was injured in the collision, towed a burned crewman to the island with a life jacket strap clenched between his teeth. His crew was subsequently rescued. For these actions, Kennedy received the Navy and Marine Corps

Medal with the following citation:

> "For extremely heroic conduct as Commanding Officer of Motor Torpedo Boat 109 following the collision and sinking of that vessel in the Pacific War Theater on August 1-2, 1943. Unmindful of personal danger, Lieutenant (then Lieutenant, Junior Grade) Kennedy unhesitatingly braved the difficulties and hazards of darkness to direct rescue operations, swimming many hours to secure aid and food after he had succeeded in getting his crew ashore. His outstanding courage, endurance and leadership contributed to the saving of several lives and were in keeping with the highest traditions of the United States Naval Service."

When later asked by a reporter how he became a war hero, Kennedy joked: "It was involuntary. They sank my boat." Kennedy also received the Purple Heart, American Defense Service Medal, American Campaign Medal, Asiatic-Pacific Campaign Medal with three bronze service stars, and the World War II Victory Medal. [2]

Q: Who is the only president to have been awarded the Medal of Honor?

A: Theodore Roosevelt. The Medal of Honor is the highest military decoration awarded by the United States government. Roosevelt was a colonel during the Spanish-American War. On July 1, 1898, he led a charge up San Juan Hill near Santiago, Cuba, with the 1st U.S. Volunteer Cavalry Regiment. Interestingly, Roosevelt was first nominated for the award on July 6, 1898, just days after the battle. However, he did not win the award at that time.

Towards the end of July, 1898, a significant number of men were coming down with malaria. Roosevelt and seven other commanders signed a letter which was sent to Washington recommending that the weakened soldiers leave Cuba immediately. Although the main author of the letter is not known, Roosevelt has often been considered the prime suspect. It was called the "Round Robin" letter. It stated in part:

> "We, the undersigned officers commanding the various brigades, divisions, etc., of the Army of Occupation in Cuba, are of the unanimous opinion that this army should be at once taken out of the island of Cuba ... that the army is disabled by malarial fever to the extent that its efficiency is destroyed, and that it is in a condition to be practically entirely destroyed by an epidemic of yellow fever, which is sure to come in the near future. We know from the reports of competent officers and from personal observations that the army is unable to move into the interior, and that there are no facilities for such a move if attempted, and that it could not be attempted until too late. Moreover, the best medical authorities of the island say that with our present equipment we could not live in the interior during the rainy season without losses from malarial fever, which is almost as deadly as yellow fever. This army must be moved at once, or perish."

The letter was leaked to the press and published around the country, which caused great embarrassment to the McKinley administration, because it made them appear cold and callous to the American public for leaving the sick troops in Cuba.

Despite Roosevelt's often expressed desire to win the award, he ultimately did not receive it at the time, although twenty-eight other participants in the Santiago campaign did. The exact reasons he did not win the award at that time are not known, although the "Round Robin" letter may have played a part. Nevertheless, Roosevelt was given the award by President Clinton posthumously on January 16, 2001, almost 100 years later. [3]

Q: This president was awarded a Silver Star, which is the military's third-highest medal, awarded for "gallantry in action against an enemy of the United States." The medal was awarded by General Douglas McArthur for the future president's role in a B-26 bombing mission in the Pacific during World War II, while serving as a commander in the Navy. However, no other members of the flight crew were awarded medals, and he was purely "observer." A biographer of his commented that "The most you can say about [this future president] and his Silver Star is that it is surely one of the most undeserved Silver Stars in history, because if you accept everything that he said, he was still in action for no more than 13 minutes and only as an observer. Men who flew many missions, brave men, never got a Silver Star." **Which president was it?**

A: Lyndon Johnson. The quote is from Johnson biographer Robert Caro.[4]

Q: Which president was the youngest pilot in the Navy during World War II, and at age nineteen, he received the "Distinguished Flying Cross"?

A: George H.W. Bush. His citation for the Distinguished Flying Cross reads:

> "For heroism and extraordinary achievement in aerial flight as Pilot of a Torpedo Plane in Torpedo Squadron Fifty-One, attached to the U.S.S. San Jacinto, in action against enemy Japanese forces in the vicinity of the Bonin Islands, on September 2, 1944. Leading one section of a four-plane division in a strike against a radio station, Lieutenant, Junior Grade, Bush pressed home an attack in the face of intense anti-aircraft fire. Although his plane was hit and set afire at the beginning of his dive, he continued his plunge toward the target and succeeded in scoring damaging bomb hits before bailing out of the craft. His

courage and devotion to duty were in keeping with the highest traditions of the United States Naval Reserve."

He also flew fifty-eight combat missions and received three Air Medals, and the Presidential Unit Citation. [5]

Q: Of the four medals won by presidents for valor in battle, which one was awarded posthumously?

A: Theodore Roosevelt's was awarded by Bill Clinton on June 16, 2001.[6]

Q: Which president paid a supporter to take his place in the Civil War?

A: Grover Cleveland because he was the sole supporter of the family at the time. He had this option due to the Conscription Act of 1863, which allowed men who were able-bodied to either serve in the army if called upon, or else to hire a substitute. Cleveland chose the latter course, paying George Benninsky, a thirty-two year-old Polish immigrant, $150 to serve in his place. Benninsky survived the War. [7]

Q: Only one president rose from the rank of private (in his state militia) to become president. Who was he?

A: James Buchanan, who was a private in the Pennsylvania militia. [8]

Q: Who is the only American president to have faced enemy gunfire while president?

A: James Madison at the Battle of Bladensburg (Maryland), which took place on August 24, 1814 during the War of 1812. Madison accompanied a military battery manned by Maryland inexperienced militiamen under the command of Brigadier General William Winder. Secretary of State James Monroe was also present. After the British started firing recently invented Congreve rockets, Winder suggested to the president that he retire from the field and take Monroe with him. The defeat of the American forces there allowed the British to capture and burn the public buildings of Washington, D.C. It has been called "the greatest disgrace ever dealt to American arms." The disorganized American retreat became known as the Bladensburg Races. As an aside, it was the use of Congreve rockets in the bombardment of Fort McHenry in the battle that inspired the fifth line of the National Anthem, "And the rockets' red glare, the bombs bursting in air." [9]

Q: Who was the only president to serve in both World Wars?

A: Dwight Eisenhower, although he did not see combat in World War I. [10]

Q: Who was the only president to serve in both the Revolutionary War and the War of 1812?

A: Andrew Jackson. During the American Revolutionary War, Jackson, at age thirteen, joined a local militia as a courier. Jackson's service in the War of 1812 included his historic victory in the Battle of New Orleans. On January 8, 1815, his 5,000 soldiers won a decisive victory over 7,500 British. At the end of the battle, the British had 2,037 casualties: 291 dead, 1,262 wounded, and 484 captured or missing. The Americans had 71 casualties: 13 dead, 39 wounded, and 19 missing. The war, and especially this victory, made Andrew Jackson a national hero. He received the "Thanks of Congress" and a gold medal by resolution of February 27, 1815. Alexis de Tocqueville later commented in *Democracy in America* that Jackson "was raised to the Presidency, and has been maintained there, solely by the recollection of a victory which he gained, twenty years ago, under the walls of New Orleans." [11]

Q: Who is the only president to have been a prisoner of war?

A: Andrew Jackson, during the Revolutionary War. Jackson and his brother Robert were captured by the British and held as prisoners. They nearly starved to death in captivity. When Jackson refused to clean the boots of a British officer, the officer slashed at the youth with a sword, leaving Jackson with scars on his left hand and head, as well as an intense hatred for the British. [12]

Q: Who was the last president to serve in the Civil War?

A: William McKinley.

Q: Which president, a noted military leader, was never actually involved in combat in any war?

A: Dwight Eisenhower. During World War I, he never left the country, though not for lack of trying. After graduation from West Point in 1915, Lieutenant Eisenhower put in for assignment in the Philippines which was denied. He served with the infantry, initially in supplies, until 1918 at various camps in Texas and Georgia. When World War I began, he requested an overseas assignment but was again denied and then assigned to Ft. Leavenworth, Kansas. In February 1918 he was transferred to Camp Meade in Maryland with the 65th Engineers. His unit was later ordered to France but he received orders for the new tank corps. He trained tank crews at "Camp Colt"—his first command—at the site of "Pickett's Charge" on the Gettysburg, Pennsylvania Civil War battleground. [13]

Q: Two presidents served in four different wars. Who were they?

A: Zachary Taylor and **Andrew Jackson**. Taylor served in the War of 1812, the Black Hawk War, the Second Seminole War, and the Mexican-American War. Jackson served in the American Revolutionary War, the War of 1812, the Creek War, and the First Seminole War.

Q: Only two people in American history have ever attained the rank of *General of the Armies of the United States* (also known as General of the Armies), which is the highest possible military rank bestowed. One was John J. Pershing who was awarded the honor in 1919 to honor his service in World War I. The other was this president, who was awarded the honor in 1976. **Who is the only president to attain the rank of *General of the Armies of the United States?***

A: George Washington. He retired as a lieutenant general (three stars) and, as a result, was technically outranked by later four and five-star generals of the Civil War, World War I, and World War II. In recognition of Washington's permanent place in United States history, on October 11, 1976, he was posthumously promoted to the full grade of *General of the Armies of the United States* by Executive Order of President Gerald R. Ford. The promotion was authorized by a congressional joint resolution on January 19, 1976, which recommended Washington's promotion and declared that no officer of the United States Army should outrank Lieutenant General George Washington on the Army list. The full text of the legislation was:

> "Whereas Lieutenant General George Washington of Virginia commanded our armies throughout and to the successful termination of our Revolutionary War; Whereas Lieutenant General George Washington presided over the convention that formulated our Constitution; Whereas Lieutenant General George Washington twice served as President of the United States of America; and Whereas it is considered fitting and proper that no officer of the United States Army should outrank Lieutenant General

George Washington on the Army list; Now, therefore, be it resolved by the Senate and House of Representatives of the United States of America in Congress assembled, That

(a) for purposes of subsection (b) of this section only, the grade of General of the Armies of the United States is established, such grade to have rank and precedence over all other grades of the Army, past or present.

(b) The President is authorized and requested to appoint George Washington posthumously to the grade of General of the Armies of the United States, such appointment to take effect on July 4, 1976.
Approved October 11, 1976."

Q: Which two presidents received the second highest military rank bestowed known as *General of the Army of the United States* (i.e. singular instead of plural)?

A: Ulysses Grant (1866) and **Dwight Eisenhower** (1944). The other three men who attained this rank were Philip Sheridan (1888), George Marshall (1944) and Douglas MacArthur (1944).

The military ranks attained by presidents other than Washington and Grant, and Eisenhower in descending order of rank, are as follows:

Army

General: **Andrew Jackson**
Major General: **William Henry Harrison, Zachary Taylor, Rutherford Hayes, James Garfield**
Brigadier General: **Franklin Pierce, Andrew Johnson, Chester Arthur and Benjamin Harrison.**
Colonel: **Thomas Jefferson, James Madison, James Polk, Theodore Roosevelt and Harry Truman.**

Major: **James Monroe, Millard Fillmore** (New York State militia)
Brevet Major: **William McKinley**
Captain: **John Tyler, Abraham Lincoln** (Illinois State militia)
Private: **James Buchanan** (Pennsylvania State militia)

Army Reserve

Captain: **Ronald Reagan**

Texas Air National Guard

First Lieutenant: **George W. Bush**

Navy

Commander: **Lyndon Johnson, Richard Nixon**
Lieutenant: **John F. Kennedy, Jimmy Carter**

Naval Reserve

Lieutenant Commander: **Gerald Ford**
Lieutenant: **George H.W. Bush**

No military service

John Adams, John Quincy Adams, Martin Van Buren, Grover Cleveland, William Howard Taft, Woodrow Wilson, Warren Harding, Calvin Coolidge, Herbert Hoover, Franklin Roosevelt, Bill Clinton and Barack Obama.[14]

Q: A president had "grave misgivings" about dropping an atomic bomb on Japan in 1945. Who was it?

A: Dwight Eisenhower. He wrote of a conversation he had with Secretary of War Henry Stimson: "During his recitation of the relevant facts, I had been conscious of a feeling of depression and so I voiced to him my grave misgivings, first on the basis of my belief that Japan was already defeated and that dropping the bomb was completely unnecessary, and secondly because I thought that our country should avoid shocking world opinion by the use of a weapon whose employment was, I thought, no longer mandatory as a measure to save American lives. It was my belief that Japan was, at that very moment, seeking some way to surrender with a minimum loss of 'face.' The Secretary was deeply perturbed by my attitude, almost angrily refuting the reasons I gave for my quick conclusions." [15]

CHAPTER TWENTY-EIGHT NOTES:

1) Seigenthaler, *John. James K. Polk: 1845-1849.* 2003
   http://teaareacomputerapplications.pbworks.com/w/page/21254746/Millard%20Fillmore
   http://www.history.navy.mil/faqs/faq60-14.htm
   http://www.reagan.utexas.edu/archives/reference/military.html
   Lardner, George Jr. and Lois Romano. *"At Height of Vietnam, Bush Picks Guard," The Washington Post,* July 28, 1999

2) Fischer, David Hackett. *Washington's Crossing.* Oxford University Press (2006).
   Hoogenboom, Ari. *Rutherford Hayes: Warrior and President.* University Press of Kansas, (1995)
   Donovan, Robert J. *PT-109: John F. Kennedy in WW II*, 40th Anniversary Edition (1961, 2001)
   http://www.jfklibrary.org/JFK/JFK-in-History/John-F-Kennedy-and-PT109.aspx
   http://enidnews.com/opinion/x1765863669/U-S-presidents-In-service-to-this-nation

3) Morris, Edmund. *Colonel Roosevelt.* Random House (2011).
   http://www.archives.gov/publications/prologue/1998/spring/roosevelt-and-medal-of-honor-4.html
   http://www.bartleby.com/51/c.html
   http://www.theodoreroosevelt.org/life/medalofhonor.htm

4) http://www.cnn.com/SPECIALS/2001/johnson.silver.star/story/storypage.html

5) http://www.history.navy.mil/faqs/faq10-2.htm

6) http://www.theodoreroosevelt.org/life/medalofhonor.htm

7) Nevins, Allan. *Grover Cleveland: A Study in Courage* (1932); Henry Graff, *Grover Cleveland*, The American Presidents Series (Macmillan, 2002).

8) www.americanhistory.si.edu/presidency/5d5.html

9) Howe, Daniel Walker. *What hath God wrought: the transformation of America, 1815-1848.* Oxford University Press (2007).
   Pitch, Anthony. *The Burning of Washington: The British Invasion of 1814*, Naval Institute Press (2000).

10) Ambrose, Stephen E. *Eisenhower: Soldier, General of the Army, President-Elect, 1890-1952*, Simon & Schuster. (1983)

11) Robert Remini, *Legacy of Andrew Jackson: Essays on Democracy, Indian Removal, and*

Slavery (LSU Press 1990)

James, Marquis. *The Life of Andrew Jackson* (Bobbs-Merrill, 1938)

Remini, Robert V. *The Life of Andrew Jackson.* (Penguin, 1990)

Remini, Robert V., *The Battle of New Orleans* Penguin Books.1999)

12) http://www.potus.com/ajackson.html

13) Ambrose, Stephen. *Eisenhower: (vol. 1) Soldier, General of the Army, President-Elect (1893-1952).* Simon & Schuster (1983).

14) http://www.history.army.mil/html/faq/5star.html
http://www.history.army.mil/books/CG&CSA/Washington-G2.htm
http://en.wikipedia.org/wiki/General_of_the_Armies
http://en.wikipedia.org/wiki/List_of_United_States_Presidents_by_military_service

15) Newton, Jim, *Eisenhower, The White House Years*, (Doubleday, 2011).
Eisenhower, Dwight, *Mandate For Change* (Doubleday, 1963).

CHAPTER 29

Wealth and Poverty

Q: This early president died penniless. Towards the end of his life, another president went to visit him and wrote in his diary: "[He] is a very remarkable instance of a man whose life has been a continued series of the most extraordinary good fortune, who has never met with any known disaster, has gone through a splendid career of public service, has received more pecuniary reward from the public than any other man since the existence of the nation, and is now dying, at the age of seventy-two, in wretchedness and beggary ... I did not protract my visit, and took leave of him, in all probability, for the last time." **Who was the writer and who was the president of which he was speaking?**

A: The writer was **John Quincy Adams**. He was speaking about **James Monroe**, under whom Adams served eight years as Secretary of State. This was his diary entry for April 27, 1831, in *Memoirs of John Quincy Adams, Comprising Portions of His Diary*, Vol. 8, edited by Charles Francis Adams (1876). [1]

Q: This president was a name partner in a brokerage house with a man named Ferdinand Ward, who was engaged in a Ponzi scheme, and who swindled the president out of his life savings. As a result of becoming destitute, he wrote and finished his memoirs just before he died, and those memoirs went on to sell 300,000 copies, earning his family a substantial sum of money. Who was this president?

A: Ulysses Grant. Grant's son Buck had formed a brokerage firm with Ward, whose early successes had earned him the nickname "the young Napoleon of Wall Street." The firm, opened in 1880, was called Grant & Ward. The president became a partner in the firm although he was not involved in actually running the business—that was handled by Ward. The company did very well at first, so Grant's old army comrades put in their money, as did Grant's widowed sister and his young nieces. Ward multiplied their money several times over. By 1884, Grant seemed at long last to have achieved the financial security he and Julia had always craved. He proudly told others that his worth was in the vicinity of two and a half million dollars.

However the reason for the success was that Ward was essentially running an early version of a Ponzi scheme. He never invested any of the money. He had an estate in Connecticut with lots of horses and a townhouse in New York.

On May 4th, 1884, Ward told Grant that the firm was short on cash. He urged Grant to go see his friend William Henry Vanderbilt about a loan. Vanderbilt wrote the general a personal check for $150,000 which Grant gave to Ward. A few days later, when Grant came down to the office on Wall Street, he was surprised to find a huge crowd gathered outside. The newspapers had picked up rumors that Grant & Ward was in trouble. Angry investors had rushed downtown, looking for the money they had entrusted to the company. Buck told Grant that they were completely wiped out, and that Ward was nowhere to be found.

Grant was back to being penniless. All the money was gone, as were the savings of every member of the Grant family and the investments of all the soldiers who had sent the General their pension checks. Vanderbilt's loan had made no difference. Ward was arrested and charged with larceny. He got ten years in Sing Sing. Although Vanderbilt was willing to forgive the $150,000 note, Grant, feeling guilty, gave Vanderbilt everything of value he owned: his military medals, uniforms, swords, and gifts he had been given on his world tour such as gold cigar boxes and an elephant tusk from the King of Siam. Vanderbilt gave the items of enduring historic value to the Smithsonian and let Grant have the rest back. He said he considered the debt repaid.

In 2012, Geoffrey Ward, who is Ferdinand Ward's great-grandson and a noted Civil War historian (he co-authored *The Civil War* with Ken Burns and Ric Burns), wrote a book about his great grandfather's life called *A Disposition to Be Rich*.

As a result of being so deeply in debt, Grant wrote a series of literary works that improved his reputation and eventually brought his family out of bankruptcy. Grant first wrote several warmly received articles on his Civil War campaigns for *The Century Magazine*. Mark Twain offered Grant a generous contract for his memoirs, including 75% of the book's sales as royalties.

Terminally ill, Grant finished his memoir just a few days before his death. The memoirs sold over 300,000 copies, earning the Grant family over $450,000. Twain promoted the book as "the most remarkable work of its kind since the *Commentaries of Julius Caesar*." Grant's memoir has been regarded by writers as diverse as Matthew Arnold and Gertrude Stein as one of the finest works of its kind ever written. [2]

Speaking of the wealth of presidents, Charles Panati, a former writer for *Newsweek*, wrote a called *The Browser's Book of Endings: The End of Practically Everything and Everybody* (Penguin, 1999) in which he writes of the wealth (or lack thereof) of the presidents at their death based on non-inflation adjusted dollars:

- **George Washington**, who wanted to free his slaves but for his widow's sake didn't, left $530,000.
- **Thomas Jefferson**, who held off death to expire on the Fourth of July left $200,000.
- **James Madison**, who contrived to keep his high-spending widow, Dolley, from poverty left less than $100,000.
- **James Monroe**, the White House's first heavy drinker left an estate in bankruptcy.
- **Andrew Jackson**, sick and senile, spent his final days singing "Auld Lang Syne." Estate: $150,000.
- **Martin Van Buren** sold off assets to keep his sons from fighting over them. Estate: $250,000.
- **William Henry Harrison**'s two-hour inaugural address (the longest in history) lead to the shortest presidency (31 days). Estate value: None.
- **John Tyler**, whose body lay for years in an unmarked grave, left more than $100,000.
- **Franklin Pierce**, who literally drank himself to death, left $70,000.
- Bachelor president **James Buchanan** (perhaps gay) left one of the largest estates up to his time: $310,000.
- **Abraham Lincoln**, who had to be buried in six feet of solid concrete, left $83,000.
- **Ulysses S. Grant** died penniless, but assured his widow a fortune.
- **James Garfield**, shot by an assassin but killed by his doctors, left $61,000.
- Former hangman **Grover Cleveland** left $250,000.
- **Benjamin Harrison**, who had the White House wired for electricity, left $375,000.
- Assassinated **William McKinley**, whose murdered body was decomposed with sulfuric acid, left $215,000.
- **Theodore Roosevelt** wrote the first 'modern' will and left $811,000.

- **Woodrow Wilson**, whose wife usurped the presidency during his stroke and prompted the 25th Amendment on 'Disability and Succession,' left $600,000.
- **Warren Harding**, who left his mistress and illegitimate daughter out of his will, left $930,000.
- **Calvin Coolidge**, the only president with Indian blood, left $500,000.
- **Herbert Hoover**, who repeatedly redrafted his will, left $8 million.
- Four-term President **Franklin D. Roosevelt** left $1.9 million.
- **Harry Truman** left bequests of as little as $5 and an estate of $610,000.
- **Dwight D. Eisenhower**, whose surgery guaranteed his death, left $2.8 million.
- **John F. Kennedy**, the wealthiest president up to this time, put an upper limit on his widow's spending and left $10 million.
- **Lyndon Johnson** willed his wife nothing, but left an estate of $10 million.
- **Richard N. Nixon**, who resigned from office, left presidential papers and tapes valued in excess of $10 million.

Washington's Will is unusual because it actually values all of Washington's assets, leaving a total of $530,000, just as Panati states.

In 2010, another study on the wealth of the presidents (or lack thereof) was done by Douglas A. McIntyre, Ashley C. Allen, Michael B. Sauter, and Charles B. Stockdale, the editors of *24/7 Wall St.* The article appeared in the May 27, 2010 edition of *The Atlantic Monthy*.

This study differs from Panati's analysis in two key respects. First, it considers their net wealth at their respective peaks. In this respect, the extremely high numbers associated with some of the presidents may not accurately reflect their degree of wealth for large portions of their lives, especially towards the end. There are numerous examples of this, especially with respect to the early presidents. Jefferson, Monroe, Jackson, William Henry Harrison and John Tyler all died relatively poor after being worth eight or nine figures (inflation adjusted) at some point in their lives, at least according to this study. It is generally agreed that at least Monroe and William Henry Harrison died as bankrupts. Second, as noted, the numbers are inflation-adjusted as of 2010. For these two reasons, the figures are wildly higher than Panati's. The comments after each president are taken from the study and the list is presented in descending order of wealth:

1. **John Fitzgerald Kennedy:** Although he never inherited his father's fortune, the Kennedy family estate was worth nearly $1 billion dollars. Almost all of JFK's income and property came from trust shared with other family members.

2. **George Washington:** $525 million. His Virginia plantation, "Mount Vernon," consisted of five separate farms on 8,000 acres of prime farmland, run by over 300 slaves. Washington made significantly more than subsequent presidents: his salary was two percent of the total U.S. budget in 1789.

3. **Thomas Jefferson:** $212 million. Jefferson was left 3,000 acres and several dozen slaves by his father. "Monticello," his home on a 5,000 acre plantation in Virginia, was one of the architectural wonders of its time. He made significant money in various political positions before becoming president, but was mired in debt towards the end of his life. Therefore, his "swing" may have been the largest of all presidents.

4. **Theodore Roosevelt:** $125 million. Born to a prominent and wealthy family, Roosevelt received a significant trust fund. He lost most of his money on a ranching venture in the

Dakotas and had to work as an author to pay bills. His 235-acre estate, "Sagamore Hill," sits on some of the most valuable real estate on Long Island.

5. **Andrew Jackson:** $119 million. "Old Hickory" married into wealth and made money in the military. His homestead "The Hermitage" included 1,050 acres of prime real estate. However, Jackson had significant debt later in life.

6. **James Madison:** $101 million. Madison was the largest landowner in Orange County, Virginia, with land holding consisting of 5,000 acres and the "Montpelier" estate. He made significant money as secretary of state but he later lost money at the end of his life due to the financial collapse of his plantation.

7. **Lyndon Baines Johnson:** $98 million. Johnson's father lost all of the family's money when LBJ was a boy. Over time, he accumulated 1,500 acres in Blanco County, Texas, which included his home, called the "Texas White House." He and his wife owned a radio and television station in Austin, TX, and had a variety of other holdings, including livestock and private aircraft.

8. **Herbert Hoover:** $75 million. An orphan, Hoover was raised by his uncle, a doctor. He made a fortune as a mining company executive, had a very large salary for seventeen years and had extensive holdings in mining companies. Hoover donated his presidential salary to charity.

9. **Franklin Delano Roosevelt:** $60 million. Roosevelt had wealth through inheritance and marriage. He owned the 800-acre "Springwood" estate as well as properties in Georgia, Maine, and New York. In 1919, his mother had to bail him out of financial difficulty.

10. **John Tyler:** $51 million. Tyler Inherited 1,000-acre tobacco plantation. His first wife, Letitia, was wealthy. Tyler bought "Sherwood Manor," a 1,600 acre estate, previously owned by

William Henry Harrison. He became indebted during the Civil War and died poor.

11. **William Jefferson Clinton:** $38 million. Clinton was born with no inheritance, and he made little significant money during twenty plus years of public service. After his time in the White House, however, he made a substantial income as an author and public speaker.

12. **James Monroe:** $27 million. Monroe's wife, Elizabeth, was the daughter of wealthy British officer. He made significant money during eight years as president, but entered retirement severely in debt and was forced to sell Highland plantation, which included 3500 acres. Monroe, Jackson and William Henry Harrison were among the poorest presidents at their deaths.

13. **Martin Van Buren:** $26 million. Van Buren made substantial income as an attorney. He was one of only two men to serve as secretary of state, vice president, and president. He owned the 225-acre "Lindenwald" estate in upstate New York.

14. **Grover Cleveland:** $25 million. Cleveland served as an attorney for twelve years, and also made significant sums on the sale of his estate outside Washington, D.C.

15. **George Herbert Walker Bush:** $23 million. Bush was the son of Prescott Bush, Connecticut Senator and successful businessman. Aided by his friends in the financial community, he made a number of successful investments. One of his major assets is his 100+ acre estate in Kennebunkport, Maine.

16. **John Quincy Adams:** $21 million. Adams inherited most of his father's land. His wife was the daughter of a wealthy merchant.

17. **George W. Bush:** $20 million. Bush was born into a wealthy family. Over ten years, he made substantial sums of

money in the oil business. The largest contribution to his net worth was the profitable sale of the Texas Rangers.

18. **John Adams:** $19 million. Adams received a modest inheritance from his father. Adams owned a handsome estate in Quincy, Massachusetts, known as "Peacefield," a working farm, covering approximately 40 acres. He also had a thriving law practice.

19. **Richard Nixon:** $15 million. Nixon was born without any inheritance, and was a public servant for most of his life including a term as a Senator from California. He made significant sums from series of interviews with David Frost and book advances. At various times, Nixon also owned real estate in California and Florida.

20. **Ronald Reagan:** $13 million. Reagan had no inheritance, but his first wife, actress Jane Wyman, had her own money. He was a movie and television actor for over two decades. "The Gipper" owned several pieces of real estate over his lifetime, including a 688-acre property near Santa Barbara, California. Reagan was highly paid for his autobiography and as a GE spokesman.

21. **James Knox Polk:** $10 million. Like his wife, Sarah Childress, Polk's father was a wealthy plantation owner and speculator. Polk made significant sums as speaker of the house and governor of Tennessee, and owned 920 acres in Coffeeville, Mississippi, as well as 25 slaves.

22. **Dwight David Eisenhower:** $8 million. Eisenhower had no inherited wealth. He served the majority of his career in the military and five years as president of Columbia. Ike owned a large farm near Gettysburg, Pennsylvania.

23. **Gerald Ford:** $7 million. Ford had no inheritance, and he spent virtually his entire adult life in public service. Over the course of his lifetime, he owned properties in Michigan, Rancho Mirage, California and Beaver Creek, Colorado. After he left the White House in 1976, he made nearly $1

million a year from book advances and from serving on the boards of several prominent American companies.

24. **Jimmy Carter:** $7 million. Carter was the son of a prominent Georgia businessman. He was a peanut farmer for almost two decades. Carter made substantial sums from writing fourteen books. He is part of a family partnership that owns 2,500 acres in Georgia.

25. **Zachary Taylor**: $6 million. Taylor inherited significant amounts of land from his family, which at one point included property in Mississippi, Kentucky, and Louisiana. He made substantial money in land speculation, the leasing of warehouses, and investments in bank and utility stocks. Taylor owned a sizeable plantation in Mississippi and a home in Baton Rouge.

26. **William Henry Harrison**: $5 million. Harrison married into money. His wife's father was a prominent judge and landowner. When Harrison's mother died, he inherited 3,000 acres near Charles City, Virginia, which he later sold to his brother. He also owned the "Grouseland" mansion and property, in Vincennes, Indiana. Despite his assets, Harrison died penniless, causing Congress to create a special pension for his widow.

27. **Benjamin Harrison:** $5 million. Harrison had no significant inheritance of his own or from his wife's family. He was a highly paid attorney for eighteen years, and served as attorney for Republic of Venezuela. Harrison owned a large Victorian home in Indianapolis, Indiana.

28. **Barack Obama:** $5 million. Obama is a former constitutional law professor and civil rights attorney. Book royalties constitute most of Obama's net worth.

29. **Millard Fillmore:** $4 million. Neither Fillmore nor his wife had significant inheritance. He founded a college that is the current State University of New York at Buffalo, and his primary holding was a house in nearby East Aurora, New York.

30. **Rutherford B. Hayes:** $3 million. Hayes' father was a shop-keeper. He was an attorney for fifteen years and owned "Spiegel Grove," a 10,000 square foot home that sat on twenty-five acres in Fremont, Ohio.

31. **William Howard Taft:** $3 million. Taft's wife's father was a law partner of former president, Rutherford B. Hayes. Taft was president of the American Bar Association, an active attorney for nearly two decades, and the only president to serve on the U.S. Supreme Court.

32. **Franklin Pierce:** $2 million. Pierce's father was a frontier farmer, and his wife was a well-to-do aristocrat. He served as attorney for sixteen years and held property in Concord, New Hampshire.

The following Presidents, all having died with a net worth of $1 million or less, are listed in chronological order:

James Buchanan: Born in a log cabin in Pennsylvania, Buchanan was one of eleven children. He worked for nine years as attorney, and spent sixteen years in public office, including four years as secretary of state.

Abraham Lincoln: Lincoln served as an attorney for seventeen years before his presidency. He owned a single-family home in Springfield, Illinois.

Andrew Johnson: Johnson's father was a tailor, and his wife was a shoemaker. He served the public for twenty years, including as Governor of Tennessee and U.S. Senator. Johnson owned a small house in Greenville, Tennessee.

Ulysses Grant: Grant's father was a tanner, and his wife was the daughter of a wealthy merchant. He lost his entire fortune when swindled by his investing partner. Grant owned a modest home in Galena, Illinois. Although he died with little money, his autobiography kept the family afloat.

James A. Garfield: Garfield was born in a log cabin in Ohio. He spent eighteen years in the House of Representatives. Garfield owned "Lawnfield," a home and small property in Mentor, Ohio. He died penniless.

Chester A. Arthur: The son of an Irish preacher, Arthur's wife came from a military family. He made substantial sums as Collector for the Port of New York.

William McKinley: Mckinley had no significant inheritance. He served thirty years in public office, including as a local prosecutor and member of the House of Representatives. He went bankrupt during the depression of 1893 while he was Governor of Ohio.

Woodrow Wilson: Wilson received a modest compensation as head of Princeton and Governor of New Jersey. He never served in any position that provided him with a reasonable income. Wilson had a stroke in office and died five years later.

Warren Gamaliel Harding: Harding obtained wealth through marriage to his wife Mabel, daughter of a prominent banker. He owned the *Marion Daily Star* and a small home in Marion, Ohio. Most of Harding's net worth came from his newspaper ownership.

Calvin Coolidge: Coolidge's father was prosperous farmer and storekeeper. "Silent Cal" spent five years as an attorney, and almost two decades in public office, which included time as Governor of Massachusetts. His net worth derived primarily from his home, "The Beeches," in Northampton, Massachusetts, the advance from his autobiography, and the money he made from his newspaper column.

Harry S Truman: Truman was a haberdasher in Missouri and nearly went bankrupt. He served eighteen years in Washington, D.C.

Another list, prepared by Forbes, listed the top ten wealthiest presidents, "taking into account a number of factors, including absolute wealth in office (some nearly went bust afterward) and, to help adjust for two centuries of both inflation and economic growth, comparative wealth within the economy of their times." It did not contain specific figures of wealth.

1. **George Washington**
2. **Herbert Hoover**
3. **Thomas Jefferson**
4. **John F. Kennedy**
5. **Andrew Jackson**
6. **Theodore Roosevelt**
7. **Zachary Taylor**
8. **Franklin Roosevelt**
9. **Lyndon Johnson**
10. **James Madison** [3]

Q: True or false: George Washington did not accept a salary as president.

A: False, although that was his original intent. In his first inaugural address, delivered on April 30, 1789, he stated:

> "To the foregoing observations I have one to add, which will be most properly addressed to the House of Representatives. It concerns myself, and will therefore be as brief as possible. When I was first honored with a call into the service of my country, then on the eve of an arduous struggle for its liberties, the light in which I contemplated my duty required that I should renounce every pecuniary compensation. From this resolution I have in no instance departed; and being still under the impressions which produced it, I must decline as inapplicable to myself any share in the personal emoluments which may be indispensably included in a permanent provision for the executive department, and must accordingly pray that the pecuniary estimates for the station in which I am placed may during my continuance in it be limited to such actual expenditures as the public good may be thought to require."

Washington's noble position raised several problems. First,

Article II, Section 1, Clause 7 of the Constitution mandates such a payment:

> "The president shall, at stated times, receive for his services, a compensation, which shall neither be increased nor diminished during the period for which he shall have been elected, and he shall not receive within that period any other Emolument from the United States, or any of them."

Second, Congress wanted to avoid setting a precedent whereby the presidency would be perceived as limited only to independently wealthy individuals who could serve without any salary. Finally, as constitutional scholar David Currie wrote:

> "If the constitutional premise was that financial independence was a crucial barrier to corruption, an officer who impoverished himself by declining his wages endangered the public interest. Moreover, if Washington was right that he need not accept this money, there would always be a risk that the President's waiver was not truly voluntary; reading the Constitution to mean what it said would obviate the need for inquiry on this unpromising score."

Ultimately, Washington agreed to accept his $25,000 salary. [4]

Q: Which two presidents donated their salaries to charity?

A: One was **Herbert Hoover**. In an interview with Charles Scott, editor of the *Iola* (Kansas) *Daily Register* in January, 1937, Hoover explained:

> "I made up my mind when I entered public life that I would not make it possible for anyone ever to say that I had sought public office for the money there was in it. I therefore kept the money that came to me as salary in a separate account and distributed it where I thought it would do the most good. Part of it went to supplement the salaries of men who worked under me and whom the government

paid less than I thought they were worth. Part of it went to charities."

The other was **John F. Kennedy**. [5]

Q: Who was the highest paid president, adjusted for inflation?

A: William Howard Taft at approximately $1,823,889 in 1909.

Q: Who was the lowest paid president, adjusted for inflation?

A: Bill Clinton at approximately $230,000 in 2000.

The level of presidential salaries over time, are as follows:

Effective Year	Presidents	Salary	Inflation-Adjusted (as of year of change)
1789	Washington to Grant	$25,000	$321,683
1873	Grant to Roosevelt	$50,000	$911,944
1909	Taft to Truman	$75,000	$1,823,889
1949	Truman to Johnson	$100,000	$919,608
1969	Nixon to Clinton	$200,000	$1,913,818
2001	George W. Bush onward	$400,000	$400,000

From 1949 on, the salaries do not include $50,000 as a non-taxable expense allowance to assist in defraying expenses relating to or resulting from the discharge of the president's official duties.

The numbers provided above for inflation-adjusted salaries can vary depending on the methodology and variables used by the person doing the study. However, the actual salaries, and the facts that Taft and Clinton were our highest and lowest paid presidents respectively, adjusted for inflation, are not in question. [6]

CHAPTER TWENTY-NINE NOTES:

1) http://boatagainstthecurrent.blogspot.com/2011/04/quote-of-day-john-quincy-adams-on-dying.html
http://www.masshist.org/jqadiaries/doc.cfm?id=jqad23_478
http://ia600400.us.archive.org/2/items/memjohnquincy08adamrich/memjohn-

quincy08adamrich_djvu.txt
2) http://www.pbs.org/wgbh/americanexperience/features/transcript/grant-tran-script/?flavour=mobile
http://www.granthomepage.com/intward.htm
Ward, Geoffrey C., *A Disposition to be Rich*, Knopf (2012).
The Personal Memoirs of Julia Dent Grant, available online at google.com
3) http://www.panatibooks.com/ends/ends.html
http://www.pbs.org/georgewashington/collection/other_last_will.html
http://247wallst.com/2010/05/17/the-net-worth-of-the-american-presidents-washington-to-obama/3/
http://xfinity.comcast.net/slideshow/finance-10richestuspresidents/the-fattest-presidential-purses/
4) Chernow, Ron. *Washington: A Life.* Penguin (2010)
http://www.bartleby.com/124/pres13.html
http://elektratig.blogspot.com/2007/12/george-washingtons-salary-as-president.html
5) http://hoover.archives.gov/info/faq.html#salary
6) http://www.presidentsusa.net/presidentsalaryhistory.html
http://coast.contracosta.edu/websites/socialsciences/economics/w_williams/SharedDocuments/CalculatingRealSalariesofPresidents.pdf
http://oregonstate.edu/cla/polisci/faculty-research/sahr/sumprpay.pdfn

CHAPTER 30

Who Was the First . . .

Q: Who was the first president born in the 20th-century?

A: Lyndon Johnson (1908).

Q: Who was the first president to appoint an African-American to his cabinet?

A: Lyndon Johnson, who appointed Robert Weaver as head of Housing and Urban Development from 1966-1968.

Q: Who was the first president to take the oath of office in Washington, D.C.?

A: Thomas Jefferson. George Washington took the first oath of office on the balcony of Federal Hall in New York City on April 30, 1789. He took the second oath of office in the Senate Camber of Congress Hall in Philadelphia on March 4, 1793. John Adams took the oath of office in the House Camber of Congress Hall in Philadelphia on March 4, 1797.[1]

Q: Who was the first president to wear pants/trousers (as opposed to knee breeches)?

A: James Madison. [2]

Q: Who was the first wartime president?

A: James Madison. The war in question was the War of 1812. There were no major military confrontations between 1789, when Washington was sworn in for his first term, and the War of 1812.

Q: Who was the first president to attend a regular season National Football League game?

A: Remarkably, it was **Richard Nixon**. On November 16, 1969, he saw Washington lose to the Dallas Cowboys, 41-28 at RFK Stadium. Thus Warren Harding, Calvin Coolidge, Herbert Hoover, Franklin Roosevelt, Harry Truman, Dwight Eisenhower, John Kennedy and Lyndon Johnson (all of whom were presidents after the formation of the NFL) never saw a regular season NFL game (although Johnson did see a pre-season game).[3]

Q: Who was the first president, and in fact the first American, to have a Medicare card?

A: Harry Truman. The Social Security Act of 1965 was signed into law on July 30, 1965, by President Lyndon B. Johnson as an amendment to existing Social Security legislation. This legislation included the establishing of the Medicare program. At the bill-signing ceremony, Johnson enrolled former President Harry S. Truman as the first Medicare beneficiary and presented him with the first Medicare card, and Truman's wife Bess, with the second.[4]

Q: Who was the first president to visit a foreign country while in office?

A: Surprisingly (again), this did not occur until **Theodore Roosevelt** visited Panama in 1906. Thus, up until the 20th-century, an American president had never left American soil while President.

Roosevelt was very enthusiastic about the Panama Canal project and he wanted to see it for himself. David McCullough wrote in his book *Path Between the Seas*:

> "Advanced preparations involved the efforts of thousands of people. . . . Streets were scrubbed, houses were painted or whitewashed, flags were hung from windows and balconies. Programs were printed, schoolchildren were rehearsed in patriotic airs. The Republic of Panama declared his day of arrival a national day of 'joy and exalted enthusiasm' and instructed the populace to behave, since 'all thinkers, sociologists and philosophers of the universe [will] have their eyes upon us in penetrating scrutiny.'
>
> At Ancon, construction of a big three-story frame hotel called the Tivoli, a structure begun the year before but still far from finished, rushed ahead with all speed as soon as Stevens learned of the visit. One wing of the building was finished and furnished in six weeks." [5]

Q: Who was the first president to visit Europe while in office?

A: Surprisingly once more, it was **Woodrow Wilson** and it did not occur until 1919. After World War I, he went to Paris to attend the Paris Peace Conference and to press for his Fourteen Points, which included establishment of a League of Nations. [6]

Q: Who was the first president to broadcast a speech on radio?

A: Warren Harding on June 14, 1922. He was making a speech at Fort McHenry at the dedication of the Francis Scott Key

Memorial. It was broadcast by WEAR (later WFBR and then WJFK) in Baltimore. [7]

Q: Who was the first Senator to become president?

A: James Monroe (although he was not a sitting Senator at the time). He was a Senator from November 9, 1790 until his resignation on May 27, 1794, when appointed by President George Washington as Minister Plenipotentiary to France. [8]

Q: Who was the first president to have his voice recorded?

A: Benjamin Harrison is believed to have delivered the oldest known recording of any U.S. President. The website for the Vincent Voice Library at Michigan State University (where the audio can be heard) states that "it was recorded on an Edison wax cylinder sometime around 1889. It lasts 36 seconds." Harrison states: "As president of the United States, I was present at the first Pan-American congress in Washington D.C. I believe that with God's help, our two countries shall continue to live side-by-side in peace and prosperity. Benjamin Harrison." Given that the first Pan-American Conference occurred between October, 1889 and April, 1890, and given that Harrison is speaking in the past tense, it seems somewhat unlikely that he made this statement in 1889. In fact, based on the wording alone, it could be argued that he made the statement after his presidency had already ended, which was in 1893. In any event, the website is http://archive.lib.msu.edu/VVL/vincent/presidents/harrison.htm. [9]

Q: Who was the first president to have an outdoor inaugural?

A: James Monroe. [10]

Q: Which president had the first telephone installed in the White House and made the first outgoing call, to Alexander

Graham Bell, of all people, who was located 13 miles away?

A: Rutherford Hayes. It was installed in the telegraph room on May 10, 1877. The Treasury Department possessed the only other direct phone line to the White House at that time. The White House phone number was "1." It would be 50 more years until President Herbert Hoover had the first telephone line installed at the president's desk in the Oval Office. [11]

Q: Who was the first president—whether or not president at the time—to sit for a photograph?

A: John Quincy Adams, the 6th president (from 1825-1829), sat for a portrait in 1843.[12]

Q: Who was the first president to appoint a Hispanic-American to his cabinet?

A: George H.W. Bush, who appointed Lauro F. Cavazos to serve as Secretary of Education in 1988. [13]

Q: Who was the first "dark horse" candidate? For extra credit, what is the derivation of that term?

A: James K. Polk was the first dark horse candidate. In 1844, the Democrats were expected to nominate Martin Van Buren, who had served one term as president in the late 1830s before losing the 1840 election to the Whig candidate, William Henry Harrison. During the first ballots at the 1844 convention, a stalemate developed between Van Buren and Lewis Cass, an experienced politician from Michigan. Neither man could get the required two-thirds majority necessary to win the nomination.

On the eighth ballot taken at the convention, on May 28, 1844, Polk was suggested as a compromise candidate. Even so, Polk received only 44 votes, compared to 104 for Van Buren and 114 for Cass. Finally, on the ninth ballot, there was a stampede for

Polk when the New York delegation abandoned hopes for another term for Van Buren (though from New York), and voted for Polk. Other state delegations followed, and Polk won the nomination. Polk, who was home in Tennessee, would not know for certain that he had been nominated until a week later.

A dark horse is little-known person who emerges to prominence, especially in a competition, and who seems unlikely to succeed. Not surprisingly, the phrase "dark horse" derives from horse racing. The most reliable explanation of the term is that trainers and jockeys would sometimes endeavor to keep a very fast horse from public view. By training the horse "in the dark" they could enter it in a race and place bets at favorable odds. If the horse won, the betting payoff would thus be maximized. The British novelist Benjamin Disraeli, who would eventually turn to politics and become prime minister, used the term in its original horse-racing usage in the 1831 novel, *The Young Duke*:

> "The first favorite was never heard of, the second favorite was never seen after the distance post, all the ten-to-oners were in the race, and a dark horse which had never been thought of, and which the careless St. James also had never even observed in the list, rushed past the grandstand in sweeping triumph." [14]

Q: Who was the first president to have been born in a log cabin?

A: Andrew Jackson. The others were Millard Fillmore, James Buchanan, Abraham Lincoln and James Garfield. [15]

Q: Who was the first president to ride a railroad train?

A: Andrew Jackson. He rode on the B&O in 1833. [16]

Q: Who was the first president to use "God bless America" in an official speech?

A: Given that the phrase seems to be heard in so many presidential speeches these days, it might seem like it has been a mainstay phrase for a long time. Surprisingly however, the first president to use it was **Richard Nixon**. On the evening of April 30, 1973, he addressed the nation live from the Oval Office in an attempt to manage the growing Watergate scandal.

It was a difficult speech for Nixon: He announced the resignations of three Administration officials, including Attorney General Richard Kleindienst, but Nixon nonetheless tried to sound optimistic. As he approached the end of his speech, Nixon noted that he had "exactly 1,361 days remaining" in his term and wanted them "to be the best days in America's history." "Tonight," he continued, "I ask for your prayers to help me in everything that I do throughout the days of my presidency." Then came the magic words: "God bless America and God bless each and every one of you."

The phrase didn't immediately catch on. **Gerald Ford** and **Jimmy Carter** both avoided it. But not **Ronald Reagan**. Reagan made "God bless America" the omnipresent political slogan that it is today. He used the phrase to conclude his dramatic nomination acceptance address at the Republican Party convention in July 1980, and once in office, made it his standard sign-off. Presidents since Reagan have followed suit.[17]

Q: Who was the first president born in the United States of America?

A: Martin Van Buren. Note that all presidents were born in America—because they have to be, but he was the first born in the USA. The first seven were born in the American Colonies.

Q: Who was the first president to have his veto overridden by Congress?

A: John Tyler. On Tyler's last full day in office, March 3, 1845,

Congress overrode his veto of a bill relating to revenue cutters and steamers. This marked the first time any president's veto had been overridden.

Q: Who was the first president to have a cabinet nominee rejected?

A: **Andrew Jackson**'s nomination of Roger Taney to be Secretary of the Treasury was rejected by the Senate in June, 1834. Taney was known for his anti-banking views. Nine months earlier, Jackson had already selected Taney as Secretary of the Treasury and he unofficially served in that post. Senators complained that the unconfirmed Taney held his office illegally. As Jackson biographer Robert Remini has written, "Whether this was true did not disturb Jackson one whit." Yet Jackson knew that sooner or later he would have to send Taney's name to the Senate and, in Remini's words, "he knew that senators would tear into the nomination like ravenous wolves to get revenge for the removal of the deposits and poor Taney would be made to bear much of the pain and humiliation."

Finally, on June 23, 1834, Jackson sent forth Taney's nomination. On the next day a pro-bank majority in the Senate denied him the post by a vote of 18 to 28, making him the first cabinet nominee in history to suffer the Senate's formal rejection. Today, Taney (pronounced Taw-nee) is best remembered as a Chief Justice of the United States Supreme Court who authored the infamous opinion in *Dred Scott v. Sandford* (1857), which ruled that African Americans, having been considered inferior at the time the Constitution was drafted, were not part of the original community of citizens and could not be considered citizens of the United States. [18]

Q: Who was the first president to appear in a sound film?

A: **Calvin Coolidge.** On August 11, 1924, Lee De Forest filmed

Coolidge on the White House lawn with DeForest's Phonofilm sound-on-film process. The title of the DeForest film was *President Coolidge, Taken on the White House Grounds*, a four minute clip. [19]

Q: Who was the first person to become president before age 50?

A: James K. Polk—age 49.

Q: Who was the first president to have his nomination disseminated by telegraph?

A: James K. Polk, after he was nominated in 1844. [20]

Q: Who was the first president to receive protection from the Secret Service?

A: Grover Cleveland in 1894 (even though the agency had been started thirty years earlier to combat counterfeiting). With Cleveland, the protection was part time. In 1902, it became full time, in 1917, it expanded to include the president's family and in 1961 it expanded to include former presidents. [21]

Q: Who was the first president to call for and use the phrase "affirmative action"?

A: John F. Kennedy. He signed Executive Order #10925 on March 6, 1961, requiring government contractors to "take affirmative action to ensure that applicants are employed, and that employees are treated during employment, without regard to their race, creed, color, or national origin." That Executive Order established the President's Committee on Equal Employment Opportunity, which later became the Equal Employment Opportunity Commission (EEOC) in the Civil Rights Act of 1964. [22]

Q: Who was the first president to have both parents alive when he became president?

A: Ulysses Grant. He assumed office on March 4, 1869. His father, Jesse Root Grant, lived from 1794-1873 and his mother Hannah Simpson Grant lived from 1798-1883. The only other presidents whose parents were both alive when they became president were John Kennedy and George W. Bush.

Q: Who was the first president to have "Hail to the Chief" regularly played when he entered a room?

A: James K. Polk. However, the song had been played for presidents previously. It was first associated with a president when it was played (under the title *Wreaths for the Chieftain*) to honor both the belated George Washington and the end of the War of 1812. Andrew Jackson was the first living president to be personally honored by *Hail to the Chief*, on January 9, 1829. The tune was among a number of pieces played for Martin Van Buren's inauguration ceremony on March 4, 1837, and for social occasions during his administration. It was Julia Tyler, the wife of president John Tyler, who first requested that "Hail to the Chief" be played specifically to announce the president's arrival on official occasions. However, it was Sarah Childress Polk who ritualized its use. As the historian William Seale stated, "Polk was not an impressive figure, so some announcement was necessary to avoid the embarrassment of his entering a crowded room unnoticed. At large affairs the band . . . rolled the drums as they played the march . . . and a way was cleared for the President."

The title of the song comes from a narrative poem written in 1810 by Sir Walter Scott called *The Lady of the Lake*:

> *Hail to the chief, who in triumph advances,*
> *Honour'd and blest be the evergreen pine!*
> *Long may the tree in his banner that glances,*
> *Flourish the shelter and grace of our line.*

In the original poem, "chief" referred to a Scottish chieftain. In America, the lyrics were altered for the president, although they are rarely sung or heard:

> *Hail to the Chief we have chosen for the nation,*
> *Hail to the Chief! We salute him, one and all.*
> *Hail to the Chief, as we pledge co-operation*
> *In proud fulfillment of a great, noble call.*
> *Yours is the aim to make this grand country grander,*
> *This you will do, That's our strong, firm belief.*
> *Hail to the one we selected as commander,*
> *Hail to the President! Hail to the Chief!* [23]

Q: Who was the first president to voluntarily retire after his first term?

A: James K. Polk. When he was elected in 1844, he promised to serve only one term and he fulfilled his promise. He died several months after his term ended anyway. [24]

Q: Who was the first president who was born west of the Mississippi River?

A: Herbert Hoover, who was from Iowa.

Q: Who was the first president to fly in a plane (though not while President)?

A: Theodore Roosevelt. At an air show at Aviation Field in St. Louis, Missouri on October 11, 1910, Theodore Roosevelt was offered a seat as a passenger in a plane for a demonstration flight. The pilot's name was Arch Hoxsey, who had just completed a record flight from Springfield, Illinois. The plane reached an altitude of about 50 feet, circled the field twice and stayed airborne for about four minutes. A video of the flight can be seen on the Library of Congress website. [25]

Q: Who was the first sitting president to fly in a plane?

A: Franklin Roosevelt in 1943, when a Boeing B314 Clipper carried him to the Allied summit in Casablanca.[26]

Q: Who was the first president to fly in a plane officially designated as Air Force One?

A: Dwight Eisenhower in 1959. Contrary to popular perception, Air Force One is not a specific airplane but the call sign for any aircraft carrying the president. The presidential call sign was established for security purposes during Eisenhower's administration. The change stemmed from a 1953 incident where an Eastern Airlines commercial flight (8610) had the same call sign as a flight the president was on (Air Force 8610). The aircraft accidentally entered the same airspace and after the incident, the unique call sign "Air Force One" was introduced for the presidential aircraft. The first official flight of Air Force One was in 1959.[27]

Q: Who was the first president to have a speechwriter?

A: Warren Harding. Newspaper reporter Judson Welliver started writing for Harding in 1921 shortly after he became President. [28]

Q: Who was the first president to be visited by a queen, namely Queen Emma of the Sandwich Islands?

A: Andrew Johnson in 1866. Her official title was Queen Consort Emma Kalanikaumaka´amano Kaleleonālani Na´ea Rooke of Hawaii. The Sandwich Islands was the name given to the Hawaiian Islands by explorer John Cook in the 1770's. [29]

Q: Who is the first president to file an income tax return?

A: Warren Harding, in 1923. He owed $18,000.[30]

Q: Who was the first president to have a stepmother?

A: Millard Fillmore. His mother Phoebe died in 1831 and his father Nathaniel married Eunice Love in 1834. [31]

Q: Who was the first president born after the death of a former president?

A: Millard Fillmore. George Washington died less than a month before Fillmore's birth on January 7, 1800.

Q: Who was the first president to assume office during wartime?

A: Surprisingly it was not until **Harry Truman** in 1945.

Q: Who was the first president to ride in a car?

A: William McKinley. However, Theodore Roosevelt rode in the first government-owned vehicle. [32]

Q: Who was the first president to meet with a pope at the Vatican?

A: Woodrow Wilson, who met with Pope Benedict XV at the Vatican in 1919 while on a European tour after World War I. Other presidents who have met with popes at the Vatican are as follows:

President	Pope	Year
Dwight D. Eisenhower	Pope John XXIII	1959
John F. Kennedy	Pope Paul VI	1963
Lyndon B. Johnson	Pope Paul VI	1967
Richard M. Nixon	Pope Paul VI	1969, 1970
Gerald R. Ford	Pope Paul VI	1975
Jimmy Carter	Pope John Paul II	1980

Ronald Reagan	Pope John Paul II	1982, 1987
George H.W. Bush	Pope John Paul II	1989, 1991
Bill Clinton	Pope John Paul II	1994
George W. Bush	Pope John Paul II	2002, 2004
George W. Bush	Pope Benedict XVI	2007, 2008
Barack Obama	Pope Benedict XVI	2009. [33]

Q: Who was the first president to meet with a pope in the United States?

A: Lyndon Johnson, who met Pope Paul VI in New York City in 1965.

Q: Who is the first president to receive a pope at the White House?

A: Jimmy Carter, who met with Pope John Paul II at the White House on October 6, 1979.

Other presidents who have met with popes in the United States are as follows:

President	Pope	Year	Place
Ronald Reagan	Pope John Paul II	1984	Fairbanks, Alaska
Ronald Reagan	Pope John Paul II	1987	Miami, Florida
Bill Clinton	Pope John Paul II	1993	Denver, Colorado
Bill Clinton	Pope John Paul II	1995	Newark, New Jersey
Bill Clinton	Pope John Paul II	1999	St. Louis, Missouri
George W. Bush	Pope Benedict XVI	2008	Washington, D.C.[34]

Q: Who is the only president who met with a pope not at the Vatican and not in the United States?

A: George W. Bush met with Pope John Paul I in Castel Gandolfo, Italy in 2001.[35]

Q: Who is the first president to be elected from the Deep South after the Civil War ended in 1865?

A: Jimmy Carter in 1976.

Q: Who was the first president to have a State Dinner?

A: Ulysses S. Grant in 1874, when he hosted King David Kalakaua of the Hawaiian Islands. [36]

Q: Who was the first president to use a teleprompter while president?

A: Dwight Eisenhower. Harry S Truman refused to use them, concluding it would make him look insincere. Eisenhower became the first president to use them but he was not a fan either, grousing about having to "use that damn teleprompter." The earliest President to use a teleprompter (though no longer in office) was Herbert Hoover in 1952, when he addressed the Republican National Convention. [37]

Q: Who was the first president to wear contact lenses?

A: According to the Optical Heritage Museum, the answer is **Lyndon Johnson** and not, as has sometimes been stated, Ronald Reagan. [38]

Q: Who was the first president to invite an African-American to the White House and who was the person he invited?

A: Theodore Roosevelt invited Booker T. Washington to the White House in 1901. That year, Washington had invited Roosevelt, who was then vice president, to visit the Tuskegee Institute of Alabama which Washington had founded. Roosevelt had planned to make the visit but it never occurred because President McKinley was assassinated that year. Roosevelt instead invited Washington to call at the White House whenever he was in town. Within weeks, Washington was in the capital and was invited to join President Roosevelt for dinner on October 16. "We talked a considerable length concerning plans about the South," Washington later recalled.

At the time of the dinner, the public was not aware of it, because efforts were made to avoid publicity. However, a reporter noticed Washington's name in a list of official callers. This touched off a wave of protests from white Southerners, who accused the president of encouraging racial mixing and social equality for blacks. *The Memphis Scimitar* wrote:

> "The most damnable outrage which has ever been perpetrated by any citizen of the United States was committed yesterday by the president, when he invited a nigger to dine with him at the White House. It would not be worth more than a passing notice if Theodore Roosevelt had sat down to dinner in his own home with a Pullman car porter, but Roosevelt the individual and Roosevelt the president are not to be viewed in the same light."

James K. Vardaman, soon to be Governor of Mississippi and a virulent racist, described the White House as "so saturated with the odor of the nigger that the rats have taken refuge in the stable," and declared, "I am just as much opposed to Booker T. Washington as a voter as I am to the cocoanut-headed, chocolate-colored typical little coon who blacks my shoes every morning. Neither is fit to perform the supreme function of citizenship."

Austro-Hungarian Ambassador Ladislaus Hengelmüller von Hengervár, visiting the White House on the same day, found a rabbit's foot in Washington's coat pocket when he mistakenly put on the coat. *The Washington Post* described it as "the left hind foot of a graveyard rabbit, killed in the dark of the moon." *The Detroit Journal* wrote, "The Austrian Ambassador may have made off with

Booker T. Washington's coat at the White House, but he'd have a bad time trying to fill his shoes." [39]

CHAPTER THIRTY NOTES:

1) http://www.whitehouse.gov/about/presidents/georgewashington
   http://www.ushistory.org/tour/congress-hall.htm
2) http://www.historycentral.com/Bio/presidents/madison.html
3) http://www.sarantakes.com/nixon-time.html
4) http://www.ssa.gov/history/lbjsm.html
5) McCullough, David. *The Path Between the Seas: The Creation of the Panama Canal, 1870-1914*, Simon & Schuster (1978).
   http://panamacanalmuseum.org/index.php/exhibits/detail/theodore_roosevelt_visit/
6) Macmillan, Margaret. *Peacemakers: The Paris Peace Conference of 1919 and Its Attempt to End War*, John Murray (2002).
7) http://www.timetoast.com/timelines/19317
   http://jeff560.tripod.com/chrono1.html (A Chronology of AM Radio Broadcasting 1900-1960
8) http://bioguide.congress.gov/scripts/biodisplay.pl?index=M000858
9) http://archive.lib.msu.edu/VVL/vincent/presidents/harrison.htm.
10) http://www.bartleby.com/124/pres20.html
11) http://www.ipl.org/div/potus/rbhayes.html.
    http://www.history.com/this-day-in-history/hayes-has-first-phone-installed-in-white-house
12) Krainik, Clifford. *"Face the Lens, Mr. President: A Gallery of Photographic Portraits of 19th-Century U.S. Presidents."* The White House Historical Association.
    http://www.whitehousehistory.org/whha_publications/publications_documents/whitehousehistory_16.pdf. Retrieved 2009-09-04.
    http://www.scholastic.com/teachers/article/fun-facts-know-about-white-house-residents
13) http://www.hispanichealth.org/news/article.aspx?ArticleId=56
14) http://history1800s.about.com/od/1800sglossary/g/Dark-Horse-Candidate.htm
    Borneman, Walter R. *Polk: The Man Who Transformed the Presidency and America*. Random House, Inc. (2008)
    Seigenthaler, John, *James K. Polk: 1845-1849: The American Presidents Series*, Times Books (2004). http://www.hotfreebooks.com/book/The-Young-Duke-Benjamin-Disraeli—2.html
15) http://americanhistory.si.edu/presidency/timeline/pres_era/3_668.html
    http://hoover.archives.gov/exhibits/cottages/
16) http://www.findingdulcinea.com/news/on-this-day/Aug/Theodore-Roosevelt-Becomes-First-President-to-Ride-in-a-Car.html
17) David Domke and Kevin Coe, *Happy 35th, 'God Bless America,'* Time magazine April 29, 2008
18) http://www.senate.gov/artandhistory/history/minute/First_Cabinet_Rejection.htm

Remini, Robert V. *Andrew Jackson and the Course of American Democracy, 1833-1845*. Harper & Row, 1984.

19) http://www.archive.org/details/coolidge_1924

20) http://history1800s.about.com/od/1800sglossary/g/Dark-Horse-Candidate.htm

21) http://www.secretservice.gov/history.shtml

22) http://www.eeoc.gov/eeoc/history/35th/thelaw/eo-10925.html
http://www.oeod.uci.edu/aa.html

23) http://lcweb2.loc.gov/diglib/ihas/loc.natlib.ihas.200000009/default.html
Bowers, Andy. *Why "Hail to the Chief"?: How it became the presidential song.* Salon.com, January 20, 2005

24) Borneman, Walter R. *Polk: The Man Who Transformed the Presidency and America.* Random House, Inc. (2008)
Merry, Robert W. *A Country of Vast Designs: James K. Polk, the Mexican War, and the Conquest of the American Continent*, Simon & Schuster (2009).

25) http://www.american-presidents.org/2009/09/first-president-to-fly-in-airplane.html

26) http://www.msnbc.msn.com/id/3606994/ns/technology_and_science-science/

27) http://potus-geeks.livejournal.com/231425.html
http://www.theaviationzone.com/factsheets/c25.asp

28) Catherine Donaldson-Evans (May 12, 2005). *"Different Writer, Same President."* FoxNews.com

29) Steven Anzovin, Janet Podell (2001). Famous first facts about American politics. H.W. Wilson. p. 136..

30) http://www.uspoliticalhistory.com/Harding_1.html

31) http://www.docstoc.com/docs/2318662/Facts-About-the-Presidents

32) http://www.theodoreroosevelt.org/life/firsts.htm
http://clinton4.nara.gov/WH/kids/inside/html/fall98-4.html
http://www.history.com/this-day-in-history/william-mckinley-first-us-president-to-ride-in-a-car-is-born

33) http://www.catholicnews.com/data/stories/cns/0903142.htm

34) http://en.wikipedia.org/wiki/List_of_meetings_between_the_President_of_the_United_States_and_the_Pope
http://www.catholicnews.com/data/stories/cns/0903142.htm

35) http://history.state.gov/departmenthistory/travels/president/bush-george-w

36) Feifei Sun, *The Right Recipe for a White House State Dinner*, *Time* magazine, January 19, 2011.

37) Peter Baker, *President Sticks to the Script, With a Little Help*, *The New York Times*, 3/5/2009.

38) http://www.opticalheritagemuseum.org/Industry/HistoricalPresEyeglassesLBJ.htm

39) Nathan Miller, *Theodore Roosevelt: A Life*. HarperCollins (1994)
Kennedy, Randall *Nigger: The Strange Career of a Troublesome Word*. Pantheon (2002)
Rubio, Philip F., *A History of Affirmative Action, 1619-1920*, University of Mississippi Press (2001)
Morris, Edmund, *Theodore Rex*, Random House (2001)
The Booker T. Washington Papers, University of Illinois Press, http://www.historycooperative.org/btw/Vol.8/html/437.html

CHAPTER 31

Who Is the Only . . .

Q: Who is the only president who also served as a vice president, senator (twice), member of the House and governor?

A: Andrew Johnson. He was vice president under Abraham Lincoln for about six weeks, from March 4, 1865 to April 15, 1865. He was a senator from Tennessee both before becoming president (1857-1862) and after (1875-1875). He was in House of Representatives from Tennessee from 1843-1853 and governor of Tennessee from 1853-1857.

Q: Who is the only president from Indiana?

A: Benjamin Harrison.

Q: Who is the only president to be born on July 4?

A: Calvin Coolidge. He was born on July 4, 1872 in Plymouth Notch, Vermont.

Q: Who is the only sitting president after Franklin Roosevelt who Queen Elizabeth II did not personally meet ?

A: Lyndon Johnson. She met every other president as a sitting president (or after their terms had ended) except for Harry Truman, since his term ended on January 20, 1953 before she was coronated. Photos of her meeting with each president since 1945 (except LBJ) can be seen online. [1]

Q: Who is the only person in American history to appear on the Republican ticket five times?

A: Richard Nixon. Richard Nixon (1952 and 1956 as Dwight Eisenhower's vice presidential running mate, and 1960, 1968 and 1972 as a presidential candidate).

Q: Who is the only president to ever win the Nobel Peace Prize after leaving office?

A: Jimmy Carter in 2002. The Nobel Committee cited his work in brokering the Camp David Accords in 1978 (and indeed seemed to imply that he should have received the award at that time) as well as for his work with the Carter Center. The text of the Committee's announcement on October 11, 2002 read in part:

> "The Norwegian Nobel Committee has decided to award the Nobel Peace Prize for 2002 to Jimmy Carter, for his decades of untiring effort to find peaceful solutions to international conflicts, to advance democracy and human rights, and to promote economic and social development. During his presidency (1977-1981), Carter's mediation was a vital contribution to the Camp David Accords between Israel and Egypt, in itself a great enough achievement to qualify for the Nobel Peace Prize. ... Through his Carter Center, which celebrates its 20th anniversary in 2002, Carter has, since his presidency, undertaken very extensive and persevering conflict resolution on several continents."[2]

Q: Who is the only president to have officially reported a UFO sighting?

A: Jimmy Carter. In Leary, GA, in 1969, seven years before he became president, and two years before he became governor of Georgia, Carter was preparing to give a speech to the Lions Club. At about 7:15, one of the guests called his attention to an object in the sky, which he described as being bright white and as being about as bright as the moon. In a 2005 interview, Carter stated:

> "All of a sudden, one of the men looked up and said, 'Look, over in the west!' And there was a bright light in the sky. We all saw it. And then the light, it got closer and closer to us. And then it stopped, I don't know how far away, but it stopped beyond the pine trees. And all of a sudden it changed color to blue, and then it changed to red, then back to white. And we were trying to figure out what in the world it could be, and then it receded into the distance."

While governor of Georgia, Carter was asked to file a report of the sighting by the International UFO Bureau in Oklahoma City, Oklahoma, which he did in September, 1973 (four years after the incident occurred). During his 1976 election campaign, he is said to have told reporters that, as a result of it, he would institute a policy of openness if he were elected to office, saying: "One thing's for sure, I'll never make fun of people who say they've seen unidentified objects in the sky. If I become president, I'll make every piece of information this country has about UFO sightings available to the public and the scientists." [3]

Q: Who is the only president who headed a labor union?

A: Ronald Reagan, who was president of the Screen Actors Guild from 1947-1952 and again from 1959-1960. His presidency of SAG coincided with the blacklist years in which efforts were made to prevent Communists or Communist sympathizers from working in the film industry. As president of SAG, Reagan testified before the House Committee on Un-American Activities (HUAC), which was investigating Communist influence in the Hollywood labor unions. He and his first wife, actress Jane Wyman, also provided federal agents with the names of actors they believed were Communist sympathizers.[5]

Q: Who was the only president who was a Rhodes Scholar?

A: Bill Clinton. After graduation from Georgetown in 1968, he won a Rhodes Scholarship to University College, Oxford where he studied philosophy, politics and economics. [6]

Q: Who was the only one-term vice president and two-term president?

A: Thomas Jefferson. He was John Adams' vice president from 1979-1801 and then President from 1801-1809.

Q: Who was the only two-term president never to veto a Congressional bill?

A: Thomas Jefferson.

Q: Which president was the only defeated vice presidential candidate to be elected president?

A: Franklin Roosevelt. His running mate James Cox lost the 1920 election to Warren Harding.

Q: Who was the only president of a debt-free United States?

A: Andrew Jackson. It occurred on or about January 8, 1835. "For Andrew Jackson, politics was very personal," says H.W. Brands, an Andrew Jackson biographer who wrote *Andrew Jackson: His Life and Times* (Doubleday, 2005). "He hated not just the federal debt. He hated debt at all." He felt that debt was "a moral failing and the idea you could somehow acquire stuff through debt almost seemed like black magic."

So Jackson decided to pay off the debt. To do that, he took advantage of a huge real-estate bubble that was raging in the Western United States. The federal government owned a lot of Western land—and Jackson started selling it off. He was also ruthless on the budget. He blocked every spending bill he could. When Jackson took office, the national debt was about $58 million. Six years later, it was all gone. Two years after that however, in 1837, the country was engulfed in the Panic of 1837, in which nearly half of all U.S. banks closed or partially failed.[7]

Q: Who was the only president who qualified for command of a submarine?

A: Jimmy Carter. Carter graduated from the Naval Academy on June 5, 1946 with distinction. After completing two years of surface ship duty, Carter applied for submarine duty. He took a six-month course at the U.S. Navy Submarine School, New London, Connecticut in 1948.

Upon completion of the course, Carter was assigned to USS *Pomfret*, where he qualified in a submarine in 1949. Detached from *Pomfret* in 1951, Carter was assigned as Engineering Officer USS *K-1* (SSK 1), the first postwar submarine built. During this tour he also qualified for command of a submarine, although he never actually did command one. After his father's death in 1953, Carter resigned from the Navy to return to Georgia to manage the family interests.[4]

Q: Who was the only president to take his entire salary in a lump sum at the end of his term?

A: Martin Van Buren. It was $100,000 for the four years combined.[8]

Q: Who were the only presidents to have a pilot's license?

A: The first to earn a pilot's license was **Dwight Eisenhower**, who qualified in 1937 when he was a 46 year-old lieutenant colonel serving in the Philippines. However he never qualified for Army wings. The others were **George H.W. Bush** and **George W. Bush**.

The most impressive record of the pilot-presidents belongs to the elder Bush. Only eighteen upon receiving his wings, he flew TBM Avenger torpedo bombers from the carrier USS San Jacinto in 1944. On a mission over the Bonin Islands, Japanese flak set Bush's Avenger afire. He remained airborne long enough to reach open water. Though his two crewmen perished after bailing out with Bush, the future president was rescued by submarine. After the war, when told that the Japanese army routinely cannibalized captured fliers, Bush quipped that he was so thin he would have made a poor meal. For his 58 combat missions, Lieutenant Junior Grade Bush was awarded the Distinguished Flying Cross and three Air Medals. [9]

Q: Who was the only president for whom English was not his first language?

A: Martin Van Buren. He spoke Dutch growing up. [10]

Q: Who was the only president not to appoint a single federal judge at any level?

A: William Henry Harrison. This was occasioned no doubt by his one-month presidency. However, even James Garfield, who was president for not much longer, managed to appoint a Supreme Court Justice (Stanley Matthews from Ohio), a Circuit Court judge and three District Court judges.

Q: Who was the only former president elected to office in the government of the Confederacy during the Civil War (though he died before he assumed said office)?

A: John Tyler. When the Civil War broke out in 1861, Tyler, a Virginian, unhesitatingly sided with the Confederacy and became a delegate to the Provisional Confederate Congress. He was then elected to the House of Representatives of the Confederate Congress. On January 5, 1862, he left for Richmond, Virginia in anticipation of his congressional service, but he would not live to see the opening sessions. He died on January 18, 1862. [11]

Q: Who was the only president who never voted and never belonged to a political office until he ran for president?

A: Zachary Taylor [12]

Q: Who was the only president not assassinated to be survived by his mother?

A: James Polk. His mother Jane died in 1852 and Polk died in 1853. The only other presidential mothers to outlive their sons were Eliza Garfield and Rose Kennedy, both of whom lost their sons to assassins. [13]

Q: Who was the only president not assassinated to be survived by his father?

A: Warren Harding. He died in 1923 and his father George died in 1928. The only other presidential father to outlive his son was Joseph Kennedy. [14]

Q: Who was the only president who had served at least one full term who had no turnover in his cabinet?

A: Franklin Pierce. There were no resignations, no dismissals and no one died. [15]

Q: Who was the only president to receive a patent?

A: **Abraham Lincoln.** On May 22, 1849, he received Patent No. 6469 for a device to lift boats over shoals. The intent was to help larger ships navigate in shallow waters. The invention was never manufactured. Part of his application read, "Be it known that I, Abraham Lincoln, of Springfield, in the county of Sangamon, in the state of Illinois, have invented a new and improved manner of combining adjustable buoyant air chambers with a steam boat or other vessel for the purpose of enabling their draught of water to be readily lessened to enable them to pass over bars, or through shallow water, without discharging their cargoes ..."[16]

Q: Who was the only president to serve in the Senate after his presidency?

A: **Andrew Johnson.** Johnson was an unsuccessful candidate for election to the United States Senate from Tennessee in 1868 and to the House of Representatives in 1872. However, in 1874 the Tennessee legislature did elect him to the U.S. Senate. Johnson served from March 4, 1875, until his death from a stroke on July 31 of that year. In his first and only speech since returning to the Senate, which was also his last, Johnson spoke about political turmoil in Louisiana. [17]

Q: Who was the only president besides FDR to attempt to serve a third term after serving two full terms?

A: **Ulysses Grant.** In 1879, the "Stalwart" faction of the Republican Party led by Senator Roscoe Conkling sought to nominate Grant for a third term as president. He counted on strong support from businessmen, old soldiers, and the Methodist church. Publicly, Grant said nothing, but privately, he wanted the job and encouraged his men. His popularity was fading however, and while he received more than 300 votes in each of the 36 ballots of the 1880 convention, the nomination went to James A.

Garfield. Grant campaigned for Garfield, who won by a very narrow margin over Winfield Hancock. However, Grant supported his stalwart ally Conkling against Garfield in the battle over patronage in 1881 that culminated in Garfield's assassination.

Theodore Roosevelt ran for a third term but he became president only because of the assassination of McKinley so his first term was not four full years. [18]

Q: Who was the only member of the clergy to serve as president?

A: James Garfield. He was a minister and an elder for the Church of Christ, making him the only member of the clergy to date to serve as president. Garfield however was a lay minister. In a 1904 book about the Church of Christ, it was written of Garfield:

> "In the early days of the Churches of Christ on the Western Reserve—and probably this was true elsewhere—it was not a difficult thing for a young man to enter the ranks of the disciple ministry, if he was a Christian, had fair gifts of body and mind, knew the alphabet of the gospel of Christ, was willing to study and had a desire to preach, he was encouraged to preach. Very few of the early disciple preachers ever 'studied for the ministry,' or were ever 'ordained' to the ministry, in the modern, ecclesiastical sense of those terms. Hence in the commonly accepted sense he was never a preacher or minister; but this may also he said of hundreds of other preachers in the Churches of Christ, at that time, before and since. He did, however, 'preach the Word.' He did hold 'revival' or protracted meetings and often with great success." [19]

Q: Who was the only president born in New Jersey?

A: Grover Cleveland

Q: Who is the only president to be elected twice to both the presidency and the vice presidency?

A: Richard Nixon.

Q: Who was the only president to win both the Medal of Honor and the Nobel Peace Prize?

A: Theodore Roosevelt. He was also the first American to win the Nobel Peace Prize. He won it in 1906 "for his successful mediation to end the Russo-Japanese war and for his interest in arbitration, having provided the Hague arbitration court with its very first case." [20]

Q: Besides Jimmy Carter and Theodore Roosevelt, who are the only presidents to win the Nobel Peace Prize?

A: Woodrow Wilson and **Barack Obama.** Woodrow Wilson's was awarded in 1919 for his crucial role in establishing the League of Nations. Barack Obama's was awarded in 2009 "for his extraordinary efforts to strengthen international diplomacy and cooperation between peoples." [21]

Q: Who was the only president whose parents were homeopathic practitioners?

A: Warren Harding. Harding's father, George Tryon Harding, went on rounds with a local homeopath for several years and attended sessions at a homeopathic college in Cleveland. Harding's mother, Phoebe, was a midwife. On the basis of this practice and assisting her husband, she was granted an Ohio medical license in 1896. She designated herself a homeopathic physician and practiced until her death in 1910. [22]

Q: Who was the only president to win a Pulitzer Prize?

A: John F. Kennedy for *Profiles in Courage*. The book came out in 1956 and described acts of bravery and integrity by eight United States Senators. Ever since the book came out there has been controversy over how much was actually written by Kennedy and how much was written by his speechwriter Ted Sorenson. In 1957, journalist Drew Pearson appeared as a guest on the *The Mike Wallace Interview* and stated: "[Kennedy] is the only man in history that I know who won a Pulitzer Prize on a book which was ghostwritten for him." Wallace replied, "You know for a fact, Drew, that the book *Profiles in Courage* was written for Senator Kennedy by someone else?" Pearson responded that he did, and that Sorenson actually wrote the book. Wallace responded: "And he got a Pulitzer Prize for it? And he never acknowledged the fact?" Pearson replied: "No, he has not. There's a little wisecrack around the Senate about Jack ... Some of his colleagues say, 'Jack, I wish you had a little less profile and more courage.'"

Years later historian Herbert Parmet analyzed the text of *Profiles in Courage* and wrote in his book, *Jack: The Struggles of John F. Kennedy* (1980), that although Kennedy did oversee the production and provided for the direction and message of the book, it was clearly Sorensen who provided most of the work that went into the end product. He found that Kennedy contributed some notes, mostly on John Quincy Adams, but little that made it into the finished product. "There is no evidence of a Kennedy draft for the overwhelming bulk of the book," Parmet wrote. While "the choices, message, and tone of the volume are unmistakably Kennedy's," the actual work was "left to committee labor. The literary craftsmanship [was] clearly Sorensen's, and he gave the book both the drama and flow that made for readability." [23]

Q: Who was the only president to appoint his brother to a cabinet post?

A: John F. Kennedy made his brother Robert the Attorney General in 1961. Although Robert graduated from the University of Virginia Law School, he never actually practiced law prior to be appointed to the position by John. When *The New York Times* said that he did not have enough experience to be up to the job, when asked about his younger brother's inexperience, President Kennedy joked, "I can't see that it's wrong to give him a little legal experience before he goes out to practice law." Following John's assassination on November 22, 1963, Robert continued to serve as Attorney General under President Johnson until September 1964, when he resigned to seek the U.S. Senate seat from New York, which he won in November. [24]

Q: Who is the only president from Pennsylvania?

A: James Buchanan.

Q: Who was the only president to be survived by both of his parents?

A: John F. Kennedy. Kennedy was the youngest president when he died (age 46) and was the only president to die before reaching age 50 besides James Garfield (age 49).

Q: Who was the only president who was *Time* magazine's Person of the Year in two consecutive years?

A: Richard Nixon in 1971 and 1972. He shared the award with Henry Kissinger in 1972.

Q: Who was the only president to become an Eagle Scout?

A: Gerald Ford, in 1927. Scouting was so important to Ford that his family asked that Scouts participate in his funeral. About 400 Eagle Scouts were part of the funeral procession, where they formed an honor guard as the casket went by. [25]

Q: Who were the only presidents whose parents were divorced?

A: **Gerald Ford** and **Barack Obama.** Obama's parents married in 1961 and divorced in 1964. [26]

Q: Who was the only president employed by the National Park Service?

A: **Gerald Ford**, who worked at Yellowstone in 1936.

Q: Who were the only presidents to sign the Constitution?

A: **George Washington** and **James Madison.**

Q: Who were the only presidents who signed the Declaration of Independence?

A: **John Adams** and **Thomas Jefferson.** There is no president who signed both the Declaration of Independence and the Constitution.

Q: Who was the only president who didn't live in Washington while president?

A: **George Washington.** Following his April 1789 inauguration, Washington occupied two executive mansions in New York City: the Samuel Osgood House at 1 Cherry Street (April 1789-February 1790), and the Alexander Macomb House at 39-41 Broadway (February-August 1790). The July 1790 Residence Act named Philadelphia, Pennsylvania, the temporary national capital for a ten-year period while the Federal City was under construction. The City of Philadelphia rented Robert Morris's city house at 190 High Street (now 524-30 Market Street) for Washington's presidential residence. Washington occupied the Market Street mansion from November 1790 to March 1797, and altered it in ways that may have influenced the design of the White House. As part of a futile effort to have Philadelphia named the permanent national capital, Pennsylvania built a presidential palace several blocks away, but Washington declined to move there. [27]

Q: Who was the only president who had been Speaker of the House and later elected president? Speaker of the House of Representatives is a powerful position because it is second in the presidential line of succession, behind only the vice president.

A: James Polk. He was Speaker from 1835-1839. However, he was not elected president until 1845.

Q: Who are the only presidents who assumed the office in even-numbered years?

A: Millard Fillmore in 1850 and **Gerald Ford** in 1974. Of the other seven presidents whose terms did not run their natural course because of death, those all occurred in odd numbered years.

Q: Who are the only presidents to have served between two and three years?

A: Millard Fillmore, Warren Harding, John Kennedy and **Gerald Ford.**

Q: Who are the only presidents whose parents were both alive when they were inaugurated?

A: Ulysses Grant, John Kennedy, George H.W. Bush and **George W. Bush.**

Q: Who was the only president to be directly elected from the House of Representatives?

A: James Garfield. Nineteen presidents served in the House of

Representatives at some point in their political career.

Date of Election or Assumed Office	Individual (Date of House Service)
1988	George H.W. Bush, Republican of Texas (1967-1971)
1976	Gerald R. Ford, Republican of Michigan (1949-1973)
1968	Richard M. Nixon, Republican of California (1947-1951)
1964	Lyndon B. Johnson, Democrat of Texas (1937-1949)
1960	John F. Kennedy, Democrat of Massachusetts (1947-1953)
1896	William McKinley, Republican of Ohio (1877-1883, 1885-1891)
1880	James A. Garfield, Republican of Ohio (1863-1880)
1876	Rutherford B. Hayes, Republican of Ohio (1866-1867)
1865	Andrew Johnson, Democrat of Tennessee (1843-1853)
1860	Abraham Lincoln, Republican of Illinois (1847-1849)
1856	James Buchanan, Democrat of Pennsylvania (1821-1831)
1852	Franklin Pierce, Democrat of New Hampshire (1833-1837)
1850	Millard Fillmore, Whig of New York (1833-1835, 1837-1843)
1844	James K. Polk, Democrat of Tennessee (1825-1839), Speaker of the House (1835-1839)
1841	John Tyler, Whig of Virginia (1816-1821)
1841	William Henry Harrison, Whig of Ohio (1816-1819)
1828	Andrew Jackson, Democrat of Tennessee (1796-1797)
1824	John Quincy Adams, Democrat Republican of Massachusetts (1831-1848)
1808	James Madison, Democrat Republican of Virginia (1789-1797) [28]

Q: Which president is the only American awarded the British Order of Merit?

A: Dwight Eisenhower. He was named an Honorary Member on June 12, 1945, about one month after V-E day.

Q: Who were the only presidents elected directly from the Senate?

A: Warren Harding, John F. Kennedy and Barak Obama.
Thirteen other senators became president, but not directly.

CHAPTER THIRTY-ONE NOTES:

1) http://bblmedia.com/destinations/longevity_reign.html
2) http://www.cartercenter.org/news/documents/doc1235.html
3) http://www.nicap.org/waves/CarterSightingRptOct1969.pdf (containing a copy of Carter's report and the response of the International UFO Bureau)
   Story, Ronald D. *The Encyclopedia of UFOs*, Doubleday (1980)
   Good, Timothy *"Above Top Secret: The Worldwide U.F.O. Cover-Up"* Quill (1989)
4) http://www.history.navy.mil/faqs/faq60-14.htm
   Bourne, Peter G. *Jimmy Carter: A Comprehensive Biography From Plains to Post-Presidency.* Scribner (1997).
5) Humphries, Reynold. *Hollywood's Blacklists: A Political and Cultural History*, Edinburgh University Press (2010).
   Hollywood: Unmasking Informant T-10, *Time* magazine, 9-9-1985
   http://www.sag.org/ronald-reagan
   http://www.cobbles.com/simpp_archive/linkbackups/huac_blacklist.htm
6) Maraniss, David. *First In His Class: A Biography Of Bill Clinton.* Touchstone (1996).
7) http://www.npr.org/blogs/money/2011/04/15/135423586/when-the-u-s-paid-off-the-entire-national-debt-and-why-it-didn't-last
   H.W. Brands, *Andrew Jackson: His Life and Times* (Doubleday, 2005).
8) http://www.potus.com/mvanburen.html
9) http://www.airspacemag.com/history-of-flight/From-Pilot-to-President.html
   http://www.history.navy.mil/faqs/faq10-1.htm
   Time magazine; *The Presidency: The Pilot*, February 8, 1954
10) Widmer, Edward. *Martin Van Buren.* Macmillan Publishers (2005).
11) Chitwood, Oliver Perry. *Champion of the Old South.* Russell & Russell (1964)
    Crapol, Edward P. *John Tyler, the Accidental President.* University of North Carolina Press (2006)
    May, Gary. *John Tyler: The American Presidents Series: The 10th President, 1841-1845* (Times Books 2008).
12) "Zachary Taylor: Campaigns and Elections." Miller Center of Public Affairs. http://millercenter.org/president/taylor/essays/biography/3.
13) http://deadpresidentsdaily.blogspot.com/2007/01/january-11-1852death-of-jane-knox-polk.html
14) http://presidentsparents.com/deaths.html
15) http://www.potus.com/fpierce.html
    Holt, Michael. *Franklin Pierce: The American Presidents Series: The 14th President, 1853-1857* (Times Books 2010).

16) Edwards, Owen Inventive Abe: In 1849, a future president patented an ingenious addition to transportation technology. *Smithsonian* magazine (October 2006). http://www.pddoc.com/skedaddle/articles/abraham_lincolns_patent.htm

17) http://www.senate.gov/artandhistory/history/minute/Death_of_Andrew_ Johnson.htmTrefousse, Hans L. *Andrew Johnson: A Biography.* Norton (1989).

18) McFeely, William S. *Grant: A Biography.* Norton (1981).
Bunting III, Josiah. *Ulysses S. Grant.* Times Books, (2004).

19) http://www.mun.ca/rels/restmov/texts/jtbrown/coc/COC1306.HTM http://www.geni.com/people/James-A-Garfield-20th-President-of-the-USA/6000000003044154591 http://www.christianity.com/ChurchHistory/11630598/

20) http://www.nobelprize.org/nobel_prizes/peace/articles/lundestad-review/index.html

21) http://www.nobelprize.org/nobel_prizes/peace/articles/lundestad-review/index.html http://www.nobelprize.org/nobel_prizes/peace/laureates/2009/press.html

22) Dean, John W. *Warren Harding.* Henry Holt and Co. (2004)
Russell, Francis. *The Shadow of Blooming Grove—Warren G. Harding In His Times.* Easton Press. (1962).
http://www.doctorzebra.com/prez/g29.htm (quoting from Deppisch, LM. *The Homeopathic medicine and presidential health: homeopathic influences upon two Ohio presidents.* Pharos. Fall 1997;60(4):5-10)
Ullman, Dana. The Homeopathic Revolution: Why Famous People and Cultural Heroes Choose Homeopathy, North Atlantic Press (2007).

23) Walls, Jeannette. *Dish: The Inside Story on the World of Gossip.* Avon Books (2000).
Parmet, Herbert. *Jack: The Struggles of John F. Kennedy.* Doubleday (1982).
http://www.straightdope.com/columns/read/2478/did-john-f-kennedy-really-write-profiles-in-courage

24) *Time* magazine, *New Administration: All He Asked . . .*, February 3, 1961
Schlesinger, Arthur, M. Jr., *Robert Kennedy And His Times*, Mariner Books (2002).

25) http://www.scoutingmagazine.org/issues/0703/a-ford.html
Townley, Alvin. *Legacy of Honor: The Values and Influence of America's Eagle Scouts.* St. Martin's Press. (2007)

26) Jones, Tim. *Barack Obama: Mother not just a girl from Kansas*, The Chicago Tribune, 3-7-2007

27) http://theboweryboys.blogspot.com/2008/01/george-washington-slept-here.html-http://www.hmdb.org/marker.asp?marker=20237 http://www.ushistory.org/presidentshouse/history/briefhistory.htm

28) http://artandhistory.house.gov/mem_bio/mem_pres.aspx

CHARTS AND LISTS

INDEX